Martial Rose Library
Tel: 01962 827306

Ambassadors from the Islands of Immortals

ASIAN INTERACTIONS AND COMPARISONS
GENERAL EDITOR JOSHUA A. FOGEL

Sovereign Rights and Territorial Space in Sino-Japanese Relations: Irredentism and the Diaoyu/Senkaku Islands
Unryu Suganuma

The I-Ching *in Tokugawa Thought and Culture*
Wai-ming Ng

The Genesis of East Asia, 221 B.C.–A.D. 907
Charles Holcombe

Buddhism, Diplomacy, and Trade: The Realignment of Sino-Indian Relations, 600–1400
Tansen Sen

Global Goes Local: Popular Culture in Asia
Edited by Timothy J. Craig and Richard King

Re-understanding Japan: Chinese Perspectives, 1895–1945
Lu Yan

Time, Temporality, and Imperial Transitions: East Asia in the Ming and Qing
Edited by Lynn A. Struve

Whither the Bronze Pillars? Envoy Poetry and the Sino-Vietnamese Relationship
Liam C. Kelley

Crossed Histories: Manchuria in the Age of Empire
Edited by Mariko Asano Tamanoi

Ambassadors from the Islands of Immortals: China-Japan Relations in the Han-Tang Period
Wang Zhenping

ASIAN INTERACTIONS AND COMPARISONS

Ambassadors from the Islands of Immortals

China-Japan Relations in the Han-Tang Period

WANG ZHENPING

ASSOCIATION FOR ASIAN STUDIES

and

UNIVERSITY OF HAWAI'I PRESS

Honolulu

Asian Interactions and Comparisons, published jointly by the University of Hawai'i Press and the Association for Asian Studies, seeks to encourage research across regions and cultures within Asia. The Series focuses on works (monographs, edited volumes, and translations) that concern the interaction between or among Asian societies, cultures, or countries, or that deal with a comparative analysis of such. Series volumes concentrate on any time period and come from any academic discipline.

© 2005 Association for Asian Studies

Printed in the United States of America

10 09 08 07 06 05   6 5 4 3 2 1

Library of Congress Cataloging-in-Publication Data
Wang, Zhenping.
  Ambassadors from the islands of immortals : China-Japan relations in the Han-Tang period / Wang Zhenping.
    p. cm. — (Asian interactions and comparisons)
  Includes bibliographical references and index.
  ISBN-10: 0-8248-2871-2 (hardcover : alk. paper)
  ISBN-13: 978-0-8248-2871-4 (hardcover : alk. paper)
    1. China—Relations—Japan. 2. Japan—Relations—China. 3. China—History—221 B.C.–960 A.D.
  I. Title: China-Japan relations in the Han-Tang period.
  II. Title. III. Series.
  DS740.5.J3W365 2005
  327.51052'09'021—dc22

                                        2005008460

University of Hawai'i Press books are printed on acid-free paper and meet the guidelines for permanence and durability of the Council on Library Resources.

Series design by Rich Hendel
Printed by Sheridan Books, Inc.

For my parents, parents-in-law,
beloved wife Fannie, and
daughter Clare

Contents

Series Editor's Preface

About twenty years ago, a European scholar of the Taiping Rebellion (1850–1864), which ravaged large parts of China and caused the deaths of many millions, mentioned to me that no sooner was the University of Washington project aimed at translating most of the extant Taiping documents completed than research on the rebellion dried up and all but disappeared. Of course, his statement was something of an exaggeration, but it contained more than a kernel of truth. A similar fate seems to have affected studies of premodern Sino-Japanese diplomatic relations. With the publication over half a century ago of English translations of the entries on "Japan" in the Chinese dynastic histories by Tsunoda Ryusaku (1877–1964) and L. Carrington Goodrich (1894–1986), research on this fascinating and extremely important topic for all intents and purposes vanished.

We are thus exceedingly proud to offer this marvelous new study by Wang Zhenping, *Ambassadors from the Islands of Immortals: China-Japan Relations in the Han-Tang Period,* the first major study on this topic in English since Tsunoda and Goodrich's translations appeared. As a look through Professor Wang's notes and bibliography will quickly reveal, however, Chinese and Japanese scholars have not been so adversely affected as their Western counterparts, having produced countless books and articles over the past century or more. Wang makes judicious use in his study of this immense body of writings as well as the rich primary documentation. We are thus lucky to have such a work in English—by one trained in the Chinese, Japanese, and Western worlds of sinology.

In his prudent examination of the primary materials—published documents, seals, and inscriptions—Wang is careful to address all sides as we now understand them: Han-Tang China, Wo-Yamato Japan, and the various kingdoms on or near the Korean peninsula. But his study goes beyond an examination of the documentary record alone. He looks at the ships that carried emissaries from "Japan" to "China," the route of travel from their port of call to the capital in Changan, Japanese efforts to acquire information from China, Chinese efforts to assimilate foreign talent, and much more.

In the end, he adopts a model of "mutual self-interest" to describe Sino-Japanese relations in this early period. Both sides saw much to be gained by keeping the relationship alive and healthy; it was not simply Chinese pompousness and Japanese ingratiation. Asian Interactions and Comparisons is pleased to be able to offer this important study to a broad readership. Let us hope that another fifty years will not pass before other works on this topic appear in English.

JOSHUA A. FOGEL

Acknowledgments

I wish to offer my gratitude to Wu Yugan, Xia Xiurui, and Li Kanghua at the University of International Business and Economics (Beijing), who gave me my initial training in economics and the history of China's foreign trade.

I also wish to extend my special thanks both to Marion Levy, chairman of the Department of East Asian Studies, and David Redman, associate dean of the graduate school of Princeton University. They gave special consideration to my application, granted me a full scholarship, and helped me eventually to arrive and study at Princeton.

I would never have studied at Princeton if John D. Langlois Jr. had not taken the time to tell me about the Department of East Asian Studies at Princeton and had not encouraged me to apply to Princeton's graduate school. Twenty years later, he has again taken the time to read and comment on the first draft of this book. To him and his wife Xinyi, I offer my whole-hearted gratitude.

At Princeton, I received from Denis Twitchett, Martin Collcutt, and James Liu rigorous training in the history of China and Japan. They helped me focus my research on the history of China-Japan relations in premodern times. They inspired me to explore the varied modes of diplomatic communication between the two countries and to study the different readings and meanings of the same diplomatic terms used in state letters as viewed from both Chinese and Japanese perspectives. I thank them for the thought-provoking conversations with me during which the major arguments of this book developed. I also thank them for their warm sense of humor that made my Princeton years so enjoyable and memorable.

A Dissertation Fellowship from the Japan Foundation allowed me to spend a year (1987–1988) in Japan, where my study and research were very fruitful thanks to Oyama Kyohei, Chikusa Masaaki, Kōzen Hiroshi, and Kamada Motoichi at Kyoto University; Tonami Mamoru and Kominami Ichirō at the Research Institute for Humanistic Studies, Kyoto University; Nishijima Sadao and Ikeda On at Tokyo University; and Ōba Osamu and Matsuura Akira at Kansai University. They provided me with further training in Japanese history and helped me locate primary sources and secondary scholarship.

Living in a foreign country could have been a frustrating experience had I not met many caring American and Japanese friends. During my first year at Princeton, Isabel Metzger met with me once a week to improve my spoken English and the drafts of my term papers. I also met her husband, Bruce M. Metzger, and son, John Metzger. It was a real joy talking with them, as they shared with me their knowledge of Christianity and their insights into contemporary issues in the United States. Through the Host Family Program at Princeton, I also came to know Louis Lardieri and her husband, Nicholas. They became my American parents. In 1987, they flew to Vancouver to attend my wedding on behalf of my parents. My wife and I are grateful for their love, care, and help. I also had the chance to live with Philip and Marilyn Garnick for two years. I thank them for their kindness and friendship. They and my other American friends made me feel like a welcome member of a big family rather than a lonely stranger in a foreign country.

During my stay in Japan, Kida Tomoo at Ryūkoku University and his wife Naoko as well as Kinugawa Tsuyoshi at Kyoto University of Technology and Fiber, Nagao Jitsuke and Sugihashi Takao at Ritsumeikan University, and Mr. Sugihara Masamichi, director of the Japan Foundation's Kyoto branch, showered my wife and me with hospitality, for which we are deeply grateful.

I must thank Frederick Mote for offering me the editorship of the *Gest Library Journal* after I graduated from Princeton. Working under his guidance was a valuable opportunity for me to collaborate more fully with other scholars, to see to the production of scholarship of quality, and to understand the publishing business more deeply.

I started writing this book after taking up an appointment in 1993 at the National Institute of Education, Singapore. I thank Ho Koon Wan, a former colleague, Lee Cheuk Yin, Yung Sai-hsing, and Timothy Tsu at the National University of Singapore for helping me overcome the initial difficulties of living and working in this tropical country.

Denis Twitchett and Martin Collcutt provided much needed encouragement for me to complete this book. They read and improved the manuscript, helped with translation of Tang poems, and sharpened my interpretation of the key issues in China-Japan diplomatic history. I am forever indebted to them for their kindness and guidance.

Timothy Brook and Julia Ching at the University of Toronto, Bob T. Wakabayashi at York University, and D. W. Y. Kwok at the University of Hawai'i read portions of the early draft of this book and made valuable suggestions for its improvement. Barbara Westergaard and Ralph Meyer offered their indispensable editing skills. I thank them for teaching me the principle of the "economy of words" and for showing me the narrative synthesis approach to scholarly writing. Their help enabled me to transform my Ph.D. dissertation written for a small number of experts to this book meant for a wider audience. Meyer also compiled the index.

In preparing the manuscript for final submission to the press, Chen Jiefang and Cao Shuwen at Princeton University helped in library research, Kida Tomoo in finding Japanese materials, and Ken Cheong in digitizing pictures for illustration.

I must thank my colleagues at the National Institute of Education: Christine Lee for arranging a semester off from teaching in 2005, which allowed me to concentrate on finishing this book, and Wong Tai Chee for help with French materials.

I must also thank Joshua A. Fogel for his keen interest in publishing this book and the anonymous external reader for invaluable suggestions to improve the manuscript. And working with Patricia Crosby, Jenn Harada, and Susan Stone at the University of Hawai'i Press has been a delightful learning experience.

My final debt of thanks goes to my parents, my parents-in-law, my beloved wife Fannie, and my daughter Clare. Without their love and support, I would have achieved little. As but a tiny recompense, I dedicate this book to them.

Ambassadors from the Islands of Immortals

Introduction

This book is an "inner history" of official relations between Japan and China from the second century B.C. to the tenth century A.D. In it I use archaeological findings and accounts in Chinese and Japanese official chronicles to build a body of knowledge about ancient Japan, which was evolving from a loose confederation of tribes into a centralized state modeled on Chinese institutions. In this process toward political unification, competing Japanese tribal leaders actively sought Chinese support and recognition to strengthen their positions at home and to exert military influence on southern Korea. They dispatched ambassadors to China and requested the bestowal of such Chinese insignia as official titles, gold seals, and bronze mirrors. To handle these requests, successive Chinese courts employed an investiture system. The system managed temporary bestowal, formal confirmation, and, when necessary, denial or deprivation of Chinese official titles for foreign rulers. Although it was designed as a control mechanism for China to conduct geopolitics in East Asia, in reality the system did not function as a unilateral tool of Chinese hegemony. The investiture system in Japan-China relations displayed a bipolar structure, with the rulers of China and Japan as the center of their respective domains. In this system, the Japanese rulers were active players, who decided whether or when they would enter or withdraw from the system. And their decision was based on careful calculation of self-interest, not on passive acceptance of China's superiority. Instead of being "Chinese-dominated," the system was flexible and responsive to the changing balance of power between China and Japan.

When a centralized power had been finally established in Japan, Japanese diplomats sent to China in the early seventh century stopped requesting Chinese official titles as a source of prestige and for domestic system-building. The investiture system ceased to be the norm of bilateral relations and was replaced by a tributary system. Although the new system defined Japan as a "tribute-paying" country (for which read "gift-presenting" country) to China, the relationship between the two countries was no longer one of "sovereign and vassal." The Tang court, however, continued to treat Japanese diplomats as subjects of China and unilaterally granted them honorary official titles in order to maintain at the ceremonial level the prestige of Tang emperors. And for the sake of successfully completing their mission, Japanese visitors accepted these titles. Both the investiture and the tributary systems were thus recipro- cal in nature. They were able to benefit both China and Japan in quite different ways and under changing circumstances.

Official contacts between China and Japan before the tenth century were conducted through "ambassador diplomacy." Both countries made meticulous preparations for their missions abroad. And both carefully chose their diplomats according to rigorous criteria and through a com- petitive procedure. Only people of high caliber were eligible for diplo- matic positions. Japanese ambassadors sent to Tang China were not only highly educated, they also had colorful personalities. Some were men of great literary talent; others were passionate lovers. After a heart- breaking parting from their loved ones at the port of departure, Japa- nese diplomats embarked on a dangerous journey to China. They often encountered unimaginable hardships and dangers when sailing on the high seas. And they would eventually arrive at the Tang capital only after a long and punishing journey in China by using the relay station system and the Grand Canal. Once in the capital, a series of elaborate court receptions awaited them.

Meticulous over details of ritual, the Tang court receptions were a mode of behavioral communication between the host and the guest. Ceremonial arrangements were designed in a way that allowed the Tang court to indicate its assessment of a foreign country's relationship with China. When a foreign ambassador acted on these arrangements, the court would interpret his behavior as acceptance of China's suzerainty. A foreign ambassador, however, might choose to object to certain cere- monial arrangements when he believed that conformity to them would be demeaning and would distort the bilateral relationship. The Tang court sometimes received Japanese ambassadors together with diplo- mats from other countries. On these occasions, arrangements for the court reception, such as the sequence in which foreign diplomats were received, the positions where they stood during an audience, and the seating arrangements for the imperial banquet held in their honor, provided a public statement of Japan's standing relative to that of other countries in the Chinese world. These arrangements sometimes became contentious issues. Making, accepting, adjusting, or rejecting ceremonial arrangements at the Tang court were thus a means for the involved parties to convey diplomatic messages and to negotiate.

Presentation and acceptance of diplomatic correspondence was another major mode of diplomatic communication between China and Japan. Most of the correspondence consisted of state letters. For its acceptance by the Tang court, a Japanese state letter had to be composed according to a set Chinese verbal etiquette. The essence of such etiquette was for all the incoming as well as the outgoing state letters to properly embody a hierarchical world order centered on China. Complex and detailed, Tang verbal etiquette stipulated the wording, the format, the type of paper, and the enclosing case commensurate to the political purpose of an outgoing Tang state letter. However, the Japanese courtiers managed to pay only lip service to these regulations. Their state letters, while superficially recognizing China's superiority, not only offered a Tang emperor no real political submission, but also dignified the Japanese ruler. This seemingly unattainable goal was achieved by an ingenious manipulation of language.

When adapting literary Chinese for use as their own written language, the Japanese adopted the *kanji* characters. Some of them, while identical in form with the Chinese characters, also had distinctive Japanese connotations and pronunciations. A number of the key diplomatic terms used in Japanese state letters to China were such *kanji* characters. Careful examinations of their pronunciations and usage in the Japanese context reveal that these *kanji* either diluted or concentrated the original meanings of their Chinese counterparts. The diluting effect weakens or cancels the honorific or the China-centered connotation of a Chinese word, converting the word in question into a less status-sensitive or a status-neutral *kanji*. The concentrating effect, in contrast, adds a tone of respect to a status-neutral Chinese word, transforming the word into an honorific. Employment of these *kanji* therefore enabled a Japanese state letter to conform to Tang verbal requirements for diplomatic correspondence and, at the same time, protected the dignity of the Japanese rulers. This understanding of the nuances of *kanji* diplomatic terms contributes to research into such controversial scholarly issues as whether

Japanese ambassadors brought state letters to Tang China and the tactics that Japanese courtiers employed in writing them.

Japanese state letters to Tang China were in fact not meant to express explicitly the changed stance of Japan toward the Chinese world order. They were merely instruments for Japanese ambassadors to activate official relations with China so that they could successfully perform their main tasks: collecting information on and siphoning knowledge from Tang, and procuring for Japan as much cultural and material benefit as possible during their visits to China. Japanese diplomats showed keen interest in many aspects of life in China, from court politics, prices for goods, natural disasters, and unrest in the provinces to new trends in the arts and recent political developments in neighboring countries of Tang. To better perform their task of introducing Chinese culture to Japan, some Japanese diplomats tried to further their knowledge of Chinese culture by studying Chinese classics under Tang instructors, some went on a shopping spree to purchase Chinese books and luxuries, and some persuaded established Tang scholars and monks to come to Japan in order to speed up the dissemination of Chinese learning at home. Japanese diplomats showed interest in all important branches of Chinese learning. They were, however, not indiscriminate borrowers of Chinese culture. The emphasis of their cultural importations was on such practical knowledge as philology, medicine, astrology, and matters relating to the calendar.

The analysis of China-Japan relations presented in this book is built on a key concept of mutual self-interest. A sustainable bilateral relationship had to have a core of overlapping self-interest of involved parties, and at the same time the official contacts between the parties had to be conducted according to mutually acceptable rules. I argue that the main objective of Japan's diplomacy toward the Sui and Tang courts was obtaining cultural and material benefits, not establishing a relationship of equality with China. The book criticizes the western tributary theory, which sees the world only from the viewpoint of the Chinese and overly simplifies the intricate domestic and international situations in which China and Japan interacted with one another. It also challenges the theory of equality, which fails to note that even though China-Japan relations during Sui-Tang times were not those between superior and inferior, bilateral relations continued to be conducted in the traditional norm of investiture and tribute. Far from forming a rigid political framework, both the investiture and the tributary systems were flexible games of interest and power between China and its neighbors. Multiple partners in these games modified the rules by which they played, or chose not to play, depending on the changing historical circumstances in which they found themselves.

The Islands of Immortals

Ancient Japan is an island of magic plants, animals, and immortals in Chinese legends. Jade greens, golden vegetables, and peaches grow on the ground, and mulberry trees of more than one thousand meters rise from the blue seas. These trees bear one-inch fruits, which are part of the diet of the immortals, who have shining golden bodies and fly like birds. As if they were two lovers embracing each other, these mulberry trees usually share the same roots, and their branches often intertwine. This vivid imagery prompts the Chinese to use the terminology "intertwining mulberry tree" *(fusang)* as a metaphor for ancient Japan.[1]

Ancient Japan in Chinese Legends

A three-thousand-year-old divine yellow beast inhabits this island. It takes the shape of a horse with eight dragon wings on the back. Flapping its huge wings, this beast flies as far as ten thousand miles a day. It once carried the legendary Yellow Emperor (r. 2697–2597 B.C.) around, allowing him to tour the vast Chinese empire at will.[2] Those who are fortunate enough to ride the beast will live for two thousand years. A type of silkworm with a horn on its head and scales on its seven-inch-long black body also lives here. Known as the "ice silkworm," it starts producing huge cocoons in five colors when covered by ice. Fine silk cloth woven from these cocoons always sheds water and cannot burn.[3]

Divine spirits are said to protect this magic island. From a distance, it looks like a floating white cloud with plants on the ground that provide immortality to whomever eats of them and palaces built of silver and gold. It is extremely difficult to reach the island; if a man attempts to approach, his ship will be obstructed by contrary winds or currents, or the island itself will mysteriously submerge into the ocean.[4]

The First Emperor of the Qin dynasty (221–207 B.C.) decided to locate this island when a report reached him to the effect that many people in the remote West had recently died of an unknown epidemic, their corpses littering the roads, but that the dead persons mysteriously revived when birds carrying some sort of plant flew over and dropped these plants on the faces of the corpses. With the report also came samples of the plant, which grew on a red stem with green leaves in the shape of water bamboo. They were immediately sent for identification. A learned man informed the emperor that the plant was the herb of immortality, a single stem of which was sufficient to save hundreds of lives. This life-saving plant, however, could be found only in the emerald field of an island in the "Eastern Sea."[5]

Obsessed with immortality, the First Emperor sent Xu Fu, an alchemist, to locate this island and to acquire the herb.[6] But Xu Fu came back empty-handed. Fearing harsh punishment for failure in an official mission, he lied to the court, claiming that on his way to the island he had encountered the Sea God, who questioned his identity and the purpose of his journey. The Sea God then led him to a mountain in the southeast, where an entire palace was built of plants of longevity. An official with a bronze face and a dragon body came out to greet Xu Fu. When he appeared, he radiated light that brightened the sky. He told Xu Fu that his meager presents would permit him only a glimpse of the plant. Xu humbly bowed twice, asking, "What would be the appropriate gifts for you?" "Bring me young boys, virgins, and craftsmen of every kind, and you may have the plant," replied the Sea God.

The First Emperor rejoiced at Xu Fu's report, never suspecting that the Sea God's request for gifts might be Xu's fabrication. Construction of a huge fleet for Xu's next mission was soon under way, and the gifts were duly prepared: three thousand each of boys and maidens, craftsmen of all kinds, and seeds of rice, millet, wheat, and beans. Xu Fu, however, knew that he would soon be sent on another impossible mission, so he decided to flee China, taking all the gifts with him.

Xu Fu and his followers thereafter found a new home in a land with large plains and lakes. There they farmed and fished to feed themselves, used herbs to cure disease, brought up their children and buried their dead. Occasionally, they also came to China to trade. They were happy and content, having no long borders to guard, no huge palaces to construct, no high taxes to pay, and no harsh punishments from which to suffer.[7] They even advised the First Qin Emperor to cease all the warfare and discontinue his wasteful projects so that he too could have an easy and relaxing life, the consequence of which would be that he would have no need to seek herbs for immortality and longevity.[8] Xu Fu's new homeland, according to these Chinese traditions, was ancient Japan.

Chinese legends trace the earliest contact between China and Japan to 1000 B.C., when a sage king ruled China. A messenger from ancient Japan was said to have arrived and paid homage to the king, expressing admiration for the prosperity and peacefulness of the Middle Kingdom. He also presented *curoma longa (changcao)*, a rare local fragrant herb for making sacrificial wine for the ancestral altar.[9]

In reality, however, the Chinese knew very little about ancient Japan. Although a Chinese metaphor compares Japan and China to "close neighbors connected by a strip of water" *(yi yidai shui)*,[10] the vast East China Sea, not a narrow strip of water, in fact separated the two countries. Primitive navigational and shipbuilding skills rendered regular contacts with each other impossible. Any information about the other party was based largely on hearsay. The Chinese usage of Wo (Japanese: Wa) is a case in point.[11] A loosely defined term, Wo refers to a variety of oceanic peoples living in southern Korea, the Japanese archipelago, and the tropical South China Sea.[12] Little is certain about the Wo except they were obedient and complaisant.[13]

The Wo People in Chinese Chronicles and Archaeology

The Chinese court found more information about the Wo in the first century B.C., when the Western Han court (206 B.C.–A.D. 8) established through territorial expansion four commanderies *(jun)* in northern Korea. A semi-military organization, the Lelang commandery became the destination for some Wo people, who came to pay annual tribute.[14] These Wo people, however, were largely Korean tribesmen from islands west of the Korean peninsula and perhaps had little to do with the ancient Japanese. Reliable information about Japan only directly reached the Chinese court in A.D. 57. That year the first Wo messenger arrived at the court of the Eastern Han (25–220).[15] To obtain firsthand knowledge of Japan, however, the Chinese had to wait until A.D. 240, when an ambassador of the Wei court (220–265) became the first Chinese official ever to set foot on Japanese soil.[16] From then until the end of the Tang dynasty (618–907), memorials to the Chinese court by Japanese embassies and Chinese ambassadors provided Chinese official historians with the valuable information about Japan that they used to compile the accounts of the ancient Japanese in their successive dynastic histories.[17] These accounts coupled with archaeological findings reveal a colorful ancient Japan with an interesting and eventful history.[18]

In the Chinese records, Japan was located in the ocean southeast of the Daifang commandery. A country of steep mountains, it was covered by dense forests of hardwood, oak, camphor, mulberry, and maple. Even the plains were full of bushes, bamboo, and trees, which grew so luxuriantly that a man could hardly see another person walking a short distance in front of him. There were no roads linking the country together, only tracks for animals. Oxen, horses, tigers, leopards, sheep, and magpies, however, could not be found in Japan.

Japanese weather was warm and mild; vegetables grew all year round. Arable land was fertile and suitable for wheat and rice, but it was in short supply. People could hardly earn a living solely by farming. Some traded with fellow islanders and Koreans, selling white pearls, green jade, amber and agate;[19] some were involved in handicrafts, producing spears, shields, wooden bows, and bamboo arrows tipped with iron or bone, and others manufactured fine paper;[20] still others fished, using nets and cormorants,[21] or themselves harvested abalone and clams. Seafood was thus a major part of the Japanese diet.[22] They ate vegetables raw and had yet to learn the use of ginger, citrus, spices, and mioga ginger as flavorings. When dining, they used their fingers to pick up food served on bamboo or wooden trays. Wine was a popular drink. Healthy eating habits brought about longevity: some people lived more than a hundred years.

The Japanese cultivated mulberry trees for sericulture and used hemp and bark to make fiber for weaving. Stone and wooden spindles and parts of a loom have been unearthed; and a design on a bronze bell shows a man holding a thread in one hand and an I-shaped weaving tool in the other.[23] Weaving, spinning, and the planting of hemp and mulberry trees had become the major economic activities of the Japanese, and these occupations have been well documented in eighth-century Japanese local records.[24] Using well-developed spinning and weaving technology, the Japanese produced a yellowish silk so strong that a six-strand thread could hold a fish of fifty catties.[25] Japanese brocade and their red and blue silks were also of high quality. A Japanese messenger proudly presented them as state gifts to the Chinese emperor in 243. Fine silk and cloth woven of various bark fibers were popular with the Japanese.[26] A ruler once wore a robe with sleeves fashioned in a white cloth made from paper mulberry fibers.[27] Clothing for ordinary people was simple: men tied pieces of cloth together without sewing; women put on a large square cloth with an opening in the center. Using seeds from tropical trees, they also wove soft, cottonlike kapok.[28] This was used as headbands for men, although they preferred leaving their hair in an uncovered coil. Accustomed to walking barefooted, they wore no shoes. Various accessories were fashionable: arm bracelets made from shells and necklaces from comma-shaped stone beads or cylindrical jewels.

To scare harmful fish away when fishing, men painted their faces black and tattooed their bodies. A decoration for both young and old, tattoos were different in size and location depending on a man's social status.[29] Women smeared their bodies with cinnabar and wore their hair in loops. Both males and females dyed their teeth black, using a jet black liquid produced by soaking iron filings in wine, tea, or vinegar to oxidize the metal.[30]

Ordinary Japanese lived in thatched huts, semi-sunken, supported by pillars, and oval in shape with a central hole in the roof for ventilation. Prominent families resided in wooden houses raised on piles. As shown in the design of a bronze mirror discovered from the Nara region, these houses were modeled on early rice warehouses. Rectangular and supported by four pillars, they had an elevated floor to prevent moisture from accumulating, making living more comfortable.[31] Family members, though, did not always live together. Sons would leave their parents on reaching adulthood. Blood ties linked families together to form the groups that were the basic production units.

As women outnumbered men, polygamy was practiced. Men of distinction often had four or five spouses, and others two or three. But polygamy caused no domestic tension since women were faithful and trusting. At social gatherings females sat side by side with males.

Divination was widely practiced to predict the outcome of an action. In a process similar to tortoise shell divination in China, the aim of the divination was announced, bones were baked, and cracks on the bones were carefully examined as clues to future events.

In a unique ritual, seafaring Japanese offered prayers to the Sea God for safety and health. When a voyage started, one person would act as the mourner, who neither bathed, combed his hair, nor washed his clothes until fleas grew unchecked on his body. He also kept a strict vegetarian diet and suppressed his lust for women. If all was well at the journey's end, fellow passengers would reward him with slaves and valuables; if, however, any passenger fell sick, or died from pirate attack, they would kill the mourner, believing that he had not faithfully observed the rituals.

Death, the Japanese thought, was provisional and potentially reversible within ten days of a person's demise. They thus did not immediately bury the deceased but kept the corpse in a coffin.[32] Family members would gather in front of the coffin, mourning and weeping, trying to call back the spirit of the dead by their voices. Friends also came. To inject energy into the feeble spirit, they generated as much noise as possible by singing, dancing, and drinking.[33] Only when revival was finally considered impossible would the burial ceremony proceed. On that day, the coffin was laid in a pit with no outer coffin. The grave was then sealed with soil and a grave mound built. Upon completion of the ceremony, mourners purified themselves by bathing. They neither ate meat nor drank wine during the entire period.

Social stratification existed in the society. The order between superiors and inferiors was well maintained. People were conscious of their status and showed respect in different ways depending on the occasion. When meeting with a great personage, a commoner slapped his hands but did not kneel or bow. When coming across a man of importance on the road, commoners would immediately withdraw to the bushes. In conveying messages to or addressing their superiors, they either squatted or knelt with both hands on the ground.

Punishment for crime was severe. For a misdemeanor, the offender would lose his wives and children, but his entire family as well as kinspeople would be exterminated if he had committed a major crime. Murderers, robbers, and rapists were sentenced to death. A thief was subject to a fine equivalent to the spoils or enslaved if he was unable to pay. Banishment or beating with a heavy stick was the penalty for other offenses, depending on their seriousness. Torture was used to induce a confession from a suspect, whose knees would be pressed by wood and his neck sawn by a bowstring. A person's innocence was sometimes tested by ordering him to pick a stone out of boiling water or dip his hand in a jar full of snakes. A scalded or bitten hand was considered evidence of guilt.[34] In reality, however, theft almost did not exist and litigation was infrequent.

The indiscriminate extension of punishment to the offender's kin indicates the existence of clans in the society. They would evolve into regional groups when agriculture developed, and coordination of the use of water for farming became necessary. In due time, common economic concerns for reclaiming land and building irrigation facilities would draw groups in the same region to form unified regional groups, whose members not only produced rice and other food crops, but also built stockade forts for self-protection. These unified regional groups were scattered in northern Kyūshū and the Kinai region around Osaka Bay. At one time there were more than one hundred of them, which the Chinese sources refer to as "principalities" *(guo)*.

These principalities were progressing toward political unification. Some thirty, such as Duima (Tsushima), Yiqi (Iki), Yidu (Itō), Touma (Toma), Gounu (Kunu), and Xiematai (Yamatai), eventually emerged as powerful contenders for hegemony, and they all sent messengers to contact Western Han authorities in north Korea in order to gain Chinese political recognition. Nuguo was one of these principalities. Located in Kasuga city, Fukuoka district, northern Kyūshū, this principality received bronze mirrors and glass *bi* disks from the Western Han court as an indication of token support for its ruler. These disks were extremely precious objects since the Chinese court used them as emblems of nobility in its own ranking system. The finding of glass *bi* disks in Kasuga city thus indicates that the Nuguo ruler had been included in Western Han officialdom and that he was considered a vassal of China. The Eastern Han court also confirmed his vassal status in A.D. 57, when it granted a Nuguo messenger a snake-knobbed official gold seal the inscription of which reads "King Nu of Wo [vassal] of Han." Moreover, the Nuguo ruler once attempted to establish a Chinese-style political hierarchy in northern Kyūshū by granting his subordinates pieces of the glass *bi* disks, which have been unearthed in different places in Fukuoka.[35]

The Myth of Yamatai
and the Rise of Yamato

Among these principalities, Yamatai subsequently evolved into one of the unified regional polities with twenty-one subordinate principalities. Scholars have debated the location of Yamatai for a long time without reaching a firm conclusion, some pointing to Kyūshū,[36] others to the Kinai region. Recent excavation conducted from 1986 to 1989 at Yoshinogari, Saga prefecture, Kyūshū, gives the Kyūshū theory more weight. Although far from solving the disagreement concerning Yamatai's location, the excavation and the reconstruction of the historical structures at Yoshinogari have revealed some physical characteristics of the center of an ancient Japanese principality.

At Yoshinogari, archaeologists have found the remains of a settlement protected by inner and outer moats. Inside the moats are two watchtowers,[37] a palace, and two burial areas with elaborately built mounds; and outside the moats, some fifty elevated storage houses. Many ritual vessels have also been unearthed alongside the path leading to the burial mounds. They were probably offerings from people of other villages controlled by the Yoshinogari ruler. The storage houses are almost double the size of average storehouses of the time, suggesting that they were granaries for rice taxes collected from neighboring regions.[38]

These archaeological findings match some of the accounts concerning Yamatai in the *Weizhi,* a third-century Chinese dynastic history. According to these accounts, the ruler of Yamatai resided in a heavily fortified palace protected by armed guards and stockades, inside which was a multistoried tower. Yamatai officials collected taxes in kind from subordinate principalities, and they also had granaries constructed to store tax grain.

Based on the *Weizhi* accounts and the archaeological evidence, modern scholars have ascertained some aspects of the Yamatai power structure. The country had been governed by male rulers, who as early as A.D. 107 sent a messenger to China, presenting 160 slaves to the Han court. However, from the latter half of the second century, Yamatai degenerated into political chaos with no recognized leader. Warfare escalated with the use of stone arrowheads of increased size and weight.[39] Power struggles, though violent and bloody, eventually led the contenders for power to reach a compromise. They agreed on Himiko to be the first female ruler of Yamatai.[40]

A mystical figure, Himiko lived a solitary life after coming to power and remained single as she grew older. Although some one thousand women served her as attendants, she deliberately avoided the public, allowing only one man to provide her with food and drink and to liaise on her behalf with her subjects. To gain strength and inspiration to govern the country, Himiko offered sacrifices and prayers to spirits, which, in the belief of ancient East Asians, had the power to influence human affairs and should therefore be served through proper ceremonies.[41] But Himiko went beyond conducting simple ceremonies and employing shamanistic skills in ruling Yamatai. She developed the "Way of Spirits" *(guidao)* to help her form a large following, outmaneuver her competitors, and stabilize her domestic situation without using force.[42]

Himiko's younger brother assisted her in the daily affairs of government; senior officials known as the "Great Wo" (Dawo), were dispatched to regulate commercial activities in each principality. And the "Great Shuai" (Dashuai) was responsible for the political control of neighboring principalities. From his headquarters in Yidu, northern Kyūshū, he supervised local rulers and kept them fearful of the Yamatai authority. He also received ambassadors from China, the Chinese authorities in northern Korea, and various Korean states when they landed in Yidu, which was then the communication hub with Asian countries. At Yidu, foreign ambassadors' ships would be inspected and their official documents and gifts forwarded to the Yamatai court.

Activities of the "Great Shuai" indicate a correlation between domestic politics and foreign relations: rulers of Yamatai, Nuguo, and other polities actively sought recognition and support from China in their quest for state-building, territorial expansion, and unification of the country. They wanted to adapt the established Chinese models for their government and political hierarchy.[43] The means they used to achieve this end was diplomacy.

The diplomacy that comprised Japan's official relations with China satisfied Japan's changing needs in different periods: it facilitated the formation of local states in the first century A.D.; it expedited Japanese progress in political centralization from the latter half of the fourth century; it was a means to elevate Japan's standing in the East Asian world when Japan achieved unification in the seventh century; and it also served to channel Chinese high culture to the Japanese archipelagos.

Japan's changing domestic situation dictated the frequency of official contact with China, which varied from short periods of frequent intercourse to long intervals of isolation. During the Eastern Han dynasty, messengers from Nuguo and Mianutguo visited the Chinese court in 57 and 107 to win Chinese support for state-building at home.[44] The thirty-odd Wo messengers that the Wei court received represented the stronger Japanese contenders for power and represented a gradual Japanese movement toward centralization; Himiko and her successor, Iyo, alone dispatched five ambassadors between 238 and 247.[45]

Bilateral contacts were spasmodic during the Western Jin dynasty (265–316). Messengers from Wo and unspecified "eastern barbarian countries" came to the Jin court in 266, 280, 281, and 282. A Wo delegation also went to southern China in 306, looking for seamstresses and working women.[46] A total break in contacts followed that lasted well past the fifth century. During this period there was an intense power struggle in Japan. Among the rival petty states, Yamato in the Kinai region in central Japan emerged victorious. The Yamato chieftains sent a delegation to China in 413, ushering in a new period of frequent official contacts.[47] Over the next ninety years, they dispatched as many as thirteen messengers to China as part of a concerted effort to consolidate political power and to strive to gain hegemony in Japan.[48]

Japan-China relations entered another quiet period in the sixth century. Near the end of the century, the Yamato court, under an ingenious leader, Prince Shōtoku (572–622), initiated reforms to transform its existing clan structure into an imperial system along the Chinese lines. China in the meantime saw the reestablishment of its own unity under the Sui dynasty (581–618), which together with the subsequent Tang dynasty were the most powerfully centralized courts in Chinese history. The Yamato rulers wished to use the complex social, political, economic, and military systems that the Sui and the Tang developed as a blueprint for their own reforms. Moreover, both dynasties were also renowned for unprecedented cultural achievement, economic development, and military expansion, which attracted visitors to their court and capital from all over the world. Again, official contact between China and Japan gained momentum: within a space of fourteen years, the Sui court received five Japanese missions;[49] during the Tang dynasty, the Japanese court appointed eighteen ambassadors to China, of whom fifteen actually reached their goal.[50]

2   Chinese Insignia in East Asian Politics

During the early spring of 1784, Jin Heiei, a farmer from Shikanoshima, northern Kyūshū, was digging a ditch when his pickaxe hit something solid in the field. It was the top of an underground chamber, in which he found a gold seal with a snake knob. A cube with sides measuring 2.4 centimeters and weighing 109 grams, the seal bore a five-character inscription in three lines that had been cut in intaglio: "The King of Nuguo, [appointed by] Han" (Han Wei Nuguo Wang). This was the seal that the Han court had bestowed upon the ruler of Nuguo in 57.[1]

Gold Seals, Military Banners, and Bronze Mirrors

The gold seal and the five-word inscription were material testimony to and verbal manifestation of the possessor's superior position at home and vassal status to China: "king" was a Chinese title that recognized him as the paramount ruler of the Nuguo and as an "outer subject" to the Son of Heaven, holding a position in China's political hierarchy that entitled him to Chinese support when needed. Indeed, any ruler of a

Imprint of the seal "The King of Nuguo (appointed by Han)." Collection of the Kuroida family; preserved at the Fukuoka Municipal Museum of Art. (Luo Fuyi, *Qin Han Nanbei chao guanyin zhengcun* [Beijing: Wenwu Chubanshe, 1987], p. 211)

Imprint of the seal "Pro-Wei Queen of Wo." This seal has not been found. The imprint first appeared in a Ming dynasty work, *Xuanhe jigu yinshi.* It was then included in the Japanese work *Kōko nichi-roku.* (Kimiya Yasuhiko, *Nisshi kōtsushi* [Tokyo: Kanasashi Hōryūdō, 1927])

principality in Wo would have wanted such recognition from China. Suishō, for example, the head of a Yamatai mission, visited the Chinese commandery at Lelang in 107 and requested a court audience at the capital. In the sixth month of 238,[2] shortly after becoming the ruler of Yamatai, Himiko sent Nashōme and Toji Gori as ambassador and vice-ambassador to Daifang, a Chinese commandery south of present-day Pyongyang, whence Chinese officials escorted them to the Wei capital Luoyang.

The court appointed Himiko "Pro-Wei Queen of Wo" (Qin Wei Wowang) and the two diplomats "Shuaishan Colonel" (Shuaishan Zhonglang Jiang) and "Shuaishan Commandant" (Shuaishan Jiaoyu) respectively. In the Wei ranking system, "Pro-Wei King (Queen) of a certain country" was the highest title for "outer subjects." The Wei court granted it only twice during its entire period in power: to Bo Tiao, chieftain of Indoscythae (Dayuezhi), a tribe occupying the banks of Amu Darya River,[3] and to Himiko.[4] Other barbarian leaders could only expect to be granted the title "Ruler in Command of His Tribesmen" (Shuaizhong Wang).[5]

Though an invaluable Wei recognition of Himiko's supremacy at home, the prestigious title "Queen," if not accompanied by other insignia, would escape the notice of both her rivals and her subordinates, most of whom were illiterate in Chinese and unable to discern the significance of any Chinese title. To effectively announce her Wei support, Himiko needed visually striking objects: military banners (*chuang*),

The bronze mirror brought back from China by the Wo ambassador who was dispatched to the Wei court in 239. Collection of the Tokyo Museum. (Naoki Kōjiro, *Nihon no rekishi* [Tokyo: Shōgakkan, 1973, vol. 1])

swords, bronze mirrors, and such imperial gifts as brocade, silk, gold, jade, and red beads. Himiko's concern was well understood by the Wei court, which not only granted her request, but also advised on how best to use these items in an edict: "You may show all the gifts to your countrymen so as to let them know that this country supports you. Therefore, in earnest, the gifts that you want are granted."[6]

A military banner symbolized the holder's status in the Chinese military establishment.[7] In the shape of a tube hanging from a pole, the banner was usually granted only to a Chinese general in chief (Dajiang).[8] When special circumstances justified a foreign holder, the banner signified his own might as well as Chinese military backing, thus effecting a psychological impact on his enemy.[9] The Sui court once bestowed military drums and banners on the Chuluo Qaghan, chieftain of the Eastern Turks. In a battle against the Western Turks, he ordered the display of these banners, which made the Western Turks believe he was backed by the Sui army; many surrendered, and the Abo Qaghan, ruler of the Western Turks, was captured alive.[10]

Given the geographic distance, Chinese military support to Himiko could only have been symbolic; but when faced with military competition from Kunu, a powerful neighbor, even such nominal backing could tip the balance of power in her favor. This motivated Himiko to dispatch four messengers to the Wei court in a short span between 240 and 247, requesting, among other things, military banners, bronze mirrors, and swords.[11]

Official Titles and Chinese Geopolitics

As previously mentioned, in 238 Himiko's two diplomats received prestigious military titles: "Shuaishan Colonel" and "Shuaishan Commandant." The colonel and the commandant were security officers for the emperor. The former led the palace guards and was often hand-picked by the emperor himself;[12] the latter was among the emperor's closest courtiers and was usually of Han nationality. Earlier in the Han dynasty, no foreigner had ever held that position. During the Wei era, however, eight Yamatai officials received the title "Shuaishan Colonel." With the exception of one Korean official,[13] no other foreigner had been given this title.

The titles queen, colonel, and commandant constituted a new power structure in Yamatai. Although quite primitive, the structure would become sophisticated when promising contenders for hegemony embarked on territorial expansion, accelerating political unification in Wo. Front-runners in this race needed to appoint an increasing number of military and civil officials to defend and govern new territories, and to redistribute power among their major supporters; in both cases official titles had to be employed, and titles obtained from China, which carried the prestige of the Chinese court, would be the obvious choice. They were the best means to convince a ruler's supporters to accept the designated positions in a new hierarchy, thus strengthening his status as the "king among lords" and promoting political stability within his own camp.[14] The Tang court once observed, "Rulers of the remote areas cannot establish their countries without receiving seals and banners from Tang."[15]

That the Wei court accepted Himiko to be its "outer subject" and allowed her subordinates to hold prestigious military titles raised a question: why had no other Wo chieftain enjoyed the same glory during the Western Han dynasty? The explanation seems to lie in divergent geopolitical considerations of the successive Chinese courts.

Western Han China was preoccupied with the Xiongnu, nomads of the steppes of Mongolia. To cope with this troublesome northern neighbor, China created a defense line in the northeast and engaged in military expansions into Manchuria and north Korea, where four Chinese commanderies were established in 108 B.C. Wo, however, was too remote from the Asian continent to play a role in China's defense strategy. No attempt was made to contact Wo, about which the court knew very little. The gold seal of 57 was the first indication that a Wo principality might have entered the world of Chinese geopolitics.

China in the third century was in political disunion; Wei (220–265), Shuhan (221–263), and Wu (220–280) were competing against one another. They used title-granting to adjust relations with neighboring countries for their desired goals. Owing to a curious misconception that southern Wo was close to its rival, Wu, in south China, the Wei court elevated the importance of Wo in its grand strategy of containing Wu. To befriend nearby neighbors, Emperor Ming (r. 227–239) changed his usual practice of not granting court audiences to barbarians and, as a special favor, received selected foreigners, among whom was the Wo messenger of 238.[16]

In the northeast, the Wei court attempted to control the unruly Korean tribes in order to consolidate its position in Korea. Enlisting the support of Wo, which was adjacent to south Korea, was part of the strategy.[17] In 238, the Wei court had just recovered the four Korean commanderies from the Gongsun family, who had taken advantage of the sharply declining power and influence of the Eastern Han court in the early years of the third century to become lords of the region.[18] It was no coincidence that the court received Himiko's messenger in the same year. But the situation in Korea remained fluid, and the local tribes were rebellious. As a measure to achieve stabilization, the Wei court granted titles to tribal chieftains. Unfortunately, however, the situation worsened; in 245 Liu Mao and Gong Zun, governors of the Lelang and Daifang commanderies, had to lead a joint force to crush the Hui, a Korean tribe.[19] Hostilities erupted again one year later, and Gong Zun was killed in battle.[20] Relations with the various Korean tribes were severed until China was unified under the Western Jin. Mahan and Chenhan again sent tributary missions to China in 277 and 280.[21]

In Chinese geopolitics, effective management of external relations leading to the establishment of a China-centered world order was the ultimate goal. To this end, China employed the investiture system, which consisted of a request for a title, its temporary bestowal and formal confirmation, and, when necessary, its deprivation. Each step in this system was designed as a control mechanism.

The system allowed a new foreign ruler to claim that he held certain Chinese military and civil titles, an action referred to as the "self-granting of titles" *(zijia)*.[22] These titles sent a message to the Chinese side, announcing the ruler's opinion of what he believed to be his appropriate status at home and abroad. These titles, however, required China's retrospective approval, before which the foreign ruler was merely self-appointed and treated as the "acting king of a certain country" *(xing wang)* by the Chinese court. This practice enabled the court to observe a new ruler and to judge his suitability to hold the titles and his ability to fulfill the duties required by the titles. A formal bestowal of a Chinese title would affect, or could even potentially go against, China's own interests. In consequence, such bestowals had to be conducted prudently. The court, after carefully weighing the potential impact approving a title might have on its own interests, would decide whether to approve, to reject, or to make certain revisions to the title.[23] This was how the Wei court handled Himiko's request in 238.

Although a bright rising star, Himiko had not yet become the sole ruler of Wo. The court seems to have been well aware of the situation: it conferred on her the title "Pro-Wei Queen of Wo,"[24] but, in the meantime, it also took the precaution of withholding full political support. Himiko was informed that the gold seal with a purple ribbon provided her as well as the silver seals with black ribbons for the two diplomats had been granted only temporarily *(jiashou)*, leaving the Wei court with the flexibility to adjust its policy toward Wo when necessary. Two years later, in 240, Ti Jun, commander of the Imperial Guard, headed the first Wei mission to Wo to inform Himiko that her title was downgraded to the less prestigious "Caretaker of Wo" (Jia Wowang),[25] an indication that the Wei had learned of the relative standing of Himiko in Wo and the inability of Yamatai to play a decisive role in Wei's containment strategy.

A Chinese title admitted a foreign ruler to a position in Chinese officialdom, but this position was not meant to be hereditary. His (or her) successor must himself undergo the two steps of request for, and approval of, a title before he became a formal member of the Chinese official world. Once granted, the title entitled a foreign ruler to bestow upon his own courtiers certain Chinese-style titles, the range of which was defined by the Chinese court according to the importance of his country to China. This practice was known as "the granting of temporary titles in accordance with imperial decree" *(chengzhi jiashou)*.[26] Titles bestowed under this arrangement had to be in good order and accord with the Chinese world order. They could neither be more prestigious than the ruler's nor be identical with those of Chinese officials. Furthermore, they had to be approved by China. Failing to abide by these rules would be deemed disloyalty to the Son of Heaven,[27] inviting punitive action from China or from one's own enemy. In 639, Emperor Taizong condemned the ruler of Karakhoja (Gaochang) for having established official titles parallel to those of Tang China. He angrily questioned the Karakhoja ambassador, "As a subject of China, how dare he [the king of Karakhoja] do this?!"[28]

Depriving a foreign ruler of his title was China's last political resort to condemn his wrongdoing. When Silla seized several cities from Paekche in 674, the outraged emperor, Gaozong (r. 650–683), deposed the Silla ruler and made his son the king.[29] By the same token, renunciation of a Chinese title indicated a foreign ruler's formal withdrawal from the Chinese world. In 752, for example, the ruler of the Nanzhao kingdom accepted from Tibet the title "Emperor of the East," thereby rejecting his Chinese title "Lord of Yunnan."[30]

Foreign rulers were not the only ones who initiated title-granting. When China was disunified, rulers of regional states sometimes granted titles on their own authority to bolster their claims to legitimacy. This was the situation in China between 220 and 589, when the Middle Kingdom was sundered and became trapped in a north-south military impasse. In the meantime, Wo experienced the rise of a central power, the Yamato court, with its increasing involvement in south Korea in the fifth century.[31] For quite different reasons, rulers of both countries now needed to contact each other. A Wo delegation to the Eastern Jin court (317–420) in 413 resumed the bilateral contacts that had been interrupted since the 240s.[32]

Liu Yu (r. 420–422), the first emperor of the southern Chinese state of Song, was most eager to inaugurate sovereign-vassal relations with foreign rulers as a means of corroborating the legitimacy of the regime he established in 420 by forcing the last Eastern Jin emperor, Sima Dewen (r. 419–420), to abdicate in his favor. Condemned for violation of Confucian politics and for usurpation of the throne, he desperately needed to legitimate his rule. On the twenty-second day of the seventh month, 420, less than one month after founding his regime, Liu Yu bestowed a series of titles on the rulers of Wo, Paekche, and Koguryŏ, as if they had recognized him as a legitimate sovereign and his regime as a suzerain state.[33]

This was a bit of pure illusion. None of the rulers upon whom titles were bestowed had requested them and none accepted them. The bestowal was purely a unilateral act arising out of the Song court's own need for prestige at home. There is no record that any Wo, Koguryŏ, or Paekche messengers visited the court at the time.[34] And had there been a Wo messenger at the court, he would have informed his host of the new ruler, Ingyō (r. 413–452), and the court would not have bestowed a title upon Nintoku (r. 313–398?), the previous Wo ruler who had been dead for more than twenty years.

Chinese Titles, Wo's Korea Policy, and Its Domestic Order

Chinese titles defined a ruler's sphere of interest and his status in the Chinese world. But nothing remained static in the volatile situation of East Asia, where the power balance often tipped, and foreign rulers sought new titles either to reflect or to attempt to reverse the changes. A foreign ruler usually received both civil and military titles. The former, such as "prince of a certain Chinese commandery" or "king of a certain country," indicated his administrative jurisdiction, and the latter specified the areas where he had established actual military control or intended to do so.[35] A military title could thus imply both Chinese sanction of intended military aggression and recognition for recently acquired lands. Such was the appeal of a military title to any ruler who, having achieved domestic unification, desired to expand his territory. For a loser whose country had been invaded, a military title that reconfirmed his previous territorial rights implied China's support for his claim to the lost territories and condemnation of the invader.

In 421, two years after the establishment of the Song, the first Wo mission arrived.[36] The second came in 425. Then in 438, the third Wo delegation paid respect to the Song,[37] requesting the approval of fourteen titles for Hanzei (r. 406–410) and his subjects.[38] Most of the titles were "general," a designation that had been created temporarily for the commanders of expeditionary forces in early China; later the designation gained importance and became a permanent position.[39] By the Song dynasty, some forty types of general existed, ranging from the second to the eighth rank.

Hanzei claimed to be "King of Wo, Area Commander in Chief

Commissioned with Extraordinary Powers, Supervising the Military Affairs of Wo, Paekche, Silla, Mimana, Qinhan, and Muhan,[40] General in Chief for Pacification in the East." If granted, these titles would have given him sweeping powers: as "King of Wo," he would have been the China-backed ruler at home; as "Area Commander in Chief Commissioned with Extraordinary Powers," he would have been a territorial magnate,[41] with broad authority over five south Korean states: Paekche, Silla, Mimana, Qinhan, and Muhan; and, as "General in Chief for Pacification in the East," he would have had latitude to carry out military operations in the region. The Song court, however, declined his request and granted him only the title "General for Pacification in the East, King of Wo."

The striking omission of "Area Commander in Chief Commissioned with Extraordinary Powers" from Hanzei's titles was a blunt denial of Wo's intended military influence in south Korea and its established interests in Mimana, the next-door neighbor to Paekche, where Wo had stationed troops since the fourth century and created a stronghold from which to exert further influence over south Korea. This most prestigious military title indicated the holder's nominal and actual sphere of interest by a series of place-names. To rulers of both the Chinese regional states and East Asian countries of the fifth century, who equated force with power and prestige, this title was much more important than the title "King." This mentality was evident in the Song dynastic history, in which only the military titles for foreign rulers appeared in the "Basic Annals of Emperors," which recorded the major events during an emperor's reign; in contrast, the whole range of a foreign ruler's titles was found in the "Accounts of Barbarians."[42] Moreover, a Chinese court would sometimes make a person king of a country and concurrently appoint someone else "Area Commander in Chief" of that same country. This was a clear indication that the former could be only the nominal ruler. In 479, for example, the Southern Qi court (479–502) made Hezhi "King of Jialuo" and "Bulwark-General of the State"; but the military affairs of this small Korean kingdom came under the supervision of Yūryaku (r. 457–479), the Wo ruler who held the title "Area Commander in Chief Commissioned with Extraordinary Powers."[43] However, the Song court denied this title to Hanzei in 438, sending him the clear message that no Wo interference in Korean states would be tolerated.

Hanzei also made himself "General in Chief" (second rank), but the Song court confirmed him only as "General for Pacification in the East" (third rank). This too was a diplomatic message to Hanzei: Wo was insignificant in the Song military strategy.[44] The low rank that Hanzei received from the Song court was in sharp contrast to the high rank the Wei court had bestowed on Himiko in the third century and with the high position provided Koguryŏ and Paekche rulers, both of whom were ranked "Area Commander in Chief Commissioned with Extraordinary Powers" and "General in Chief" by the Song court.[45]

Wo's diminished importance was no surprise. It was now dealing with Song, a southern Chinese regime whose geopolitics aimed at encircling the Northern Wei, successor of the third-century Wei Kingdom whose rulers had befriended Himiko. The eastern link of this ring consisted of several states: Beiyan (407–436, capital in present-day Chaoyang, Liaoning province), Wo, Koguryŏ, and Paekche, of which the latter two figured more prominently than Wo owing to their geographic closeness to the Northern Wei.[46]

This link was, however, vulnerable: Koguryŏ and Paekche had been foes for decades, and both were weakened by this prolonged mutual hostility. Koguryŏ had maintained relations with the Northern Wei, making its loyalty to the Song questionable. The Song court had to rely increasingly on Paekche to keep the link in place. Any further Wo penetration into south Korea could easily worsen the intricate situation, badly damaging the link. To save the link from collapse, the Song court raised the status of Koguryŏ and Paekche rulers by prestigious titles and in the meantime tried to discourage Wo intervention in the region by granting less prestigious titles to Hanzei.

But Wo rulers persisted in gaining control of Paekche, which was strategically too crucial to the security of Mimana to be ignored. Ingyō attempted to acquire the title "Area Commander in Chief Commissioned with Extraordinary Powers" in 443, but to no avail. He had to wait until 451 to become "King of Wo, Area Commander in Chief Commissioned with Extraordinary Powers, Supervising the Military Affairs of Wo, Silla, Mimana, Jialuo, Qinhan, Muhan, General for Pacification in the East."[47] But the notable omission of Paekche from this title underlined the Song court's determination to prevent Wo dominance over Paekche. To emphasize the importance of Paekche, the court appointed its king "General in Chief," a title one rank higher than Ingyō's "General." Later, when Ankō (r. 453–456) succeeded Ingyō, the Song court granted him the same title in 462,[48] reiterating its unyielding stance toward Wo.

Repeated setbacks did not render the Wo rulers despondent. After enthronement, Yūryaku also pressed for Chinese sanction for Wo ambitions toward Paekche. In a series of self-granted titles, he made himself "Area Commander in Chief Commissioned with Extraordinary Powers" and promoted himself from "General" to "General in Chief." This time, some of Yūryaku's efforts were successful. In 478, the Song court approved his title "General in Chief," which was on a par with that of the Paekche king.[49]

The year 479 witnessed the establishment of the Qi dynasty (479–502). The court, in celebration of the new dynasty, promoted Yūryaku to "General in Chief for Defense in the East" and reappointed him "Area Commander in Chief Commissioned with Extraordinary Powers."[50] The succeeding Liang court (502–557), despite promoting Yūryaku to "General in Chief for Expedition in the East" (second rank) in 502,[51] also omitted Paekche from his military titles. In fact the successive southern dynasties had always rated Wo inferior to Koguryŏ and Paekche. Even after his promotion in 502, Yūryaku was still junior to the Koguryŏ and Paekche rulers, both of whom held the first-rank titles "Chariot and Horse General in Chief" and "General in Chief for Expedition in the East."[52] The relative standing of Wo in East Asia was best summarized in the *Dynastic History of the Liang:* "Of all the eastern barbarians, Korean states are the major ones."[53] Persistent requests from Wo had not softened the stance of the southern Chinese dynasties that Wo should not be permitted to augment its military presence in southern Korea, and they used the investiture system to deter Wo from dominating southern Korea.

But the Wo rulers stayed in the system. The utility of Chinese titles in domestic politics outweighed the disadvantage that some of the titles inflicted on Wo in international politics. For Wo to develop from a loose tribal federation into a unified country, Chinese titles were indispensable. In 107, when Suishō, the messenger of Yamatai, came to the Eastern Han court, he was accompanied by other petty warlords. These warlords, although inclined to do so, had not yet totally committed their loyalty to Yamatai.[54] Wo's political disunion and instability lingered on for many years. In 425, to promote internal stability, Hanzei requested thirteen Song military titles: "General for Pacification in the East" for himself, "General for Stabilization in the West," "General for Expeditions against the Barbarians," "General Commanding the Troops," and "Bulwark-General of the State" for Wazui and others. These were all third-rank titles, but status distinctions existed among the possessors: "General for Pacification in the East," which Hanzei received, was the highest, whereas the titles for his subjects were ranked tenth, eleventh, and twelfth respectively.[55] These titles thus officially confirmed Hanzei's supreme position among his supporters and helped him build a hierarchial system subordinate to the Chinese world order.

Under this system, Wo was, on one hand, the "eastern fence" of the Middle Kingdom and its ruler an "outer subject" to the Son of Heaven; on the other hand, however, Hanzei was himself the center vis-à-vis his generals. The title "General for Pacification in the West" underlined the centrality of Yamato in this system: the title holder was Hanzei's subject responsible for upholding Yamato authority in the West. Here, "west" referred to areas west of the Yamato court, mainly Izumo and northern Kyūshū, not the areas west of the Song capital, Jiankang (present-day Nanjing).[56] Indeed neither the Song nor the Wo wanted a Wo general to pacify any area in China.

As political stabilization and centralization progressed in Wo, the hierarchical system grew more sophisticated, and demand for Chinese titles increased. The number of Chinese titles acquired from the Song almost doubled: from thirteen in 425 to twenty-three in 451. These titles were also diversified from military to civil; now, officials holding a civil title such as "Grand Protector" were stationed in new territories to establish Yamato authority.[57] In a state letter to the Song court in 478, Yūryaku hinted at the utility of Chinese titles: "I humbly granted the title 'Commander Unequaled in Honor' on myself and other titles on my fellow countrymen so as to persuade them to offer fidelity [to the Song emperor]."[58] Under the pretext of advising supporters to offer loyalty to the Song emperor, Yūryaku institutionalized himself as the paramount ruler by taking an honorific title for eminent generals.[59]

The Evolution of the Investiture System

However, in 600, when a Wo ambassador eventually contacted the Sui court after bilateral relations had been suspended for almost a century, acquisition of a Chinese title was not an item on his agenda. With the achievement of greater unification in the seventh century and the establishment of a centralized power structure in which the "Tennō," the Heavenly Sovereign of Wo, was at center stage, Chinese titles as a means of system-building were no longer of political use. The sovereign-vassal relations between the two countries ceased, and a new bilateral relationship emerged that depended on diplomatic maneuvering to advance Wo's interests in southern Korea as well as its assimilation and adaptation of Chinese governmental structure and culture.

These bilateral relations, however, were conducted in the same way they had been for centuries. Title-granting as a diplomatic activity at the Tang court persisted well into the ninth century. Although the Wo ambassadors requested no titles from their host, neither did they reject the titles unilaterally granted them by the Chinese court. There was no open challenge to Chinese suzerainty, nor was there pressure for an equal footing with China.

Mostly honorific, these titles had no significant political implications; their bestowal and receipt became a ceremonial activity at Tang court audiences. In 703 Awada no Ason Mahito was made Vice-Director of the Court of Imperial Entertainment (Sishan Yuanwai Lang).[60] In 754, Fujiwara no Kiyokawa was appointed "Lord Specially Advanced,"[61] and his two vice-ambassadors "Overseer for the Grand Master of Imperial Entertainments with Silver Seal and Blue Ribbon."[62] In 805, before his departure for Japan, Fujiwara no Kadonomaro was awarded an "Appointment Order" with no specific position,[63] and, in 839, Fujiwara no Tsunetsugu was granted the title "General of the Cloudlike Flags of Great Tang,[64] Acting Chamberlain for Ceremonial,[65] and concurrent Left General of the Imperial Insignia Guard."[66] They were all titles of supernumeraries at the Tang court.

If these titles were of minimal political substance, their bestowal was nevertheless of symbolic significance to the Tang court. It was useful in maintaining China's image as a suzerain state, and, as long as Wo ambassadors paid "tribute" (for which read "gifts"), accepted titles, and behaved according to court protocols, the investiture system remained intact, at least on the ceremonial level.

The system was of practical use to Wo also. Acceptance of Chinese titles was the prerequisite that enabled the Wo to use the investiture system as a channel by which to assimilate Chinese high culture. Self-interest urged the Wo not to withdraw from the investiture system, yet at the same time to distance itself from the China-centered world order. Although this stance might seem self-contradictory and unsustainable, it was, in fact, plausible: as long as the Wo ambassadors made no formal requests for Chinese titles, their action would already have conveyed the message: the Tennō had no intention to serve the Son of Heaven as an "outer subject."

China was not unaware of the profound changes in its relations with the Wo, but the Tang court did not attempt to establish a sovereign-vassal relationship because of a shift in its military priority from the northeast to the northwest and then the southwest. An attitude had prevailed in the Sui and early Tang courts to the effect that northern Korea was lost Han territory that ought to be recovered. Both courts therefore considered an active policy in the northeast justified. They made Koguryŏ the primary target and resorted to large-scale military operations and diplomatic maneuvers to subjugate Koguryŏ. Wo was also drawn into this conflict.[67]

The Tang court conquered Koguryŏ in the 670s but found it ungovernable. Emperor Gaozong decided to retreat, leaving the Korean states to settle their own affairs. But the northeast again drew the attention of the Tang court when the Khitans and later Parhae disrupted the region in the 690s.

In the meantime, however, events in the northwest and southwest constrained the Tang court to pay that region more attention. The Tuyuhun, a tribe in the region that is now modern Qinghai province, which had served as a buffer between China and the Tibetans, fell in the 660s; then the Turks revived in the 680s and Islamic forces intruded into Central Asia, threatening the Silk Road. The Tibetan empire rose to power in the seventh century and the Nanzhao kingdom in the 730s. After a period of passive reaction, the Tang court began systematically from the 710s to develop a western strategy, the essence of which was to enhance China's position by forging alliances and sovereign-vassal relations with countries in the northwest.[68]

If still a marginal player in Tang diplomatic maneuvers against Koguryŏ, Wo was totally irrelevant to the Tang western strategy; that strategy marginalized Wo as a remote country that was cut off from regular contact with China (*jueyu*). No effort was made to set up sovereign-vassal relations with them; a "loose-rein" policy was considered sufficient.

The gist of this policy was that "all courtesies must be returned."[69] No foreign ambassadors would be rejected provided they observed court protocol and fulfilled their duties and obligations. This was a low-key foreign policy that stressed the necessity of keeping in touch with remote and rebellious countries but did not suggest substantive relations with them. An edict of 619 mirrored well the thinking behind the policy: "Mountains and rivers define the boundaries between China and barbarian countries; in distant lands and inaccessible countries, laws and administrations are different from those in China. Therefore our previous emperors conciliated people from remote countries and implemented the 'loose rein' policy, rather than making them subjects of China."[70] The "loose-rein" policy transformed Tang-Wo relations into contacts desirable and beneficial to Wo rulers, who wanted access to Chinese culture but did not want to give allegiance to the Son of Heaven.

The investiture system in China-Wo relations displayed a bipolar structure. Although unipolar and China-centered from the Chinese perspective, the system in fact had two foci: a Chinese emperor and a Wo ruler, each of whom was a center at a different level. Since its implementation took two willing parties, the system could not be operated by one dominating party alone. Rather than rigid and "Chinese-dominated," the system was flexible, responsive to the changing balance of power in East Asia; it was not a tool through which China arbitrarily handled its external relations.

The investiture system was reciprocal in nature. Participating countries joined the system as a result of a careful calculation of self-interest, and the system benefited them in fairly divergent ways. No foreign ruler entered the system because of a passive acceptance of a China-centered world order or of mere "admiration of the truthful and righteous conduct of the Son of Heaven (muyi)."[71]

By the same token, Chinese rulers did not grant titles simply to uphold the system. For the system to take shape and stay in place, it had to be mutually advantageous to all parties.

A sovereign-vassal relationship brought about by the investiture system was often nominal. Chinese titles mirrored to a considerable extent China's strategic ideals, not the actual realities of a bilateral relationship. China, when in disunion, lacked the military muscle and political will to enforce the world order embodied in its titles; the titles' bestowal became a unilateral action to boost the prestige of a Chinese regional ruler or to make his intentions known to his foreign counterparts. Similarly, acceptance of Chinese titles often concealed fundamental changes in the relationship between the parties, as was exhibited in the China-Wo relations over the centuries. This usefulness of the investiture system to the parties to it worked to save the system from extinction; its framework survived, but its contents evolved so as to benefit the participating countries as they were faced with new circumstances.

The Messenger of the Emperor

The mission of a messenger was to represent his ruler in seeking the best possible results from the mission with regard to his court's interests.[1] He either handled domestic issues or dealt with international affairs. But Chinese rulers did not differentiate between these two types of messengers. In their thinking there was no clear-cut line between internal and external affairs. A Chinese ruler considered himself the Son of Heaven and believed that the whole world therefore came under his jurisdiction. A Chinese saying that well reflected that mentality stated: "Under the wide heavens, all is the king's land. Within the sea boundaries of the land, all are the king's servants."[2] As a result of this conception, the Chinese court adopted similar regulations and practices both for dispatching domestic messengers and for sending ambassadors abroad.

A messenger of the emperor could play a crucial role in both domestic and international politics.[3] Emperor Taizong once acted on the advice of his chief minister, Wei Zheng, and dispatched a messenger to south China, who successfully persuaded the local lord to offer loyalty to the newly founded Tang dynasty. "A single messenger is more efficient than one hundred thousand soldiers in bringing peace to south China!" a delighted Taizong acclaimed. "I must reward Wei Zheng!"[4]

The Task, Qualities, and Criteria
for Selecting Ambassadors

In international politics, a Chinese ambassador was sometimes a messenger who conveyed China's opinion on a specific issue to a concerned party, or he might be a representative of the Chinese court sent to grant a title to a foreign ruler in an investiture ceremony. He sometimes appeared at the funeral of a loyal "outer subject" of China, offering condolences upon the subject's death; he could also be a commissioner entrusted with a royal marriage, escorting the Chinese princess who was to be married to a foreign ruler. On all these occasions, an ambassador was appointed only for an ad hoc task. Not a permanent representative of his court, he had no official residence in the capital of his host country but stayed at a guest lodge. He returned home after completing his mission and had no successor.

In China-Japan relations, an ambassador was a messenger sent to convey a message to the host court by word and in writing. A message from Japan usually requested China to take such desired actions as granting political and military support, or supplying specific goods; a message from China often aimed at enforcing the perceived lord-vassal relationship with Japan and maintaining a China-centered world order in East Asia.

Irrespective of the nature of their specific duty, both Japanese and Chinese diplomats were, in a broad sense, cultural ambassadors. Every Japanese ambassador had the responsibility to introduce Chinese high culture to his country. And when abroad, he embodied the cultural advancement of his homeland, which he consciously used to project a civilized image for Japan and to elevate Japan's international standing among other East Asian countries. A Chinese ambassador in contrast shouldered the duty of "spreading Chinese customs and moral codes abroad,"[5] which was part of the grand Chinese strategy of making "barbarians" more amenable to that strategy by edifying them with Chinese rituals, music, and Confucian teachings.[6]

Ambassadors were also spies. Tang ambassadors sought a broad range of information about foreign countries: their topography, their customs, their cities, their political situation, and their national strength. A Tang ambassador to Koguryŏ in the 640s was the director of the Bureau of Operations (*Zhifang langzhong*)—an agency under the Ministry of War. When he arrived at a Korean city, he would present fine Chinese silk to the local officials, saying: "I am fond of landscapes. I have heard of a beautiful place nearby and would like to visit." The officials, having received his gifts, would happily show him around, not knowing that they had allowed him access to places that could be of strategic importance.[7] A Tang ambassador to Tibet in the 780s induced his Tibetan servants to talk about the number of war horses and the size of the population in the country. He learned that there were some eighty-six thousand horses and fifty-nine thousand people. But of the fifty-nine thousand Tibetans, only some thirty thousand were fit for battle; the others were the elderly and the young.[8] The information gathered by these ambassadors was invaluable to China since the Tang had been at odds with both Koguryŏ and Tibet, and would shortly set in motion massive military operations against them.

Before he could conduct official business, an ambassador had to secure an audience with the host court. Such an audience was not guaranteed in premodern diplomacy. Whether or not the host court would formally receive a foreign ambassador depended on the opinions of its officials, both central and local, who formed their impression of a foreign country by observing the appearance, speech, and deportment of its ambassador. They regarded an ambassador as a mirror of his master because they believed that "to know a ruler, you have only to observe his messenger, for a clear-sighted subordinate indicates an awe-inspiring master."[9]

Given the circumstances in which he operated in the host country, an ambassador had to possess certain qualities if he was to carry out his duties successfully: he had to be presentable, making a favorable impression on his host; he had to be cultured, demonstrating his country's cultural achievement by carrying himself with dignity so that the host court would consider his requests favorably. And, most important, he had to be articulate so that he could defend the interests of his country and ensure that the protocol accorded to him during a court audience or an official banquet properly reflected the nature of the bilateral relationship between the host country and his nation, and of the multilateral relationships between his country and other nations when their ambassadors were also present.[10]

The Chinese court adopted stringent criteria when choosing its ambassadors. They were required to be of Han nationality; foreign nationals serving the Chinese court were ineligible for the post. Foreigners might be assigned as deputies to an ambassador but would not be allowed any crucial functions such as translating a Chinese edict to a foreign court.[11] Since much of his communication with the host court would be conducted orally, an ambassador was required to have excellent skills in oral communication, which was widely used in both domestic politics and interstate diplomacy in ancient China. Messengers from the Son of Heaven during the Western Zhou dynasty (eleventh century B.C. to 771 B.C.), for example, announced his instructions orally to his subjects.[12] And Chinese lords during the Spring and Autumn period (770–476 B.C.) often appeared at each other's court for face-to-face discussion of important bilateral issues.

An ambassador also had to be well versed in the Chinese classics, for his communication with the host court was expected to be brocaded with appropriate quotations from the classics.[13] This too was a tradition from antiquity, when messengers from various Chinese states met, conveyed their opinions to each other, and answered questions posed to them by creating extempore verses containing quotations from the *Odes (Shi jing)*. Chinese sources refer to this skill as *zhuandui;* it was a prerequisite for both diplomats and statesmen, and one of the nine indispensable skills by which a capable subject could effectively serve his lord and rule the country.[14] Confucius once sharply criticized bookish scholars for lacking these skills: "Though a man may be able to recite the three hundred odes, yet if, when entrusted with a government charge, he knows not how to act, or if, when sent to any quarter on a mission, he cannot give his replies unassisted *(buneng zhuandui)*, notwithstanding the extent of his learning, of what practical use is he?"[15]

A messenger had to have the ability to successfully carry out his master's mandate.[16] While abroad, he needed to be able to discern a changing situation and to use his own discretion accordingly.[17] This required him to be a man of benevolence and courage.[18] He had to be straightforward, expedient, unyielding, and prudent so that he could deal with the indifference, the deceit, the anger, and the doubt that he might encounter at a host court.[19] The Chinese court considered any messenger short of these qualities incapable of appeasing the "barbarians." And official historians would give him a negative appraisal for his performance. Gao Biaoren, a Tang ambassador to Japan in 631, was one such example. Owing to a dispute over the ceremonial arrangements for his reception, Gao decided not to deliver the Tang edict to the Japanese court. His action duly earned him an entry in *The Magic Mirror in the Palace of Books (Cefu yuangui)*, a Song dynasty encyclopedia, but in a section entitled "failures on missions."[20]

An ambassador received no specific verbal or oral instruction regarding how he should accomplish his mission and how to respond to unexpected events. He had total freedom to act as the occasion demanded and to speak in whatever way he deemed instrumental in achieving his goal. He could offer congratulations to his host on auspicious occasions or extend condolences over ominous events without prior approval from his own court.[21] He could compromise his dignity by putting aside his insignia and blackening his face with ink in order to meet with a nomadic chieftain in his tent;[22] he could even ingratiate himself with a

Turkic leader by saying that both the leader and the Chinese emperor were "Sons of Heaven of great countries."[23] He was indeed licensed to lie when needed for the good of his country while abroad.

The Rank of an Ambassador and His Insignia

Chinese ambassadors were officials of various ranks. The court would choose an ambassador of appropriate rank for the circumstances under which he was dispatched. This practice was first used in domestic politics in ancient China. For the annual meeting with the Son of Heaven, a Chinese lord would send a grand master *(dafu)* to attend; for the major gathering held every three years, a minister *(qing)* would represent his master; and once every five years, the lord himself was expected personally to pay tribute to the Son of Heaven.[24] The status of an ambassador thus indicated the importance of his mission. In external relations, the rank of a Chinese ambassador to a country signified the relative importance of this country vis-á-vis other countries in the Chinese world order. Pei Shiqing, the Sui ambassador to Japan in 608, was an official of the lowly ninth rank, holding the title of Gentleman-Litterateur (Wenlin Lang). This indicated the insignificance of Japan in the eyes of the Sui court.[25] During the Tang dynasty, however, the court recognized Japan as a major country compared to other East Asian countries.[26] As a result, Gao Biaoren, the Tang ambassador to Japan in 631, held the fourth rank.[27] In contrast, Tang ambassadors to the three Korean states of Silla, Paekche, and Koguryŏ were usually of the fifth or sixth rank.

The rank of a Chinese ambassador could become a contentious issue in bilateral relations. The chieftain of a powerful steppe people who was hostile to the Han court openly stated, "I would not have a substantive conversation with a Han messenger if he were not a ranking official." It was the practice of the Xiongnu to try to intimidate young low-ranking Han ambassadors. They believed that such an ambassador intended either to sell a harmful idea to their ruler or to assassinate him.[28] Indeed, a Tang ambassador was once refused a meeting with a rebellious general of Paekche on account of his low rank.[29] To avoid the embarrassment of its ambassador being rejected by a foreign country, the Tang court usually dignified its ambassadors on important missions with temporary or concurrent high court titles.[30]

The number of ranking officials and the size of the entourage in a Chinese delegation to a particular country also indicated this country's importance to China. Tang ambassadors to the Uighur and the Tibetan states in the ninth century would have had thirteen and eight ranking officials on their staffs respectively, while the number of such officials would be less than five in a Tang delegation to the Nanzhao kingdom. Similarly, Tang ambassadors to the Uighur, Tibetan, and Nanzhao kingdoms usually had an entourage of fewer than thirty people; a Chinese ambassador to Silla would have been accompanied by fewer than twenty people.[31]

An ambassador declared his identity by an insignia in the shape of a rod *(jie)*.[32] The Chinese term for ambassador *(shijie)* literally means "an ambassador carrying an insignia."[33] Primary sources often specify that an ambassador "carried the ensign" *(chijie)*, as in the case of Gao Biaoren, head of the Tang mission to Japan in 631.[34] The ensign also indicated that the court had temporarily entrusted a person with the power to conduct official business. This practice could be traced to high antiquity, when the Son of Heaven granted a rod made of jade or horn to one of his representatives who was in charge of a state or a city. When messengers from various Chinese lords interacted with each other during the Spring and Autumn period, they identified themselves by golden ensigns carved in shapes that were determined by the geographic features of their countries. The shape of the insignia for a messenger from a mountainous state was a tiger. A man was the insignia for a flatland state and a dragon for a state containing swampy territory. These messengers also carried bamboo arrows engraved with a description of their task.[35]

A Tang ambassador received his insignia from the Chancellery (Menxia Sheng).[36] The ensign entrusted him with such sweeping power as to enable him to execute any member of his delegation on his own authority. However, to prevent an ambassador from abusing his power, the Tang court usually allowed him to handle only one specific issue, and his power was valid only for the period of his mission. An ambassador was not supposed to involve himself with other matters. Doing so would subject him to the punishment of a beating with the heavy stick or penal servitude if his unauthorized act resulted in any damage or loss. He was not to overstep his office and encroach on other officials' duties. Upon completing his mission, an ambassador was required to make a report to the court.[37] His report would, to a large extent, influence China's decision concerning its next move toward the host country, be it political support and recognition, or punitive military action.[38] Following his report, he was obliged to submit his insignia to the court as soon as possible. A delay of one day or ten days would subject him to a penalty of fifty blows with a light stick or one year of penal servitude.[39]

The Funding of Missions

The Tang court earmarked none of its revenue as a regular expenditure for missions sent abroad. Until the 730s, bolts of silk of various qualities were used to fund such missions. Court ordinances would set aside some as "state gifts" *(guoxin)* to foreign rulers and others as "personal presents" *(sidi wu)* to be put at the disposal of the ambassadors themselves.[40] A Tang ambassador had to use his "personal presents" to pay the expenses of his journey as soon as he left China. But the amount of silk provided often was insufficient to cover all the expenses of an ambassador on a long journey, during which he might face unexpected events. The only Tang ambassadors who might not face running short of funds were those who escorted a Chinese princess to be married to a foreign ruler. When an ambassador on that mission arrived at the border, officials from the host court would greet him and have all the necessary arrangements made for him.

To solve the problem of underfunding, the Tang court allowed prefectural authorities whose territories a Tang mission passed through to sell up to ten governmental positions *(sidi guan)* and to use the money as funding for receiving the mission. This practice continued into the early ninth century, when the court decreed that the Bureau of General Accounts under the Ministry of Revenue should issue five hundred thousand copper cash to each of its ambassadors.[41]

Inadequate funding for Tang diplomats caused them financial difficulties. To cope with the situation, some brought their own valuables and traded with foreigners to generate funds for themselves; some acquired Uighur horses and expensive foreign goods and sold them upon their return to China in order to recoup their losses; some even demanded bribes from foreign officials and their rulers.[42] The corrupt practice of taking bribes became so common among Tang diplomats that many even regarded it as the virtue of following local customs.[43] A Tang ambassador to the Turgesh (Tuqishi) was urged by his own staff to accept the gold offered to him as a gift. After he left for home, his hosts were surprised to learn that the ambassador had left all the gold behind him, buried in the tent in which he had been lodged.[44] To correct the problem of corruption, the Tang court commended a few Chinese ambassadors upon their refusal of bribes;[45] the court also made it an offense punishable by death for any metropolitan official to take bribes from foreigners.[46] In the mid-ninth century, it furthermore issued the following edict:

> The court has learned that when officials are dispatched to outer barbarian countries, [foreign rulers] usually offer them gifts. This is their way of cultivating a sense of respect for the Chinese emperor, and the quantity of the gifts varies. People refer to this practice as "human affairs." It started in earlier times and has since become a common practice. Now when authorities on the borders receive a court order to pacify the barbarians, they all have to dispatch messengers. If every messenger is allowed to follow the old practice, the neighboring regions will become impoverished. And if the court does not regulate and check such a practice in advance, a messenger will find it difficult to refuse such gifts. [It is therefore stipulated that] messengers to the border areas should not accept more than a single gift.[47]

Corruption, however, remained a problem among some top Tang diplomats. Shen Weiyue, the Tang ambassador to Japan in 762, was one of them. Within five months of his arrival in Japan, Shen's infamous behavior prompted Ji Qiaorong, his own deputy, Yan Ziqin, the military administrator *(sibing)*, and thirty-eight mission members to boycott him. They took the unusual move of reporting the matter to the Dazai Headquarters, which was the Japanese governmental branch in charge of receiving foreign visitors in Kyūshū. They accused Shen of having accepted bribes and having illegally sold Chinese goods. They also requested that the Dazai Headquarters appoint the vice-ambassador as their leader since Shen had discredited himself and was unsuitable to head the mission. The Japanese court handled the incident with great caution and sophistication. It turned down the request of the insubordinate Tang diplomats and continued to treat Shen with respect and generosity. In the meantime the Japanese court made preparations to send Shen back to China. Shen, however, failed to cross the sea and returned to Kyūshū in 762. There the court provided him with all the

daily necessities as usual. In fact Shen, his deputy Yan, and other ranking officials of his delegation were to remain in Japan for the rest of
their lives. In the late 780s, the Japanese court granted Shen the junior
fifth rank, lower grade, and a new family name, Kiyomi, and allowed him
to reside in the capital. Others received similar treatment.[48] Although it
was not unusual for some diplomats to remain in a host country owing
to unexpected circumstances, it was nevertheless a diplomatic scandal
that members of a Tang mission to Japan had openly criticized their
superior for his inappropriate behavior and had appealed to the Japanese court to put the vice-ambassador in charge of them.[49]

A Tang ambassador traveled in style when he was on an official mission. He was accompanied by an armed escort with banners flown to his
left and right.[50] His mission, however, became less glamorous and full of
danger the moment he left Chinese territory. Dealing with the "barbarians" could be frustrating or even dangerous. One Tang official visited
the Turkic headquarters five times and several times almost died on the
mission.[51] Neither China nor its neighbors granted diplomatic immunity to foreign ambassadors. Many ambassadors suffered the mistreat-
ment of detention by the host court.[52] The Turks detained a Tang ambassador because they suspected that he had poisoned their leader, who
had fallen sick shortly after the ambassador's arrival.[53] When a Koguryŏ
ambassador came with the news that the legitimate ruler of his country
had been murdered and a new ruler was now in power, the Tang court
accused him of not avenging his former ruler and of speaking for the
new one. He was subsequently handed to the Court of Judicial Review
(Dali Si) for a trial.[54] Once detained, an ambassador became a bargain-
ing chip his captor could use to achieve the goals he desired. The captor
might also transfer a detained Chinese ambassador to a third party to
cement an alliance against China.[55] The detention, transfer, and release
of ambassadors were thus themselves a means of diplomacy. Hardship on
a mission abroad was such a frustrating experience that some Tang diplomats abandoned their mission halfway through it and were disciplined by
demotion;[56] some failed to report to the court upon returning home and
were banished for one year;[57] and some were even compelled to agree to
speak on behalf of a foreign court when they were back in China.[58]

It was no wonder that some ranking Tang courtiers shied away from
a mission abroad. They considered such a mission an undesirable task
since it entailed a long separation from family members. A poem pre-

sented to a Tang ambassador before his second trip to Tibet describes him as "having returned home only once in five years, when even his wife could not recognize him."[59] To make things worse, a long journey abroad would also keep an ambassador out of touch with court politics, and this could be detrimental to advancement in his career.[60] In the early eighth century, for example, the emperor chose the director of the Chancellery *(Menxia shizhong)* as the ambassador in charge of marrying a princess to the Tibetan ruler since the director was familiar with Tibetan affairs and good at pacifying neighboring states. The director, however, stubbornly turned down the job on account of inexperience in foreign affairs. The emperor then assigned the job to the vice-director of the Secretariat *(Zhongshu shilang)*. He was quite unhappy with the appointment and feared falling into imperial disfavor. The chief minister of the Court of the National Granaries *(Sinong qing)* told him: "As a premier of the country, you have now been made a mere messenger. How degrading!" The director, however, managed to stay in the capital after much maneuvering behind the scenes.[61] Indeed, powerful players of politics at the Tang court sometimes removed their rivals by sending them away as ambassadors to remote foreign countries.[62] The Tang court thus was not always able to appoint the most suitable person as its ambassador.

The Japanese Mission to China in 834

New Year's Day of 834 in Japan did not seem different from the previous one: the emperor, following court routine, received his subjects and treated them to a banquet. The next day, he paid a courtesy call on the abdicated emperor and received from his predecessor sparrow hawks, eagles, and bird-hunting dogs as gifts. Beneath the normality, however, there was an air of anticipation. Why did the abdicated emperor present his successor with creatures known for their ability to spot prey quickly and catch it at an explosive speed? Was this a message to the emperor that he should move quickly to achieve his goals? Nobody in the court knew the exact answer; but everybody knew that changes would occur since Japan had a new ruler, Emperor Nimmyō (r. 833–850), who had ascended the throne nine months previously and who would certainly use the new year as the occasion on which to signal the official start of his rule. On the third day, the emperor promulgated an edict that

Imprint of the seal "Envoy Dispatched to Tang." The seal has not been found. The imprint is from a document submitted to the Japanese court by an envoy. (Kimiya Yasuhiko, *Nisshi kōtsūshi* [Tokyo: Kanasashi Hōryūdō, 1927])

announced the adoption of a new reign title and that indicated he would forge ahead into the future by carrying forward the cause of his predecessors. He quickly approved a series of senior appointments;[63] and the court, on the nineteenth day of the first month, decided to organize a mission to Tang China.

This decision surprised nobody in the court since the Tang cultural influence on Japan was at its apex in the early ninth century, and the new emperor himself was the embodiment of such influence: he excelled in music, painting, and classical Chinese poetry. One of his Chinese poems, which he wrote when he was the crown prince, was included in the *Collection of National Polity (Keikokushū)*, a contemporary work compiled in 827.[64] He was determined to base his policies on the moral teachings of Confucius and to keep his court in touch with events in China so that Japan could receive new impetus from the Asian continent.

Emperor Nimmyō's China mission was the eighteenth, and incidentally the last, to actually reach China. The first mission had set off for China in 630. In the course of the following two centuries, most of the China missions had successfully reached their destinations, but a few had been canceled. These missions started in a small way, with one or two diplomats aboard a single ship. When Japan made adoption of Chinese culture the major goal it would pursue in its relations with China, the missions grew progressively larger in scale and more complex in organization. They evolved into the principal vehicle for channeling Chinese culture, technological expertise, and the finer Chinese products to Japan. Emperor Nimmyō's China mission was, in fact, the largest ever of such missions, comprising over six hundred people aboard a fleet of four giant ships. This event therefore provides an exemplary opportunity for observing how the Japanese court organized a mission to China.

A China mission was led by four types of key diplomats: the ambassador, usually of the fourth rank,[65] the vice-ambassador of the fifth rank, the administrative officer, and the secretary. This arrangement resembled the organizational structure of a government office, where the chief officer was assisted by his deputy, the administrative officer, who was in charge of daily affairs, and by the secretary, who was responsible for documentation. The number of each type of diplomat varied depending on the importance of a mission. The second China mission in 653, for example, had two ambassadors and two vice-ambassadors. Its 242 members boarded two ships, each of which had an ambassador and a vice-ambassador in charge.[66] This arrangement was to ensure that at least one major diplomat would survive and eventually reach China should the mission suffer an untoward incident such as a shipwreck.[67]

The importance of a mission sometimes justified the appointment of either an "escorting ambassador,"[68] a "supervising ambassador,"[69] or an "ambassador to Tang bearing the sword of authority" *(ken Tō jissetsu-shi)*.[70] Appointees to these positions were senior to the ambassador. In contrast, a mission of relatively low level might have but one ambassador and no vice-ambassador. The ambassador of 759, for example, had the simple task of fetching a fellow Japanese ambassador from China, and a primary source speaks of him as a "single ambassador," a term that carried an overtone of insignificance.[71] Similarly, the head of a mission would not be referred to by his full title "ambassador" *(taishi)* if his task was unspecified,[72] or if he was simply to escort a Tang ambassador home.[73] He would be mentioned in passing simply as a *shi*.

Not all the appointed diplomats actually traveled to China. For the mission of 716, the supervising ambassador was assigned another duty, and the ambassador was also replaced by someone else.[74] Appointed diplomats sometimes became victims of domestic politics and were discharged from their duties. This happened to the vice-ambassador of the mission in 761, one year after his appointment. The mission itself was consequently canceled under dubious circumstances.[75]

A group of service staff attended to the daily needs of the diplomats and ensured their personal safety. The service staff included low-rank-

周古柯   倭國

Portrait of a Wo ambassador attributed to Gu Deqian, a painter of the Southern Tang dynasty (937–975). This portrait is a copy of the original work by Emperor Yuan (r. 552–555). (Collection of the National Palace Museum, Taiwan, Republic of China)

ing officials, guards, archers, servants, and interpreters from Korea, Amami, and other Ryūkyū islands. They formed the second group of mission members. The third and the largest group of mission members was the group of navigational personnel who were in charge of operating, managing, and repairing the ships: the shipmaster, the chief craftsman for shipbuilding, the boatswain, the oarsmen, the helmsmen, the navigators, the sailors, the shipwrights, the overseer, and the carpenters. Among them, oarsmen were numerous since they had to row the ships when the winds were unfavorable. Although their exact number was unrecorded, usually one-third to one-half of the people on board an eighth-century oceangoing ship were oarsmen and sailors.[76] The China mission in 834 could therefore have had as many as two hundred to three hundred sailors.

The fourth group of people on a China mission were the specialists. Their number was small, but they shouldered the important task of introducing recent advancements in their respective fields in China to Japan. Among them were astrologers, diviners, physicians, practitioners of the Yinyang arts, musicians, painters, chanters, chant masters, jade workers, and metal workers. Their task was twofold: they served the members of the mission, but once in China they focused on improving their skills by learning from Chinese experts. Lay students and student monks also belonged to this group. They studied Buddhism and various other aspects of Chinese culture and institutions. The length of these students' stays varied. Some remained in China for a long time to acquire an in-depth knowledge of a chosen subject; others had a short stay since they were already advanced scholars and wanted only to have specific problems solved.[77]

These students and diplomats were to have a fundamental impact on the Japanese government when they returned home to hold high-ranking positions. Because of their firsthand experience with and thorough understanding of Chinese culture and political institutions, their opinions on governmental affairs at home carried much weight and often became the basis for court decisions. Yamato no Nagaoka (698–769), the son of an assistant minister of justice, was one example. He went to China in 716 to study the Tang legal system. Returning home after a short stay in China, Nagaoka became a leading authority on law and one of the authors of the Yōrō Code compiled in the second year of the Yōrō period (718). Thereafter his opinions and interpretations of the law were often sought by other legal scholars.[78] Kashiwade no Ōoka, assistant professor from the Bureau of Great Learning, was another example in point. He had traveled to China in 752, and in 768 he informed the court rather belatedly that while in China he had learned that the Tang court had granted Confucius the new canonized title "Wenxuan Wang." He then pointed out that Japan's Education Code still referred to Confucius by the outdated title "Kong Xuanfu" and suggested that the code in question be amended to show proper respect to this Chinese saint. His suggestion was accepted.[79]

Most of the Japanese diplomats to China were scholar-officials. They were selected by stringent criteria through a competitive procedure to ensure that Japanese diplomats were men of high caliber, great communicators, and showmen, capable of personifying the virtue of their ruler and the cultural achievements of their country. It was on the basis of these considerations that the Japanese court promulgated an edict in 560, stipulating that only men of noble birth could be appointed diplomats.[80] In addition to a distinguished family origin, the court judged a diplomat by his knowledge of history and literature, his achievements in calligraphy and composition, his personal ability and intellect, and last but not least, his impressive physical appearance.[81] These criteria in fact applied not only to diplomats to China, but also to officials at home who received foreign visitors.[82]

For an ambassador to fulfill his task, his ability to use written Chinese when communicating with the host court was crucial. In 777, Japan decided to send a China mission without the ambassador, who had to quit the delegation owing to serious illness. Knowing that China might reject such a mission, the emperor instructed the vice-ambassadors to "explain the matter in detail" if they were questioned by the Tang court.[83] Earlier in 659, a servant from a Korean delegation made false allegations against some Japanese diplomats in China. The Tang court found them guilty of the charge and sentenced them to banishment. It was Iki no Muraji Hakatoko's skill at written communication that rescued them from this embarrassment: he successfully appealed to the Tang emperor, with the result that the punishment was remitted.[84]

An ambassador's showmanship—his ability to impress and please his Chinese host—was equally important in diplomacy. Upon arrival in China, Awada no Ason Mahito (?–719), the ambassador to China in 702, impressed both the Chinese officials and the Tang emperor by his polite

An early-sixteenth-century portrait of Sugawara no Michizane. He was appointed "Ambassador Dispatched to China" in 894 but never traveled to China since the Japanese court later decided to abandon the mission. Collection of Okayama Prefectural Art Museum. (Yoshiaki Shimizu, *Japan, The Shaping of Daimyo Culture, 1185–1868* [Washington, D.C.: National Gallery of Art, 1988], p. 147)

and refined conduct. Having met with him, a local official remarked: "I have often heard that eastward in the sea there is a Yamato no Kuni [i.e., Japan]. They say it is a country of gentlemen, whose behaviour is extremely polite. Now seeing this ambassador, his appearance is most favourable, how could it be possible not to believe what I formerly heard."[85] Tang courtiers at the capital described Mahito as a man "well versed in classics and history and knowledgeable in literary works." The Tang court made him vice-director of the Court of Imperial Entertainment owing to his gentle appearance and cultivated behavior.[86]

An ambassador had to display his accomplishments with care and appropriateness, never leaving the host court with any impression of insincerity or arrogance that could lead to a diplomatic blunder and distrust. The Japanese ambassador of 670, however, mishandled his mission. Tang officials considered him conceited, untruthful, and boastful. They believed that he had exaggerated the size of Japan's domain by stating that "[Japan] covers many thousands of square meters and extends to the ocean on the south and on the west. And in the northeast, the country is bordered by mountain ranges."[87]

The Star Diplomats

KIYOKAWA: THE SHOWMAN

Of all the Japanese diplomats, Fujiwara no Kiyokawa (706–778) was the greatest showman. During an audience in 752, Emperor Xuanzong told his guest: "I have heard that there is a virtuous ruler in your country. Now having observed your distinctive manner of walking and bowing, I would name Japan a country of ritual, righteousness, and gentlemen." Xuanzong was so impressed by Kiyokawa that he ordered portraits of Kiyokawa and his two deputies to be made and stored in the palace, an imperial favor that foreigners seldom received. He also created a poem for Kiyokawa upon his departure for home.

FAREWELL TO THE JAPANESE AMBASSADOR
The Customs of all countries under the sun do not differ,
Their ambassadors all gather auspiciously at court in the Central
　　Kingdom.
I am mindful that you came from so far because you cherish
　　Righteousness,

It is a pity you have to make so awesome a journey to your distant
    home.
On the swelling ocean, vastly spread under the Autumn moon,
May your homebound ships speed on the westerly gales.
I am truly amazed by you gentlemen:
That our cultural influence should shine so brightly in your
    distant land.[88]

KIYONAO: THE LITERARY TALENT

Unlike Kiyokawa, Fuse no Ason Kiyonao—Japan's ambassador to
China in 778—was a man of both showmanship and considerable literary acumen. He won the acclaim of Tang and Song officials for attainments in calligraphy.[89] While adoring him as a man of noble manner,
they commented with admiration on his brush strokes, which showed a
rhythm similar to that of Wang Xizhi (321–379), the famous fourth-
century Chinese calligrapher. Many years after Kiyonao's visit to China,
a Song official showed his friends two pieces of calligraphy, which he
claimed to be Kiyonao's works that his ancestor had acquired when
serving Kiyonao as an interpreter. They were poems from the early-sixth-
century Chinese anthology *Selections of Refined Literature (Wen xuan)* written in the simplified form of the cursive script. Not only was the style of
the script unique, but so also was the quality of the two pieces of paper
that Kiyonao used: one was prune purple and the other glossy white.
The surface of the paper was as smooth as a mirror so that the writing
brush could easily slide away. Only accomplished calligraphers could
use such paper.[90]

OTOMARO: THE GREAT LOVER

An ambassador of considerable literary talent tended to have tender
feelings and a strong personality. Isonokami no Otomaro was such a
person. His life was full of twists and turns, making him the most colorful figure of all the Japanese ambassadors to China.

The third son of the minister of the left, Otomaro was of true blue
blood. Like most people of his background, Otomaro was well versed
in the Confucian classics and talented in composing poems and prose,
some of which appear in the *Yearnings for the Ancient Chinese Style (Kai-*

fūsō), the *Collection of Ten Thousand Leaves (Man'yōshū)*, and the *Collection of National Polity*.[91] He proved himself a promising young man in 724, when the court put him and a group of courtiers in charge of the preparation for the Great New Food Festival—a Shinto ceremony held at the time of a new emperor's enthronement. He rose to the junior fifth rank, upper grade, in 732. Otomaro was an exceedingly handsome man, and his physical appearance distinguished him from other courtiers. He was also a man of elegance, leisure, and poise, and a man who knew exactly how to demonstrate a graceful demeanor. These qualities undoubtedly helped him secure the position of ambassador to China in the early 730s. He had conducted himself so well during a court audience held specifically for selecting the ambassador that he enjoyed popular confidence when the court offered him the job.[92] But Otomaro did not travel to China. The court assigned him another job: governor of Tamba (occupies parts of present-day Hyōgo prefecture, Kyoto, and Osaka). After a few years away from the capital, he returned to the center of politics in 738, when he was appointed controller of the left in the State Council, holding the junior fourth rank, lower grade.[93] His future seemed boundless.

Otomaro's career, however, soon took a nosedive. A man prone to personal sentiment, he had an affair with a lady. Nobody knew how it happened, and perhaps nobody would have cared if the affair had been with a beauty found in the back streets of the capital Heiankyō (the modern city of Kyoto). But Otomaro's lover was no commoner. She was Kume no Wakume, a noble lady and the widow of Fujiwara no Umakai (694–737).

Umakai was one of the four sons of Fuhito (659–720), a powerful player in court politics and a power broker. Fuhito rose to prominence by helping the court strengthen its power as a centralized government; he then consolidated his own power by marrying his daughters into the imperial family. Umakai inherited his father's political wisdom and rose rapidly in the court ranks. A remarkable man well versed in both polite letters and martial arts, Umakai was chosen in 717 as the vice-ambassador to China. This appointment apparently represented the court's recognition of his literary talent, which was eventually fully manifested in his two-volume collected works. A number of his poems also were included in the *Yearnings for the Ancient Chinese Style* and the *Collection of Ten Thousand Leaves*.[94] Returning from China in 718, Umakai, taking advantage of his firsthand experience with Chinese institutions, positioned himself for bigger jobs. Six years later, in 724, he headed the Ministry of Ceremonies, holding the senior fourth rank, upper grade. In the same year, an opportunity presented itself that allowed Umakai to demonstrate his military talent: he was appointed general in chief to suppress the rebellious Emishi people in northeastern Japan. Returning victoriously from this military campaign, Umakai was promoted to the junior third rank. In the late 720s and early 730s, Umakai held other important jobs: construction supervisor of the new palace in Naniwa (modern city of Osaka) in 726, and military governor of the Western Sea district (present-day Kyūshū) in 732. But Umakai's promising career came to a sudden end in 737, when he died of smallpox during an epidemic that devastated most parts of the country, forcing the court to close offices and to exempt peasants from the year's rent.[95] Umakai was only forty-four years old at his death; but he was already adviser of the State Council, ceremonies minister, and concurrent director of the Dazai Headquarters, holding the senior third rank.[96]

The affair between Otomaro and Wakume might have developed shortly after the unexpected death of her husband.[97] Little did Otomaro know that he was playing with fire since the powerful Fujiwara clan was keeping a watchful eye on Wakume. The affair was soon discovered and brought Otomaro serious trouble: he was sentenced to exile for life in Tosa (present-day Kōchi prefecture) in 739. Nor was Wakume spared humiliation and punishment. Referring to the legal codes, the Fujiwara clan insisted in court that Wakume's conduct was also punishable since she was a rank-holding lady. She was consequently stripped of her rank and exiled for life in Shimousa (present-day Chiba prefecture) in the same year as her lover.[98] In fact, they were lucky, for the normal penalty for adultery was penal servitude. Exile for life was a mitigated punishment for them.[99]

Wakume did not live in Shimousa for the rest of her life, however. Having stayed there for only a year and a half, she was permitted to return to Kyoto under an amnesty announced in the sixth month of 749. It pardoned all prisoners except those under a death sentence. The court gradually rehabilitated her. She was restored to the junior fifth rank, lower grade, in 767, and promoted to higher ranks in 768, 772, and 776. Apparently the Fujiwara clan, especially Fujiwara no Momokawa (732–779), her own powerful son who eventually rose to councillor of the State Council, forgave her. When she died in 780, Wakume held the junior fourth rank, lower grade.[100]

Otomaro was, however, less fortunate than his lover. Hands bound and guarded by bowmen, he was sent off to Tosa after the sentencing. Family members and a few friends came to bid him farewell, presenting poems to a despondent and humiliated man:

> You great man from Furu,
> Because of your mistake,
> Getting that woman in trouble,
> You are like a horse
> Drawn along by a rope,
> You are like a boar,
> Hemmed in by bows and arrows.
> By the command
> of our dread sovereign,
> You must depart for a province
> Distant as the heavens
> Off there on the tatters
> Of Matsuchi Mountain—
> Will you come back from there?[101]

Taking pity on Otomaro, the author of this poem doubted with good reason whether his friend would ever come back from exile. As for Otomaro's wife, she not only suffered the heartbreak of parting, but was also deeply concerned for her husband's safety and health:

> By the command
> Of our dread sovereign
> You are taken off,
> Going away to some province.
> Dear and beloved,
> my lord husband,
> may the fearsome gods
> dwelling at Suminoe
> Take on human shape
> And condescend to guard
> At the prow of your boat,
> staying close beside you

Delivering you safe
From the juts and points of shores,
keeping your boat free
From the rough waves and the winds,
Keep in good health
And protected against disease,
And with no delay
Bring you back home again
To your native land.[102]

Did Otomaro ever regret his reckless behavior? We do not know. But parting with his parents and his family certainly saddened him:

My lord and father
Held me his beloved son,
My lady and mother
Held me her beloved son.
Travellers from the eighty clans
Come back to the capital
Up the awesome Koshiko Slope,
Making offerings at the shrines
Tugging at the sacred rope,
While I press on and on
Over the road to distant Tosa.[103]

In this poem, Otomaro, guarding his feelings closely, shows little of what he thought of the exile. But the short text *(hanka)* that follows the poem, betrays his true feelings:

The Ōsaki strand
Where the god rules the shore
Is a constricted place—
Unlike the many boatmen going north,
I must remain in exile here.[104]

Otomaro might also have dreamed of quick forgiveness by the court. But the court completely shattered his dream: in the edict that proclaimed the general pardon in 740, the court singled out Otomaro as one of those who were "ineligible for the amnesty," for those inelegible "had committed liaison with other people's wives."[105] Obviously, the Fujiwara clan was still angry with him. They were not about to forgive him that quickly. During his years in exile, Otomaro devoted himself to writing poetry. He often stood still for a long time, gazing at deep water and weighing the words for his poems, which eventually became the two-volume work *Harboring Grief*.[106]

But neither did Otomaro spend the rest of his life in exile. After four years in Tosa, he bounced back onto the political scene. The court eventually pardoned him in 743 and granted him junior fourth rank, upper grade. The intricate court politics that resulted in Otomaro's comeback were never made clear in the primary sources. It might have been the work of the friends of his powerful father, who was once minister of the left; or perhaps the emperor himself had changed his mind. It would have indeed been a terrible waste to leave so gifted a scholar permanently in exile. After all, a romance with a lady, no matter how noble she was, was only a minor stray from correctness in a man's life. Otomaro's career was soon back on track. He served as commissioner of the Western Sea Circuit for two years before the court brought him back to the capital. From 746 to 749, he held such leading positions as regulatory minister, controller of the right, and minister for central affairs. He died in 750 as associate councillor, holding the junior third rank.[107]

After Otomaro's death, his story faded from the memory of many courtiers, who were accustomed to scandal and intrigue in court politics. But some eighty years later, the story seems to have been resurrected, at least in the mind of Ono no Takamura (802–852).

TAKAMURA: THE GIFTED VICE-AMBASSADOR

Takamura would have no particular reason to remember Otomaro; the two lived at different times and came from unrelated families. But the court appointed Takamura vice-ambassador of its China mission in 834.[108] The two men were now linked with each other. Both were literary geniuses,[109] and both were chosen as diplomats to China. Takamura pondered over the implications of this appointment to his career. When he was deep in thought, the experiences of Otomaro and other diplomats to China may have come to mind. Little would Takamura know that three future incidents would make his life as eventful as Otomaro's: he would not travel to China; he would also be sentenced to exile, though for reasons other than romance with women, and he too would manage to stage a miraculous comeback in politics.

A sense of achievement must have welled up in Takamura's heart when he accepted the appointment, for he knew how stringent the criteria for diplomats were and how competitive the open court audience for the selection of diplomats was.[110] The emperor wanted only the best to be diplomats to China, and he, being selected above other competitors, became one of them. Many of Takamura's predecessors were outstanding China experts. Some had studied in the Middle Kingdom before their appointment to a China mission; some had served more than once on these missions. Inukami no Mitasuki, the first ambassador to Tang in 630, had served as the ambassador to Sui fifteen years earlier in 614.[111] His deputy, Yakushi Enichi, had studied medicine in Sui before returning to Japan in 623. And in 654, Enichi was again made vice-ambassador.[112] Similarly Takamuko no Genri (?–654) had spent more than twenty years in Sui before he returned to Japan in 631. He was then appointed "supervising ambassador" in 654.[113] Kibi no Makibi, the vice-ambassador in 750, had also been a student in China from 716 to 732.

Takamura also knew that the court often chose its diplomats from the well-known "diplomatic families." The Hatas were one such family. The father, Benshō, was ordained a monk while still young. The court decided to send him to Tang as a student in the early eighth century because of his quick wit, eloquence, and knowledge of metaphysics. While in China, he became friendly with Li Longji, the future Emperor Xuanzong (r. 712–756), who highly regarded and patronized him as a *go* player. Benshō also courted a Chinese woman and fathered two sons, Chōkei and Chōgen. Chōgen, the younger son, returned home after his father and elder brother had died in China. He became a court official and was made the administrative officer on the China mission in 732. In the Tang capital, Emperor Xuanzong received Chōgen warmly and generously rewarded him. He still fondly remembered Chōgen's father and their friendship from many years previous.[114]

The Hakuris were another "diplomatic family," though a less prominent one. The father, Yoshimaro, was a servant to Abe no Nakamaro—the famous Japanese student who went to China in 716 and made a distinguished career in the Tang court. In China Yoshimaro married a Tang lady and had two sons. After their return to Japan in 734, Tsubasa, one of the teenaged sons, became a monk. The court, however, decided to put his talent to better use. It ordered Tsubasa to resume secular life and made him a scribe on the China mission in 775. He was promoted to administrative officer before the mission left for China in 777.[115]

The most prominent "diplomatic family" was perhaps the Fujiwaras. The father, Fujiwara no Kadonomaro of the senior third rank, was appointed ambassador in 801. His delegation had twice attempted the voyage before they eventually reached China in 804. Thirty years later, Tsunetsugu (796–840), the seventh son of Kadomaro, followed his father's footsteps in heading another China mission. Like his father, Tsunetsugu had a distinguished career. When he died at forty-five in 840, he held the junior third rank. Official historians of his time highly praised Tsunetsugu as a refined man who "since he was young studied history and classical Chinese in the Great Learning Bureau, thoroughly familiarized himself with the *Selections of Refined Literature,* and was skilled at composition and calligraphy.[116] He was a man of wisdom, capability, and decorum." "In recent history," the historians commented, "only the Fujiwara family produced a father and a son both of whom were selected as ambassadors to China."[117] And Tsunetsugu happened to be Takamura's boss, the ambassador of the China mission in 834.

A promising official and a bright scholar, Takamura considered himself on a par with, if not more distinguished than, any diplomat on his own or previous missions. A man of noble birth, he had a high-powered father who at the time of his death was adviser of the State Council, holding the senior fourth rank, lower grade. But since childhood, Takamura was different from other privileged youths who were merely "city boys" and spent their time mostly in the capital. He lived a large part of his early childhood in Michinoku (present-day Aomori prefecture in northeastern Japan), where his father served as governor in the 810s, trying to subjugate the unruly local tribes and establish the authority of the court. The wilderness and the warfare in the remote north left a lasting impact on Takamura; he was transformed from a timid boy to a tough-minded, outspoken young man skilled at horsemanship and archery. Aloof and proud, he wanted to stay above politics and worldly considerations. Takamura maintained his temperament after he returned to the capital. He showed no interest in learning and other scholarly pursuits until Emperor Saga (r. 809–823) heard about the unique behavior of this young man. The emperor, a fine poet and calligrapher in his own right, did not consider the martial arts a suitable pursuit for Takamura.

"The son of such a distinguished courtier," lamented the emperor, "why would you want to be a horseman and a bowman?!" The emperor's words shocked Takamura. Perhaps for the first time, he felt ashamed of himself and began to pursue studies seriously. At twenty, Takamura passed the competitive examinations to become a student of literature at the Great Learning Bureau. There his learning and scholarship progressed considerably; in particular, he demonstrated keen understanding of legal issues. Two years later, he was made patrolling censor of the Censors Board, and next year, a junior secretary of the board. Takamura's attainments in legal studies made him one of twelve experts whom the court commissioned in 826 to compile the *Commentary on the Yōrō Code (Ryō no gige)*, which interpreted the laws and statutes that the court had established in 718, the second year of the Yōrō period (717–723). Takamura's expertise in legal and administrative matters landed him a series of relatively junior but very promising jobs: palace secretary in 828, assistant executive secretary for the Ministry of Ceremonies in 830, and assistant director of the Dazai Headquarters in 832. That year Takamura was only thirty years old but already held the junior fifth rank, lower grade. The next year, he was appointed scholar for the Heir Apparent; he then became junior assistant president of the Censors Board and the concurrent assistant governor of Mimasaka (in present-day Okayama prefecture, central Japan).[118] Takamura was now one of the rising stars of officialdom. Over six feet in height, he was a man of strong physique. He also enjoyed a reputation as a man who was filial—dedicated to his mother and generous to relatives and friends. From time to time, he willingly parted with his entire salary to help them.[119] Takamura knew that with his reputation and the new appointment to the China mission, which was clearly an imperial favor and a court recognition of his career potential, he would rise even higher in the court hierarchy once he returned from China.

Indeed many vice-ambassadors were like Takamura: as talented as their bosses and more distinguished than the ambassadors in literary achievements. Isonokami no Yakatsugu (729–781), for example, came from an aristocratic family. His grandfather was minister of the left of the State Council, holding the junior first rank, and his father, associate councillor of the State Council, holding the junior third rank. Yakatsugu was frank, open, and quick to grasp new ideas. Handsome, poised, and graceful, he was well read and was particularly fond of Chinese classics, history, composition, and calligraphy. His poems were refined and well known among his contemporaries. Whenever he encountered picturesque scenery, Yakatsugu would reach for his writing brush and create a poem. He became one of the leading poets from the 750s, and his works, amounting to several dozen, were on the lips of the people of his time. Passionate about learning and books, Yakatsugu decided to let other scholars access his book collection. He had a temple built on the site of his own home. At one corner within the temple, a pavilion was constructed to store Confucian classics. This pavilion might well have been the first public library in Japan, where anybody eager to learn could use the collection as he wished. Yakatsugu's love for books and his achievements in learning earned him a position in the China mission of 761. He was appointed vice-ambassador.[120]

Takamura was quite satisfied that the court had assembled a group of talented people to serve him as subordinates on the China mission. Matsukage, the administrative officer, was a Fujiwara and son of the junior assistant minister of justice. He was known for his seriousness and integrity as well as for his beautiful eyebrows and beard.[121] Sugawara no Yoshinushi, another administrative officer, was also of noble birth. His father was a courtier of junior third rank, and he was himself a child prodigy, who grew up to become a student of literature at twenty-three. He was a man of refined manners and an eloquent speaker.[122] In contrast, Nagamine no Takana, the acting administrative officer, had started as a commoner from the capital. He was brought up by his brother, an official of the junior fifth rank, lower grade, and became a student of literature at twenty-one. He lived in austerity. Having not even a peck of rice at home, he was nonetheless fond of receiving literary friends and forming adopted brotherhoods with them. People respected him as an incorruptible and honorable man who was conscientious about his duty and seldom thought about personal interest.[123] Fujiwara no Sadatoshi, another acting administrative officer, was a talented musician. He was to study the *pipa,* a Chinese string instrument, with a Tang performer, who came to like him so much that he married his daughter to Sadatoshi.[124] Sugawara no Kajinari, the physician, was an accomplished doctor who specialized in acute diseases. He had already thoroughly familiarized himself with the Chinese medical classics when the court included him in the China mission as an advanced scholar. He eventually became an acupuncture professor and a palace doctor.[125]

The Reward System

Takamura knew that appointment to the China mission would bring him not only promotion, but also a string of generous material rewards. Starting from the late seventh century, the Japanese court increasingly resorted to both promotion and material rewards to encourage officials to accept appointments to its China mission and to perform their duties attentively. The court had to dangle rewards in front of the courtiers since many of them came to perceive the voyage to China as a dangerous task. Many delegations had suffered shipwreck and hardship in traveling to a remote foreign country. Many considered the task undesirable, for it would send them away from the capital for at least a year and perhaps for good should they fail to return safely.

To boost the morale of its mission members, the Japanese court routinely granted them ranks that were usually one rank or one grade higher than their current ones.[126] As perquisites, major diplomats received concurrent provincial appointments that allowed the appointee a salary package that was the same as an incumbent's without actually taking up the office.[127] The court also provided its diplomats, practitioners of the Yinyang arts, physicians, diviners, and shipmasters with laborers to till their lands at home.[128]

Takamura needed only to look at his leader, Tsunetsugu, and fellow diplomats to figure out the rewards that were coming his way. His boss was promoted by one grade to junior fourth rank, upper grade, in the eleventh month of 833.[129] He was then appointed concurrent governor of Sagami (present-day Kanagawa prefecture) in the first month of 834.[130] These appointments were obviously rewards for Tsunetsugu, for his appointment to the mission was announced seven days later. In the fifth month, nine of Tsunetsugu's subordinates, ranging from the administrative officer to the shipmaster, also received concurrent provincial appointments.[131] Before departure for China, Tsunetsugu would obtain a governorship in Bitchū (present-day Okayama) and Ōmi (part of present-day Shiga prefecture) in 834, the position of concurrent controller of the left in 835, and the senior fourth rank, lower grade, in 836.[132]

For Takamura, however, career advancement after his appointment to the China mission came much later. He had waited for almost a whole year before he was promoted from the junior fifth rank, lower grade, to the upper grade of the same rank in early 835.[133] Four days later he also received a concurrent governorship in Bizen (present-day Okayama prefecture).[134] A few months later he became senior assistant minister of justice. At the end of 835, the court decided to "temporarily lend higher rank" (shakui) to Tsunetsugu and Takamura. The former received the senior second rank and the latter the senior fourth rank, upper grade. These ranks gave the diplomats more importance and would help them fulfill their task in China. But these ranks were not officially granted to Tsunetsugu and Takamura. Their bestowal was therefore announced orally, and no certificate of appointment was issued.[135] A measure similar to the temporary grant of titles was to allow officials of lower rank to wear the court robes appropriate for senior officials. The vice-ambassador to China in 777, who held the junior fifth rank, upper grade, was permitted to wear a court robe in purple, which was the official color for courtiers of the third rank and above.[136] The court granted him this special privilege since he was to perform the duty on behalf of the ambassador, who was ill.[137]

The reward system benefited sailors, monks, archers, and other mission members as well. All of them would be given an official rank if they were commoners.[138] Officials from the Ministry of War and the ambassador interviewed and tested the archers. If recommended, an archer would receive a rank from the Ministry of Ceremonies.[139] In 751 as many as 113 members of the China mission received official titles of various ranks.[140] Titles of nobility were also conferred on an interpreter, a scribe, and a shipmaster on Takamura's mission.[141] If a mission member died of sickness, attack by pirates, or shipwreck while he was on duty, a rank would be posthumously granted to him,[142] and his adult sons of twenty-one years of age or older would become eligible for official ranks, which were determined according to the Selection and Promotions Code.[143] Such a deceased mission member was treated as one who had established a lower grade of merit to the country and was therefore entitled to "merit rice fields," which were then granted to his sons and daughters for use during their lifetime.[144]

After returning home safely, mission members were showered with more rewards: promotion to higher ranks or grades,[145] grants of such gifts as silk floss, cloth, spades and rice,[146] and lands. The court usually granted its diplomats tax and corvée exemption for one year. But it was particularly generous to members of its China missions; for them, the exemption period was extended to three years.[147] On one occasion, sailors and other mission members were even granted a tax exemption for ten years.[148] A mission member was sometimes detained in a foreign country owing to unexpected circumstances. When he eventually came home, he would be granted additional tax and corvée exemptions, the duration of which would be determined by the number of years that he had spent abroad.[149] The court rewarded monks on a China mission even more lavishly: some received lands and sustenance households, and others, youthful servants.[150] In the case of the monk Fushō, even his mother received a rank.[151]

In rare exceptions, the court rewarded its chief diplomats while they were still away in China. Fujiwara no Kiyokawa was appointed minister of ceremonies in 760 and governor of Hitachi (present-day Ibaraki prefecture) in 763; both were prominent concurrent positions.[152]

For those who had demonstrated courage and devotion while performing their duty, the court would promote them more than one grade at a time. Kawabe no Sakamaro was the helmsman on the fourth ship in 752 when he was sailing back to Japan with a wind from astern. Suddenly the stern caught fire, which quickly spread toward the bow. Most people on board panicked, not knowing what to do about the fire. But Sakamaro remained calm. He altered course so the wind was abeam in order to let the wind blow the fire away from the ship. His hands were soon burned by the fire, but Sakamaro held on to the rudder with all his strength until others had managed to extinguish the blaze. The people and the goods on board were saved, but Sakamaro's hands were damaged. For his bravery, the court promoted Sakamaro ten grades to become the brigade recorder (shuchō) of his home province and granted him the fifth rank some twenty years later in 775.[153]

A promising career prospect and enticing material rewards, however, could not erase the worst fear some mission members had: the fear of the dangers of an ocean voyage. Fujiwara no Matsukage was so frightened that he repeatedly petitioned the court to release him from duty almost as soon as he was appointed administrative officer for the mission of 834. The court eventually granted his request on the ground that his mother was very elderly.[154] This development must have alerted Takamura, for he, along with Katsukage, harbored the same fear and was quite convinced of the danger awaiting him.

In fact, most ninth-century Japanese aristocrats were oceanophobic.

They considered the ocean to be a vast living hell, and the stories of voyagers frightened them: many voyagers suffered from sickness due to lack of fresh water and food; some died from shipwreck when heavy seas broke their ships apart; some drifted for days after their ships had been blown off course. And when they eventually landed on the shores of an unknown place, they were sometimes captured or even cannibalized by aborigines. The fear of sea voyages was so deep-rooted and lasting that it still haunted Kiyowara no Toshikage, the hero in *The Tale of the Hollow Tree (Utsubo monogatari),* a novel written in the late tenth century, when the Japanese court had dispatched no missions to China for almost a hundred years.[155]

Takamura, however, knew that his fear was well founded in reality, thanks to the experiences—albeit sometimes exaggerated—of some renowned people. One of them was the Tang monk Jianzhen. He and his disciples left Yangzhou for Japan on the sixteenth day of the tenth month, 753. They encountered what they considered strange phenomena and scary sea creatures: they saw a mirage in the southeast that disappeared mysteriously at noon; white-spotted congers crowded the sea; flying fish covered the sky; and they saw albatrosses whose wingspan was over two meters. But it was the ocean itself that was most frightening. Beyond sight of shore, Jianzhen and his followers were on the empty open sea. The color of the ocean began to change, and soon it turned as dark as ink. High winds created mountainous seas and sent their ships surging atop waves as if they were on mountains; yet before they realized what had happened, their ships shot down as if they were falling into a deep valley. No one could keep his feet—it was as though they were all drunk—and the only thing they could do was to pray for safety by repeating the name of the Buddha. After but a few days at sea, they ran out of drinking water and had to live on raw rice. When they tried to eat it, however, the rice stuck in their throats. They were unable either to swallow or to spit it out. Some drank salt ocean water, and their stomachs were soon bloated. "Never in my life," one disciple lamented, "have I suffered anything as terrible as this!" They were, in fact, on the verge of dying from dehydration, and they were saved only when clouds started to gather and rain fell on the deck. Everyone rushed to collect the rainwater with bowls. They were able to satisfy their thirst fully the next day, when it rained again.[156]

Once the voyagers were on the high seas, they considered their fate to be in the hands of the gods. They tried everything humanly possible that they could think of to stave off disaster, be it offerings to the Sea God or even the sacrifice of human lives.

Dōshō, a Japanese monk who had studied in Tang in the 650s, parted with a three-legged tripod vessel as a sacrifice to please the dragon king. This tripod was no ordinary cooking utensil but a treasure. It was a gift from Master Xuanzang (602–664), the famous Tang monk who studied Buddhism in India for seventeen years, before coming back to China in 645 with many volumes of Buddhist sutras to launch a grand translation project in the capital.[157] Dōshō was one of his favorite students and had the privilege of sharing a room with his master for a few years. Upon Dōshō's departure for home, Xuanzang presented him with the tripod: "I brought this all the way from the Western Region,"[158] said the master. "I use it to prepare my food whenever I fall sick, and the food has always been mysteriously efficacious in curing my illness." With tears in eyes, Dōshō parted with his master and traveled to Dengzhou, a seaport at the tip of the Shandong peninsula, where a Japanese mission was to sail for home. Unfortunately, many mission members fell sick at the port. Dōshō brought out the tripod and made porridge for them. To everybody's surprise, they all recovered on the same day, after eating the porridge. Setting sail with a following wind, the mission headed for home. When they reached the open sea, however, Dōshō's ship, instead of sailing forward, started to circle. It circled for seven days. People on board were puzzled: "The wind has been favorable and strong; we should reach home in a few days. But the ship does not move forward. There must be a reason." "The dragon king wants the tripod!" the diviner stated. But Dōshō protested: "My master granted this tripod to me. How dare the dragon king request it?" "If you begrudge the dragon king the tripod," his fellow voyagers shouted at him, "everyone on this ship will become fish food!" Rather unwillingly, Dōshō tossed the tripod into the sea. According to the story, the ship immediately sailed forward.[159]

It was fortunate that it had not been thought that Dōshō needed to sacrifice his life to satisfy a greedy dragon king. But that was exactly what happened in 763 to the Chinese wife of a Japanese student, his baby girl, her wet nurse, and a lay Buddhist. That year they traveled from China to Parhae to board the ship of Itafuri no Kamatsuka, the shipmaster of a Japanese mission to Parhae. The mission had just fulfilled its task and was about to sail for home. After leaving the harbor, the ship soon encountered a storm and lost its way; the helmsman and some sailors were killed. Kamatsuka believed that four people on board caused the misfortune: the three Chinese females and the eccentric lay Buddhist who ate only a few grains of rice but remained energetic throughout the day. He ordered the sailors to throw them overboard. These human sacrifices, however, did nothing to calm the heavy wind gusts, and their ship drifted for more than ten days before it finally reached Japan. For his crime, Kamatsuka was tried and sentenced to imprisonment.[160]

The most appalling story was the misfortune the China mission suffered in 732. Heguri no Ason Hironari, the administrative officer, reported to the court that the Japanese fleet was enveloped in a fog bank on its way home. Hironari's ship—with 115 people on board—lost both direction and contact with other ships. A contrary wind then blew his ship all the way to southern Vietnam. Unable to utter a word of the local language, they were totally lost in this strange land. To make matters worse, they encountered brigands, who attacked and captured them. In captivity some were executed, some escaped, and some were sold into slavery. More than ninety died of tropical diseases. Only Hironari and three others survived and managed to meet with the king, who granted them grain but put them in a dilapidated shelter. Their nightmare ended only when some locals who had traveled to and lived in Tang found them almost a year later. They smuggled them out and returned them to China.[161]

The Voyage to China

The detailed reports that Japanese diplomats filed on their return vividly recounted the hardships, dangers, and tragedies that they and their deceased colleagues had experienced. This information induced the court to make necessary arrangements and provide equipment for its mission of 834 in the hope of minimizing the risks to the mission members. Among the arrangements, the construction of ocean-going ships was most crucial to the mission's success.

Early in the second month of 834, the court appointed a commissioner and a vice-commissioner, both of the fifth rank, to supervise the project. In the fifth month, an engineer *(daikō)* was also made the deputy commissioner. By putting a number of officials in charge of shipbuilding, the court indicated the great importance of the task. The court soon seems to have become dissatisfied with the progress that was being made, as, during the eighth month, it replaced the commissioner and appointed a supervising artisan.[1] To encourage him to speed up the work, the court also made the artisan a concurrent secretary of Awa province (present-day Tokushima).[2]

Shipbuilding and Other Preparations

Over the centuries, the Japanese developed a shipbuilding technology that produced flat-bottomed junks for the China missions. These ships measured twenty meters in length, seven meters in width, and weighed some 110 tons. Their hulls were built of camphor, and their decks, sailing rig, and so forth, of cedar, pine, and cypress. Clamps joined sections of a ship together, and iron plates hanging outside a ship protected its crucial joins.[3] Four or five cabins each with an opening to the deck divided a ship. These cabins were not connected to each other: one had to reach the deck first to access other cabins. This design was intended to prevent leakage in one cabin from spreading to the rest of the ship. Mission members used these cabins as both storage and living areas. But the ambassador, the vice-ambassador, and the students had their own quarters in the forecastle and the poop. Two sails powered these ships. When the ship was becalmed, sailors rowed the ship using oars, each of which was hewed from a single length of wood. Along both sides of a ship ran wooden walkways from which the sailors rowed or poled the ship.[4] Decoration followed the pattern of the famous three-colored Tang clay figures: the Japanese painted the hulls of their ships white; the masts, forecastles, and poops vermilion; and certain other parts green.[5] Small boats were kept aboard each ship for transportation from ship to shore. In cases of emergency, they were used as lifeboats.[6]

The Japanese court established a series of policies and practices to coordinate matters related to shipbuilding, the allocation of ships, and the safety of mission members. Most ships were built in Aki (present-day Hiroshima prefecture). Other prefectures, such as Ōmi (present-day Shiga prefecture), Tamba (which occupies parts of present-day Hyōgo prefecture, Kyoto, and Osaka), Harima (present-day Hyōgo prefecture), and Bitchū provided timber as well as laborers for its transportation to the shipbuilding site.[7]

China missions in the seventh century employed only two ships. Beginning with the eighth century, the fleet usually consisted of four ships. The term "four ships" (yotsu no fune) was to become synonymous with the ships built specifically for a China mission.[8] These ships were named, some after the place of the shipyard, such as Saeki, and some after the expectation of the ship's performance, such as Harima Hayatori (Fast Bird of Harima).[9] These ships were gigantic by the standards of the time; and the court as well as the mission members regarded them as embodiments of the ship god, for whom reverence must be shown. The court thus granted each ship itself the junior fifth rank, lower grade, and a crown made of tapestry with purple tassels.[10] Officials from the Office of Rites (Jinjikan) made offerings and prayed for a safe journey for mission members at Shinto shrines in the capital, Ise, the metropolitan area, and in seven districts.[11] When the ships were ready, the ambassador would number and allocate them to his subordinates. He usually boarded ship number one.[12]

Takamura, however, did not want anybody to decide which ship he should board, for he knew his safety at sea depended on the ship's quality. Taking matters into his own hands, Takamura rushed to the shipbuilding site and chose the one of best quality for himself. He then numbered and named his own ship. By so doing, Takamura overstepped his authority and violated the long-established precedent that only the ambassador had the authority to choose and number mission ships. Knowing, however, that Takamura was an arrogant man, the ambassador tolerated his conduct.[13]

In the meantime, other preparations for the China mission proceeded according to specific court regulations.[14] Everyone on the mission, from the ambassador to the sailors, received silk fabric, silk floss, and cloth of various quantities and qualities.[15] The mission members were expected to use them to pay for daily necessities and purchases in China. There were also presents provided for the Chinese emperor: silver, silk of various qualities, silk floss, cloth, crystal, agate, oil from camellia seeds, juice from the kudzu vine, and paint.[16] Also prepared for the mission members were one hundred suits of cotton armor and helmets, four hundred protective skirts,[17] and eleven kinds of prepared medicines as well as the herbs and equipment needed to make these medicines.[18] Officials were put in charge of ensuring that mission members were all dressed properly.[19] Given their great size, China missions were usually very costly for the Japanese court.

Events before Departure

On the first day of the second month, 836, preparations for the China mission had finally been completed after more than two years. To pray for the mission's success, the court halted government business for a day in order to hold the ceremony of presenting offerings to the gods of heaven and earth in Kitano (a northern suburb of Kyoto). This began the series of official ceremonies that preceded the mission's departure. On the seventh day, the ambassador himself made offerings to the Kamo shrine.[20] Two days later, the emperor received the major mission members at the Ceremonial Court (Shishinden) in the inner palace and rewarded the ambassador, the vice-ambassador, administrative and acting administrative officers, secretaries, the shipmaster, interpreters, and student monks with silks and cloth of varied quantities. During the same month, the court issued certificates of appointment and granted new ranks to mission members.[21] In the fourth month, major mission members paid a courtesy call to the court. As was usual on such an occasion, the emperor did not appear, only the ministers and the advisers of the State Council.[22]

After their courtesy call to the court, mission members knew that

their departure for China was approaching. But despite the preparations, they never felt fully prepared for that dangerous and challenging
task. Takamura remembered that many of his predecessors turned to
friends for consultation and to bid them farewell. Tajihi no Mahito
Hironari, the ambassador to China in 732, visited Yamanoue no Okura
(660?–733?), a poet who had been a junior scribe on the China mission
in 702.[23] He wanted to benefit from the former diplomat's experience
in China. But instead of giving sound advice to his visitor, Okura dedicated a eulogistic poem to him two days later, in which he praised Japan,
its deities, and the court; showed much admiration for Hironari's
appointment as ambassador; and wished him a safe journey to and from
China:

> Since the age of kami it has been said
> That Yamato, whose mountains fill the sky,
> Is a majestic land of the imperial kami,
> A land blest by the mana of words.
> It has been so retold
> From mouth to mouth, age to age.
> All of us, living today, see and know it.
> Though worthy men are many,
> The Mikado of the High-Radiant Sun, divine,
> Out of fond affection,
> Has chosen you, a scion of a minister's house.
> You have received his solemn command,
> And to the far-off land of China
> You will be sent, and you will go.
> The kami who dwell by the shores and in the deep
> Of the expanse that is their domain—
> The great, exalted kami—
> Will guide you at the prow.
> The great, exalted kami of heaven and earth
> And the spirit of the Great Land of Yamato
> Will wing about the heavens and scan the expanse
> From distant celestial heights.
> When you return, your duties done,
> The great, exalted kami shall, again,
> Lay their hands on the prow

And speed you along a course,
Straight and direct as an ink line,
From the cape of Mitsu, where your ship will moor.
Fare well, let there be no mischance.
Come back quickly![24]

Jubilation, however, was hardly the feeling evoked by parting; the real sentiment was sadness and anxiety, which the two short texts *(hanka)* that followed the poem revealed:

(1) I shall await you
   In Ōtomo at the pine grove[25]
      of Mitsu, its sand
   Swept clean by my broom
   Come back quickly.

(2) I shall hear
   Of your ship casting anchor
      At Naniwa Bay;
   Then will I unite my waistband
   And hasten to your side.[26]

Kasa no Kanamura, another well-known poet, also lamented on the same occasion:

   Beyond the waves
A small island vanishes
   Behind the clouds.
Were we to be so parted
Oh, the choking grief.[27]

The most touching poem of parting was perhaps one written by a mother to her son. It expressed deep anxiety for the hardship that her son would suffer during his journey to China:

   When hoarfrost falls
On the moor where travelers
   Seek shelter for repose,
Enfold my child with your wings,
O flock of cranes of heaven![28]

To the family members of diplomats, separation from and the possible death of their beloved relatives on the trip to China caused bitter sorrow. Fujiwara no Teika, a thirteenth-century literary scholar, vividly described these feelings in his fictional tale *The Tale of Matsura (Matsura no miya monogatari)*. This was the story of Ujitada, who traveled with the ambassador on a China mission. Before his departure,

> Ujitada's mother gazed out over the sea stretching endlessly into the distance. She thought she had prepared herself for this parting, and yet now, when the time was actually before her, tears flowed anew as all her worst fears for her son pressed upon her mind:

> From this day forth
> I shall be the more attached
> To the setting sun and moon
> As I prayerfully await my son's safe return
> In my place on a mountain of Matsura.

> Her husband also composed a poem:

> Alone in the capital,
> With even the mountain of Matsura
> So far, far away,
> Must I abide in solitary anguish,
> My gaze ever cast toward China?

> ... The majestic ship released its moorings and moved away from shore. Before long it looked like no more than a fragile fallen leaf tossed helplessly upon waves. Ujitada's mother raised her blind and gazed sadly after the vessel disappeared among the clouds and haze on the horizon.[29]

The sadness of parting and fear of a perilous journey must also have welled up in Takamura and his fellow mission members. But the court could not afford to let parting grief dampen its diplomats' commitment, as their task was too important to be undermined by personal feelings. To boost the morale of his diplomats, in the late fourth month, the emperor treated them to a grand banquet at the Ceremonial Court.

Officials of the fifth rank and above attended the banquet. To add an atmosphere of jubilation to the occasion, participants were ordered to compose poems using the farewell party as the theme. During the banquet, Tsunetsugu expressed his desire to wish the emperor longevity. When he received permission, Tsunetsugu left his seat to move toward the throne, prostrated himself, wished the emperor longevity, and stood up. The emperor raised a wine cup for Tsunetsugu, and a courtier poured wine for him. He kneeled down to receive and drink the wine, and then moved back to the lower steps of the palace, where he bowed, executed ceremonial dance steps to show gratitude, and returned to his seat. Now it was the participants' turn to present their poems. We read in the *Ten Thousand Leaves* the following poem, which is undated and by an unknown author:

> To the ambassador to China
> I've prayed [to] the Sea God
>   for you my friend;
> so on your outward sail and in,
>   may your vessel speed to journey's end![30]

As an imperial favor, the emperor also wrote and granted a poem to the ambassador, which Tsunetsugu gratefully accepted and carefully put in his robes. Drinking now started. While wine was being served, the ambassador and the vice-ambassador also received gifts from the emperor: imperial robes, white or red imperial silk quilt, and placer gold.[31] These were the emperor's personal belongings. Giving them to the diplomats was the emperor's way of showing them his personal attention and care. The banquet usually ended with its participants dead drunk.[32] Tsunetsugu and Takamura were indeed honored, for the emperor did not always attend the farewell banquet in person, nor was the banquet always held at the Ceremonial Court. Sometimes a high-ranking courtier would entertain the diplomats on behalf of the emperor and grant the imperial poem to the ambassador at the seaport.

The emperor once again received Tsunetsugu and Takamura on the twenty-ninth day of the fourth month. This time, he granted the ambassador the "sword of authority" *(settō)*, which was an insignia *(setsu)* to symbolize that the ambassador had been officially entrusted with limited authority to carry out his task.[33] In fact, the full title for an ambassador was "Ambassador Bearing the Sword of Authority" (Jisetsu Taishi).[34] The swordholder used to have sweeping power in the eighth century; he could discipline his subordinates in whatever way he considered necessary, even adjudicating the death penalty to mission members who were junior to the administrative officer.[35] But the court redefined Tsunetsu-gu's authority, prohibiting him from executing any of his subordinates. It also authorized Takamura to use the sword of authority.[36] The sword was such an important insignia that the court requested its immediate return if the sword bearer was unable to carry out his duty owing to illness or when he had completed his mission and come back to the capital. Saeki no Imaemishi, for example, returned the sword to the court in 776, when he fell sick. The court then instructed the vice-ambassador, Ono no Iwane, to bear the sword and to perform the ambassador's duties.[37] Tajihi no Mahito Agatamori, the supervising ambassador of 716, came back to the capital on the thirteenth day of the twelfth month, 718. Two days later, he submitted the sword to the court.[38] Late submission of the sword carried severe punishment for the offender: a delay of one day was punishable by fifty blows with a light stick; if the delay was ten days, the punishment was one year of penal servitude.[39]

The court also issued an edict to instruct its diplomats how to conduct themselves in China: "You ambassadors in dealing with Tang officials must speak gently to comfort them and do nothing to surprise them."[40] After the bestowal of the sword of authority, the mission was ready to depart for China as soon as the weather permitted. From that point on, no one on the mission was allowed to stay overnight at home without a legitimate reason.[41]

From the late fourth month to the early fifth month, the court made some last minute decisions to satisfy the needs of certain mission members: it allowed the physician to change his place of abode from Yamashiro (in the southern suburbs of Kyoto) to the left district of the capital; it granted the junior fifth rank, lower grade, to an administrative officer, to the ambassador's mother, and, on recommendation by Takamura, to a commoner; it also conferred titles of nobility on a clerk and a scribe.[42] On the ninth day, a courtier announced another edict to Tsunetsugu, wishing the mission a safe journey. Three days later, the diplomats boarded their ships. On the same day, Fujiwara no Tasuke, a middle captain of the right from the Headquarters of the Inner Palace Guards, arrived at Port Namba (present-day Osaka) with an imperial instruction. He entertained the China mission on behalf of the emperor and announced an edict urging the mission to embark on its task.[43] On the fourteenth day, after more than two years of painstaking preparations, the four ships weighed anchor. They sailed southwest to Fukuoka, northern Kyūshū, which was their last stop in Japan before they attempted to cross the East China Sea.

A few days after the mission's departure for Fukuoka, a storm ravaged the capital during the night. Gusting wind and pouring rain uprooted trees and blew off roofs. Few houses were spared in the disaster. The storm was considered a bad omen for Tsunetsugu. That night his fleet was anchored at Port Wada (in present-day Hyogo, only some one hundred kilometers southwest of Kyoto), which was also hit by the storm. Worried, the court sent a minor officer to find out what had happened to its mission, but flooded rivers blocked his way. The court then dispatched another minor officer to make sure that its diplomats and the fleet were safe and sound.[44]

Convinced that danger awaited its China mission, the court ordered an adviser of the State Council and two other high-level officials to present offerings at the tombs of four rulers, trying to call down the protective power of the deceased sovereigns for its mission.[45] In the meantime, it added another interpreter to the mission and allowed a painter and a musician to change their place of abode to the right district of the capital.[46]

The Rescue Arrangements with Neighboring Countries

Over the centuries, the Japanese court had adopted a practice of informing Silla about its China missions and requesting the Silla court to render help to Japanese mission members should such a need arise. Silla also sometimes functioned as intermediary between the Japanese court and its ambassadors. For example, in 770 and 774, while performing his duty in China as the ambassador, Fujiwara no Kiyokawa entrusted the Silla officials who were also visiting the Tang court with his letters. His letters were then brought back to Silla and forwarded to the Japanese court by a Silla ambassador.[47] When the Silla court found a missing Japanese diplomat, it would inform its Japanese counterpart to bring him home.[48] In 804, Mine no Masato, an assistant executive secretary of the Ministry of Military Affairs, arrived at Silla with a letter of the State Council. It informed the Silla court that four Japanese ships had been dispatched to China early in the seventh month of the previous year. Whereas two had been turned back by contrary winds, the other two had gone missing. "Having observed the wind direction," the letter reads, "we believe that [the two ships] must have reached Silla. Therefore Mine no Masato has been dispatched to look for them. If they have indeed drifted [to your shores], it would be appropriate to render them assistance accordingly so that they can return home. If they are not in your territory, we hope you will send an ambassador to China to look for them and report [the findings] to us."[49]

In the intercalary fifth month, 836, the Japanese court sent Ki no Mitsu to make a similar request of Silla. He presented the Silla court with an official letter of the State Council, informing Silla of Japan's planned mission to China. "When our mission departs," the letter reads, "the ocean should be calm. We know the journey will succeed. But winds and waves are changeable, and that worries us tremendously. Should any ship of the mission drift into your territory," the letter requests, "please render help and send it on to China so that there will be no delay."[50]

Mitsu, however, mishandled his job. Instead of stating his task truthfully, Mitsu tried to ingratiate himself with the Silla officials at the seaport, claiming that he was a goodwill ambassador on a special mission to strengthen bilateral ties between Japan and Silla. His claim contradicted his mission as stated in the official letter and aroused the suspicion of the Silla court. It immediately sent a central official to interrogate Mitsu. But Mitsu, good at neither written nor oral explanations, failed all the queries.[51] The Silla court decided not to receive Mitsu formally in the capital. It also sent a strongly worded official letter to the Japanese court, expressing doubts about Mitsu's real identity: "[Although] the imprint of the State Council seal on the official letter is clearly discernible...there have been [cases whereby] islanders benefited themselves from trade by using counterfeit official seals and documents to trick our coast guards." The letter went on to lecture the Japanese court: "The conduct of bilateral relations should not involve deceit. But your ambassador is unable to produce satisfactory replies to our queries. His words are totally untrustworthy." Mitsu must have also claimed that he was the ambassador to China and that Takamura's ship had already left Japan for China. These inventions angered his host: "If Takamura has indeed departed for China, the Japanese court would not necessarily have dispatched Mitsu as another ambassador to Tang. Besides, your China mission has an ambassador, and Takamura is a mere deputy. Why did Mitsu brush aside the highest ranking diplomat and indiscreetly mention only his subordinate?" The Silla court had in fact learned of Takamura's whereabouts from its own source of information: "Takamura is still in Japan. He has yet to cross the sea. But Mitsu claimed that Takamura's ship has sailed for China. These words are hearsay from maritime traders. They are pure nonsense!... Moreover, Mitsu is merely a low-ranking official who wears the green court robe and comes aboard a single ship.[52] How can he pretend to be an ambassador to Tang? What he says is absurd—like slander or a lie." Silla justice officials even requested several times that Mitsu be tried so as to deter other criminals. But the Silla court, desirous of not damaging bilateral relations with Japan further, released him after five months of detention. Mitsu eventually returned to the Dazai Headquarters in the late tenth month. It would take him another two months to gather enough courage to report his failed mission to the court.[53] This incident was such an embarrassing diplomatic blunder that it earned a detailed account in the *Later Chronicles of Japan Continued*. "If we preserve only the gist of this event but do not detail how it happened and ended," the official historians wrote, "we are afraid that readers might not be able to learn a lesson from our account. We have therefore transcribed the official letter from Silla and attached it to the account."[54]

Attempts to Cross the Ocean

Without proper arrangements with the Silla court and haunted by a bad omen, Tsunetsugu led his fleet to brave the East China Sea on the second day of the seventh month. Two weeks later, an urgent report from the Dazai Headquarters arrived at the court: the winds had turned the first and the fourth ships back to Hizan province (present-day Nagasaki).[55]

The court immediately instructed the Dazai officials to accommodate the mission members at their headquarters, provide them with daily necessities, and wait for further instructions. To repair the damaged ships, the court selected and sent artisans to the Dazai Headquarters. It also deployed sentries along the coasts of the Chika Islands (present-day Hirado and Goto archipelagos) to watch for other ships should they too drift back to Japan. Locals were dispatched to the far-off islands. They were to be rewarded with grain and cloth if they spotted any goods or members of the mission.[56]

Takamura, who had boarded the second ship, was no luckier than his boss. After a week at sea, his ship was beaten back to the shores of Hizen. The ship itself sustained only minor hull damage, although the lifeboats were lost. As mission members gradually returned to Japan in the following month, their horrible experience became known to the court. People aboard the first, the second, and the fourth ships were lucky, for their ships had at least survived the heavy seas and returned home intact. Those on the third ship, however, were less fortunate. Mountainous waves damaged the rudder, ripped off the sidetracks, and flooded the cabins. Some people drowned. The ship was beyond control, drifting aimlessly on the sea. The shipmaster and the administrative officer feared that people on board would soon die of thirst, so they decided to let the people dismantle the ship's deck and use the timbers to make rafts that they could use to look for drinking water. Most people rushed to make rafts and soon left the ship, but some remained. When the ship eventually touched shore at Tsushima Island in the late eighth month, only three people aboard remained alive.[57]

After his near-death experience on the ocean, Takamura could not help but wonder why their first attempt had failed. Had they not received all the blessings from the emperor, the deceased sovereigns, and their fellow courtiers? He still fondly remembered the poem by Empress Kōken (r. 749–758), whose warm and sincere blessing had encouraged the mission members on their journey:

In this god-blessed country of Yamato,
people sail as safely as walking on the ground;
And they board ships as comfortably as staying in bed.
The four ships shall sail stern to stern,
and swift come home again.
. . .[58]

But a journey to China was like anything but the pleasure of staying in bed. It had always been perilous; it had humbled many of Takamura's predecessors and had taken some of their lives. What Takamura did not quite understand was that, when tragedy struck, it was not so much because of the bad luck of mission members, but because of their lack of knowledge of the monsoons, their primitive shipbuilding technology, and their lack of navigational skills.

In their poetry, Chinese writers compared China and Japan to close neighbors separated by a mere strip of water as narrow as a clothing belt. But this belt—the East China Sea—occupies a vast area of nearly 1.25 million square meters. The sea route linking the two major ports of Nagasaki and Shanghai stretches some 850 kilometers, and a modern ocean liner at thirteen knots would take a day and a half to cover the distance. The best chance for the ninth-century Japanese to reach China in ships powered only by men and sails was to sail with the wind astern. And that required an understanding of the changing monsoons.

From October to December, a northeastern monsoon blows from the Japanese archipelagos toward the Asian continent, making it the best season to sail to China. Starting in May and continuing into September, the wind changes to the southwest, which would facilitate a return journey from China to Japan.[59] But Tsunetsugu and the Japanese court apparently had not learned to use the monsoon. Their first attempt to cross the sea was on the second day of the seventh month—August 17 on the solar calendar—when the southwesterly wind was still strong, thus beating their ships back to Japan.

Tsunetsugu and his subordinates were fortunate that they at least had returned home safely. Some members of the earlier China missions had never made it. Of the forty ships that the successive Japanese courts had dispatched to China, as many as twelve sank. That almost one-third of the China mission ships suffered shipwreck testified to their poor quality. These giant flat-bottomed wooden boxes had no keel to support the hull, nor was the hull watertight. Water weed instead of putty was used to caulk the joints of the ship.[60] Oversized and structurally unsound, these ships were not seaworthy. One ship that the mission of 762 used ran aground at Port Namba even before its departure for China. A damaged rudder immobilized the ship. Waves beat relentlessly against its stern and soon broke it up. The court decided to abort the mission out of concern over the ship's poor quality.[61] When battered by strong winds and high seas, these ships were like leaves in a hurricane. Heavy seas so worked their hulls that the ships flooded and foundered, with the loss of passengers and cargoes; high winds snapped masts, rendering ships helpless; and the combined forces of the high winds and waves pounded joints loose, sometimes causing a ship to break in half.[62] Even when a ship managed to reach the Chinese shore, it was usually damaged beyond repair. The Tang court had to build new ships to send the Japanese delegation home. Some Japanese ships were still usable after their voyage to China, but the ambassadors as well as the student monks preferred to abandon them and obtain ships constructed by Silla for their journey home.[63] In 839, the Japanese court ordered that new ships should be built to the specifications of Silla ships, for the latter could better "resist the wind and the waves."[64]

Furthermore, ninth-century Japanese had not mastered the skill and knowledge necessary for safe ocean navigation. They had yet to learn how to use the compass to determine the direction in which a ship was sailing. Communication between ships was also difficult. They had to use torchlights to keep in touch with each other at night.[65]

It was therefore no surprise that the Japanese missions before the 660s chose the "Northern Route" for their journey to China. Starting from Port Hakata (in Fukuoka, northern Kyūshū), this route stretched northwestward to cross the Korean Straits. It then turned west and north, running along the west coast of the Korean peninsula. At about 38 degrees north latitude, the route turned west again, cutting across the Yellow Sea. It ended at Dengzhou, a seaport on the northern tip of the Shandong peninsula.

Sailing the Northern Route had several advantages. Major Korean landmarks and islands that could be used as objects of reference to determine a ship's location and to keep it on course were often in sight. In case of emergency, a ship could always pull in to shore for help. The route was safe, for Koguryŏ and Paekche—the two Korean states that occupied the west coast of the Korean peninsula—had been friendly to Japan. And the Japanese as well as the Chinese delegations during the previous Sui dynasty had already sailed along the Northern Route.[66]

The route, however, became dangerous in the 660s, when the Tang military campaign against Koguryŏ and the wars for unification among the three Korean states reduced Korea to chaos. In consequence, the Japanese court decided to have its China mission avoid the perilous Korean peninsula and sought to find a new route to China. It was a wise decision since Silla unified Korea in the late 660s and thereafter became disrespectful to Japan. Bilateral relations between the two countries deteriorated further in the eighth century, to the point that the Japanese court even contemplated a military expedition against Silla in 759.

The Japanese court opened the "Southern Island Route" in the early eighth century after its officials had visited some of the southern islands in 698. The next year, chieftains of Tane, Yaku, Amami, and Tokuno-

shima presented gifts to the Japanese court and accepted its titles.[67]
These developments convinced the court that it was now safe for its missions to use the southern islands as transfer ports on their way to China.

Taking the Southern Island Route, a China mission would sail all the
way to Tokunoshima. There the mission would cross the East China Sea.
If all went well, they would arrive near the mouth of the Yangzi River.[68]
Then, beginning in the 770s, China missions shortened their trips by
taking the "Southern Route." This route first took a China mission to
the Gotō archipelago west of Kyūshū; there the mission would wait for
a following wind to send its ships directly to the mouth of the Yangzi
River. A China mission could now avoid possible harassment by Silla by
taking either the Southern Island Route or the Southern Route. But
these routes also subjected a mission to the mercy of the ocean. Once
mission members sailed from Port Hakata, only the vagaries of wind and
wave would determine whether or not they arrived in China.

Tsunetsugu's mission attempted the Southern Route. After their first
attempt failed, Tsunetsugu and Takamura returned the sword of authority to the court in the middle of the ninth month, 836. This was not,
however, the end of their ordeal. The court allowed them to rest at home
but in the meantime appointed a chief officer and a deputy to supervise
the repair of their damaged ships. Within three months, the repairs
were completed. The court immediately set in motion other preparations for the mission's second attempt to reach China. In the early second month, 837, it urged Tsunetsugu to worship the gods of heaven
and earth in Kyoto. To solemnize this ceremony, government offices in
the capital suspended business for a day. The court also granted Tsunetsugu a concurrent governorship of the Dazai Headquarters and gave
some of his subordinates noble titles. It then held a farewell banquet in
honor of the mission, during which participants composed poems using
the theme "in company with the ambassador to Tang at a farewell banquet in late spring." The joyous drinking continued into dusk, when
ranking officials and Takamura started presenting poems to the emper-
or. But the ambassador, with the imminent China trip on his mind, soon
became drunk; he had to excuse himself from the banquet. Two days
later, major mission members paid the court a courtesy call. And on the
fifteenth day of the third month, Tsunetsugu and Takamura again
received the sword of authority. They were now authorized once more

to lead the mission to China. Takamura, as vice-ambassador of the mission, had so far faithfully performed his duties. For example, he carried the sword of authority on his left shoulder for Tsunetsugu after the ambassador had received it from a court official. In a humble gesture to show respect to the court and the ambassador, he then walked in quick short steps in front of his superior when leaving the court.[69] But Takamura's attitude toward his duty was soon to change.

Tsunetsugu left the capital for the Dazai Headquarters in Kyūshū on the nineteenth day of the third month; Takamura followed suit five days later. To pray for the mission's safety, the court ordered offerings to be presented to the Sun Goddess at the Ise Shrine; it also granted the ambassador's ship the junior fifth rank, lower grade, and named it *Taiheira* (Grand Safety and Goodness).[70]

Despite all the meticulous preparations and sincere good wishes, the mission's second attempt also failed. Late in the seventh month, an urgent report from the Dazai Headquarters reached the court to the effect that the first and fourth ships had drifted to Iki Island (northwest of Kyūshū), the second ship to the Chika Islands, and the third ship had gone missing. The date of the Dazai report revealed that the mission had left for China sometime in the seventh month—August on the solar calendar. Its ships had thus sailed directly into a contrary wind.[71]

The mission's second failure puzzled the court, and it took more than half a year to come up with a solution. "The ambassador to China has been forced back to Japan in recent years, unable to cross the sea," an edict dated the twenty-seventh of the third month, 838, reads. "It has been the way of the spirits in the imperceptible darkness that they will respond only to devoted believers and that the virtue of the radiant god is such that he will surely protect people who have accumulated merits." Out of this belief, the court ordered officials at the Dazai Headquarters to work with the provincial authorities to identify candidates who were at least twenty-five years of age and devoted to the study and practice of Shinto. Among the candidates, nine were to be ordained into the priesthood and posted in four major Shinto shrines. They were to practice various religious ceremonies rigorously so as to bring peace and safety to the mission on its way to and from China. In the meantime, offerings were to be presented to the state-established provincial Buddhist monasteries and Shinto shrines. A few days later, in the early fourth month, the court also ordered monks and priests to chant the *Sutra of the Dragon-King of the Sea* from the day of the mission's departure until its return.[72]

In the south at Port Hakata, however, there was no sign that the mission would make a third attempt any time soon. The leaders apparently had cold feet and did nothing during the entire fourth month. Their inaction displeased the emperor, who, at the end of the month, had an edict issued to both Tsunetsugu and Takamura, urging them to act. "You ambassadors are expected to lead a mission to cross the sea. Things, however, have not proceeded as you wished, and you have been delayed at the lodge. I am mindful of the difficulties on your trip, and I often have you in mind. Now the trade wind has started blowing, and your arduous journey should start. Why should you wait?" The emperor in fact became so concerned that he dispatched Fujiwara no Tasuke, who, in the fifth month of 836, had entertained the mission members on behalf of the emperor at Port Hakata. This time, however, his task was to supervise the departure of the China mission—a measure unprecedented in the court's history of dispatching missions to China.[73]

Tsunetsugu, however, tried to find every possible excuse to postpone the trip. "Although it was the weather that caused us to miss the seasonal wind," he wrote in his memorial to the court, "unforeseen hindrances seem to have troubled our departure more than once. Besides, a journey across the vast ocean is both arduous and unpredictable. How can we expect a successful crossing without resorting to the blessing and protection of the spirits? I therefore humbly request that [monks] in various provinces read the *Large Sutra on Perfect Wisdom*."[74]

Takamura was even more innovative in dodging his duty. Possibly he recalled the case of Saeki no Imaemishi, the ambassador to China in 775. After his courtesy call on the court, Imaemishi left for the port of departure. But he stopped at the Rajōmon, the southern gate of the capital, and claimed that he was sick. He was nonetheless carried to Osaka in a palanquin. There the whole mission waited for days for him to recover. There was, however, no sign of improvement. The court then ordered the vice-ambassador to take over Imaemishi's responsibility to lead the mission to China.[75] Now Takamura also became conveniently sick, hoping that the court would release him of his diplomatic duty.[76]

The court ignored Takamura's claim to be ill. But it had to pay attention to Tsunetsugu when he reported that his ship was leaking. Tsunetsugu had no way to determine the seriousness of the leak; but having twice experienced peril at sea, he knew that he depended on his ship's soundness. He must still have resented Takamura's having taken the liberty a few months earlier to choose the best ship for his own use. Tsunetsugu decided to memorialize the court requesting that the ships be renumbered and that he take over Takamura's ships. His request was granted.

The court decision infuriated Takamura. He decided to use it as an excuse for not carrying out his diplomatic duty. "The court decision [regarding the ship allocation] has been inconsistent and has changed several times," he voiced his objection in a memorial. "When it first sequenced the mission ships, the court made the best one ship number one. After the allocation, the ships drifted back to Japan. Now all of a sudden the court has changed the ships' sequence and assigned one of inferior quality to me. This is a decision that benefits oneself at the expense of others; it is against both common sense and humane feeling. [Tsunetsugu's conduct] has caused him to lose face. How can he lead his subordinates now? Besides, my family is poor, and my parents are getting old and unwell. I should fulfill my filial duty by drawing water and gathering firewood for them. Are my arguments not correct? I have decided not to command any mission ship."[77] As if he thought the words in his memorial were not audacious enough, Takamura composed a "Ballad of the Way West," which ridiculed the court policy of dispatching missions to China. His words were so sarcastic and disrespectful that they angered the abdicated emperor, Saga, who ordered the court to punish Takamura. But Takamura did not mind the punishment, for his offense had automatically disqualified him as a diplomat of the court. His wish was fulfilled.

Takamura, however, had to pay a heavy price for his behavior. His ridicule of court policy constituted the serious offense of "criticizing the emperor," which fell into the category of "great irreverence" and was punishable by decapitation. His refusal to obey the court order conveyed to him by Fujiwara no Tasuke was equally serious, for the penal code stipulated that "opposing commissioners with imperial decrees or lacking the proper behavior that a subject owes to his emperor is punishable by strangulation."[78] The verdict regarding his punishment came down in the mid-twelfth month: "Takamura, having received an imperial order to serve on a mission abroad, falsely claimed illness and failed to carry out the order of the state. According to the law code, he could be sentenced to death by strangulation. But it is appropriate to mitigate his sentence to life exile in a remote place. [Therefore he should] be sent into life exile in Oki province [present-day Oki Islands]."[79] Stripped of his senior fifth rank, lower grade, he was made a commoner. This setback in his career, however, did not seem to have dampened Takamura's poetic inspiration. He compiled ten poems on his way to Oki province. One of them reads:

> You on your fishing boats—
> please tell this to my loved ones:
> that my boat has passed
> safely through the Eight Isles
> on the broad plain of the sea.[80]

Showing no regret for his misconduct, Takamura apparently consoled himself with the thought that he was not the only diplomat who had defied the court and decided not to go to China. Several members on board other ships, including a shipmaster, a scholar of the calendar, and a student of the calendar also refused to carry out their duties. They fled their ships and went into hiding before they were arrested and sent into life exile on Sado Island.[81] In fact, some thirty years before, some members of the China mission in 805 had already expressed negligence in their duties. Mimune no Imatsugu, an administrative officer, rushed ashore for safety when his ship was washed back to a remote island and caught between rocks. He left the official gifts and the private goods on board in the care of only a few archers. The ship drifted away when waves broke the rope tying it fast. The court issued Imatsugu a strongly worded edict: "It is the duty of a diplomat to take great care of the state gifts, and only manpower could keep them intact. But you ignored your official duty and shamefully sought personal safety. How could your ship be saved when it was left unmanned and drifting? Is this the way of a diplomat? You will be punished by law so as to prevent the same offense from happening in the future."[82]

Takamura spent two years in exile before he was called back to the capital in 840, when he showed remorse for his unruly behavior. The emperor, who had always recognized Takamura's literary reputation, which was growing even as he was serving his sentence, pardoned him. He was restored to the senior fifth rank, lower grade, in 841. A series of promotions followed one another from late 841 to the end of 852. He held a number of important positions in the court and in local governments. At one time, he again became involved in diplomacy. The court dispatched him to the lodgings for foreign guests in the capital to grant an imperial edict and an official document of the State Council to a Parhae ambassador. He died at fifty-one.

Takamura was remembered as a man who had lived a poor but honest life, filial to his mother and generous to relatives and friends.[83] Moreover, his and other fellow mission members' reluctance to travel to China prompted the court to reconsider its China policy. Tsunetsugu was the last ambassador to lead a China mission. Some fifty years later, the court again organized such a mission but decided to abandon it once and for all.

What the court did not realize was that Takamura's reluctance to follow the court's orders and the consequent delay in the mission's departure in fact contributed to the success of the mission's third attempt. Closely watched and repeatedly urged by Tasuke, the first and the fourth ships left for China early in the seventh month of 838; and when the second ship eventually set sail from the port, it was already the end of the month—the end of August on the solar calendar. The southwesterly wind had died down, making it easier for Tsunetsugu to sail to China. He reached his destination safely and immediately began to conduct the requisite ambassador diplomacy in China.

The Journey to Changan

As soon as a Japanese ambassador came ashore in China, he sought to contact local Chinese authorities to inform them of his arrival, to request supplies of daily necessities for his subordinates, and to apply for permission to use the Tang official transportation system to travel to the capital, Changan.

This transportation system offered two types of services. The first, known as *yi* in Chinese, was a speedy relay service that supplied fresh horses at every relay station to couriers and officials on urgent business; the second, referred to as *zhuan* in Chinese, was a slower service that provided carts to officials traveling on routine government matters.[1] Vast and complex, this transportation system could be considered the nervous system of the Tang empire. An eighth-century writer once summarized its importance and basic features: "The prosperity of the illustrious Tang is due to an ancient [transportation] system. It starts from the capital and extends in four directions throughout the ten circuits. At a distance of ten miles [thirty *li*] from each other, relay stations line the roads. They are allocated horses of upper, middle, and lower quality. Their buildings are spacious, and their meals are delicious. [Staff at the stations] strive to satisfy every need [of the official travelers]. [Thanks to this system] the emperor's orders can be easily transmitted to places where there are hardly traces of human beings. There is no other system that can reach these remote regions."[2]

The Relay Station System and Its Management

Stations were the major facilities for the relay service. They were built in the metropolitan area in Changan and in Luoyang,[3] as well as in the prefectures. Prefectural stations were classified into six grades according to how often they were used. The total number of stations varied over the course of time, ranging from 1,300 to 1,700 in all. Most of them were situated along main roads, some on the coast, and some at the junction of a road and a river. The distance between the stations was not rigidly

邸驛

三才圖會 宮室一卷

驛邸宿也史記作諸侯却卻刺卻之義也公莫也司豊也官

二千

A Ming dynasty relay station. (Wang Qi and Wang Siyi, *Sancai tuhui,* 1609 edn.; facsimile rpt. [Shanghai: Shanghai Guji Chubanshe, 1988], vol. b, p. 996)

fixed. In the mountainous south and the remote northwest, the distance between stations was sometimes stretched from twenty to thirty-three miles (sixty to a hundred *li*) in order to build the station at a suitable site, such as one near water or grass. In the metropolitan areas, where station services were heavily used, the distance between them could be shortened to as little as five miles (fifteen *li*).[4] Once a station was named, any change to the name was subject to the approval of the court.[5]

A relay station was enclosed in a compound surrounded by high walls with an arch over the gateway. Sometimes bamboo and mulberry trees were planted around the compound. Inside the station, there was a main hall and a side hall as well as rooms of various sizes suitable to house travelers of different ranks. There were separate living quarters for travelers' companions and servants. There were also kitchens, stables, areas to stack firewood and forage, and storehouses for wine, tea, and pickles. In some major stations, there were several-storied buildings, pavilions, and painted boats on a pond to entertain travelers.[6]

Officials traveling on business were required to keep to a rigid timetable. To ensure that official travelers adhered to their schedule, a timing device was installed in front of the metropolitan post station (Duting), which was situated at the center of both Changan and Luoyang.[7] Most metropolitan officials on business trips were required to depart from the station on time. Those of the third rank and senior, and elite members of officialdom would leave from their office. When the relay horses arrived, they had to embark on their trip without delay.[8] To help travelers check the distance, one mark would be established at every 1.7 miles (five *li*), and two marks at every 3.3 miles (ten *li*) along the road. These marks were in the shape of a pyramid about four to six feet high.[9] A courier was required to travel on schedule, and doing so could be a matter of life and death under certain circumstances. The court, for example, once ordered the execution, at a relay station, of a minister from the Ministry of Personnel who had been dispatched to Hebei and was suspected to have been involved in a local mutiny. Later, the emperor decided to pardon him and had a courier sent to stop the execution. The courier, however, dozed off in the saddle and failed to keep his schedule. When he eventually arrived at the station, the execution had already been carried out.[10] An official traveler was not supposed to stay at any station for more than one night without legitimate reasons. If he needed to stay longer, he had to acquire permission from the prefectural government;[11] and his stay could not exceed three days, after which he was required to move into a private inn.[12] Most official travelers traveled on a tight schedule. They usually left the stations very early in the morning. In his poem titled "Early Departure from the Jindi Station," a Tang poet wrote:

> The insects are singing in the fields
> and the city is bathed in the moonlight.
> When everybody is sleeping behind closed doors,
> the travelers are already about to leave the station.[13]

Horses were another major facility provided for the relay service. Depending on its location and grade, each station was allocated a number of horses. The Duting station in both Changan and Luoyang had from 75 to 90 horses in service when the emperor was away from the capital. When he stayed in the capital and held court, the number of horses was increased to 105 to handle the frequent communication between the emperor and his subjects.[14] A prefectural station of the first grade would have 60 horses. Stations from the second to the sixth grades had respectively 45, 30, 18, 12, and 8 horses. A station would be equipped with both horses and boats if a ferry existed within its jurisdiction.[15] Stations along waterways were classified according to the most frequently used, the frequently used, and the less frequently used, and were equipped with four, three, and two boats respectively.[16]

Relay horses differed in breed. Most stations used the larger horses from the Longyou region (present-day Gansu, Qinghai, and Xinjiang provinces).[17] But stations in the mountainous and humid south used smaller horses from modern Sichuan province, as they were used to traveling in mountainous terrain and were accustomed to hot and humid weather. To ensure the quality of relay horses, an administrator from the War Section (Bingcao Sibing Canjun) of a prefectural government would supervise the selection of locally bred horses. Qualified horses would be branded with the character "station" (yi) and the name of the prefecture on the left shoulder and neck. Horse pasturage supervisors (jianmu) from the Court of the Imperial Stud (Taipu Si) would then examine them. If a horse passed, both its cheeks would be branded with the character "dispatch" (chu).[18] The vice-director of the Bureau of Equipment (Jiabu langzhong yuanwailang) from the Ministry of War supervised the management of relay horses and stations.[19]

In the early Tang, county and prefectural authorities assigned rich local families to head relay stations. These families used their own resources to finance the stations.[20] This practice, however, soon became too heavy a financial burden on them. Consequently, local government took over the management of relay stations after the mid-eighth century by making a specially appointed administrator *(zhuanzhi guan)* the station-master.[21] A few subofficial functionaries, some servicemen, and boatmen assisted him. Their number was determined by the number of horses or boats at the station: one serviceman would take care of three horses, and three boatmen would be in charge of a boat.[22] The performance of a stationmaster was subject to the scrutiny of either the metropolitan governor or a prefect, depending on the location of his station. Sometimes a surveillance and supervisory commissioner or a censor was dispatched to inspect the operation of stations or to investigate the wrongdoing of a station head.[23]

Once horses had been allocated to a relay station, it was the sole responsibility of the stationmaster to keep them in good shape. Prefectural officials checked the condition of these horses annually.[24] If a horse died of mismanagement, the stationmaster had to replace it at his own cost.[25] But if relay horses died of natural causes or were injured while in service, the prefectural government would use its funds to purchase new horses to replace them. A prefectural government sometimes acquired additional horses for stations where the number of official travelers had sharply increased.[26] It had also to submit an annual report to the Ministry of War, detailing the number of horses that were injured or had died, and listing those that were strong or weak.[27]

A relay station had an operating budget for the purchase of such articles and goods as bedding, table linen, kitchen utensils, saddlery and tack for the horses, forage, and foodstuffs for daily use and consumption. This budget came from the prefectural government, which allocated revenue from the household levy to stations to pay for these expenditures.[28] In the meantime, the court assigned some six acres of land to each horse; grain and clover were grown on this land to supply fodder for the stations.[29] Relay stations in the greater metropolitan area of Changan and in certain prefectures usually served a large number of official travelers, and they needed bigger budgets. To help the stations in Changan and Wannian counties, both of which were situated within the capital, Changan, the court allocated a one-time cash grant to the county authorities. They were to use the money for loans to generate a profit from the interest that would become part of the station's budget.[30] Prefectural governments adopted the same practice to finance some of the stations under their jurisdiction.[31]

In the early Tang, the use of the relay service was strictly regulated because the service was "basically provided for urgent military matters."[32] Metropolitan and prefectural officials could avail themselves of the service only when they were handling matters of the greatest importance and urgency. There was no exception even for the crown prince, who had to obtain permission from Emperor Taizong in 645 before delivering urgent documents to his father.[33] There were, however, a few special occasions when prefects and metropolitan officials of the fifth rank or senior who were away from the capital on business could send their congratulations to the capital by relay service. These occasions were when "the emperor ascends the throne or is crowned, or the emperor's mother is given a temple name, or an emperor or an heir apparent is announced, or there is an amnesty or new year's day."[34]

To prevent misuse of the relay service, the *Tang Code* stipulated that "all cases of documents... that are not required to be sent by the postal relay service and are, are to be punished by one hundred blows with the heavy stick."[35] Prefects who had overused the relay service by having issued more than 127 certificates within a year would receive no salary for three months.[36] The Tang court also made the following matters offenses since they adversely affected the function of relay stations: wrongful entry into and improper acceptance of services from relay stations; misuse of station facilities;[37] using relay horses under false pretenses;[38] using excessive numbers of relay horses;[39] taking the wrong route while riding a relay horse; going to places beyond the destination; passing a station without changing horses; causing the death of a relay horse without good reasons;[40] carrying private goods other than necessary clothes, quilt, and weapons;[41] and illegally lending or borrowing relay horses.[42] To avoid waste, all services and supplies to an official traveler stopped one day after his arrival at the capital.[43]

The strict regulations for use of the relay service were gradually relaxed when the court made the service available to more officials. Among these were newly appointed governors-general and prefects traveling to their posts to assume office; military commissioners, surveillance commissioners, eunuchs, censors, officials holding the third and higher rank, and those from the Secretariat-Chancellery or the Department of State Affairs traveling on official business. Under these relaxed regulations and with the permission of central or local authorities, some private travelers as well as members of foreign missions could use the relay service. Sometimes demoted metropolitan officials and criminals were also sent from the capital by relay service.[44]

The vice-director of the Chancellery authorized the use of the relay service by officials departing from the capital. They had to apply to the Chancellery for a paper certificate. The supervising secretaries first examined the individual applications and the vice-director then determined whether an applicant was eligible either for the relay service or for the transportation service.[45] Official travelers from other regions acquired their certificate from the regent at the secondary capital, Luoyang, or from the military administrator of the War Section of a prefecture.[46]

The certificate set a schedule for its bearer by stipulating how many stations he must pass daily. If he was on urgent business, he would be provided with horses of superior quality and was expected to pass at least six stations a day.[47] If he fell behind schedule, he would be punished by flogging or penal servitude.[48] A traveler's eligibility to use the relay service would be double-checked by the local authorities if he happened to pass through Luoyang or by the headquarters of any of the five Chief Military Commissions. They would countersign his certificate or cancel it if they deemed that necessary.[49] Except for the Chancellery, prefectural authorities were not to issue two-way certificates that allowed a traveler to use the relay service both on his way to carry out his duty as well as to return home. Upon arrival at his destination, he had to turn in his certificate to the local authorities; upon completion of his duty, he would be instructed to use the transportation service for his return trip.[50]

Depending on his rank, an official traveler would be provided with one of the five grades of services.[51] When allocating horses, for example, "active duty officials of the third rank and above and princes are to be provided with four post horses. Officials of the fourth rank and dukes of state and above are given three. Officials of the fifth rank and nobles of the third rank and above are given two. Titular officials and former officials are each proportionately given one less than active official.... Former officials of the sixth rank and below, titular officials, guard officials, couriers dispatched by a department, and those on urgent business are all given [a single] horse."[52]

Not all official travelers were entitled to use the relay service. The vice-director of the Chancellery would examine the application by any metropolitan official to use the service and assess the importance of his business. If his business was deemed routine, the applicant would have to use the transportation service.[53] In general, an official on a return trip after completion of his official task would also have to use the transportation service.[54] A prefectural military administrator was expected to use the same discretion when scrutinizing local applications submitted to his office.[55]

The Transportation Service

The Tang transportation service carried people and goods to their destinations mainly by carts and was therefore a slower mode of transportation. It provided official travelers with horse-drawn carriages or ox-drawn carts as the major conveyance. This service was tailored to Chinese travelers, who, unlike the nomads, preferred riding in carriages or carts to riding on horseback.[56]

Horses used in the transportation service were called "transportation horses" (zhuanma). They were mainly draught animals and were inferior in quality to the "relay horses" (yima).[57] Besides their difference in quality, these two types of horses were also managed differently. Whereas relay horses were allocated to each station and a traveler had to change his mount at every station, the transportation horses were kept at county seats, managed by the county authorities, and traveled long distances between counties or even prefectures.[58] Prefects and the deputy commander of local militia annually inspected the transportation horses as well as the oxen and the donkeys that were used. Old and sick animals unfit for service would be sold "after their condition has been verified by prefectural officials."[59] The prefectural authorities also needed to report annually to the Bureau of Equipment, Ministry of War, detailing the condition of the transportation horses and donkeys, including those that had died or been injured.[60]

Eligible travelers received an "exchange document" (didie) as authorization to use the transportation service.[61] The surveillance commis-

sioners, military commissioners and vice-commissioners, and the commander and vice-commanders of military garrisons could bring a number of companions with them when traveling to and from the capital.[62]
They stayed overnight at lodges (*guan*), which were established at a distance of ten miles (thirty *li*) from one another.[63] Unlike the relay stations, these lodges provided travelers only with accommodation but no
means of transportation.[64]

Until the early eighth century, carts remained a major conveyance
for official travelers, who received a number of carts as well as drivers
and oxen according to their ranks. A court edict stipulated that only "at
places where carts and oxen are unavailable are horses and donkeys to
replace them [as riding animals]."[65] Court regulations also specified the
daily travel distance for official travelers using the transportation service.[66] The court, however, found it increasingly difficult to implement its
regulations regarding the use of carts for travel on official business.
After almost a century of governance in China, the Tang royal family
saw aspects of their nomadic way of life, such as horse riding, becoming
fashionable among their Chinese subjects. In his memorial to the court
in 708, the left mentor to the crown prince pointed out that in antiquity, grand masters and other senior officials all rode in horse-drawn carriages. From the Wei and the Jin until the Sui dynasties, court officials
used carts pulled by oxen. But the custom changed during the Tang
dynasty. The emperor still used ceremonial carriages when visiting the
imperial tombs and temples, or when conferring titles on princes and
dukes; and ordinary people did the same in wedding ceremonies. "On
other occasions, people no longer ride in carriages. Nobles or commoners use only saddle horses to travel."[67] Carts were employed mainly for
cargo transportation. In the 730s, officials eligible for transportation
service were often granted permission to ride transportation horses.[68]
When these horses were in short supply, they would try illegally to use
relay horses as mounts.[69] This major change in the mode of official travel
was evident in a contemporary court regulation that specified the number of transportation horses for officials of various ranks but mentioned
no carts or oxen.[70] In the meantime, riders of transportation horses
were ordered not to pass more than four stations in a day.[71]

The Tang transportation system was now more integrated: horse riding became a standard mode of travel for official as well as for authorized private travelers,[72] who could avail themselves of services by both

the relay stations and the lodges.[73] One thing, however, remained unchanged: the transportation system still provided two kinds of service: the fast relay service and the slower transportation service; and the kind of service provided a traveler was still determined by the importance of his business.

The Tang transportation system was highly efficient when it was well managed. A courier could quickly transmit information to or an order from the capital when an emergency occurred. A Tang poem reads:

> Station after station, a relay horse gallops like a shooting star.
> Having left Xianyang at dawn, [the courier] arrives at Mount
>   Long at dusk.[74]

This courier indeed traveled very fast, covering 153 miles (465 *li*), the distance between Xianyang and Mt. Long (in present-day Gansu province), in one day.[75] On an urgent mission to pacify a military uprising, another poet wrote, "I feel late even when traveling at 300 *li* [99 miles] a day."[76] Relay horses in Tang poems were often described as "flying relay horses"[77] and as "coming down from the mountains like falling stars."[78] On occasion, couriers traveled day and night.[79]

The delivery of fresh lychees from south and southwest China all the way to Changan was a well-known example of how efficient the Tang relay service could be. Produced in the two prefectures of Jiannan (in parts of modern Sichuan, Yunnan, Guizhou, and Gansu provinces) and Guangzhou (in parts of modern Guangdong and Guangxi provinces), lychees were a delicacy that ripened in hot summer and turned bad easily. Once harvested, "the color of the lychee would differ after a day; its smell would alter after two days; after three days, its taste would change; and beyond four or five days, both its fragrance and its flavor would be totally lost."[80] Lychees were therefore a fruit to be enjoyed locally. But Consort Yang, Emperor Xuanzong's lover, who came from Sichuan, happened to have a craving for lychees. To please his favorite lady, the emperor ordered that lychees from Jiannan prefecture be transported to the capital as quickly as possible by the relay service. "A single horseman smothered in red dust—and the young Consort laughs," a Tang poet wrote, "but no one knows that it is the lychees which have come."[81] When these lychees arrived in Changan, it was said, they still maintained their original flavor.[82] They must have traveled at least 265 miles (793 *li*) daily in order to reach the capital within three days, since the distance between Changan and the prefectural capital of Jiannan was 785 miles (2,379 *li*).[83]

Overuse and abuse of the Tang transportation system, however, often hindered its efficient functioning. The court, for example, allowed such officials as those of the fifth rank and above on active duty, titular officials of the second rank and above, and dukes and those of higher noble titles to use relay stations for private purposes. They could "pass the night at a station." "At places on the frontier and where there is no local inn, officials of the ninth rank and higher, honorary officials of the fifth rank and above, as well as nobles who come to a station in a military colony…will be allowed to pass the night. But they may not take anything."[84] This practice rendered relay stations liable to abuse and was eventually abandoned in 834. But five years later, in 839, ranking officials were again permitted to use relay stations when traveling for ancestor worship on Tomb-Sweeping Day in the lunar third month if they did not need to travel to other prefectures.[85]

Moreover, the low status of a stationmaster and his assistants made it difficult for them to enforce relevant regulations when receiving ranking officials or eunuchs. Sometimes they were not even given the chance to inspect the certificate of an overbearing official so that they might provide him with services appropriate to his status. The door to misuse of relay stations was left wide open. There were cases whereby lawless persons pretended to be imperial messengers. They acted like tyrants when using station facilities, claiming that they were on a mission to find and present herbs to the emperor or to pursue and capture criminals.[86] Even some genuine official travelers abused their privilege and incurred tremendous waste to relay stations. Some, when traveling in south China, used overland stations themselves but asked their companions to use stations along the waterways.[87] Some totally ignored the stationmasters; they refused to produce their certificates, bullied stationmasters to acquire whatever goods they wanted, and refused to comply with the limits on the weight of luggage and on the number of companions they could bring. Some demanded the use of a number of horses that far exceeded the number to which they were entitled. And when relay stations were short of horses, they even commandeered horses from private persons, causing much grievance among a station's local population.[88] The court in 821 had to promulgate an edict specifically instructing eunuchs to "produce certificates to relay station subofficial functionaries so that they could provide horses according to [the number specified in] the certificate."[89] But this edict does not seem to have deterred presumptuous eunuchs from abusing their privileges. In the 840s, a eunuch, angry at the coarse pancake that a relay station provided him, flogged a station serviceman until he bled. The local surveillance commissioner sealed and presented a piece of the pancake to the court. Emperor Xuanzong (r. 846–859) was outraged. He called the eunuch in and scolded him, "Don't you realize that it is not easy for a station in the deep mountains to prepare this pancake for you?"[90] On another occasion, a status-conscious eunuch had a clash with a censor over who had the priority to use the best station facilities. The clash resulted in bodily injury. The court in the early ninth century had to make it a regulation that when a censor and a eunuch arrived at the same station, the one who arrived first should have the use of the best room.[91]

Corruption among some prefects also damaged the transportation system. Instead of properly managing the relay stations, they ordered stations within their jurisdiction to provide services to ineligible personnel.[92] They issued official notes instructing stationmasters to provide free meals to the note bearer. These notes were therefore known as "meal notes" (shidie),[93] and some were even recognized by the authorities of other prefectures.[94] The prefect of Guangzhou was one such person. His "meal notes" often read: "To lodges and stations along the road: provide [the note bearer] with meals only (eryi)." But some greedy note bearers, having enjoyed their free meal, tried to take advantage of illiterate station staff and demanded a supply of eryi. Unable to read, when poor station staff asked for an explanation of eryi, they were told: "Well, it is bigger than a donkey but smaller than a mule. If you do not have one for me, you may pay me cash. Each eryi is worth three to five thousand copper cash!"[95]

A bizarre incident of abusing the transportation system occurred in 809 when a military commissioner ordered that the coffin of a deceased local army supervisor be transported to Changan. His audacity prompted the court to reiterate that "[anyone who] enters relay stations should be issued an official certificate. There has been no such case as providing relay services according to a note. Moreover, transporting a coffin is a private matter. [The coffin] should not be allowed to enter or stay at any station without authorization. Nor should horses or laborers be provided [for its transportation]."[96] The court was clearly losing control over the management of relay stations in the early ninth century. When it came to the late ninth century, military commissioners with inflated powers actually determined who should use the stations within their jurisdiction and how a traveler should be received.[97]

To make matters worse, many relay stations were overused, and the users did not always treat the station facilities with due care and attention. Some stations quickly deteriorated. A late Tang writer observed:

> A relay station might receive more than one hundred batches of travelers a year. They could barely get a place to sleep in the evening or get a meal when hungry. Coming in the dusk and leaving in the morning, why should they care about [the station facilities]? When enjoying boating [in the station pond], they stop only when they have broken the punt-pole, damaged the hull, or smashed the bow. And when they fish [by the pond], they stop only when they have emptied [the pond], jumped into the mud, and caught all the fish. Some feed their horses in the corridor; others leave their hunting birds in the hall. This is how the rooms become dirty and dilapidated, and the utensils broken. Subordinates of minor officials, though quick-tempered, can still be controlled; but those of the ranking officials are tyrannical and very difficult to manage. That is why [some relay stations] deteriorate daily.[98]

A Tang scholar wrote about the Yicheng relay station (in present-day Yicheng, Hubei province) in 819: "Buildings [in the station are said to have been] very grand and magnificent in the past. But now only one thatched house still stands."[99] The situation of the Baocheng relay station (in present-day Baocheng, southwest Shaanxi province) was a graphic testimonial to the decline of the transportation system during the late Tang. Known as "the first station in China," the station had its glorious days. A late Tang scholar, however, was shocked by the scene when he visited the station. "When I look at the pond," he wrote on the wall of the station, "it is shallow, muddy, and silted up; when I look at the boat, it is broken, decayed, and barely held together by glue. The station courtyard is left unattended, and the hall and the corridors are ruined. Nowhere can I see a sign of its [past] grandeur and magnificence."[100] Some stations were so shabby that they were even said to have been haunted.[101] An edict of 837 openly admitted that "most of the relay stations are in bad shape and unable to provide horses when needed."[102]

This was the condition of some of the relay stations when the eighteenth Japanese mission headed by Fujiwara no Tsunetsugu arrived at China in the early seventh month, 838.

From the Port of Entry
to the Capital via Yangzhou

Tsunetsugu landed at Juegang (some 43 miles [130 *li*] east of present-day Rugao, southern Jiangsu province).[103] He had his subordinates contact the authorities of a local garrison and present them with a document. He was fully aware that he had to secure from the local authorities both supplies and protection for his delegation, as certain areas in ninth-century China had become unsafe owing to banditry and unrest.

The ambassador of the seventeenth Japanese mission to China in 804, for example, decided to sail directly to the seat of Fuzhou prefecture after they had gone ashore at Changxi (north of present-day Xiapu, Fujian province) and the county magistrate told him the mountainous road to the prefectural seat was unsafe for travel.[104] Another Tang dynasty story vividly describes the danger that foreign diplomats might face in China. In the 740s a Japanese mission of five hundred members arrived at Haizhou (present-day Lianyungang, Jiangsu province) aboard ten ships loaded with treasures worth several million copper cash. The prefect, a corrupt and greedy man, housed them in an official lodge and treated them cordially but confined them to the lodge. He ordered that, during the night, their ships be sunk after all the treasures aboard had been unloaded. The next morning he told the Japanese: "Rising tides last night washed the ships away. They are nowhere to be found now." The report of this fabricated incident reached the court, which ordered the prefect to supervise the construction of ten ships and the dispatch of five hundred sailors to send the Japanese home. Before departure for Japan, the sailors came to the prefect for instruction. "Well," said he, "the journey to Japan is far. How could you come back safely from the surging waves and strong winds on the sea? Do whatever you deem convenient." The sailors, taking the prefect's hint, murdered all the Japanese one night when they had let down their guard.[105]

A few days after Tsunetsugu's subordinates had contacted the Chinese authorities, a commissioner from a garrison came to check the Japanese ships, which had run aground and been damaged. The commissioner offered Tsunetsugu wine and cakes, and arranged musical entertainment for him as a welcoming ceremony. In the meantime, garrison officials filed a report with the Yangzhou Area Command, informing the authorities of the Japanese mission's arrival. A commissioner from Yangzhou arrived shortly after with provisions for the members of the mission.[106] They were soon on their way to Yangzhou under escort. They were allowed to use the official lodges and were greeted by local county officials who presented them with coins as a gesture of hospitality. Some twenty days after their landing, Tsunetsugu and his entourage reached Yangzhou.[107]

Rectangular in shape, Yangzhou measured 3.63 miles (11 *li*) from north to south and 2.3 miles (7 *li*) from east to west.[108] "Ten thousand households in a world all its own," was the way a late Tang poet praised Yangzhou in his writing.[109] Although its exact population was unclear, Yangzhou was no doubt an international metropolis with a sizable foreign community of several thousand members.[110] The city must have been densely populated since a blaze in 834 was said to have destroyed several thousand houses in its residential area.[111] Yangzhou was a transportation center with a port on the banks of the Grand Canal that started from the city of Hangzhou in Zhejiang province and linked south China with the Tang capital. The canal greatly facilitated north-south transportation and turned Yangzhou into the busiest port in China. "Thousands of sails enter the ancient port," wrote one Tang poet.[112] "Coming like clouds, the sails block the bridge [in the port]," described another scholar.[113] Many cargo ships, painted pleasure boats, boats loaded with reeds, and other smaller boats filled the port. "The boats in the port are innumerable!" exclaimed a Japanese monk on viewing the scene.[114] Yangzhou was a bustling commercial hub. Shops stood next to one another in the business district. They carried luxurious and exotic goods not only from China but also from as far away as Persia and Arabia.[115] Commerce and trade generated such enormous wealth for Yangzhou that the city earned the reputation of "number one" in China.[116] Yangzhou was also a city that never slept. When night fell, tens of thousands of red gauze lanterns lit up office buildings and shops. Most shops stayed open for business, and guests crowded the restaurants and the pleasure quarters, where music and song continued until dawn. The city fascinated both foreigners and the Chinese so much that a Tang scholar claimed he felt as though he was wandering in a fairyland when strolling the main streets in Yangzhou at night. Another Tang poet even wrote that if he were to die, he would prefer to die in Yangzhou.[117]

In this international metropolis, however, and in other Chinese cities as well, foreign diplomats did not enjoy much freedom. Their activities were closely supervised by the Chinese authorities, and all their movements were subject to approval in advance. The court wanted to minimize contacts between foreigners and the Chinese so as to reduce the chances of unnecessary conflicts occurring between them. In the *Ordinances Governing Foreigners,* the court stipulated: "When foreigners enter China and are on the road, they are not allowed to mix with or talk to the Chinese. Prefecture and county officials who have no business with the foreigners are not allowed to meet with them."[118] Foreigners, for example, could not visit a local Buddhist temple without permission.[119] And when a monk from Tsunetsugu's mission expressed his wish to travel to temples outside the jurisdiction of Yangzhou, the local authorities informed him that his request was subject to approval by the central court.[120] Nor could foreigners go to the marketplace and purchase goods at will. As early as 714 the court had forbidden trading with foreigners for a range of commodities. It classified pearls, gold, silver, iron, a variety of silk fabrics, and other goods as "items under imperial prohibition" *(jinduan se)* that should not be sold to foreigners.[121] The prohibition was enforced in all cities. When Tsunetsugu arrived in Chuzhou (present-day Huaian, Jiangsu province) on his way back to Japan in 839, the local authorities summoned from Tsunetsugu's entourage the supervisor of the tribute articles, a shipmaster, and an interpreter for their illegal purchase of spices and medicine. They were questioned and detained but subsequently released. Four other mission members, including the attendants of an administrative officer and a scholar-student, tried to do the same. When local officials questioned them, they fled, leaving behind them two hundred strings of copper cash.[122]

While Tsunetsugu waited in Yangzhou, the local government filed a memorial with the court detailing the number of Japanese visitors and requesting instructions for further action.[123] In the meantime, the government sent more than ten boats to transfer the goods on the damaged Japanese ships to Yangzhou. It ordered a commissioner to inspect the goods,[124] and it put another commissioner and several other low-ranking officials in charge of receiving the Japanese mission.[125]

Prefectural authorities, however, did not always wait for court instructions when handling Japanese visitors. After the mid-eighth century, they sometimes speeded matters up by sending a Japanese ambassador and some key members of his entourage on after they had filed a report with the court. The court, having received the report, would decide on the appropriate size of the ambassador's entourage and inform him accordingly.[126] In 777, for example, authorities at Yangzhou instructed sixty-five members from the Japanese mission to proceed to Changan. Having traveled some thirty-three miles (one hundred *li*), they received a court order that reduced the number of the Japanese delegation to only twenty. At the request of the Japanese ambassador, the number was increased, and eventually forty-three people arrived in Changan.[127]

Japanese diplomats often traveled under escort; and they, like other Chinese official travelers, used official transportation facilities,[128] proceeded on a tight schedule, and stayed at each place for only one night. "We are already on the road when stars are shining in the morning sky," one Japanese diplomat wrote, "and we rest only after the stars have appeared in the sky in the evening."[129]

Tsunetsugu waited in Yangzhou for about two and a half months before receiving court permission to proceed to the capital. As part of the preparations, the court instructed the relevant prefectures en route to supply provisions to the Japanese diplomats when they passed through their jurisdictions. These provisions were transported from the prefectural seats to the villages and counties along their route, and were distributed under the supervision of a commissioner.[130] With all the arrangements for his journey to Changan in place, Tsunetsugu was now ready to leave Yangzhou. However, some members of his mission could not travel with him, as the court permitted only thirty-five people to accompany him. Among them were two administrative officers, two secretaries, an interpreter, a scholar, and a monk. The rest, amounting to some 270 persons, had to stay in Yangzhou. After a farewell banquet in honor of Tsunetsugu held by the local government, the Japanese mission boarded five relay boats and sailed to Changan along the Grand Canal.[131] Thereafter, the primary sources do not tell us much about Tsunetsugu. But the experiences of other Japanese ambassadors who had visited China earlier allow us to glimpse how Japanese diplomats were treated in the capital.

Diplomacy in the Tang Capital

A Japanese mission usually spent some two months on the road before reaching the Changle relay station in the suburbs east of Changan.[1] The station was the starting point of two major roads, one leading to the eastern capital, Luoyang, the other to modern Hubei and Hunan provinces. The Changle station was also the site where official welcome and farewell ceremonies were conducted for ranking officials and where eunuchs, on behalf of the emperor, hosted banquets for or granted gifts to officials. Many private travelers and their friends also met or parted with each other at the station.[2]

Japanese diplomats would rest at the station for two days to wait for a welcome ceremony before entering the capital.[3] This ceremony followed an ancient practice whereby an official representing the Son of Heaven welcomed and presented gifts to the tribute-paying princes and dukes in the suburbs of the capital.[4] During the Tang, this ceremony evolved into an elaborate ritual. It started with a Tang "respect-paying commissioner" arriving on horseback. He greeted the Japanese ambassador, announced to him an imperial edict extending the emperor's welcome,[5] and treated him to a banquet.[6] In appreciation for their efforts in having completed a long and arduous journey to China, an "imperial commissioner for greeting foreign guests" *(yingke shi)* came up to present the ambassador and his companions with fine imperial "flying dragon horses" and saddles. The saddle for the ambassador was gorgeously decorated with "seven treasures": gold, silver, pearl, coral, agate, glass, and shell; and those for his subordinates were painted.[7] The ceremony and the generosity of the Tang court moved the Japanese visitors to tears. They then mounted the horses and entered the capital with thousands of people looking on.[8]

Changan, the City of Eternal Peace

The Tang capital, Changan, was formerly Daxing Cheng (City of Great Prosperity), which had been the administrative center for the previous Sui dynasty. The first Sui emperor decided to build Daxing Cheng

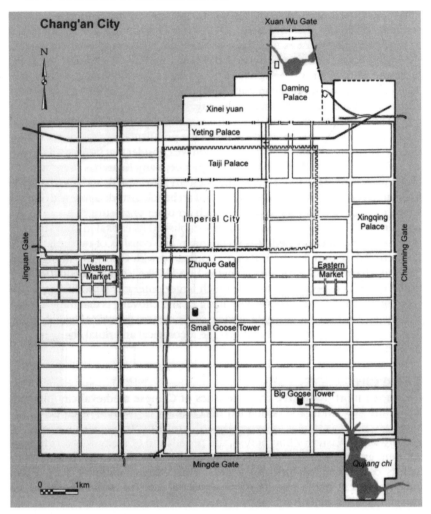

Map of Changan City. (Wang Tao, "A City with Many Faces: Urban Development in Pre-Modern China," in *Exploring China's Past*, ed. and trans. Rederick Whifield and Wang Tao [London: Saffron, 1999], p. 118)

because he considered the ruined ancient Han capital, Changan, unsuitable to be the capital for his empire. The city was cramped and dilapidated; it also lacked quality drinking water. Situated southeast of Changan, Daxing Cheng was believed to have good geomancy. It also had easy access to rivers in the north and the east. Through connecting canals, these rivers would provide the new capital with ample water and a convenient means of transportation. Construction of Daxing Cheng started in 582. The city was renamed Changan (City of Eternal Peace) and was further expanded after the Tang dynasty was established.[9]

Changan was a grand city. Surrounded by thick walls, it measured 9,721 meters from east to west and 8,652 meters from north to south. The city took the shape of a rectangle and occupied an area of 84 square kilometers. Vermilion Bird Avenue (Zhuque Jie), which was more than 150 meters in width, was the widest avenue in town and served as the north-south axis for Changan. Nine north-south avenues and twelve east-west streets divided the city into 108 wards. Half of these wards and a market were situated east of Vermilion Bird Avenue; the rest and another market were located west of the avenue. The wards and the two markets came under the jurisdiction of Wannian and Changan counties respectively.

The center of Changan was in the north, where the "palace city" *(gongcheng)* was located. A walled inner city in its own right, the palace city comprised three sections: the middle section in which the emperor conducted court audiences and handled state affairs; and the eastern and western sections, which served as residences for the crown prince and the emperor respectively. Due south of the imperial palace was the "imperial city" *(huangcheng)*, where many government offices were located. The wards occupied the rest of Changan and surrounded the palace and the imperial city on the south, east, and west. Enclosed by rammed earth walls, these wards were squarish and in varied sizes. Those due south of the imperial city were smaller and had only one gate on the east and on the west but none on the north or the south. This design was based on geomancy considerations. It ensured that energy generated by people living in those wards would not be channeled toward the north and adversely affect the imperial palace. Wards due east and west of the palace and the imperial city were bigger; and the rest were medium-sized. They all had one gate in each of the four directions. A road in the shape of a cross divided each ward into four sections; and each section was further split into four parts. Characterized by a symmetrical north-south axis with the palace in the north, the layout of Changan was symbolic of imperial power: the emperor was positioned at the top and in the center of the city to control his subjects and people.[10]

Changan was a city with tight security. As the political center of the Tang, Changan had the largest congregation of imperial family members and ranking officials. The safety of the ruling elite was the top priority for the court. Detachments of the Imperial Insignia Guards (Jinwu Wei) patrolled the palaces and the capital.[11] Commissioners for street inspection maintained public security in the six major avenues. Scuffles, improper use of roads, and illegal trade were deemed unlawful activities and were banned in the capital.[12] Guardhouses were established at city gates and police posts in the wards. They were manned by guards and cavalrymen whose number amounted to one hundred at a major guardhouse or a mere five at a minor police post.[13] The court regulated commoners' movement by keeping a fixed schedule for the opening and closing of city and ward gates. In the early Tang, government employees would travel the streets at dawn and dusk to remind people by voice that they should leave or return to their wards on time. Drum beats replaced human voices during Emperor Taizong's time.[14] Every morning at about five, a drum signal from the Gate of Obedience to Heaven indicated the start of the day. In response, drums placed at various avenues were beaten three thousand times. City gates and ward gates were opened to people at the drumrolls, and the city came to life. When daylight ended, the Gate of Obedience to Heaven was locked after four hundred drumbeats. There would be another drumroll of six hundred drumbeats to remind people of the impending closure of ward gates. When the drumroll died down, a curfew was imposed on the entire city. People could now move around only within their own wards. Violators were punished by twenty blows with the light stick.[15] Commissioners for street inspection sent cavalrymen to patrol the streets and remind people to observe the curfew. Plainclothes military men also went out on patrol to look for violators. When the guards noticed someone suspicious abroad, they would order such a person to identify himself or herself. If the person did not respond, they would warn him or her by striking their bow strings; if there was still no response, they would shoot; a person could be shot to death if the warning was ignored.[16]

Xu Di, assistant minister of the Court of Judicial Review, had a rough encounter with the Imperial Insignia Guards when he was galloping in the capital after the sunset drumroll. A general who was leading the guards patrolling the area stopped him for violation of curfew, had him flogged, and forwarded his case to the court for sentencing. Xu claimed that he was innocent since he had been on official business that night. His case was dropped only after a scholar-official recommended in a preliminary judgment that Xu had already been penalized by flogging and that there were no grounds to bring a new charge against him.[17]

Tang dynasty legends also tell interesting stories of ordinary people's experiences with the curfew. According to one tale, having spent a night of wining and dining with a beautiful woman, a debauchee arrived at a ward gate before dawn. As it was still early, the gate was yet locked. To kill the time while waiting for the gate to open, he chatted with the owner of a cake stall who was preparing for early morning sales. He learned with astonishment that the house where he had stayed overnight was haunted, and the woman with whom he had spent a night was a ghost! A civil service examination candidate, for his part, had to cope with the sunset drum. He had come all the way to Changan from another prefecture, but instead of preparing for the examination, he wasted his time drinking and singing with a woman in the pleasure quarters. He refused to leave even when the sunset drum was being beaten. The procuress urged him to return to his inn, but he stayed overnight, thus having to squander more money and time on the lady.[18]

For effective enforcement of the curfew in the capital, houses in the residential wards had to be built according to a unique regulation: no commoner was allowed to break through the ward wall to construct a gate for his house that would allow him direct access to a street outside the ward. A house gate had to open onto a street or an alleyway inside the ward. The ward walls thus served as a means both to protect the residents and to control their movement. Residences for officials of the third rank and senior, or for people of special status, however, were not required to comply with this construction regulation: a privilege that enabled them to move about easily during the night should they need to handle urgent official business.[19] Commoners could also move around outside their wards at night if they had to attend to matters related to death, marriage, or the sickness of family members. Before doing so, however, they had to acquire a permit from their respective district or ward office.[20] On certain holidays, such as the fifteenth day of the first month, people were allowed to celebrate until the wee hours of the morning. In general, curfews were relaxed during the late Tang. "It is customary that Luoyang has no curfew," a mid-ninth-century Tang poet wrote. "Returning on horseback at night, the fragrance [of a lady] fills my bosom."[21] Night markets even appeared in Changan, and the court had to ban them by an edict in 840.[22] Still, in the late Tang, residents of

Changan enjoyed a livelier and more colorful nightlife than formerly. We read that the Chongren ward, the entertainment quarter situated due east of the "imperial city," was livelier than the two metropolitan markets, buzzing with excitement and activities that continued day and night.[23]

Changan was an international metropolis with a population of over one million people, perhaps the largest and most populated city in the world at the time.[24] Inside the city, the Eastern and Western markets functioned as vibrant centers for overland trade,[25] where local products from all over China and foreign goods from Samarkand, Persia, and Syria changed hands. The markets, each rectangular in shape and covering an area of about one square kilometer, roughly the area of two residential wards, were enclosed by four walls. Two north-south and two east-west streets split each market into nine subdivisions, with numerous shops and stores lining the streets and alleyways. Although the exact number of shops was unknown, a Japanese monk visiting Changan in 843 noted in his diary that, in the sixth month, a great fire during the night burned down more than four thousand shops in the Eastern market, reducing a large amount of copper cash, goods, silver and gold, silk, and spices to ashes.[26]

The government regulated trading activities by setting up an office for the market director, a price-regulating office, and a price-equalizing office in the markets. These offices sought to prevent unfair trade by controlling weights, measures, and prices. Merchants were compelled to observe fixed business hours since gates to the markets did not open until noon, and they closed before sunset.[27] The Eastern and Western markets in Changan, however, were not meant to satisfy all the daily needs of commoners. Although in the Western market there were jewelry shops, wine shops, eateries, restaurants, commission shops, and shops carrying such daily necessities as fish, drugs, silk, clothing, candles used in the Buddhist mass, and saddlery and tack for horses,[28] the two markets functioned mainly as places where the court acquired the goods it needed and sold surplus tax goods.[29] Many other commercial activities were therefore conducted outside the two markets. This practice was a continuation of an age-old tradition according to which services related to butchery, music, wine making, and funerals were performed outside the major markets of a city.[30] During the Tang, we find that outside the Eastern and Western markets there were shops that produced and repaired musical instruments in the Chongren ward,[31] a grocery store in the Pingkang ward,[32] a silk festoon shop in the Xuan-yang ward,[33] a peddler of oil in the Xuanping ward,[34] cake houses in the Shengping and Fuxing wards,[35] and an eatery in the Changxing ward that served *biluo,* a kind of stuffed pastry.[36] These stores operated in wards near the Eastern market. And in wards near the Western market we find a store that specialized in gold, silver, pearls, and jade in the Yanshou ward and a store that sold items for funerals in the Fengyi ward.[37]

A large number of foreigners lived in these wards. There were, among others, merchants from the Western Region (the vast area including the middle and the western part of the Asian continent, the Indian penin-sula, the eastern part of Europe, and the northern part of Africa); missionaries who preached various religious beliefs; monks from East Asia in search of the Buddhist laws; princes of foreign countries who remained in Changan as hostages; "barbarians" who, by court permis-sion, lived permanently in the capital or who overstayed their permitted time of residence illegally by disguising themselves in Chinese costume and mixing with the Chinese;[38] and lastly, diplomats, such as the Japa-nese ambassador Tsunetsugu and his entourage.

The strong presence of foreigners in the capital and the open-mind-edness of the Tang ruling elite toward foreign cultures and religions transformed Changan into a cosmopolitan city. More than one hun-dred temples of such varied religions as Buddhism, Daoism, Nestorian Christianity, Zoroastrianism, and Manicheanism were established in the city. Acrobats and conjurers from India entertained Chinese audiences. They fascinated the Chinese by sword swallowing and breathing fire; using magic, they sometimes also staged shows of self-inflicted injury, stabbing the abdomen with a sword, or cutting the tongue with a dag-ger. Concerned about their adverse effects on the morality of its people, the court eventually banned such bloody performances in the 650s and sent the magicians home.[39] The influence of the "western barbarians" on the Chinese was most evident in the changing lifestyles of people in Changan, who were becoming increasingly bold and unrestrained: *biluo* and baked flatcakes were now their favorite foods;[40] western dress fea-turing lapels, buttons down the front, and narrow sleeves became the latest fashion; they listened to music introduced from Central Asia and played polo; and they entertained themselves by a wild game in

Tang dynasty maidservants wearing the clothes and hats of the northern tribal people. The drawing is based on stone inscriptions in the Tang dynasty tomb of Wei Xu in Xian, Shaanxi province. (Lü Yifei, *Huzu xisu yu Sui-Tang fengyun* [Beijing: Shumu Wenxian Chubanshe, 1944], plate no. 14)

mid-winter, during which naked, barefooted, and masked participants crowded the major streets, singing, dancing, splashing water on each other, and throwing mud at one another.[41]

Such western influences on the Chinese way of life were so overwhelming that Yuan Zhen, an early-ninth-century Tang poet, wrote with great amazement about this phenomenon:

> Ever since the Western horsemen began raising smut and dust,
> Fur and fleece, rank and rancid, have filled Xian and Luo.
> Women make themselves Western matrons by the study of
>   Western make-up;
> Entertainers present Western tunes, in their devotion to Western
>   music.[42]

Residents of Changan were indeed fascinated by all things foreign. Their greatest fascination seemed to be western waitresses working in the wine shops. Sweet and low in alcohol content, wine was a national beverage during the Tang.[43] It served to quench people's thirst and was readily available at stalls along the major roads[44] or at wine shops in cities. In Changan, wine shops hired western waitresses to solicit customers.[45] And not a few Tang poets fancied these beautiful lasses with fair complexions, flaxen hair, and blue eyes. "A Western houri beckons with her white hand," the fairy poet Li Bai wrote, "inviting the stranger to intoxicate himself with a golden beaker."[46] Indeed Li Bai was himself very much intoxicated by these western beauties:

That Western houri with features like a flower—
She stands by the wine-warmer, and laughs with the breath of
    spring
Laughs with the breath of spring,
Dances in a dress of gauze!
"Will you be going somewhere, milord, *now,* before you are
    drunk?"[47]

Untrammeled, materialistic, but also cultured and sophisticated— that was the lifestyle of the people in Changan. Foreign diplomats in the capital would also have had a chance to sample aspects of this lifestyle.

The Court of State Ceremonial

Having entered Changan, a Japanese ambassador and his entourage would be lodged in the guest house managed by the Court of State Ceremonial (Honglu Si) under the Ministry of Rites. A chief minister headed the Court of State Ceremonial, which had three subordinate units: the Office of State Visitors (Dianke Shu), the Ceremonial Office (Siyi Shu),[48] and the Foreign Relations Office (Libin Yuan).[49] The chief minister was the principal official responsible for receiving foreign diplomats. In collaboration with the director of the Bureau of Receptions in the Ministry of Rites, he managed court receptions and banquets for foreign ambassadors, determined their ranks, and accorded them the appropriate treatment.[50] But his primary task was to manage foreign guests' behavior by enforcing the court policy of minimum and controlled interaction between visitors and the Chinese. Unauthorized people were denied entry to the compound of the Court of State Ceremonial and the guest house. An edict of 731 ordered the compilation of a register that listed the names of all personnel working for the Court of State Ceremonial. Guards would check the name of a person against the register before letting him or her enter the compound where foreign guests stayed. Interpreters and stewards (*zhangke*) received warrants from the chief minister that authorized them to have direct contact with foreign visitors.[51] They had to produce the warrant for the guards who would then escort them to enter and leave the compound.[52] Unauthorized liaison with foreigners was subject to severe punishment. In the 710s, a scribe from the Secretariat accepted gifts from foreigners. When his misdeeds were exposed, Emperor Xuanzong decided personally to interrogate him and sentenced him to death. It was fortunate that the court later mitigated his punishment to flogging and banishment.[53]

The court justified its policy of minimizing contact between foreigners and the Chinese by claiming it was in the interest of national security to do so, as it believed information concerning important matters should not be divulged to unauthorized persons, especially foreigners. The court considered the following items to be "important matters": a plot to rebel, a plot fomenting sedition, plans of a campaign to surprise the enemy, and plans to arrest anyone plotting treason.[54] Some items, although not classified as "important matters," were also to be kept secret. Student observers of astronomical phenomena, for example, had to make secret reports to the emperor if they noticed "changes in the wind, clouds, ethers, or clouds of the sky."[55] The content of their reports was treated as classified information since the phenomena mentioned in the reports were deemed indicative of current or future political events of the dynasty. It was only to be expected that Tang laws would specify that "all cases of divulging important matters that must be kept secret are to be punished by strangulation. If what was divulged is not an important matter that is to be kept secret, the punishment is one and one-half years of penal servitude. For disclosing matters to the ambassadors of foreign countries, the punishment is to be increased by one degree."[56]

The court restricted the movements of foreigners in the capital to minimize unnecessary contacts with the Chinese. Foreigners could not leave the guest house without permission.[57] Irritated by this unpopular measure, in 772 some Uighurs twice took the liberty to leave the house and kidnaped some Chinese; they even murdered people in broad daylight in 774.[58] In response, the Tang court established the left and right "battalions for subjugation of distant countries" *(weiyuan ying)* as a special task force to deter such violence and appointed the chief minister of the Court of State Ceremonial its commissioner.[59] The court further strengthened the two battalions by putting them under the command of the Imperial Insignia Guards in 780.[60]

Foreign visitors could engage themselves in a desired activity only after they had secured court permission. They first had to direct their requests, such as shopping for fine Chinese products, to the Court of State Ceremonial, which would forward them to the court for decision. The Court of State Ceremonial, for instance, reported in the 710s that "the Tibetan ambassador knows the [Tang] products well. He desires such items as silk brocade, bows, and arrows, and has requested permission to purchase them." His request was granted after a scholar-official had recommended that "[the court] should allow the purchase since this would demonstrate [China's] prowess to remote barbarians. Even if we let them acquire these items illegally, it would not harm China."[61] The court also granted the Japanese ambassador's request to shop in 717 and ordered the Imperial Insignia Guards to deploy a detachment to keep public order in the marketplace while they did so. Even so, the ambassador could not purchase "items under imperial prohibition."[62] Tsunetsugu, however, was less fortunate. When his mission arrived in Changan in 838, its members were not allowed to buy or sell anything in the capital.[63] The court in 749 opened a Southern market next to the camp for the battalions for subjugation of distant countries. This market catered specifically to foreigners, and its location enabled the nearby battalions to enforce a degree of control over their trading activities.[64] Trading without permission was a crime considered equivalent to robbery. Not only would the offender's goods be confiscated, he could also receive "the maximum punishment of life exile at a distance of three thousand *li* [990 miles]" from the capital.[65]

No member of any foreign mission enjoyed "diplomatic immunity." They would be arrested just like common criminals if they had committed a crime.[66] They might eventually be released, but this would result from an act of clemency by the Son of Heaven, not from their status as diplomats.[67] The Tang court might also detain a foreign ambassador without his being charged if considerations of international politics justified such a move. In 659, after a successful court audience with the emperor in which the Japanese ambassador had been praised as "the most distinguished" among all the foreign ambassadors being received, things suddenly took a turn for the worse. The Tang court first neglected the Japanese visitors and then issued the ambassador an imperial decree: "This government has determined to take administrative measures regarding the lands east of the sea [i.e., Korea]. Therefore you, the visitors from Wa, may not return to the east." A member of his entourage reported that "they were placed in separate seclusion, their door was closed and exit prohibited, and they had no liberty of movement. In such misery they passed the year."[68] The Japanese visitors must have been profoundly confused and frustrated. They could have had no idea that their misery was due to a massive joint military operation planned by Tang and Silla for the seventh month of the following year. The aim of the operation was to destroy the Korean state of Paekche, the common foe of Tang and Silla but an ally of Japan. To prevent any leakage of the plan, the Tang court detained all members of the Japanese mission in Changan, thus making them victims of a military intrigue against Korea.

Japanese diplomats were not the only victims of international politics, and they certainly were not the most unfortunate. During Emperor Daizong's reign (762–779), Tibet dispatched eight peace missions to China. But since the Tibetans also continued their border skirmishes, the Tang court doubted the real purpose of the Tibetan missions and detained all their members. Some languished for years in China and died of old age.[69]

Providing foreign visitors with daily necessities and provisions according to detailed court regulations was another major daily task for the Court of State Ceremonial.[70] They received such items as tents, curtains, carpets, mats, bedding, and charcoal for heating.[71] Most of the items bore the month and year of issue, and were supposed to last for a fixed period: a mat for three years, a carpet for four years, and bedding for seven years. A user would have to pay a fine if an item was worn out prematurely.[72] At the beginning of each season, the Court of State Ceremonial received from the Bureau of Receptions food ingredients,[73] which were sorted into five groups and supplied to visitors according to their ranks for daily consumption.[74] These foodstuffs were known as "regular ingredients" (changshi liao).[75] An aide supervised the preparation of meals for the guests.[76] Senior diplomats of the fifth rank and above, however, did not eat with their subordinates. The Tang court treated them as "consultants-in-ordinary" *(changcan guan)*, who were expected to attend regular court audiences.[77] They would have lunch in the palace after a court meeting, with the Court of Imperial Entertainment (Guanglu Si) preparing their meal.

A different kind of food would be served at a banquet held upon a foreign ambassador's arrival in Changan or before his departure for home. The food used on these occasions was especially rich and was called "ingredients for entertainment" *(sheshi liao)*. On lunar New Year's Day or the winter solstice, senior diplomats would attend a feast after the congratulatory audience with the emperor. The dishes prepared for them would be made of "ingredients for court banquets" *(shehui liao)*.[78] Little is known about precisely what food was provided for foreigners on different occasions, but the "regular ingredients" provided for Chinese officials show that they consisted mainly of grain (rice and flour), oil, seasonings (fermented soy beans, salt, ginger, vinegar, soy paste, honey, and pepper), vegetables (scallions and leeks), fruits (melons, pears, and dried dates), meats (mutton, pork, and fish), and wine. Firewood (charcoal) was also provided.[79] The exact amount and type of the ingredients varied according to the rank of an official. Censors supervised the supply of foodstuffs and the preparation of meals for foreign guests and impeached officials who neglected their duties.[80] Liu Xiu from the Shayuan Directorate was one of these officials. Situated north of present-day Dali county, Shaanxi province, this directorate was in charge of breeding and supplying horses and domestic animals to the court. Liu had allegedly concealed sheep of better quality and provided thin and small ones for a state banquet in honor of an Eastern Turkic ambassador. The guests complained bitterly, and the censor impeached him. In support of the impeachment, the court handed Liu's case over to the Court of Judicial Review. One official pointed out in his preliminary judgment that Liu must be punished since his misconduct had "brought about animosity [against China]. [The ambassador] must have considered it a shame for a great country to have such an uncourteous custom. And other proud foreigners might also harbor ill will [toward China] if they despise the superficial court ceremonial of the Middle Kingdom."[81]

The way in which the Tang court handled the Liu Xiu incident clearly indicates that receiving foreign visitors, managing their movement, and taking care of their needs was no trivial business. In fact, it was through these tedious daily activities that officials at the Court of State Ceremonial implemented a pivotal principle of Tang diplomacy: "displaying order to visitors in grand ceremonies." This principle is best revealed in the term *honglu,* the Chinese name for the Court of State Ceremonial.[82]

The Ideology and Practice of the Tang Guest Protocol

From antiquity, the gist of Chinese court protocol for receiving visitors had always been to "treat ambassadors from greater countries with respect" and to "display order to all guests."[83] This order exhibited a China-centered world system, in which countries acknowledged the Middle Kingdom's supremacy, enjoyed a relatively stable standing, and existed harmoniously in an orderly fashion with one another. The central task for the Court of State Ceremonial was to demonstrate this hierarchical order by granting visitors suitable treatment according to rank. An imperial decree of investiture appointing Jiang Huan, chief minister of the court in question, specified that his task was to "adhere to the established practices when receiving [ambassadors from] various states so that there would be criteria for manifesting their grades *(deng)* and prestige *(wei).*"[84] A Tang scholar further explained that the vice-minister should "receive [foreign diplomats] in grand ceremonies and identify their grades and prestige."[85]

A hierarchical world order required the distinction of China's neighbors from one another. The Tang court therefore classified some countries as its "outer fences"[86] and some as countries in the "remote region" *(jueyu).* The "fence countries" were situated primarily within the geographic confines whose boundaries were the Korean states in the east; Cambodia (Zhenla) in the south; Iran (Bosi), Jiankun (a tribe active at the upper reaches of Yenisei River, Central Siberia), and Tibet (Tufan) in the west and southwest; and the Qidan, the Mohe, and the Turks in the north. Countries beyond these places were considered "remote countries," whose rulers were unable to maintain regular contact with China and who were considered unimportant to China.[87] Japan was also deemed a "remote country."[88]

There were subtle but important political differences between a "fence country" and a "remote country" in terms of their relations with China. An "outer fence" was supposed to protect China, and a "fence country" was therefore a vassal state of the Middle Kingdom. Having pledged political allegiance to the Tang emperor, its ruler was granted Chinese court titles, which secured him a proper place in the court hierarchy and made him an "outer subject" of the Tang emperor. He was obligated, at least in theory, to pay annual tribute to the Son of Heaven and would in return be eligible for Chinese assistance. But the Tang court deliberately avoided accepting too many countries as its vassal states so as not to overburden itself with the obligations of assisting its vassals.[89] The ruler of a "remote country," in contrast, either refused to offer loyalty to the Son of Heaven or had had its request to become an "outer subject" of China declined. Such a ruler was an outsider, having no designated position in the Chinese court establishment, but when his ambassador attended audiences in Changan, the Tang court needed to indicate the relative standing of his country in the international community. To do so, the Tang court used a five-grade system to distinguish the "remote countries" from each other.

This grading system employed "greater" and "lesser" as the criteria to determine the status of foreign rulers. The reputation of a country among its neighbors (fanwang) and the extent of its acceptance of Chinese culture were the major considerations when determining a country's grade.[90] The Court of State Ceremonial compiled a record of the grades for various countries, which it used as the basis for granting a suitable reception to a foreign ruler or his representative. The term "grade" was used in making arrangements on three major occasions: a court audience with the emperor, state banquets, and the supply of daily meals. At a court audience during which all foreign participants had to stand in their proper order, the term "grade" determined the position that a visitor took in the palace courtyard.[91] More specifically, visitors of the third, fourth, and fifth grades took their positions behind Chinese military officers of the third, fifth, and sixth ranks respectively. Guests of the first and second grades would follow the Chinese prefectural delegates coming from the same direction that they themselves had. A Japanese ambassador, for instance, was to stand behind the delegates from prefectures in eastern China. The standing positions for diplomats of the same grade were in two lines, and the positions decreased progressively in honor. The place of honor was in the north since it was the nearest to the Tang emperor. Foreigners who were already "outer subjects" of China stood with Chinese officials of the same rank, and they

probably took up the least prestigious places in the south.[92] The standing order and the specific position for a foreign ambassador during a
court audience thus became a graphic display of the status of his country relative to that of other countries.

The term "grade" was used to denote a specific group of "ingredients
for entertainment" or "ingredients for a court banquet" when it was
used in the context of preparation for a welcome or farewell party in
honor of a foreign guest of a given status or for a feast held on New
Year's Day or on the winter solstice in which the foreign guest would
participate. Diplomats of the first, second, and third grades would be
provided with the same foodstuffs as the Tang officials of the third,
fourth, and fifth ranks respectively. Ambassadors from countries of low
prestige would receive food ingredients that amounted to only half of
those provided Chinese auxiliary officials (sanguan), who had no specific administrative positions and were minor officials in the court.[93]
When used in the context of preparing daily meals for foreigners, the
term "grade" referred to one of the five groups of "regular ingredients"
catered specifically to visitors. Food supplies for foreign diplomats of
the third rank and above would be equivalent to those for a Chinese
official of the third grade; foreign visitors of the fourth and fifth ranks
as well as the chieftain of a major tribe would receive food ingredients
that were the same as those for a fourth-grade Tang official; and the
foodstuffs for the chieftain of a minor tribe or foreign visitors of the
sixth rank and below would be the same as those for a fifth-grade
Chinese official. It is worth noting that an "outer subject" holding a
Chinese rank did not receive the same "regular ingredients" as his Chinese counterpart.[94]

The Tang court was willing to recognize the superior position of a
country in relation to certain other countries provided that China's own
supremacy over them remained unchallenged. Japan in the eighth century, for example, was identified as "a greater country among countries
east of the sea."[95] In general, a country whose ruler submitted himself to
China earlier was a "greater country," and one that did so later, a "minor
country."[96] This principle guided China in handling the relations between
its neighbors. In 639, disputes broke out between the Xueyantuo (a tribe
active in the Mt. Khangai area in western Mongolia) and the Western
Turks. The Tang court tried to solve the problem by sending the chief
minister of the Court of the National Granaries as its special envoy to

confirm the status of Xueyantuo as a "greater country," for its king had accepted a Chinese title as early as 629 and had since helped the Tang defeat the Eastern Turks. The Western Turks were still at odds with China in 639, however, and the Tang envoy announced that their country could be regarded only as a "lesser country."[97] Using the five-grade system, the Tang court created a world order that some contemporary Tang scholars vividly compared to the solar system: China was the sun and other countries were its planets, each of which had its own satellites.[98]

The hierarchical world order of the Tang court was the basis for its reception of foreign ambassadors. Tsunetsugu and other foreign ambassadors might not have been clearly aware of the political implications of their reception by the Chinese when they were received by local governments individually. Once they congregated in Changan, however, they would immediately notice the different arrangements for their stay in the capital. And lodging, as one of these arrangements, served as the first manifestation of China's assessment of the strategic importance of a country in the world order it perceived.[99] Most of the foreign visitors would stay at the guest house west of the Court of State Ceremonial in the "imperial city." Some, however, deemed the house a place of no prestige, for notorious and uncivilized "barbarians" such as the Xiongnu during the Han dynasty and the Turks in the early Tang had once stayed there. Furthermore, the street outside the house had been an execution ground where rebellious barbarian leaders had been executed and their heads displayed as a warning to foreign visitors during the Han period.[100] Throughout the Tang, criminals were usually executed under the "lone willow" in the Western market, which was only two wards southwest of the guest house.[101] Over time, the guest house became known as the "residence for the barbarians" (manyi zhidi), suitable only for minor visitors.[102]

A foreign ambassador who considered himself a representative of a "civilized country" would feel deeply embarrassed if he had to stay at the guest house with "uncivilized barbarians." He would acknowledge it as a special imperial favor if the Tang court assigned him a residence elsewhere.[103] This was what happened in 630 to Illig, the ruler of the Eastern Turks after the Tang forces had captured him and sent him to Changan. There Emperor Taizong treated him leniently. As an especially courteous treatment, the emperor ordered the return of all Illig's companions and housed them at the Court of the Imperial Stud (Taipu

Si).[104] Among Japan's eighteen ambassadors to China, four reported having received such an imperial favor. The first two, arriving in China in 753 and 778 respectively, were lodged in an "outer house" *(waizhai)*, the third at the Xuanyang ward west of the Eastern market in 804,[105] and Tsunetsugu himself at the Foreign Relations Office in 839.[106] The symbolic importance of the lodging they were assigned often made foreign ambassadors in the Tang capital apprehensive. If they accepted the arrangement, they would be deemed to have accepted China's assessment of their countries' international standing.

The Tang reception arrangements for its visitors were also meant to be a process of edification. "Coming to China, foreigners study the classics and the mode [of governing a country]," Emperor Xuanzong once wrote in his poem for the king of Silla.[107] To edify foreign diplomats with Chinese culture, the court arranged tours for them to observe the teaching of Confucian ethical codes at the State University (Guozi Jian);[108] the court in the 680s also had the best answers to the civil service examination questions transcribed and displayed to them;[109] and in 752 the Japanese ambassador had a rare chance to visit the worship halls for Confucianism, Buddhism, and Daoism built specially for the emperor and the imperial family in the inner palace.[110] To prepare a foreign ambassador and his entourage for the grand audience with the emperor, the Court of State Ceremonial would send officials from its Office of Receptions to teach them how to express gratitude to the Son of Heaven and other related matters of etiquette.[111] The court hoped that through these activities the "uncivilized barbarians" would learn to act properly and acquire some understanding of their countries' position in the world.

The Tang court referred to its protocol for receiving foreign kings or their ambassadors at the palace as the "guest protocol" *(binli)*.[112] This protocol applied to the following events: (1) the ceremony that an imperial messenger conducted at the guest house to welcome and reward a foreign king, (2) the announcement that an imperial messenger made at the guest house to inform a king of the date for his audience with the emperor, (3) the grand court audience with the emperor, (4) acceptance of a foreign state letter and gift, (5) a banquet in honor of the foreign king or (6) of his ambassador.[113] The conventional English rendering for *bin* has been "guest," but usage of the term in premodern diplomatic language had a rather different connotation than

Painting from the eastern wall of the entrance passage of the tomb of Tang prince Zhanghuai. The first person on the left is the chief minister of the Court of State Ceremonial. The second and the third are his ministers. Fourth from the left is the ambassador from the Eastern Roman empire; and fifth and sixth are ambassadors from Silla and Malgal (Mohe, a tribe in northeastern China) respectively. (Wang Weikun, "Tang Zhanghuai taizi mu bihua keshi tu bianxi," *Kaogu,* no. 1 (1966), p. 66)

the English word "guest." When used as a verb, *bin* signifies the action "to submit" and "to follow,"[114] and thus the following usages of the term are found in primary sources: "submit and follow" *(bincong),*[115] "submit and obey" *(binfu),*[116] "submit and offer tribute" *(bingong),*[117] "refuse to obey" *(bubin),* and "yet to submit" *(weibin).*[118] When employed as a noun, the term refers to a person who "cherishes the righteousness (of the Chinese emperor) and obeys (his orders)"[119] or "comes to pay tribute and offers his loyalty to the Chinese court."[120] Unlike in modern diplomacy where a host will treat a state guest as an equal no matter how small a country he or she represents, a "guest" of the Tang court was never on a level with his host. *Bin* was therefore a term laden with political implications. This explains why the Tang court in 684 changed the name for the Court of State Ceremonial to the Court in Charge of Guests (Sibin Si).[121]

The Tang "guest protocol" defined the ritualistic movements of a foreign visitor and his host during the six events. The purpose of these movements was to demonstrate by body language Chinese political dominance and foreign obedience. The way the major participants conducted themselves in each of these events was a vivid expression of the China-centered nature of the "guest protocol."

As preparation for an imperial messenger's call on a foreign king at the guest house, officials from the Canopies Office had a tent pitched outside the gate of the guest house. On the day of the visit, a tent handler guided the messenger into the tent. Inside the guest compound, the king, in the costume of his own country, was ushered to the top of the eastern stairs of the main hall. The messenger then left the tent to proceed to the west side of the compound gate, and his subordinates followed him carrying rolls of silk. An official appeared at the gate and inquired the purpose of the messenger's visit. "Entrusted with an imperial command, I come to reward the king," replied the messenger. The official returned to the compound to inform the king of the news. Upon receipt of the news, the king came out. He made Chinese obeisance twice to the messenger by genuflecting and bowing. The two then entered the compound side by side. Once inside the compound, the messenger and his subordinates ascended to the top of the western stairs of the main hall first, and the king moved to the top of the eastern stairs. Holding a roll of silk with both hands, the messenger declared: "A decree arrives." Following the Chinese practice, the king would be about to descend the stairs and kneel, but the messenger again announced: "Here is another decree that the foreign king need not descend and kneel." Upon hearing this, the foreign king turned to the north, where the emperor lived, as an expression of his gratitude. He made obeisance twice and kowtowed. After the announcement of the decree, the king stepped forward to receive the imperial gifts, returned to his position, and handed the gifts over to his followers. He once again made obeisance twice and kowtowed. The king and the messenger then walked out of the compound.

Outside the compound gate, the king bowed to the imperial messenger, clasping his hands in front of the chest. This movement signaled the start of the second part of the event for the king to present his own gifts to the messenger. The two men, having entered the compound together, bowed to each other and asked the counterpart to take the lead in walking up the stairs of the main hall. The king, acting as the host, proceeded to the top of the eastern stairs first. Once the messenger was also at the top of the western stairs, the king displayed the gifts he had brought to the messenger, who made obeisance twice before accepting them. After another obeisance by the king, the presentation of gifts was completed. The king followed the messenger in descending the stairs and exiting the compound. The two then left for the palace together.

At the palace, an official from the Court of State Ceremonial came out to greet the king and guided him to his designated standing position. A palace attendant then appeared and announced: "Here comes the edict of greetings." On hearing this, the foreign king made obeisance twice. He repeated the movement after the announcement of the edict. At this point, the business of the day ended. A court official then guided the king back to the guest house.[122]

The movements required of the foreign king during this event were an indication that the Tang court treated its foreign visitors as subjects of the Tang emperor. As a special favor, the court exempted the king from descending the stairs and kneeling down to listen to the imperial edict at the guest house.[123] But he had to kowtow to acknowledge the imperial favor, and he had to do so again after receipt of the imperial gifts. Kneeling and pressing both hands and his forehead to the ground,[124] the king offered his deepest respect to the Tang emperor. This action was expected of Chinese as well as foreign subjects who were honored to have received an imperial edict and gifts, and who had to show gratitude to the Son of Heaven. Moreover, the carefully designed movements for the king precluded any possibility for him to imply that he was in a position superior to that of the Tang emperor. His gifts presented to the messenger, for example, were to be worth the same as the gifts for him from the emperor, but not more.[125] And the movements of the messenger reminded the king that he was merely a peer of the messenger, who only genuflected but did not kowtow to him when receiving his gifts.

Rituals for other major events in the Tang "guest protocol" were equally formalistic and tedious. Tang scholars described the gist of these events using a set phrase: "offer the jade tablet [to the emperor] and set out the protocol [for the audience that the Son of Heaven granted to his lords]" (banrui sijin).[126] This phrase is another revelation of the

China-centered nature of the Tang "guest protocol," for "offering a jade tablet" was a metaphor for the symbolic action of "paying tribute," or the actual presentation of local products to the Chinese emperor. And the protocol itself *(jin)* was one once used between the Son of Heaven and his feudal lords.[127]

The Chinese "guest protocol" had always been politically oriented. As early as the eleventh century B.C., the Zhou court (eleventh century B.C.–221 B.C.) had specified that "a guest *(binke)* is a subject or a lord coming to pay tribute [to the court]."[128] The Zhou "guest protocol" was to "befriend the states of the various marquises" *(bangguo)* so as to make their rulers feel "close and attached" to the Zhou king.[129] The Tang "guest protocol" inherited this tradition that stressed the status difference in relations between a Chinese sovereign, his lords, the foreign kings, and their ambassadors.[130] The Chinese sources, for example, universally described the purpose of any Japanese mission as "coming to pay tribute" *(laichao)*,[131] "asking to become [China's] subject" *(qingli)*,[132] or "coming back to offer [tribute]" *(guixian)*,[133] although Japan certainly never intended to be a vassal state to the Tang. Moreover, a Tang ruler considered the visit of a Japanese ambassador evidence of his widespread moral influence outside China. Foreign ambassadors, he believed, would come to pay homage to him only when he had been exercising moral leadership in domestic and foreign affairs.[134] Their visits were a recognition of his political achievement, which was particularly important to a Tang emperor of weak leadership, who needed foreign recognition to shore up his position at home. Due to its symbolic political significance, the arrival of foreign diplomats was often mentioned in the Tang sources along with such "great auspicious omens" as the Yellow River running clearer, the Yellow River and the Yangzi River turning five colors, or the sea becoming calm and tranquil.[135] A Japanese prince, for instance, was said to have visited China in 853. His arrival and the recent auspicious phenomenon that the Yellow River was running clearer were reported to the emperor together.[136]

The political implications of the "guest protocol" prompted the Tang court to take stringent measures to ensure proper and smooth conduct of all related arrangements for foreign diplomats. Negligence was not tolerated, and offenders were subject to punishment. An example in point would be the incident that occurred during a banquet in honor of a Japanese ambassador.[137] To entertain the guests coming from the east, court musicians were supposed to perform "eastern barbarian music."[138] They, however, mistakenly performed folk music and dances from the "Western Region" (sanyue). A censor impeached them. Admitting no wrongdoing, the musicians claimed that they had staged the performance according to instructions from officials in charge of court music. Their case was referred to Confucian scholars for preliminary judgment. Not surprisingly, they all found the musicians guilty of negligence and recommended punishment.[139] They based their judgments on an age-old Confucian tradition that music should never be intended for mere entertainment. Music was "an instrument with which the sages in antiquity had molded the temperament [of people]." Music played at court audiences and state banquets was considered to have an edifying effect that was believed to be instrumental in establishing order between the Chinese sovereign, his subjects, and ambassadors from vassal states.[140] Playing music appropriate to the occasion was compared to the strengthening of dikes, a measure necessary to prevent barbarians from rebelling against China.[141] Lu Deming, an early Tang writer, summarized the importance of music in governance: "A ruler must have his musicians play the music of the four barbarians. This is the way to unify the world."[142]

Not only Tang officials but foreign visitors as well were liable to punishment if they failed to follow the appropriate court protocol. In the 710s, an ambassador from the Caliphate (Dashi) offered fine horses and belts embedded with precious stones and mother of pearl to the Tang court. He, however, refused to bow to the emperor and stood upright throughout the reception. The censor wanted to impeach the ambassador, but the Secretariat director objected. "The customs of Dashi differ [from those of Tang]," he argued. "Its ambassador came from afar to admire the righteousness [of our emperor]. He should not be punished." The emperor pardoned the ambassador. A few years later a Dashi ambassador again visited the Tang court. He tried to explain to Tang officials that people in his country did not bow even to their own ruler; they did so only to the god of heaven. But this time Tang officials repeatedly questioned and blamed him, and he eventually agreed to bow in the Chinese fashion.[143]

Events in the emperor's presence were the core of Tang "guest protocol." When ambassadors from various countries were present during these events, they became international gatherings, displaying the prestige and the standing of a participant's country in the Chinese world. Depending on the occasion and the purpose, such a gathering could be held in the "inner court," the "middle court," or the "outer court."

The "outer court" was a space south of the Chengtian Gate, one of the three southern entrances to the "palace city." Known as the Lateral Place (Hengjie), this space was in fact a street that measured 411 meters in width—the widest in Changan. It functioned as a square for grand congratulatory gatherings during which a Tang emperor would ascend the gate tower and hold an audience with his subjects. Celebrations on New Year's Day, the winter solstice, and the Longevity Festival (Emperor Xuanzong's birthday) were some of the events that took place at the "outer court."[144] North of the Chengtian Gate was the Taiji Hall. It served as the "middle court" where an audience with the emperor was conducted twice a month on the first and the fifteenth day. Further to the north was the Liangyi Hall. This was the "inner court," where the emperor attended to his routine business, received foreign ambassadors, accepted their national letters and state gifts, and feasted them. The three courts at the palace city functioned for some fifty years after 618. In the meantime, in 634, the Tang court started to build the Daming Palace, a new complex northeast of the palace city in the imperial park. The new palace occupied an elevated area of 3.2 square kilometers, which was part of Dragon Head Hill. The northern section of the palace was in the shape of a trapezoid, and its southern section a rectangle. When Emperor Gaozong made the Daming Palace his main residence in 663,[145] the new palace replaced the palace city to become the center of activities for him and his successors. Now the Hanyuan Hall in the palace became the "outer court," the Xuanzheng Hall the "middle court," and the Zichen Hall the "inner court."

When a visitor entered the Daming Palace through one of its southern gates, he would step into an open rectangular space that measured some six hundred meters from north to south. This square and the Hanyuan Hall at the northern end served as the "outer court." Three parallel "dragon tail stairways," which were made of stone and brick and seventy-eight meters in length, led the visitor up to the Hanyuan Hall. South facing, the hall was in an inverted U-shape and was built on high ground with the base some fifteen meters above the level of the square.[146] When the visitor ascended this towering structure, "leaned against the railing, and looked downward, South Mountain would seem [to be a

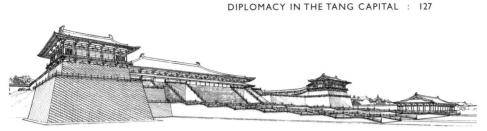

Artist's impression of the reconstructed Hanyuan Hall. (Liu Dunzhen, *Zhongguo gudai jianzhu shi* [Beijing: Zhongguo Jianzhu Gongye Chubanshe, 1984], pp. 120–121)

small object] in his palm." But if he "looked upward [from the square], the jade throne [in the hall] would seem to exist in the sky."[147] This was exactly the visual and psychological effect that the Tang court wanted the Hanyuan Hall to have on the participants in an audience: a sense of magnificence and dominance for the emperor but a feeling of intimidation and subordination for his subjects.

Participants in a court audience had to rise in the wee hours to dress for the event because they had to arrive at the palace gate before five. Tang emperors had the habit of receiving their subjects before daybreak, a practice known as the "early audience,"[148] and nobody was supposed to be late. It would not be too unbearable to get out of bed on a midsummer night. But to attend the New Year's Day celebration, one had to brave subzero temperatures, or even a winter snow,[149] and stand outdoors throughout the ceremony. To warm themselves up, some would have a quick snack before the audience. They bought steamed buns, put them in their sleeves to keep them warm, and ate them while waiting for the palace gate to open.[150] To kill time, some chatted. Others became so bored with the formalities that they did not stand or walk in good order, held their jade tablets askew, and walked or rose deliberately slowly.[151] Some made an uproar and cursed when speaking; others were heedless or disrespectful in sitting or standing, or acted in an offensive manner to others present. The court had to make such behavior a punishable offense and dispensed punishments ranging from blows with the light stick, deprivation of salary for a month, or impeachment for repeated offenders.[152]

When the palace gate opened at five, participants in an audience to receive a foreign king would notice that a series of arrangements had been carefully made. Inside the audience hall, the imperial throne with a canopy was placed under the northern wall, as was a seat for the king southwest of the throne. In the palace courtyard, a tent for the king was pitched; chimes of bells were deployed in the shape of a square to resemble the walled imperial palace;[153] twelve sections of drums and fifes were arranged; and ceremonial chariots and carriages were displayed. The standing positions for the major participants in the audience were marked by black tablets bearing their names in red characters. The king would stand south of the bells, and his subordinates followed him in double ranks. The master of ceremonies would stand northeast of the bells. Behind and slightly south of him would be the two court heralds.

The "Huanghui Guards of Honor" were the first to move into the courtyard.[154] Then came the chief musician and his staff led by the grand music director. Carrying halberds and spears, the emperor's bodyguards deployed themselves. The supervisor of rites and the court heralds also took their positions. In the meantime, the escort guided the king into the tent outside the palace. With everybody in place, the audience was about to commence.

The director of the Chancellery appeared and ordered the imposition of a state of maximum security within the palace. Armed and in uniform, officers of the palace guards and the seals secretary, with the imperial seal in his hands, gathered at the palace gate to meet the emperor. At the same time, the king, in the costume of his own country, stepped out of the tent. A secretarial receptionist led him to the west side of the palace gate. The director of the Chancellery now ordered the imposition of a state of maximum security outside the palace and along the roadways where the emperor's palanquin would pass.

Wearing the imperial crown and a deep-red gauze robe, the emperor arrived in a palanquin shaded by a canopy. When he was about to come out of the palanquin, the guards of honor started waving their weapons to pay respect to the emperor. The grand music director ordered the musicians to toll the *huangzhong* bell first and then the five bells to its right. The chief musician raised the tube-shaped imperial banner and beat the *zhu*, a square wooden tray used as a percussion instrument, to signal the musicians to start performing the "music of grand harmony." This piece of music was the seventh in the twelve-piece imperial music. It was used at all important ceremonies to herald the appearance of the emperor[155] and was played along with the rhythmic striking of the *guxi* bell.[156] The music stopped after the emperor had seated himself on the throne.

Led by a secretarial receptionist, the king entered the palace courtyard to take his standing position. As soon as he stepped into the palace, the musicians struck up the "music of leisure and harmony," which was used to accompany the entrance or exit of princes and dukes.[157] The music died down when the king had arrived at his position. The supervisor of rites announced, "Make obeisance twice!" A court herald conveyed the order to the king, who obeyed the order and kowtowed. Now the director of the Chancellery descended the stairs to inform the king of an imperial decree. The king made obeisance twice and kowtowed before and after the proclamation of the decree. The director returned to the audience hall to receive another decree of greetings to the king. He then ordered the king to ascend the stairs and take his seat in the hall. The king again made obeisance twice and kowtowed. The secretarial receptionist led the king to proceed toward the seat to the accompaniment of music. The music died down when the king had reached the top of the stairs. The receptionist then guided him to his seat. He prostrated himself before sitting down. By imperial decree, the director of the Chancellery came over to greet the king. The king prostrated himself and left the seat. As he was about to descend the stairs and make obeisance, the director informed him of a decree exempting him from doing so. The king returned to his position to listen to the decree. Now the director returned to the throne to receive yet another decree permitting the king to return to his lodge. The receptionist guided him to descend the stairs, and the escort directed him back to his position in the square. There the king made obeisance twice and kowtowed. The audience ended in music when the king had exited the palace.[158]

During this court audience, the king performed three types of motions: obeisance, kowtow, and prostration. These motions were key vocabulary in the body language that the Tang court requested of a foreign king or his ambassador in expressing submission to the Tang emperor. Foreign guests, except the king, were obliged to use the same body language frequently when attending an imperial banquet in their honor, making the otherwise joyous feasting event over formal and rather unbearable. In a long drawn-out voice, the supervisor of rites would order the guests to take their seats upon their arrival at the banquet hall. The selected few ranking diplomats who had the honor to dine with the emperor would sit on low couches placed in the banquet hall southwest of the seat for the emperor and the rest on mats in the corridor. All of them were to prostrate themselves before sitting down. But soon they had to stand up, prostrate themselves, and stand behind the seats when wine was brought to the banquet hall. They made obeisance twice, stuck their tablets of office into the girdle of their robes to receive the wine, and sat down. But they had to prostrate themselves once more before they could eventually enjoy the wine. The guests had to repeat these ritualistic motions every time a dish or a cup of wine was served and when a gift was bestowed on them.[159]

Using body language to indicate political submission was merely one requirement of foreign visitors in the Tang "guest protocol." Such submission was also to be demonstrated by deeds—thus the ceremony for the visitors to present gifts. The Tang court treated a visiting foreign king as a subject of the emperor. He was obliged, as any Tang prefect, regularly to send tribute to the central court. The court therefore regarded these goods as "local" tribute to the Son of Heaven. The Japanese state gifts, for example, were recorded as tribute from either Henan, Lingnan, or Yangzhou,[160] depending on a Japanese mission's port of landing in China and the local Tang authorities who handled the gifts.

Besides their value as a symbol of political submission, foreign goods also had important practical use. The Tang court established a procedure to manage these goods. When a foreign mission arrived at China, local authorities would examine its goods and retain any item that they considered unworthy of being brought all the way to the capital.[161] Among the foreign goods, horses, medicines, and spices unavailable in China attracted special attention from the court.[162] The court issued instructions to local authorities to pack and seal up the rare medicines and spices, and send them to the manager of receptions. He made a detailed list of the amount and name of each item and handed them over to the Court of State Ceremonial.[163] There the chief minister checked the amount of each item against the list and informed the Directorate for Imperial Manufactories as well as the Market Exchange Office. Officials from these two offices came with experts to determine the value for these items[164] and to choose some to be presented to the emperor. When all was done, a report was filed with the Secretariat.[165]

A foreign visitor presented his gifts to the Tang emperor before the start of an imperial banquet or during an audience. He would have the heavy gift items displayed in the palace courtyard and the portable ones carried by his subordinates. When presenting the gifts, he was supposed to employ both body language and verbal expressions to demonstrate his subordination to the Tang emperor. After making obeisance twice, he held a gift in both hands and stated, "The outer subject so and so from such and such a country dares to present a gift." A courtier conveyed these words to the emperor, who would then issue a decree through the director of the Chancellery accepting the gifts. Officials from the Imperial Manufactories then came out to collect them.[166] Moreover, if a foreign visitor presented his gifts during the congratulatory audience on New Year's Day, he would have to shout "Long live the emperor!" three times just like any Chinese officials present on the occasion.[167]

Fighting for Precedence at the Tang Court

In the cold winter of 725, Ōtomo no Furumaro, the Japanese vice-ambassador to China, stepped into the "outer court" to attend the Chinese New Year's Day gathering at the Hanyuan Hall. He looked around and immediately noticed that Tang officials had designated his superior the second standing position, which was west of the throne and next to that for the Tibetan ambassador. In contrast, the ambassador from Silla enjoyed the first position, which was east of the throne and ahead of the position for the ambassador from the Caliphate. This arrangement deeply troubled Furumaro. Japan had always treated Silla as its own vassal and tribute-paying state, but now the arrangements for their reception implied that Japan was inferior to Silla. He therefore decided to protest to the Tang court. The positions in which foreign visitors would stand in the palace courtyard were in fact only one of the causes for serious disputes among foreign participants in an audience. The sequence in which they were received, the seating arrangement for an imperial banquet, and other ceremonial arrangements for court gatherings could also become contentious issues, for the ambassadors saw these arrangements as tokens of their countries' relative standing in the

Chinese world as well as of their own status in the Tang court.[168] The Chinese sources refer to such disputes as "fighting for precedence" (*zhengzhang*).

Dispute over precedence in court gatherings had been part of Chinese political culture ever since the spring of 712 B.C., when the marquises of Teng and Xue (both located in present-day Teng county, Shandong province) appeared at the court of the state of Lu and contended over who should have precedence.[169] This tradition continued into the fifth and sixth centuries A.D., when several regional states existed in China. In 489, for example, the ambassador of the Southern Qi (479–502) arrived at the Northern Wei court (386–534) for a celebration on Chinese New Year's Day. He staged an angry protest to his host when he saw the ambassador from Koguryŏ standing side by side with him:

> Entrusted with the imperial edict of our emperor, I come to visit your country. The Northern Wei is the only country that can be called a match [to the Southern Qi]; therefore, [ambassadors from] outer barbarian countries should certainly not enjoy the same position as mine, not to mention that Koguryŏ is only a lesser country among the eastern barbarians, which also pays tribute to my country. How dare its ambassador stand side by side with me today?

Urging the host court to change the arrangement, another Southern Qi diplomat reminded his host, "Our imperial court has never treated any [Northern] Wei ambassador as one of a lesser country, nor have we ordered him to stand among ambassadors from these countries."[170]

Neighbors of Tang China also learned to use "fighting for precedence" as a tactic to advance their interests at the Chinese court. In 730, the Turgesh (Tuqishi) ambassador attended a banquet in his honor. Before a Tang official ushered him to the seat of honor, the ambassador from the Western Turks (Xi Tujue), who was invited to the same banquet, voiced an objection. He asserted that Turgesh was a minor country whose king used to be the subject of his ruler; it was therefore inappropriate to let the Turgesh ambassador occupy the seat of honor. The Turgesh ambassador immediately fought back. He argued that it would be a grave impropriety if he were to sit next to his Turkish counterpart since he was the guest of honor. Officials from the Secretariat gathered to discuss the matter. They solved the dispute by issuing an imperial edict that ordered the preparation of two separate seats with curtains hanging overhead. The Turgesh ambassador would sit on the west side of the banquet hall and the ambassador from the Western Turks on the east side.[171]

In 758, the Uighur ambassador disagreed with his counterpart from the black-clothed Tadzik Arabs (Heiyi Dashi) about who should enter the audience hall first. The dispute was so furious that a court translator had to separate them and order them to enter the hall simultaneously through two side gates.[172]

Although not knowing all the previous incidents of "fighting for precedence," Ōtomo no Furumaro did not hesitate to complain to General Wu Huaishi about the ceremonial arrangements. "Silla has from ancient times been a country paying tribute to Japan. Today, however, the Silla ambassador would take the first position on the east side of the hall, and the position for our ambassador is next to his. This [standing arrangement] is not in line with righteousness." Furumaro's assertiveness must have impressed General Wu. He decided to swap the standing positions for Japan and Silla. Now the Japanese ambassador stood in the first position on the east side of the hall, ahead of the ambassador from the Caliphate.[173]

Furumaro's fruitful efforts in raising Japan's prestige at the Tang court impressed some Tang scholars. Shortly after the incident on New Year's Day in 753, Wang Wei (699?–761), a celebrated Tang poet, wrote a poem for Abe no Nakamaro (698–770), a Japanese genius who came to China as a youngster in 716, adopted the Chinese name Chao Heng, and eventually became an official at the Tang court holding the title Assistant Director of the Palace Library. After years of service at the court, Nakamaro received permission to leave for home in 754 with Fujiwara no Kiyokawa, the Japanese ambassador and the superior of Furumaro.[174] Wang's poem was a farewell gift to Nakamaro. Its preface reads:

Among countries to the east of the sea, Japan is the major one. It follows the instructions of the Sage and its people have the manners of gentlemen. Its calendar is modeled on that of China, and the costume [of its officials] is the same as the Chinese. Although it takes time [for the Japanese] to reach China, the old friendship [between the two countries] has been maintained by [court visits of] its ambassadors. Despite the surge of the boundless sea, its tribute is presented to the Son of Heaven. The supervisor of rites promoted [the Japanese ambassador] to a higher rank, putting him in a position before those for other lords and marquises. The tent handler changed his residence, [allowing him] not to reside among other barbarians.[175]

In fact, a change in his standing arrangement was not the only preferential treatment that Kiyokawa had received from the Tang court. He also had the rare opportunity to tour the imperial warehouse and the three worship halls for Confucianism, Buddhism, and Daoism in the inner palace.[176] Emperor Xuanzong even presented him with a poem upon his departure for Japan.[177] Fujiwara no Kadonomaro, the Japanese ambassador to China in 801, also reported: "The great Tang dynasty has always given Japanese ambassadors special treatment as respected guests of state. We have audiences before the emperor's dragon face and hear his phoenix words. His generous concern for us has already exceeded expectations."[178]

The way in which the Tang court handled disputes over precedence among foreign visitors reveals the dual characteristics of its "guest protocol": rigidity and flexibility. As an expression of China's notion about the standing of a country in the Chinese world, the protocol in question was rigid. Any alteration to the established practice that implied a change in China's attitude toward a country, be it favorable or unfavorable, was subject to approval from the court, sometimes from the emperor himself.[179] But the Tang "guest protocol" was also flexible since it was merely a means to an end, and that end varied at times. The court sometimes changed its usual style of reception to convey a special message to a visitor. A common practice was to "raise the level of reception" (*jiali*)[180] or to accord a visitor "special treatment" (*shuli*).[181] The Turks during the first years of the Tang received such treatment, for the court was preoccupied with bringing the rebellious prefectures in central China under control and was apprehensive of the Turks taking advantage of the situation to pose a military threat to China. The Tang court ingratiated itself to the Turks by tolerating the arrogant and imperious Turkish diplomats, granting them preferential treatment, and ignoring their discourtesy during court audiences.[182] After the An Lushan rebellion, when the Tang depended for a while on an alliance with the Uighurs, they too enjoyed great tolerance. In the ninth century, the Tang court also accorded Japanese ambassadors a sort of "special treatment." It appointed eunuchs, not ordinary officials from the Court of

State Ceremonial, to take care of the Japanese visitors. From time to time, private messengers from the emperor would carry messages and rewards to the Japanese ambassadors.[183] Rigidity and flexibility were therefore complementary, not contradictory, elements in the Tang "guest protocol."

Tang "guest protocol" was a mode of state action. It employed ideological, cultural, and economic means to realize China's diplomatic goals. This mode of action could be very efficient. Differentiating foreign visitors from each other by their standing positions during a court audience, their seating order at a state banquet, or their lodging, or other ceremonial arrangements, the Tang court could exert psychological and emotional pressure on the participants. In 804, a rousing welcome ceremony in the suburbs of Changan was said to have moved the Japanese ambassador and his entourage to tears.[184] This impact, when brought home by a foreign ambassador, could become a catalyst for domestic reforms in line with Chinese institutions. Reforms in late-sixth-century Japan, for instance, brought about a new court rank system, the twelve cap ranks, which showed strong Chinese influence and helped Japan enhance its prestige at the Chinese court.[185] This was exactly what the Tang court expected of its "guest protocol"—the edification of foreigners by Chinese culture and institutions so that they, it was hoped, would share in Chinese values and remain on good terms with China.

The Tang "guest protocol," however, did not always produce the results the court expected. The neighbors of Tang also considered it a mode of state action in their own national interest when dispatching ambassadors to China. Contrary to what the Tang court hoped, an ambassador's participation in an audience with the Tang emperor was due not so much to a simple wish to acknowledge China's superiority but to an intention to use the protocol as a manifestation of the kind of international power relationship that the ambassador's ruler envisioned. Therefore he would conform to the Tang ceremonial arrangements when they embodied a recognized status quo or his country's superiority in a bilateral relationship, but he would dispute the arrangements if they would put his country in an unacceptable position of inferiority. It was also characteristic that disputes over precedence at the Tang court usually occurred between ambassadors from the same region, over which both countries wanted to exert dominant political or military influence.

Fighting over precedence at a Tang court gathering seldom happened between ambassadors from countries that were far away from each other. The Tang emperor, for example, received five ambassadors in the first month of 839. During the audience, the ambassador from Nanzhao stood in the place of honor, ahead of the Japanese ambassador.[186] No dispute over precedence occurred between the two.

The Rise of a Japan-Centered Ideology

Ironically, the Tang "guest protocol" also produced a result contradictory to the court's intended purpose of edifying "barbarians" with Chinese culture. Using the knowledge of Chinese political culture gained by their diplomats, Silla and Japan gradually developed their own world view. This world view claimed the existence of an East Asian political hierarchy whose center was not China but was either Japan or Silla. It totally ignored, if it did not overtly deny, China's supremacy. Consequently, China's effort to enforce its political cosmology through the "guest protocol" did not bring about order and peace in Asia but facilitated the emergence of competing political world views in the region. Systems of interstate dependency grew up in the West (Tibet-Arabs-Nanzhao), the Southwest (Tibet-Nanzhao-Lower Burma), the North (Uighurs-Kirghiz-Qidan and Uighur-Arabs), and the Northeast (Silla-Japan-Parhae). All of these were spheres from which China was excluded. In many cases the individual participants in these local spheres of influence also had a political relationship with China.[187] Such competing views of the political world motivated Silla and Japan to contest for regional dominance. One example was Silla's decision in 734 to change its name to the "State of the King's City" (Wangcheng Guo) without acquiring Japan's consent in advance. Japan interpreted Silla's move as a deliberate challenge to its suzerainty since the Japanese court had long regarded Silla as a vassal state. The relations between the two states worsened, and, in 759, Japan even contemplated invading Silla.[188]

In the meantime, a "Japan-centered cosmology" (chūka shisō) also developed. A phenomenon associated with the rise of the Yamato court as a centralized power in Japan, this political cosmology was employed to consolidate control of the court in domestic politics as well as to support Japan's claims to superiority over other East Asian countries in international relations. In this world view, the "Central Land" (Chūgoku) was a key concept.[189] When used in domestic affairs, the term "Central Land" referred to the areas under the direct control of the Yamato court: the sixteen prefectures in southwestern Honshū where the authorities could efficiently levy taxes and corvée on the local people. In contrast, the court considered the southwestern islands, southern Kyūshū, northern Honshū, and Hokkaidō as remote regions inhabited by tribes (i),[190] whose members were inferior to people of the "Central Land" and should be treated differently.[191] This differentiation between the people of the "Central Land" and the tribes laid the cornerstone for a hierarchical social order in Japan.[192]

In diplomacy, the court employed the term "Central Land" to mean Japan.[193] Japan's neighbors were all "barbarian countries."[194] These comprised Koguryŏ, Silla, and Paekche as the "outer barbarian countries" (gaiban)[195] and Tang China as a "remote barbarian country" (enban).[196] Although none of these countries had a substantial lord-vassal relationship with Japan, the Japanese court unilaterally treated their delegations as "tribute-paying" delegations and their diplomats as "barbarians" (banjin). The court thus created a hierarchy among foreign diplomats in Japan. As for foreigners who were in Japan but were not on any "tribute-paying" delegation, they were universally regarded as "tribesmen."[197] The Japanese world view therefore consisted of four major components: the "Central Land," the "tribes," the "outer barbarian" countries, and the "remote barbarian" countries.

This world view was instrumental in helping Japan assert a leading position over other East Asian countries. Silla and Parhae in the eighth century acknowledged Japan's superiority and indicated their obligation of fealty by addressing the Japanese emperor as the "Heavenly Emperor" (Tennō), or the "Brilliant Emperor" (kōtei) in state letters to Japan.[198] The Sui and Tang courts also recognized Japan as a major country in East Asia. They dispatched to Japan ambassadors whose ranks were senior to the ranks of those sent to the Korean states.[199] However, implementation of this Japan-centered cosmology was confined largely to the Japanese court protocol for receiving foreign visitors. Beyond the scope of ceremonial, the Japanese court lacked the ways and means to impose its world order effectively on any Asian countries.[200] As a result, the formation of a Japan-centered cosmology led neither to Japan's open challenge to China's suzerainty nor to any effort to assert an equal footing with China. Nevertheless a gradual and almost undetectable centrifugal trend away from the China-dominated world order did emerge in Japan's policy toward China. Some Tang officials already sensed this new trend in the way Japanese diplomats conducted themselves at the Tang court, and they described these Japanese as arrogant, boastful, and untruthful in answering questions posed by them.[201] What the Tang officials could not discern were the subtle expressions of Japan's own world view that its state letters to Tang China exhibited.

Weight and Nuances in State Letters

During the third month of 608, Emperor Yang (r. 605–618) arrived at his audience hall in a good mood to receive ambassadors from Paekche, Japan,[1] Chitu (on the Malaysian peninsula), and Jialuo-she (in western Thailand).[2] Emperor Yang, the second ruler of the Sui dynasty (581–618), considered the ambassadors' visits to be the initial results of the active foreign policies he had adopted immediately after ascending the throne—policies whose purpose was the restoration of China's predominance in Asia. China had enjoyed that predominance during Western Han times but had lost it when the Eastern Han dynasty fell in 220, a fall that cast the long shadow of political disunity over China for the next three centuries. Nevertheless, by the early seventh century China again enjoyed economic prosperity, political unity, and strong military potential. Emperor Yang believed the time was ripe to recover that lost Han glory. With the help of his highest-ranking ministers, he conceived a grand strategy of diplomatic maneuvers and military operations in hopes of realizing his ambition.[3]

In the northwest, the Sui targeted the Western Turks. Pei Ju, a chief foreign policy adviser to Emperor Yang, shuttled between Wuwei and Zhangye (both located in present-day Gansu province) in the attempt to persuade local tribal chieftains to sever their ties with the Turks. Pei urged them to dispatch ambassadors or to come in person to China, promising them lavish gifts from the Sui court once they had arrived. The court hoped that these valuable gifts would lure them to transfer their loyalty from the Turks to the Sui. Further, to enhance Sui influence in the Western Region, Emperor Yang, himself, toured the northwestern frontiers in 607. There he received Yami (Qimin) Qaghan, the leader of the Eastern Turks, who were the Western Turks' rivals. These efforts paid off. During the next year, the king of Karakhoja (Gaochang) and chieftains from as many as thirty tribes traveled to the Sui court to establish official ties with China.[4]

In the northeast, Emperor Yang attempted to subjugate Koguryŏ. Previously, in 598, Koguryŏ troops had defeated a Sui expeditionary force, a major military setback for the Sui court that had deeply humiliated the first Sui emperor. Emperor Yang wanted to settle this old score with Koguryŏ for his father. It so happened that while touring the northwestern frontiers, he learned from Yami Qaghan that a Koguryŏ ambassador was staying at the *qaghan*'s headquarters. Summoning the ambassador, Emperor Yang directed him: "Quickly return home and inform your king that he should come to pay tribute soon. Otherwise, Yami Qaghan and I shall tour his territories!"[5] These were not empty words. A quickly assembled force of over one million Sui soldiers conducted three massive military operations in Korea none of which succeeded and all of which would eventually contribute to the fall of the Sui dynasty.

In 605, in the South and the Southeast, the adventurous Sui court marched troops to Champa (in central and southern Vietnam) and established three military colonies.[6] In addition, in order to look for countries unknown to the court, a low-ranking Sui commandant sailed in 607 to the South China Sea. He arrived at Liuqiu (a spot probably located somewhere in Taiwan, the Philippines, or the southern Japanese islands) and tried to coerce the local ruler into political submission to the Sui court. However, the only tribute he was able to bring back to the Sui ruler was a captured local tribesman. The following year he again traveled to Liuqiu. This time he came home with only a suit of cloth armor.[7] In spite of such meager "tribute," the Sui initiatives in the region proved fruitful. Of the four ambassadors whom Emperor Yang would receive in the third month of 608, two came from Southeast Asia. The emperor considered their visits sufficient evidence that Sui China was regaining the predominance in Asia he desired. This conviction, however, was proved to be but an illusion at Emperor Yang's reception of the Japanese ambassador.

A Letter from the Son of Heaven in the Land of the Rising Sun

The audience with Ono no Imoko, the Japanese ambassador, began smoothly enough. Imoko charmed his host by praising Emperor Yang as "a bodhisattva of the sovereign west of the ocean" who "reveres and promotes Buddhism" and by telling the complacent emperor that the flourishing of Buddhism in China had prompted his master to send him and other monks to Sui China. However, the atmosphere of the reception soured decidedly when Emperor Yang's courtier read the letter Imoko carried. It began: "The Son of Heaven in the land of the rising sun addresses a letter to the Son of Heaven in the land of the setting sun. We hope you are in good health." The emperor was taken aback. Had the Japanese ruler really been so haughty as to have called himself the "Son of Heaven"? Emperor Yang took the letter himself and read it. There in black and white were indeed the two titles: "the Son of Heaven in the land of the rising sun" as the title the Japanese ruler had used for himself and "the Son of Heaven in the land of the setting sun" as the title he had used for him. Emperor Yang was displeased. "In the future," he instructed the chief minister of the Court of State Ceremonial, "no discourteous state letters from barbarian countries should be brought to my attention."[8] Nonetheless, though quick-tempered, the emperor refrained from expressing his anger.[9] Unhappy though he was, he neither cut short the audience nor lashed out at Imoko. Instead, he treated the ambassador courteously and for good reason: preparations for war against Koguryŏ were well under way; harsh treatment of Imoko could push Japan to side with Koguryŏ in China's future military operations in Korea.

Emperor Yang wondered whether the misuse of the title "Son of Heaven" in Imoko's letter might have resulted from a lack of common sense on the part of the Japanese. He still remembered how an ambassador's description of the outlandish Japanese ruler had amazed his father eight years previously in 600: his father had been told that the Japanese ruler held court before dawn but stopped attending to state affairs after sunrise, asking his brother to handle the daily government business on his behalf.[10] "That is outrageous!" Emperor Yang's father had commented, and he had then instructed the ambassador that such an eccentric way of governance should be abandoned.[11] Was it possible that the audacious wording in the letter Imoko had brought was due also to customs peculiar to the "eastern barbarians"? Emperor Yang decided to satisfy his curiosity by following the example of the enlightened Chinese sovereigns of the past who investigated local customs when trying to establish able leadership over people in remote places.[12] Soon Pei Shiqing, a steward of the Court for State Ceremonial holding the prestigious title "Gentleman-Litterateur" (Wenlin Lang), was on the way to Wo.[13]

Emperor Yang's self-restraint had defused a potential diplomatic crisis. In fact, however, he had good reason to be upset with Imoko's letter, as its wording had violated the verbal etiquette for diplomatic correspondence that successive Chinese courts had developed over the centuries.

Using the Right Word: Chinese Verbal Etiquette for Diplomatic Correspondence

With the spread of Chinese culture, some Asian countries adopted literary Chinese as a common written language of culture and as the lingua franca for diplomatic communications with China. The Tibetans, for examples, had "invited Chinese men of letters to polish their letters."[14] Official correspondence from Paekche "all followed the Chinese regulations concerning court documents."[15] And quite a number of diplomatic letters from Silla, Koguryŏ, the Turks, Karakhoja, and Nanzhao were also written in Chinese.[16]

Asian rulers could ill afford careless treatment of state letters, whether they were incoming or outgoing. State letters were instrumental in maintaining friendly relations and solving minor disputes with neighbors during times of peace. When tensions arose or when war broke out, a state letter was the vehicle for seeking external support, neutralizing potential enemies, and negotiating a truce. In international politics, a well-written state letter sometimes served a country's interests better than sheer military force.[17]

China employed state letters mainly to express the nature of the world order as China perceived it and to ensure the proper function of its investiture system. State letters conveyed diplomatic messages, bestowed official titles, and announced rewards or punishments to foreign rulers. For proper verbal embodiment of the centrality China perceived itself to hold, successive Chinese courts had developed a set of rules that were to be applied in composing a state letter. The letter's wording,[18] its form of address, and the choice of paper and of letter case were required to be strictly compatible with the status of both the sender and the addressee in the Chinese world. These rules enabled a state letter to convey the sender's message not only by its contents, but literally by means of every one of its technical details. The Chinese court expected foreign rulers to follow the same rules as well. No mere red tape, these rules were instrumental in implementing China's geopolitical strategy.

China did not benefit unilaterally from the exchange of state letters. Nor did a foreign ruler submit a state letter merely to offer political compliance to China. He did so out of consideration for domestic and international politics. His letter was sometimes sincere, sometimes superficial or full of flattery. But the letter was required to conform to Chinese verbal etiquette to ensure acceptance by China.

Over the centuries, Japan's diplomatic correspondence with China remained unchanged in form. Its contents, however, evolved from expressions of loyalty whose purpose was to secure Chinese support before the seventh century, to projections of ostensible political subordination in exchange for access to Chinese high culture during the Sui and Tang eras. Moreover, seventh-century Japanese state letters began to use Chinese characters to transliterate the native title for the Japanese ruler. The Chinese, however, failed to understand that this title was based on a newly formed Japan-centered cosmology and was a subtle sign of Japan's divorce from the Chinese world order. They believed that the Japanese state letters remained politically correct and acceptable.

The nature of a bilateral relationship dictated a state letter's forms of address, which were the titles for the sender and the addressee respectively. Appearing right at the beginning of a state letter, these titles served as an appraisal of the sender's relative standing in relation to the addressee. They therefore also conveyed a diplomatic message. It was crucial that a state letter employ the correct titles. Failing that, the host court would reject the letter, and the sender's initiative would not yield any of the desired results.

The Chinese court addressed the ruler of a military rival by his native designation: *shanyu* for the ruler of the Xiongnu during the Han, and *qaghan* for the ruler of the Western Turks during the Tang. In letters to China, these tribal leaders used neither personal names nor the degrading term "subject" for themselves. Nor, after surrendering to China, did they immediately become a full-fledged member of the Chinese world. The Chinese court considered them too barbaric to be fully sinicized and preferred keeping them at a political distance. In this subtle relationship, the Chinese court allowed these foreign rulers to call themselves "subjects" to the Chinese emperor but not to mention their personal names when writing to China, since the use of a personal name implied political closeness to the Chinese emperor.[19]

Once a foreign ruler had formally become a subject of China, his letter to China followed the format of a "memorial" *(biao)*[20] that a Chinese courtier used when writing to the throne. The ruler was now supposed to call himself an "outer subject" and to mention his personal name.[21] As a special imperial favor, the Chinese court sometimes allowed him not to call himself a "subject."[22] However, the court deemed any unilateral omission of personal name or of the term "subject" from a foreign state letter as a de facto termination of the sender's vassal status and thus a challenge to China's authority. In the meantime, the Chinese court adopted a specific form of address and wording in its state letters to indicate the sovereign-vassal nature of a bilateral relationship.

Diplomatic Correspondence between China and Wo: From the Wei to the Northern and Southern Dynasties

In 238, the Wei court (220–265) dispatched a "dictation of investiture" *(zhi)* to Himiko, the female ruler of Japan, as follows:

A DICTATION OF INVESTITURE ISSUED TO
THE PRO-WEI QUEEN OF WO, HIMIKO

The governor of Daifang, Liu Xia, has sent a messenger to accompany your Grand Master, Nashōme, and the vice-ambassador, Toji Gori [to the Wei capital]. They have arrived here and presented your gifts: four male and six female slaves, and two pieces of patterned cloth, each twenty feet in length.

Although living far away [from China], you have sent an ambassador to pay tribute. [This action shows] your loyalty and filial piety [toward me]. [Thus] I am very fond of you. I now confer upon you the title "Pro-Wei Queen." A gold seal with purple ribbon has been encased and entrusted to the governor of Daifang, who will grant it to you temporarily. [By so doing, I wish] you to rule your people in peace and to endeavor to be devoted and obedient (to me).

Your ambassador Nashōme and [vice-ambassador] Gori came from afar, and must have had a fatiguing journey. I have, therefore, appointed Nashōme the "Shuaishan Colonel" and Gori, the "Shuaishan Commandant." I have also bestowed upon them the silver seals with blue ribbon, granted them audience in appreciation of their visit, and sent them home with gifts. The gifts are five pieces of crimson brocade with dragon designs, ten pieces of crimson tapestry with dappled pattern, fifty lengths of bluish-red fabric, and fifty lengths of dark blue fabric. These are in return for your tributary goods. As special gifts, I bestow upon you three pieces of blue brocade with interwoven characters, five pieces of tapestry with delicate floral designs, fifty lengths of white silk, eight taels of gold, two swords five feet long, one hundred bronze mirrors, and fifty catties each of jade and of red beads. All these things are sealed in boxes and entrusted to Nashōme and Gori.

When they arrive and you acknowledge their receipt, you may exhibit all of them to your countrymen, and let them know that these gifts are bestowed upon you at your request, and that my country supports you.[23]

This "dictation of investiture" is the earliest surviving sample of diplomatic correspondence from China to Japan. In this document, the Wei court used the title "Pro-Wei Queen Himiko" to address Himiko. This title, comprising the term "queen" (or "king") and a personal name, appeared only in Wei official dispatches sent to "outer subjects." Also indicative of the nature of these bilateral relations was the use of such words as "loyalty," "filial obedience," and a reference of Himiko as a "daughter" of the Wei emperor. Loyalty was the fundamental moral character that a Chinese emperor expected his subjects to exhibit and filial obedience the basic obligation that sons and daughters owed to their father.[24]

Using the terminology "dictation of investiture," not "conferment" (ceshu), to inform Himiko of her appointment as the "Pro-Wei Queen of Wo" also revealed her relatively low standing in Wei officialdom. A dictation of investiture was used for the appointment and removal of a chamberlain (qing), or of a metropolitan official,[25] while a conferment was used with respect to the bestowal or annunciation of more prestigious posts—those of the three dukes (sangong), prince, and marquis.[26] Himiko was therefore shown by the language used to be considered inferior to a Chinese prince or a marquis.[27]

The Southern Song court (420–479) during the Southern and Northern Dynasties (420–581) also issued edicts to announce the bestowal of Chinese titles on successive Japanese rulers. The rulers were addressed in those edicts as the "King of Wo," with their first name transliterated into Chinese characters. For example, a Song edict of 421 called the

Japanese ruler "Wo Zan" (Zan, the King of Wo), the term "Zan" being the transliteration for the first name of Emperor Nintoku "Ōsazaki."[28] The first name of a Japanese ruler in Chinese transliteration also appeared in the Song edicts issued to Japan in 438,[29] 451,[30] 462,[31] 478,[32] 479,[33] and 502.[34]

The Japanese court quickly learned that the proper means for communication with China was a "memorial." An official dispatch from Chinese officials to the Son of Heaven, a memorial informed a Chinese emperor of important matters[35] and indicated the sender's loyalty.[36] In her memorial of 240, Himiko expressed gratitude for the titles, the gifts, and the official seal granted her by the Wei court. The court regarded her memorial as a gesture of political subordination to China.[37]

The fourth century saw a hiatus in China-Japan relations. When it eventually resumed contact with China in the fifth century, the Japanese court again used the memorial when communicating with China.[38] In 478, a memorial from Emperor Yūryaku (r. 457–479) reached the Northern Wei court in which he repeatedly called himself a "subject" and described Japan as a "remote principality" and an "outer fence" for China. He showed determination to follow the footsteps of his father, who had offered loyalty to and maintained a sovereign-vassal relationship with China.[39]

Diplomatic Communication between Sui China and Japan

Progress toward political unification in seventh-century Japan profoundly changed the foundation for Chinese-Japanese relations. Having systematically consolidated its control over most parts of the country,[40] the Japanese court believed that seeking Chinese political recognition and using it in their power struggle had now became irrelevant to domestic politics. The Japanese court began to distance itself from the China-centered world order, and its ambassadors stopped requesting Chinese titles for Japanese officials. This newly acquired sense of independence embodied itself in a Japanese state letter dispatched to Sui in 600. Signifying the changed political tone, the letter omitted both the Chinese-style title "Wowang" (King of Wo) and the belittling term "subject" as references to the Japanese ruler. The ruler's first name also disappeared from the state letter. In its place were the eleven Chinese characters *abei jimi amei duolisibigu*. They were the Chinese transliteration for "Ōkimi Ametarashihiko," the native designation of the Japanese ruler that proudly expressed his authority and dignity.[41]

Ironically, the Sui court missed those bold signs of Japan's withdrawal from the Chinese world order.[42] Misperceiving the real meaning of those eleven Chinese characters, the court interpreted them as transliteration of the Japanese ruler's first name, the mention of which had been the minimum Chinese requirement for state letters from an "outer subject." Tang scholars recorded this diplomatic blunder in the 650s when compiling the *Dynastic History of the Sui*, stating: "In the twentieth year of Kaihuang [600], the ruler of Wo sent an ambassador to the [Sui] court. The ruler's family name was A-mei and his first name was Duolisibigu. He had a title: *abei jimi*."[43] Although quite correct in pointing out that *abei jimi* was a title, the Tang officials, as had their Sui predecessors, mistook "Duolisibigu" for the first name of Suiko (r. 593–628), the Japanese ruler who had dispatched the ambassador to Sui China. They had no idea that "Duolisibigu" had nothing to do with Suiko. In actuality, it comprised the phonetic marks for *tarashihiko*,[44] which appeared in the names that such Wo male rulers as Keikō (r. 71–130), Seimu (r. 131–190), and Chūai (r. 192–200) employed.[45] But Suiko was a female, and her name was "Toyomikekashikiyahime." In fact, "Ōkimi Ametarashihiko" means "Heavenly Emperor." It was the designation for every Wo ruler, male or female.[46] It was not until the late seventh century that the Tang scholar Zhang Chujin became the first to realize that "the meaning of *abei jimi* is the same as Son of Heaven *(tianer)* in Chinese."[47]

The use of Chinese characters to transliterate the native designation of a Wo ruler was indeed an ingenious invention in diplomatic communication. This practice allowed Japanese officials to express the dignity of their ruler and his or her new political stance toward China without risking China's rejection of their state letters. The Japanese ambassadors to China in 608, 610, and 614 must also have presented the Sui court with state letters using the same designation.[48]

The Sui court would certainly have rejected all the Japanese state letters had it discerned the real meaning of the eleven Chinese characters. But it accepted the Japanese state letter in 600 and thus unintentionally conveyed the misleading message to Japan that China now treated Japan as a peer state. Acting on this misconstruction, the Japanese court took an even bolder move in 607 by sending Imoko to present another state letter in which *tianzi* (Son of Heaven) was used as the title for both the Japanese and Sui rulers.

Aside from the misused titles, the rhetoric of Imoko's letter was also unacceptable. An "outer subject" was not supposed to describe his written communication with the Chinese overlord as "sending a letter" *(zhishu)*.[49] Nor was he permitted to greet a Chinese emperor by saying, "I hope you are well" *(wuyang)*. Only state letters exchanged between China and its peer states—Nanyue and Xiongnu in the Han dynasty and the Western Turks and the Tibetans during Sui and Tang times— were supposed to use these expressions.[50]

To reiterate that the Japanese ruler was an "outer subject" to China, Pei Shiqing traveled to Wo in 608 and delivered the following state letter:

THE EMPEROR GREETS THE EMPRESS OF WO

Your ambassador, the provincial governor, the Dairei, So Inkō [the Chinese name for Imoko], and his suit have arrived, and have given us full information.

We, having reverently received the precious command [of Heaven], rule over the universe. It is our desire to diffuse abroad our civilizing influence so as to cover all living things, and our sentiment of loving nurture knows no distinction of distance.

Now We learn that Your Majesty, dwelling separately beyond the sea, bestows the blessings of peace on your subjects, that there is tranquillity within your borders, and that the manners and customs are mild.

With the most profound loyalty, you have sent us tribute from afar, and we are delighted at this admirable token of your sincerity.

Our health is as usual, notwithstanding the increasing warmth of the weather.

Therefore we have sent Pei Shiqing, official entertainer of the department charged with the ceremonial for the reception of foreign ambassadors, and his suit, to notify you of the preceding. We also transmit to you the products of which a list is given separately.[51]

The political tone of this letter troubled Empress Suiko. She suspected the Sui court of using the verb "greet" *(wen)* in the opening line to indicate her inferiority, and she raised the question with Prince Shōtoku. "The form of this letter," replied the prince, "conforms to what the Son of Heaven uses in correspondence to his princes and marquises."[52]

The prince's reply was no surprise, for Pei's mission was to assert China's superiority over Wo. That being the case, however, why should Pei's letter have addressed Suiko as "empress" *(huang),* thus putting her on a par with the Sui emperor and violating a cardinal rule for composing a state letter?

Quoting the *Biography of Prince Shōtoku (Shōtoku Taishi denryaku),* a tenth-century work that has since been lost, Zuikei Shūhō (1391–1473) defended the alleged use of "empress" in the Sui letter. He further suggested that Prince Shōtoku had explained to Suiko: "The use of *'huang'* is universal. Employing the term [to address you], the Sui emperor has signified his politeness."[53] But as a man of considerable erudition, the prince would not have made those contradictory remarks, for a Sui state letter whose style was identical with that of a Sui official dispatch to a Chinese prince or marquis would certainly not address its recipient as an "empress."

Incidentally, Shūhō also quoted another work that offers circumstantial evidence that the Sui letter called Suiko the "ruler *(wang)* of Wo."[54] This was the proper title for Suiko, since the successive Chinese courts had always used "ruler" as a reference to a foreign leader, and the title "ruler" also agreed in political tone with the verb "greet" in the Sui state letter.

The controversy over the title for Suiko was most likely caused by the traditional Japanese scholars who authored the *Chronicles of Japan (Nihon shoki)* and the *Biography of Prince Shōtoku.* Politically conscious and eager to protect the prestige of their master, they seem to have deliberately replaced the title "ruler" with "empress" when transcribing the Sui state letter of 608 into their works.[55]

The Characteristics of Tang Diplomatic Correspondence

A Tang diplomatic letter conveyed the will of the Son of Heaven. The letter was analogous to other court dispatches, since the court saw all the addressees, Chinese or foreign, as subjects of the Tang emperor.

Those dispatches were known collectively as the "words of the emperor" (*wangyan*), or simply as the "letters" (*shu*).[56] Among the seven different types of official dispatches, "conferment" (*ceshu*), "dictation" (*zhishu*), "decree of requital" (*weilao zhishu*), and "edict to handle specific matters" (*lunshi chishu*) were the four most frequently used in diplomacy.[57]

A conferment announced the bestowal of an official title;[58] a dictation proclaimed grand rewards and severe punishments, granted high official ranks, or pardoned surrendered enemies;[59] a decree of requital praised the distinguished and the capable, and encouraged the industrious;[60] and an edict for specific matters conveyed the emperor's kindness, sent his instructions to dukes and ministers, and regulated the behavior of his subjects.[61] Together these documents adequately handled Tang external affairs, which involved, among other things, granting titles to foreign rulers, praising their appropriate actions or blaming their wrongdoings, issuing them instructions, and expressing condolences on their deaths.

Sophisticated in style and nuanced in wording, Tang diplomatic letters did not always faithfully reflect the changing—or the changed—relations between Tang and its neighbors. Apart from being vehicles for messages, these letters were embodiments of China's perceived world order. The concept of "all under heaven" had always guided Tang officials when drafting a state letter. To them, changes on the foreign front alone, no matter how fundamental, did not justify a revision of the concept. Consequently, Tang state letters routinely depicted China as the suzerain[62] and its neighbors as vassals even when a new pattern in Tang-Japan relations that emphasized cultural assimilation had already replaced the sovereign-vassal norm prevailing before the Sui.[63] The only exceptions were letters dispatched after 756 to Tibet, to the Uighurs, and to Nanzhao over which Tang China was unable to exert real military pressure.

The Tang court developed detailed regulations to ensure that a state letter sustained China's image of a suzerain among friendly countries, reflected the reality of its relations with military rivals, and embodied the standing of a foreign ruler in the Chinese world.[64] The *Previous Regulations of the Hanlin Academy (Hanlin xueshiyuan jiugui)*[65] reveal that the regulations were concerned mainly with three aspects of a state letter: wording, the use of paper, and the type of enclosing case.

STATE LETTER TO SILLA OR PARHAE
A letter is to begin with "Edict to the ruler *(wang)* of a certain country" and mentions both his family and first names. It ends with "[I] hope recently all has been well with my chamberlain. There are more matters than I have mentioned in this edict granted on you." A letter uses white paper in golden flower pattern with the right side in five colors and is enclosed in a case of the second category. An imperial seal is affixed.[66]

The state letter to Silla or Parhae was short in length but not in political implications. Silla and the Parhae kings emerged merely as "rulers." They were mentioned not only by their family and first names, but also as "chamberlains" *(qing)*. Originally a term that the Chinese monarch of the Qin and the Han had used to address his high ministers, "chamberlain" lost its noble undertones during the Northern and Southern Dynasties to become a term that referred to anyone who was inferior to the user.[67] It was also used as an adjective for a country of lower standing in the Chinese world. The late-eighth-century Tang poet Zhang Ji, for example, used "chamberlain country" as a reference to Silla.[68]

This state letter employed a glossy whitish paper scroll, which was made of silk fiber.[69] The Tang court used this high-quality paper only when issuing edicts to handle important state affairs: appointment or dismissal of generals and chief ministers, declarations of war, announcements of amnesty, and comfort to people in disaster areas.[70] Edicts that dealt with less important matters employed yellowish jute paper.[71] Of lower quality, this paper was also used for letters sent to a foreign ruler's subordinates—Tibetan or Uighur ministers, or the generals and ministers of the Nanzhao kingdom.[72]

The right edge of the paper was colored green, red, yellow, white, and black: hence the name "five-colored edict" *(wuse zhao)*.[73] These colors represented China and its neighbors: green for countries in the East, red for those in the South, yellow for China, and white and black for countries in the West and the North respectively. The yellow, in the middle of the five colors, symbolized China's centrality.

A tradition dating back to the Han dynasty, the court used letter cases of various categories depending on the addressee's status.[74] The state letter to Silla was enclosed in a case of the second category, which used white sandalwood of the second quality and was inlaid with mother-of-pearl and emerald produced in Hetian. A silver lock was applied to the case.[75] But the Tang letters sent to the two Tibetan rulers during the Yuanhe period (806–820) used a letter case of higher quality, since they were then China's foes. It was made of white sandalwood of the first quality and was inlaid with mother-of-pearl, emerald, and pearl. In contrast, letters to Tibetan and Uighur ministers were put into cases of lower quality. They were made of red sandalwood and were inlaid with only mother-of-pearl.[76]

STATE LETTER TO THE KIRGHIZ (XIAJIASI)

The paper and the enclosing case are the same as those for the letters sent to Silla. The letter begins with "Decree to the Kirghiz" and mentions both the family and the first name [of its ruler]. It ends with "[I] hope recently all has been well with my chamberlain. There are more matters than I have mentioned in this edict granted to you." An imperial seal is affixed.

STATE LETTER TO THE UIGHUR TIANMU QAGHAN

A letter is to begin with "The emperor, father-in-law [of the *qaghan*], respectfully greets his son-in-law the Uighur Tianmu Qaghan." It ends with "[I] think it is appropriate to let you know [these matters]." [A remark on the weather of] the season.[77] "[I] hope recently all has been well with my chamberlain. My regards to your generals, chief ministers, and fellow tribesmen."

A striking characteristic of this letter is the use of two kinship terms: "father-in-law" (*jiu*)[78] and "son-in-law" (*sheng*). The Tibetan, Uighur, Turkic, and Kirghiz rulers had married Tang princesses, forming kinship ties with the Tang imperial family.[79] A dynastic marriage put a Tang emperor in a senior position. He was now the "father-in-law" and the foreign ruler, his "son-in-law."[80] Stressing status distinctions, these kinship terms were not politically neutral. They helped to maintain on paper the "superior" position of a Tang emperor.[81]

A dynastic marriage also imposed filial obligations on an otherwise recalcitrant and unpredictable foreign ruler. He was now supposed to be loyal and obedient to his Chinese father-in-law.[82] Delighted at the marriage with Princess Wencheng, the Tibetan ruler performed the ritual of a son-in-law to a Tang prince who had escorted the bride to Tibet in 641.[83] If a son-in-law turned disobedient, his Chinese father-in-law then stood on the moral high ground and was able to condemn his behavior.[84]

The opening line of the state letter to Tianmu Qaghan used the phrase "respectfully greet" (jingwen) to indicate the relatively high status of the addressee. This was a phrase borrowed from private letters to esteemed persons, in which "respectfully greet" appeared at the beginning or the end, or at both ends of the letter.[85] A Chinese emperor sometimes used the same phrase in letters sent to ranking officials[86] or to individuals who enjoyed a special relationship with him.[87] In diplomacy, the phrase in question was the rhetoric for communication between peer states.[88] An "outer subject" or a low-ranking Tang official deserved no such courtesy. The Tang court letters they received only "greeted" them.[89]

Using or dropping the adverb "respectfully" often implied a change in the nature of a bilateral relationship. The two letters from Emperor Xuanzong to the two Eastern Turkic rulers were cases in point. The first, which "respectfully greeted" the Qapaghan (Mochuo) Qaghan, was sent in 717 when the two countries were at odds with one another.[90] But the second, a letter of condolence sent to the Bilgä Qaghan in 731 on the death of his younger brother, dropped the adverb "respectfully," for the Tang court had reached a peace settlement with the Eastern Turks in 721–722, and the Bilgä Qaghan had agreed to form a father-son relationship with Emperor Xuanzong.[91]

STATE LETTER TO THE QIDAN

A letter is to begin with "Edict to Abaoji, the Qidan ruler."[92] It ends with "[I] think it is appropriate to let you know [these matters]. [Then, a remark on the weather of] the season. "[I] wish that recently all has been well with my chamberlain." (The following words are the same as those in a letter to the Kirghiz).[93] Previously, a letter used jute paper. No blank space was left [at the beginning of the letter],[94] and no imperial seal was affixed. [Qidan courtiers were allowed to] announce a letter in their court. Now, a letter uses five-colored paper, an imperial seal is affixed, and a case of the second category encloses the letter. (After the Qidan ruler illegally adopted the title "emperor," most

letters to Qidan dealt with military secrets. For expedience, those letters drafted by the Secretariat did not follow the composition rules.
And no sample has been preserved at the Editorial Office.)[95]

STATE LETTER TO THE ZANGGE

A letter is to begin with "Edict to the Zangge" and mentions both the
family name and the first name [of its ruler]. It ends with "[I] think
it is appropriate to let you know [these matters]. [Then, a remark on
the weather of] the season. "Does everything go well with my chamberlain recently? There are more matters than I have mentioned in
this edict granted to you." The letter uses five-colored paper, but no
imperial seal is affixed.

STATE LETTER TO THE TUYUHUN AND THE TANGUT
(DANGXIANG) CHIEFTAINS, AND THEIR AMBASSADORS

A letter is to begin in the same manner as a letter to the Zangge does.
It uses jute paper. No imperial seal is affixed.

STATE LETTER TO THE BIAOXIN OF NANZHAO

A letter is to begin with "The father-in-law and emperor respectfully
greets his son-in-law and the Biaoxin."[96] It ends in the same manner
as a letter to the Uighurs does. After the sentence "There are more
matters than I have mentioned in this edict granted to you," the titles
and names of the four [Tang] chief ministers are affixed. A letter
uses white paper,[97] and an imperial seal is affixed.[98]

The three major aspects of a state letter survived the Tang dynasty.
Officials at the Later Tang court (923–936) concerned themselves with
the same issues in 928 when preparing an edict to Koguryŏ: "We are
unsure whether to address [the Koguryŏ ruler] as 'chamberlain' or to
call him 'you,'" they told the court. "Nor are we certain about the kind
of paper to be used, and the way to seal and to enclose [the edict]."[99]

To draft a state letter, a courtier had to be capable of word-splitting.
When depicting the transfer of an object from one party to another, he
had to choose from a wide variety of status-sensitive verbs the most suitable one that not only denoted the action, but also appropriately
embodied the status of the respective parties. Emperor Taizong, for
example, pondered the shades of meaning of these verbs before dictat-
ing an edict to be sent with some cherries as gifts to the Duke of Xi (in

present-day Zibo city, Shandong province): "'Offer up' sounds unduly respectful [to the duke], but 'grant' is too belittling." Unable to select the suitable verb for the occasion, the emperor consulted his erudite director of the Palace Library. The director advised him to follow the example of Emperor Wu (r. 502–549) of the Liang and use "give" *(xiang)*. "The emperor," explained the director "used this verb when sending things to the Prince of Baling [located in present-day Yueyang city, Hunan province] of the Qi."[100]

Asian rulers themselves also became aware that China's perception of a bilateral relationship determined the use of verbs in its state letters. To ensure that the perception reflected the reality, the Tibetan ruler sent a minister to query the wording of a state letter that a Tang ambassador brought to him in 781: "The Tang edict reads: 'I [Emperor Dezong] have received the things that you offered up. Now, I shall confer certain gifts upon you, my son-in-law. You will receive them when they arrive.' Great Tibet and Tang are countries like father-in-law and son-in-law. Why am I treated as a subject?" He requested that the ambassador send his assistant back to China for clarification.

The Tibetan ruler was not overreacting to the rhetoric of the Tang edict. As son-in-law to the Tang emperor, he had kinship ties with the Tang imperial family. Certain verbs in the edict, however, obscured this special relationship and portrayed him as just another "outer subject" to China. Although both described the transfer of gifts from one party to another, "confer upon" *(ci)* required a superior to initiate the action,[101] whereas "offer up" *(gongxian)*, an inferior.[102] It is no wonder that the two verbs in the Tang edict displeased the Tibetan ruler. He had also spotted the verb "receive" *(lingqu)* that hinted at a monarch-subject relationship between the gift sender and the recipient.[103]

The assistant to the Tang ambassador came back with a revised edict. It changed "offer up" to "present" *(jin)*, "confer upon" to "send" *(zhi)*, and "receive" *(lingqu)* to "take them" *(lingzhi)*. He also conveyed an oral explanation from the Tang court: "The former chief minister Yang Yan did not follow the established rules; hence the errors in the previous edict."[104] The new verbs for gift exchanging gave the revised Tang edict a softer tone analogous to that in letters between a Tang emperor and his family members. "Present," for example, described a junior sending gifts to his senior,[105] and it was thus a verb suitable for the Tibetan ruler, who was a son-in-law to the Tang emperor. Similarly, the Uighur ruler, another son-in-law to the Tang emperor, was also recorded to have "presented" local goods to the Tang court.[106] In contrast, "send" depicted gift exchange between friends or people of the same social status.[107] As for "take them," a list of gifts usually preceded this verb. This usage indicates the recipient's distinctive status. Not an ordinary "outer subject," the gifts for him had to be specially selected and itemized in a state letter.[108]

Officials of other East Asian countries learned the art of using status-sensitive words as well. In works for domestic readers, Japanese courtiers seldom used "offer up" to refer to an ambassador bringing gifts to China.[109] But to enhance the prestige of their master, they sometimes deliberately wrote that China "offered up" goods to the Japanese court.[110] In diplomacy, Japanese officials were particularly strict about the wording of state letters from Silla, which they considered a vassal state of Japan. In 774, they questioned a Silla ambassador: "[Your letter reads:] 'We make a request for renewing the old friendship, and for conducting a regular visit [to each other's court].' These words sound like the rhetoric of a peer state, not of a country that performs tributary duties to Japan. Moreover, what is the intention of sending a letter that has substituted 'state gifts' *(guoxin)* for 'tax goods' *(tiao)*, thus straying from the old and usual norm?" Later the court issued the Silla ambassador an edict of condemnation: "[The king of] Silla calls him a subject and offers up tax goods [to Japan]. This has been a well-known fact since ancient times. But [your state letter], instead of following the established routine, takes the liberty to use novel expressions, referring to 'tax goods' as 'state gifts' and replacing 'paying tribute' with 'fostering cordial relations.' Judging by the precedents, the letter is rather impertinent in wording." The court denied the Silla ambassador a trip to the capital and sent him home directly from the port where he had landed.[111]

Similarly, to reject the claim that Japan was their suzerain, Parhae officials employed the verb "present" when writing to Japan.[112] The Japanese court consequently softened its stance toward Parhae, using "respectfully greet" and "take them" in its state letters as a gesture of respect to the addressee.[113]

The rhetoric for diplomatic communication among Asian countries developed into an art of great sophistication, capable of manifesting the subtle status differences between the sender and the recipient of a state letter. And, when the power relations in the region evolved, diplomatic language was often the barometer of change.

Tang State Letters to Japan

"Once you are back at home, / open the heavenly letter *(tianshu),*" the Tang poet Zhu Shaorui wrote in 806 to Kūkai, the famous Japanese monk who had come to China to study in 804 and was now about to leave for home.[114] The scarce Japanese records also confirm that the Tang court had sent letters to Japan earlier, in 671 and 673.[115] Unfortunately, all these letters have since been lost, except the one that Emperor Xuanzong granted to Nakatomi no Nashiro in the winter of 735.[116]

Nashiro came to China in 733 as vice-ambassador of the ninth Japanese delegation to China. Having stayed in China for a year, he and Tajihi no Mahito Hironari, head of the delegation, left Suzhou for home in the tenth month of 734.[117] But their ships were soon blown off course. Some of the diplomats managed to return to China and reported the incident to the Tang court. Following a practice among East Asian countries, Emperor Xuanzong issued the following edict to inform the Japanese ruler of the whereabouts of his diplomats.[118]

EDICT TO WANG-MING-LE-MEI-YU-DE,
RULER OF THE STATE OF JAPAN

Your country is a land of Confucian teachings and righteousness protected by the deities. [And your ambassadors] have never had any trouble sailing across the vast sea. But last year they somehow encountered peril.

Tajihi no Mahito Hironari and those who accompanied him came to pay tribute. On their way home, the sky clouded over and hid the North Star soon after they had left the mouth of the [Yangzi] River. They lost direction. Then, a severe storm rose, and their ships drifted off course.

One ship headed by [Tajihi no] Mahito Hironari floated to the jurisdiction of Yuezhou prefecture,[119] from whence he was later sent back [to Japan]. I reckon [he has] already arrived at home.

Another ship headed by [Nakatomi no] Ason Nashiro drifted to the South [China] Sea. They suffered from danger and hardship in every possible way and barely survived.

Before [Nakatomi no Ason] Nashiro was sent home, a memorial from Guangzhou prefecture reached me: the ship that Heguri no Ason Hironari and his fellows boarded had floated to Linyi [the central coastal part of Vietnam around Hue]. They were in a foreign land and could not speak the native language. Moreover, they were captured and robbed. Some were killed, and some were sold into slavery.[120] I could hardly bear to read of all the disasters and hardships [that they have suffered].

However, Linyi and other countries [in that area] often pay tribute [to China]. I have already instructed the protector-general at Annan[121] to issue an edict to [their rulers], ordering them to escort [the Japanese diplomats] to [the protectorate, should] any of them be spotted. I have also instructed [the protector-general] to comfort and send the Japanese home.

The whereabouts of the other ship is, however, unknown, and this often bothers me deeply. Probably the ship has already reached your shore. If a [Japanese ambassador] comes [to China], he should report this matter to me in detail.

Disasters and accidents such as these are indeed unpredictable. Loyal and faithful as my chamberlain and your diplomats have been to me, why did the deities let them down and make them suffer these terrible disasters? My chamberlain, I think you will also be shocked upon learning all this. Nonetheless, the fate of everyone is predestined in this vast world.

The midwinter is very cold. I wish my chamberlain, your chieftains, and your people well.

Now, [Nakatomi no Ason] Nashiro is returning home and will make a detailed oral report to you. There are more matters than what I have mentioned in this edict granted to you.[122]

Emperor Xuanzong emerges from this letter as a compassionate man. He informs the Japanese ruler in great detail of what has happened to his delegation and of the arrangements to look for the missing Japanese diplomats. In essence, however, the wording Emperor Xuanzong uses leaves no doubt of his authority: Japan is an "outer fence" (*bifan*) for China and the Japanese sovereign merely a "ruler," an "outer subject," and a "chamberlain." The Japanese emperor is addressed by name—

Wang-ming-le-mei-yu-de—and his ambassador should "report in detail" to the Tang court. The pomposity of Emperor Xuanzong is most evident in his omission of the opening sentence of greetings to his Japanese counterpart.

When circumstances required its use, however, a sentence of greetings would appear in Tang official correspondence to Japan. In 753, poet Wang Wei wrote about Japanese ambassadors bringing home "edicts bearing the expression 'respectfully greet.'"[123] A Tang correspondence to Japan used the same expression earlier, in 664, when tension caused Tang-Japan relations to deteriorate after a Tang-Silla joint force crushed, in southern Korea, a Japanese fleet that had attempted to help Paekche resist Tang aggression in 663.[124] Tang occupation of Paekche sent a shock wave to the Japanese courtiers. Fearing an imminent Tang attack on the homeland, they hurriedly deployed troops to protect the islands of Tsushima, Iki, and northern Kyūshū.[125] Instead of invading Japan, Liu Renyuan, the Tang area commander in chief stationed in Paekche, sent Guo Wuzong as his ambassador three times to Japan between 664 and 671 to ease the tension across the Korea Strait.[126] The timing of Guo's visits apparently required him to show respect to the Japanese emperor, whose forces had confronted the Tang troops in southern Korea not long before.[127] It would have been a diplomatic blunder if any of Guo's letters did not use the phrase "respectfully greet" or addressed the recipient as a "chamberlain."[128]

In addition to defusing the tension between China and Japan, Guo set the precedent for diplomatic contact on the local level. Because he carried with him only "certificates" (die) issued by Liu Renyuan, not "letters from the Son of Heaven," the Japanese court decided to accord Guo a low-level reception: he was to stay at the Dazai Headquarters in Kyūshū and was not to travel to the capital. The local officials made an oral report of his certificates to the throne but did not forward them to the court. The general in chief in northern Kyūshū also issued Guo a certificate before he left Japan.[129] Exchanging certificates between local authorities became a new game beneficial to all. The host court substantially reduced the cost of receiving a foreign guest, who, instead of journeying all the way to the capital, conducted his official business at a local administrative center. Moreover, both China and Japan could, if necessary, handle important diplomatic issues in the name of local authorities. This prevented an embarrassing dispute from occurring at the host court, leaving much needed face-saving room for diplomatic maneuvering in the future.

A Japanese Messenger without a Written Message?

Did the Japanese court entrust state letters to its ambassadors dispatched to Tang China? Some traditional and modern scholars believe not, asserting that the court refrained from doing so in order to avoid controversy over the wording of its state letters.[130] Others disagree.[131] They point to the lack of concrete evidence for Japan's unilateral abandonment of the use of state letters, reliance on which had been an essential feature of Japan's relations with China before the Tang dynasty. They further emphasize that this assertion rests on a misinterpretation of a single piece of documentary evidence: a letter to the surveillance commissioner at Fuzhou.[132]

The author of this letter was Kūkai, who drafted it on behalf of Fujiwara no Kadonomaro, the Japanese ambassador dispatched to China in 803–804.[133] Addressed to Yan Jimei, the local Tang surveillance commissioner,[134] this letter complained about the officials at Fuzhou who had allegedly accorded the Japanese delegation ill treatment.[135] These officials had questioned Kadonomaro about the lack of proper official documents *(wenshu)*, searched his ships, and registered the goods on board.[136] "Bamboo and bronze tallies were originally used as a protection against fraud," argued Kūkai. "[When as in Japan], customs are unaffected and the people are straightforward, what is the use of such documents? . . . [Therefore] no list of gifts bearing the impression of an imperial seal *(yinshu)* has ever been used when offering presents [to the Tang court]." The term *yinshu* has been interpreted as "state letter" and used as evidence that Kadonomaro did not bring a state letter with him.

The term in question, however, had nothing to do with a Japanese state letter. It was a list of the official gifts to be presented to the Tang emperor, and using such a list had been a practice in gift exchange between East Asian courts. For example, a Tang decree to the Silla ruler reads: "There are some gifts listed in a separate enumeration *(juru bielu)*."[137] Similarly, when presenting gifts to the Japanese court, ambassadors from Silla, Paekche, and Koguryŏ usually "offered a separate list of gifts" *(bie shangbiao)*.[138] And a Japanese state letter of 815 informed the Parhae ruler: "[The Japanese emperor] has some gifts [for you], which are listed separately *(semu rubie)*."[139] Since he came to China to "proffer national offerings and special gifts" *(guoxin biegong)* to the Tang emperor,[140] Kadonomaro was supposed to produce for the Fuzhou officials a list of gifts as well. This list together with the total number of people on Kadonomaro's mission would provide the court with the necessary information to decide the number of Japanese diplomats and the types and amount of gifts that would be transported to the capital.

The treatment that Kadonomaro had received at Fuzhou was not at all discriminatory. Checking and listing a traveler's goods had been a routine procedure that the Tang authorities applied to all travelers, foreign or Chinese. When Zuda, a Japanese prince, arrived in Mingzhou in 862, local authorities also inspected his ships and made a detailed report of the goods on board and of his entourage.[141] Tang officials needed to perform these duties before issuing a travel permit, which specified, among other things, the traveler's personal belongings.[142] Similarly, Japanese officials at the Dazai Headquarters inspected and listed all his gifts when Guo Wuzong arrived there in 664.[143] In any case, officials at Fuzhou were authorized to inspect only Kadonomaro's goods, not his state letter. They had neither the power nor the means of doing so, since the letter was sealed in a letter case.[144] Some forty years later, in 846, Ennin, who had arrived in China with the last Japanese mission, reported in his diary that officials at Yangzhou observed the same practice when handling official documents from Japan: "Li Shen, the Regional Commander of Yangzhou and the Grand Overseer, did not himself dare to open the (Japanese) Council of State document and the Enryakuji document and (the letter from) the Deputy Vice Governor (O)no, because they were sealed, but sent them sealed to Changan."[145]

Even more significantly, Ennin's eyewitness account of the activities of the last Japanese ambassador dispatched to China confirms that the ambassador brought with him a "Council of State document." The diary also recorded that the Tang court instructed Ennin and seven other monks to wait "until the Japanese credentials *(benguo biaozhang)* had arrived" at the court before they left for the Guoqing Temple at Taizhou to study.[146] Kujō no Kanezane (1147–1207) wrote in his diary that

Kiyowara no Yorinari (1122?–1189), a Confucian scholar holding the title "Doctor of the Classics" (Myōkyō Hakase), once said, "Referring to the emperor of that country [Tang China] as the Son of Heaven, [the Japanese] court also sent official documents [to Tang China]."[147] In both diaries, the "Council of State document," the "Japanese credentials," and the "official documents" clearly refer to Japanese state letters.[148]

The Tang court would never have received any of the sixteen Japanese ambassadors in the capital had they not produced proper official documents. His state letter along with his insignia, national offerings, and special gifts were the four authenticating objects that established a Japanese ambassador's identity. Only when he presented a state letter that specified his task would the Tang court accept him as the genuine and legitimate representative of Japan and grant him a court audience.[149]

The Japanese court acted in the same manner. It required all foreign ambassadors, those from Silla in particular, to submit a state letter. In 752, the court informed a Silla ambassador that a mere oral explanation of his visit was insufficient and inappropriate.[150] The same message also reached Silla in 779 and 780.[151] The court would waive the requirement for a state letter only when the Silla king came to Japan in person. It deemed a foreign ambassador as having violated the "protocol set for barbarian countries" (banrei) if he failed to produce a state letter. The court treated Jin Lansun, a Silla ambassador sent to Japan in 780 without a state letter, as a "casual messenger" (keishi), denied him a court visit,[152] and sent him home directly from the port of entry.

As a matter of fact, several Japanese state letters reached the Tang court. One was a memorial that wished the Tang emperor good health (tong qiju) in 648.[153] Also, a Japanese ambassador congratulated the Tang emperor on his military conquest of Koguryŏ in 670.[154] The ambassador could not have fulfilled this duty without a state letter. And, on numerous occasions, Japanese ambassadors were described as having come "to present a memorial and to offer up local products to the Son of Heaven."[155]

Not only did they send state letters to Tang China, the Japanese officials were also deeply concerned about the wording of those letters. They discussed at great length the appropriate way to open a letter.[156] If they had decided to stop using state letters, they would certainly not have bothered themselves with such an issue.[157] Japan simply could not have sent a messenger to Tang China without entrusting him with a written message.

Reconstructing a Japanese State Letter to Tang China

By submitting a state letter to the Tang court, a Japanese ambassador took the first crucial step in activating Japan's official relations with China. But he would have the chance to fulfill his task only after the court had accepted his letter. To ensure Tang acceptance, Japanese state letters had to be written in such a way that they ostensibly satisfied a Tang emperor's ego as the "Son of Heaven," although actually maintaining Japan's independence from the Chinese world order. Unfortunately, none of those letters has survived in Chinese or Japanese sources. To understand how the Japanese managed to meet such a challenge, we need to reconstruct a Japanese state letter to Tang China. The reconstruction must be based on clues gathered from Japanese court documents, relevant Chinese records, and the diplomatic correspondence between Japan and other East Asian countries.

The Japanese court employed the terminology "decree to extend regards" *(irō shōsho)* and "decree to a barbarian ambassador" *(tai banshi shō)* to convey messages from the emperor to a foreign ruler or his ambassador. The court furthermore classified the occasions on which these two documents were used as major state affairs.[158]

Palace secretaries *(naiki)* at the Ministry of Central Affairs (Nakatsukasashō) drafted decrees.[159] The emperor read them, added the date, the month, and the year, and returned them to the ministry. Using the formal script, officials at the ministry copied a draft decree to a piece of yellow paper.[160] After the minister, the vice-minister, and the associate ministers had affixed their signatures, this fair copy of the decree was forwarded to the State Council (Daijōkan) for the chancellor *(daijō daijin)* to sign. The decree was ready for promulgation when the senior councillor *(dainagon)* had reported it to and received approval from the emperor.[161] It was then stamped using an imperial seal,[162] enclosed into a letter case, and sealed with wax.[163] A special representative of the emperor, accompanied by a palace secretary, delivered the decree to a foreign ambassador at the guest house.[164]

Although both were written messages from the emperor, a "decree to extend regards" and a "decree to a barbarian ambassador" differed in the opening sentence and in the way they were delivered.

Depending on the occasion, a "decree to a barbarian ambassador" began with one of five opening sentences. The sentence would read, "The imperial decree of the heavenly Japanese emperor, the incarnation of God who rules Japan," if the decree handled a matter of great importance.[165] But the term "Japanese" would disappear from the opening sentence if the decree dealt with a matter of secondary importance. And the court used a "decree to a barbarian ambassador" when issuing orders to both visiting foreign ambassadors and its own diplomats.[166]

A courtier delivered a "decree to a barbarian ambassador" by proclaiming, "The emperor decreed, saying *(iwaku)* . . ."[167] The word "saying" indicates that he only announced the decree but did not hand it over to the recipient.[168]

In contrast, a "decree to extend regards" was entrusted to the recipient to bring home.[169] If he came from a "greater barbarian country," the decree began with a simple but dignified sentence, "The Heavenly Emperor respectfully greets so and so." But the decree would omit the adverb "respectfully" if the recipient was from a "lesser barbarian country."[170]

Japanese state letters for Silla, Koguryŏ, and Parhae opened with the same sentence, "The Heavenly Emperor respectfully greets the king of such and such a country."[171] Identical with the opening sentence of both the "decree to extend regards" and the Tang sample state letters dispatched to Nanzhao and the Uighurs, this sentence should be the documentary base for reconstructing the opening line of a Japanese state letter to Tang China.

Nishijima Sadao, however, disagrees. He bases his study on the "decree to a barbarian ambassador" and suggests that the reconstructed opening line should read, "Zhu ming le mei yu de, the incarnation of God who rules Japan, with respect, begs to inform the Emperor of the Great Tang" *(Mingshen yuyu Riben Zhu ming le mei yu de jingbai Da Tang huangdi).*[172]

This approach is problematic. A "decree to a barbarian ambassador" was for oral announcements only, not for a foreign ambassador to bring home. Moreover, the reconstructed opening line should not have been based on that of a "decree to a barbarian ambassador," since the Japanese court had always considered the wording of its letter to China a special case.[173]

More specifically, the Tang court would take issue with the use of *mingshen* and *yuyu* in the opening line that Nishijima reconstructed.

Pronounced *akitsukami* in Japanese, *mingshen* means "the incarnation of God" and is an exclusive title for the Japanese sovereign.[174] But the term has a much broader and very different meaning in the Chinese context: it is a metaphor for the Supreme Deity, who created and governed the universe, and was superior to any secular ruler.[175] Not a title for any particular Chinese emperor, *mingshen* never appeared even in the posthumous title of any Tang emperor.[176] Had a Japanese state letter used *mingshen*, the Tang courtiers would certainly have been amazed, thinking that the letter had compared the Japanese ruler to the Supreme Deity, even though this is not at all what *akitsukami* means in Japanese.

The term *yuyu*, pronounced *ame no shita shirasu* in Japanese, would also cause controversy. *Ame* in the Japanese legends is a place in the heavens for Izanagi and Izanami, the couple who created Japan; *ame no shita* refers to "the place under the plain of the high sky," which is a metaphor for the Japanese archipelagos;[177] and the whole expression means "to rule Japan."[178]

But in Chinese *yuyu* denotes a Chinese emperor's control over his empire as well as the barbarian countries by moral virtue.[179] The phrase emphasizes the supreme position of the Son of Heaven over all his subjects, Chinese and foreign.[180] If a Japanese letter used *mingshen yuyu* to describe a Japanese ruler, Tang courtiers would have taken the phrase to mean "the king of Japan, the incarnation of God who rules the whole world"[181] and would have considered it a challenge to the suzerainty of the Tang emperor.

The title "Tianhuang" (Heavenly Emperor) would be the most problematic phraseology should a Japanese state letter ever use it in its opening line.[182] The Chinese understood *huang* as the "pervasive shining virtue (of the Chinese emperor)."[183] They often used *huang* as the abbreviation for *huangdi* (emperor), a titular honor that belonged exclusively to the Chinese sovereign. It was therefore a political taboo for anyone else to use this title that symbolized supreme power. In the early Tang, Li Gui, area commander in chief of Liangzhou (near present-day

Wuwei, Gansu province), sent Emperor Gaozu a letter in which he called himself "the emperor of the Great Liang." This action immediately invited a punitive expedition from the Tang court.[184]

The title "Heavenly Emperor" was in fact a Chinese, not a Japanese, invention. It started as a reference to one of the three legendary Chinese kings.[185] Han dynasty writers were the first to apply the title to a living ruler.[186] The title gained greater political significance during the Tang. In 674, "Heavenly Emperor" became the designated title for Gaozong (r. 650–683) and "Heavenly Empress" (Tianhou) for Wu Zetian (r. 685–704).[187] After the death of Emperor Gaozong in 683, "Heavenly Emperor" became a segment in his posthumous title and later, in 749 and 754, in his revised posthumous title.[188] From the time of these two Tang rulers, "Heavenly Emperor" also appeared widely in handwritten copies of Buddhist scriptures and in inscriptions on images of the Buddha.[189]

Silla was the first East Asian country to use "Heavenly Emperor" in domestic politics as well. The title appeared around 694 in the inscription on a stone tablet erected in memory of Jin Renwen, the second son of the king of Silla. The Koreans probably also informed the Japanese court of the use of this title in Tang China.[190] The Japanese should also have learned firsthand that "Heavenly Emperor" was the title used for Emperor Gaozong by the early eighth century, when Awada no Ason Mahito, the eighth Japanese ambassador dispatched to China, returned home in 704.[191] Therefore, Japanese state letters, at least those sent to China after 704, were unlikely to use the Chinese-style title "Tianhuang" when addressing the Japanese sovereign.

I do not suggest that Japanese courtiers willingly sacrificed the dignity of their ruler every time they wrote to the Tang court. They did not drop his rightful title of Heavenly Emperor for the sake of ensuring Tang acceptance of their state letters. They worked out a way to maintain the dignity of their master and to feed the sinocentric arrogance of the Tang emperor in the same letter: replacing the Chinese-style title "Tianhuang" with six Chinese characters, *zhu ming le mei yu de,* which were phonetic marks for *sumeramikoto,* the Japanese equivalent of "Heavenly Emperor."

Using Chinese characters to transliterate the title of a Japanese ruler in diplomatic communication with China had originated much earlier, in 600, when *abei jimi* appeared as the title for the female Wo ruler in her letter to Sui China. In the early eighth century, Japanese codified law finalized this practice, making it a routine for Japanese courtiers to follow when drafting official documents to be used in both domestic and foreign affairs.

According to the codified law, there were seven Chinese-style titles for the Japanese emperor, and their use depended on the occasion. An imperial decree should use "Tianhuang" (Japanese: Tennō).[192] But if it was to be delivered orally, the decree must address the Japanese sovereign as *sumeramikoto*. Four groups of Chinese characters had been designated as transliterations for *sumeramikoto*. *Xu ming le mei yu de* was one of them.[193] The codified law thus allowed the Japanese officials flexibility when addressing their emperor in a state letter to Tang China. They substituted *xu ming le mei yu de*, the Chinese transliterations for *sumeramikoto*, for the Chinese-style title "Tianhuang." They could also use the other three groups of Chinese characters to avoid giving the Tang court the impression that all Japanese rulers had the same name.[194]

A letter by Emperor Xuanzong offers circumstantial evidence that Japanese courtiers had acted on this authorized flexibility. Sent to Japan in 735, this letter called the Japanese emperor *zhu ming le mei yu de*.[195] Except for the first one, the six Chinese characters were identical with *xu ming le mei yu de*. This could hardly be a coincidence, for Tang courtiers could not have picked up these words just by accident. Only one explanation is plausible: when drafting the letter, the Tang courtiers transcribed these words from the state letter presented to the court earlier in 733 by Tajihi no Mahito Hironari, the tenth Japanese ambassador sent to China.[196]

The reconstructed title for the Japanese emperor should therefore read "Riben Zhu ming le mei yu de." This title avoided the term *guowang* (king), the usual way a Chinese court addressed a foreign ruler,[197] and thus maintained the dignity of the Japanese emperor. Ironically, the title was also acceptable to the Tang officials, who took "Zhu ming le mei yu de" to be the personal name of the Japanese ruler and considered a Japanese state letter that mentioned this name as having satisfied the minimum Tang requirement for incoming foreign correspondence.[198]

A Japanese state letter sent to China in 608 also confirms the use of this reconstructed title. The title appears in a slightly different form, "Emperor of the East" (Dong Tianhuang).[199] At first glance, the two titles bear no resemblance to one another. But Dong Tianhuang turns out to be another version of Riben Zhu ming le mei yu de. This is the case because the Japanese pronunciation for Dong Tianhuang is Yamato no Sumeramikoto, and Yamato stands for Riben (Japan).[200]

The letter of 608 also provides a clue to the way the Tang emperor might have been addressed in the opening sentence of a reconstructed Japanese state letter. The first line of the letter reads: the Japanese emperor, "with respect, begs to inform the Xi Huangdi [Emperor of the West]." *Xi* reads *morokoshi* in Japanese.[201] A metaphor for China, *morokoshi* can be rendered "Da Tang" (Great Tang) in Chinese. Xi Huangdi is therefore an equivalent of *Da Tang Huangdi* (Emperor of the Great Tang). Thus, the reconstructed opening line of a Japanese state letter to Tang China would read: "Zhu ming le mei yu de of Japan, with respect, begs to inform the emperor of the Great Tang" *(Riben Zhu ming le mei yu de jingbai Da Tang huangdi)*.[202]

In addition to a major linguistic twist to the Japanese emperor's title in a "decree to extend regards," this reconstructed opening line also substituted "with respect, begs to inform" *(jingbai)* for "respectfully greet." The verb *bai* described an inferior providing information to his superior.[203] Modified by the adverbial phrase "with respect," the whole expression "with respect, begs to inform" constituted a proper tone of subservience.[204]

Components of a Japanese State Letter to Tang China

A Japanese state letter comprised seven components: (1) an opening sentence that used "greet," "respectfully greet," or "with respect, begs to inform," according to the addressee's status; (2) the main body; (3) a comment on the recent weather; (4) an acknowledgment of the incoming foreign state letter; (5) regards to the addressee; (6) an account of the sender's situation; and (7) ending words.[205]

Not every Japanese state letter had all seven components, and the components did not always appear in the same order. The Japanese state letter of 608 was, for example, ceremonial in nature. It omitted the main body and put component 4 in front of component 3.

Component 1: The Emperor of the East, with respect, begs to inform the Emperor of the West.

Component 4: Your Ambassador, Pei Shiqing, official entertainer of the Department of Foreign Receptions, and his suit, having arrived here, my long-harbored cares are dissolved.

Component 3: This last month of autumn is somewhat chilly.

Component 5: How is Your Majesty? We trust well.

Component 6: We are in our usual health. We now send the Dairei So Inkō, the Dairai Wonari, and others to you.

Component 7: This is respectfully presented but does not express all.[206]

In contrast, a Japanese state letter sent to Silla in 706 had a lengthy main body but dropped components 4 and 6.

Component 1: The Emperor respectfully informs the King of Silla.

Component 2: That we, completely lacking virtue, nevertheless have received an exalted destiny. We are ashamed that, without the abilities of the polisher with stones, yet we have been entrusted with the holding of the mirror. Till evening we forget to partake of food, our worries whether our acts have been good or bad gradually increasing; till deep in the night we do not sleep, the doubts about our acts still increasing. We fervently hope that our benevolence penetrates unto far-away realms. You, Sir, have been in your realm since generations, loving your subjects. Inspired by the greatest sincerity, for a long time your ships have been bringing tribute to our court. We pray that by making rock-like foundations you will bring about that beautiful sounds penetrate unto the shy doe's retreat, that by strengthening the castle a beautiful model be provided for the goose-pond, so that peace and happiness prevail (in the State), and honest and quiet customs (among the population).

Component 3: The cold season being at its severest,

Component 5: We wonder how you are nowadays.

Component 7: Now we have dispatched a special mission of our ambassador...to inform you of our intentions, [which are not fully expressed in this letter].[207]

Although similar in components, these two letters differ notably in the time of compilation—almost one century apart from each other.

This similarity raises the issue of whether the first letter was indeed written in 608, ten years before the founding of the Tang dynasty. If it was, the letter is then unsuitable as documentary evidence to be used in reconstructing a Japanese state letter to Tang China. But both internal and external evidence suggests that the letter in question was contemporary with the Tang dynasty.

The first piece of evidence for this is the title "Heavenly Emperor." This title could not have come into use as early as in 608, since it was not until Emperor Jitō's time (r. 687–696) that the title first appeared in the *Penal and Administrative Code (Asuka Kiyomihara Ryō)* issued in 689 by the court at Asuka.[208]

The seven-component format of the letter of 608 is also evidence against its authenticity as an early-seventh-century work. This format was borrowed from works by Wang Xizhi and Wang Xianzhi. Commonly known as the "Two Wangs" *(er Wang),* both were fourth-century Chinese scholars famous for calligraphy and letters of fixed components.[209] Some of their letters began with "Xizhi [or Xianzhi] respectfully greets *(jingwen)*" or simply with "greets" *(wen),* depending on the status of the addressee.[210] This was followed by a comment on the recent weather, an acknowledgment of the incoming letter, regards to the addressee, an account of the sender's own situation, and finally the ending words.[211] Those well-composed letters were to become part of the "etiquette for letter-writing" *(shuyi),* which provided model letters for contemporary Chinese to emulate.[212]

A comparison between the components in the Japanese state letter of 608 and those in the letters by the Two Wangs reveals striking similarities. They are so similar that it seems the former was modeled on the latter. But seventh-century Japanese officials could not have availed themselves of the works by the Two Wangs. They had to wait another century for Awada no Ason Mahito and Tajihi no Mahito Agatamori, who were dispatched to China in 701 and 716 respectively, to bring those works home.[213] It was no coincidence that during the same period, in 720, Japanese courtiers completed the *Chronicles of Japan,*[214] in which the Japanese state letter of 608 first appeared.

Moreover, China-Japan relations in the early seventh century also precluded the letter in question addressing the Japanese ruler as "Tianhuang." Merely one year previously, in 607, Emperor Yang had expressed displeasure at a Japanese state letter that used a similar title, "Tianzi" (Son of Heaven), for the Japanese ruler. He sent Pei Shiqing to make his displeasure known to his Japanese counterpart. In a conciliatory tone, the Japanese ruler explained to Pei: "We are an uncivilized people, living as we do at the far end of the waters, with no knowledge of civilization.... We beg that you will inform us regarding the new order of things in your great country."[215] Given the atmosphere of this court audience, would the Japanese courtiers deliberately offend the Sui emperor again by sending him a state letter in 608 that used "Tianhuang" as the title for their master?

The internal and external evidence thus seriously discredits the Japanese letter of 608 as a genuine work of the early seventh century. The letter was probably a work by the compilers of the *Chronicles of Japan,* who, having consulted the letters by the Two Wangs, fabricated it to boost the prestige of their ruler.[216]

But this eighth-century fabrication is also a treasure. It confirms the use of the state letter in Sui-Japan relations. It also offers useful clues to the opening line as well as the seven components in a Japanese state letter to Tang China.

The *Kundoku* Method: Modifying a Chinese Diplomatic Term by Reading It in Japanese

When they adopted literary Chinese as their written language, the Japanese adapted the language for their own use. They sometimes read a Chinese character using a distinctive Japanese pronunciation without revising its original meaning. But sometimes they assigned both a Japanese reading and a Japanese connotation to a Chinese character. These two Japanese ways of handling Chinese characters are known collectively as the *kundoku* method.

Originating in Korea,[217] the *kundoku* method was introduced to Japan in the early sixth century.[218] For a long time, the method was inconsistent, with monks and laymen reading Chinese characters in varied ways. Even among the monks, the reading of a Chinese Buddhist sutra could be different if they did not belong to the same sect.[219] The method moved gradually toward standardization in the early Heian period, when scholars from the Great Learning Bureau (Daigaku Ryō) employed similar ways to read Chinese characters in their lectures on Chinese classics and on the *Chronicles of Japan* that were delivered to court officials and candidates for government positions.[220]

The *kundoku* method that assigned both Japanese meaning and reading to a Chinese character was a powerful linguistic tool. It subjected a Chinese word to Japanese interpretation and transformed it into a *kanji*, a word of distinctive "Japanese flavor" *(washū)* that was identical or near identical merely in the written form, but not in meaning, with its Chinese correlative.[221]

The invention of *kanji*, however, totally escaped Tang courtiers. Owing to limited knowledge of Japan, they assumed that the "eastern barbarians" in Korea and Japan used literary Chinese in the same way they did.[222] They were unaware that in their reading of a Japanese state letter as a document in literary Chinese, they had injected Chinese mentality into the letter and distorted its diplomatic signals. Nor did they have any idea that the *kundoku* method could modify or redefine the meaning of a Chinese diplomatic term.

Such modification and redefinition was inevitable. The Japanese found that some Chinese words were permeated with nuances too peculiar to Chinese culture to be used for the adequate expression of Japanese thoughts. Ō no Yasumaro (?–723), author of the *Records of Ancient Matters,* once wrote about the frustration of trying to render intrinsically Japanese ideas in Chinese: "In high antiquity both speech and thought were so simple that it would be difficult to arrange phrases and compose periods in the characters. To relate everything in an ideographic transcription [read Chinese characters] would entail an inadequate expression of the meanings; to write altogether according to the phonetic method [read *man'yōgana*] would make the story of events unduly lengthy."[223] Compilers of the *Chronicles of Japan* faced the same dilemma: Chinese words often brought about associations with Chinese idioms and Confucian terminology rather than indigenous Japanese way of thinking.[224]

The invention of *kanji* solved the problem, but it also introduced linguistic differences between a *kanji* character and its Chinese correlative. To develop a proper awareness of those differences, we need to study the Japanese reading of a *kanji* term, since it offers clues to a term's meaning in the Japanese context.

Regrettably, information on pronunciations of many *kanji* that are contemporary with the Nara and Heian periods has been insufficient. Although fragmentary sixth-century records on the sounds of a few *kanji* exist, the earliest surviving text to which the *kundoku* method was systematically applied dates as late as the Enryaku period (782–806).[225] As for the *Chronicles of Japan,* the main source materials for the present study, the earliest available edition that bears the old markings and the Japanese syllables is the Iwazaki Bunko edition compiled during Emperor Ichijō's time (r. 987–1011).[226] No record shows the pronunciations of *kanji* in earlier periods. Consequently, a time gap exists between my discussion of a *kanji*'s meaning contemporary with the Nara and Heian periods and the source materials that I use to support the discussion. But this gap does not totally discredit the effort to unveil the meaning of a *kanji* term by studying its pronunciation. Admittedly, the readings for some *kanji* changed over time. But those for the main body of Japanese words have remained relatively stable. There are grounds to believe that the *kanji* pronunciations preserved in the Iwazaki Bunko edition of the *Chronicles of Japan* are tied in many ways to those in the Nara and Heian periods.[227]

Dilution and Concentration Effects

When applied to a Chinese word, the *kundoku* method sometimes results in a dilution of the word's original meaning. The effect of this dilution weakens or cancels the honorific or the sinocentric connotation of a Chinese word. For example, Da Tang (Great Tang) was a laudatory Chinese term, which resonated with Chinese pride toward their homeland.[228] When it appeared in a Japanese state letter, Tang officials assumed that the term praised a Tang emperor's far-reaching moral virtue, recognized his suzerainty, and acknowledged Japan's political deference to China.

This was, however, a misconception. The Japanese employed Da Tang merely as a geographic term and read it *morokoshi*.[229] Coined in the early Heian period (794–1185), *morokoshi* referred to present-day Zhejiang, Fujian, and Guangdong provinces in southern China as well as to northern Vietnam. This was the region where the Japanese missions to Tang China landed, and the mission members purchased various foreign goods *(moro)* and brought *(koshi)* them home.[230] Later, *morokoshi* became a metaphor for the whole of China.[231] *Morokoshi* was also the reading for several other geographic terms related to China or Korea: "the West" *(sei)*,[232] "the Western Land" *(seido)*,[233] "the Western Sea" *(seikai)*,[234] and "Kan" (Chinese: Han).[235] None of these terms conveyed admiration for the Middle Kingdom.

Apparently, Da Tang was used in state letters to China to satisfy the ego of a Tang emperor, since the term seldom appeared in articles and poems for domestic readers. In those writings, China emerged as "the State of Tang" (Karakuni)[236] or "a foreign land" *(ihō)*.[237] Both terms carried an obvious tone of indifference.[238]

Tang officials would surely also have been surprised had they learned that one of their value-laden diplomatic terms, *daguo* (greater country), was read as *morokoshi* in Japanese.[239] In the Chinese world, the only "greater country" was China;[240] its neighbors were "insignificant countries" *(weiguo)*.[241] But *morokoshi* diluted *daguo* from a metaphor for Tang supremacy to a mere geographic term for China.

The meaning of another value-laden term, *fanguo* (fence country), was similarly diluted when it was pronounced *tonari no kuni* in Japanese. In the dichotomous Chinese world order, a "fence country" had formal sovereign-vassal relations with China, whereas a "neighboring country" *(linguo)* was China's peer.[242] In reality, however, a large number of countries fell into neither of the two categories. They were too far away from China to have regular official contact with the Tang court. And when their ambassadors occasionally reached the Middle Kingdom, they offered no political submission to the Son of Heaven. Nevertheless, the Tang court regarded these countries also as "neighbors" *(lin)*, but only in a geographic sense.[243] Japan was one of them.[244]

In the mind of many Tang writers, however, the Japanese ruler had always been an "outer subject of China." In a poem presented to Abe no Nakamaro on his return to Japan in 754, Bao Ji wrote:

> Although a super genius, you were born in a lesser country;
> The Eastern Sea is the western neighbor [of Japan].
> Through multi-interpretation, you came as the ambassador of
>   the ruler of a vassal state;
> For a thousand years to come, you will remain the subject of our
>   sage emperor.[245]

Bao vividly revealed his feelings toward Japan by using such words as "a lesser country" *(xiaguo)* and "the ruler of a vassal state" *(fanjun)*.

Other Tang writers such as Zhu Qiancheng, Zheng Ren, Hongjian, and Wang Wei shared these feelings. In poems presented to Kūkai, they described his trip to China as "coming to China in response to the Confucian teachings" or "paying tribute to the Tang court."[246] Wang Wei even bluntly called the Japanese emperor "an outer subject" of China.[247]

Of course, the poetic descriptions of Japan and its ruler by Tang scholars did not mean that Japan had ever officially accepted "fence country" status in relations with Tang China.[248] But on several occasions, the Japanese themselves also used *fan* (Japanese: *ban*) as a metaphor for Japan. For example, Sugawara no Kiyotomo, the administrative officer of the sixteenth Japanese mission to China in 805, used "eastern fence country" *(tōban)* as a metaphor for Japan in his poem to Wang Guofu, a Chinese imperial messenger:

> I am a guest from an eastern barbarian country;
> Cherishing a deep feeling [for the benevolence of the Chinese
>   emperor], I came to the holy Tang.
> About to return, I have not fully expressed my gratitude [toward
>   the Son of Heaven];
> Tears of parting wet my robe.[249]

In the meantime, Ennin addressed himself as an "ordinary monk from an outer fence country *(gaiban)*" when requesting permission from the Tang court to travel to Mt. Tiantai.[250] And the *Chronicles of Japan* used "visitors from various barbarian countries *(shōban)*" to describe the participants of a party held in 659 on the winter solstice. Among them, there were Japanese diplomats.[251] Did the term *ban* in those accounts imply Japan's vassal status to China?

Unlike its Chinese correlative *fan* (a fence country), *ban* was a geographic term without a definite political implication.[252] This unique usage resulted from Japan's inability to establish substantive sovereign-vassal ties with East Asian countries. Although Japanese codified law defined Koguryŏ, Paekche, and Silla as tribute-paying "outer fence countries" *(gaiban)*,[253] in reality none of them was "a fence country" to Japan. The Japanese court was unable to impose a notion of Japanese centrality on those countries, except when receiving their ambassadors. On this sole occasion, over which it had complete control, the court called a foreign delegation a "tribute-paying" mission and its members, "barbarians" *(banjin)*.[254] Japanese courtiers also composed poems that portrayed the ambassadors from Silla and Parhae as "subjects of bar-barian countries" and "tributary ambassadors."[255] But on other occasions, all countries, including China, were "neighboring countries" *(rinkoku)* to Japan. The court did not distinguish a "fence country" from a "neighboring country." And Japanese courtiers read both terms as *tonari no kuni,* effectively erasing the fundamental political difference between the two terms in Chinese diplomatic language.[256]

The Japanese use of "fence country" *(ban)* explains why neither Kiyotomo nor Ennin hesitated to call his homeland an "eastern fence country."[257] Similarly, China sometimes also appears in the Japanese sources as a "fence country" *(bankoku),* "a remote fence country" *(enban),* or "a country in the remote region" *(zeiiki).*[258] To ensure that readers of the *Chronicles of Japan* did not misunderstand the term *shōban,* traditional Japanese scholars assigned *kuniguni,* which means "several countries, as its reading."[259]

The most fascinating dilution effect occurred in the use of two titles of the utmost importance in Chinese politics—Son of Heaven *(tianzi)* and emperor *(huangdi).* When writing to the throne, Chinese courtiers and "outer subjects" had to use these titles,[260] which signified the role of a Tang sovereign as the sole ruler of the universe who implemented the mandate of Heaven, whose shining virtue reached every corner of the world.[261] But this posed a problem to traditional Japanese historians, since codified law stipulated that they must also use the same two titles to address their own master.[262] How did they handle the thorny issue of having to mention the two sovereigns simultaneously in their work? They addressed both of them as Son of Heaven *(tenshi),*[263] making them peers to one another.

Carrying the game of words one step further, they even downgraded a Tang sovereign by assigning *kimi* as the reading for his title, *huangdi* (emperor).[264] Originally a reference to the royal family members living outside the capital,[265] *kimi* was a less prestigious title than *ōkimi,* which was reserved for the Japanese ruler.[266] When used as the reading for *huangdi, kimi* canceled the China-centered connotation of the Chinese title. In the meantime, Japanese scholars did not bother to use an honorific title for the Tang emperor in documents for domestic use. He was merely "the ruler of the Tang" (Tōō).[267]

Status-sensitive Chinese verbs suffered the dilution effect as well. For example, "to pay tribute" *(chaogong)* and "to visit" *(pin)* had long been linguistic tools of the Chinese court to indicate the different natures of its relations with its neighbors. Both came into use during the Western Zhou dynasty (eleventh century B.C.–771 B.C.). "To pay tribute" implied a formal monarch-subject relationship in which Chinese princes regularly paid a court visit to the Zhou king *(chao)* to offer local products *(gong)* as an action betokening the fulfillment of their obligations.[268] This term also described a call on the Chinese court by a foreign ruler who had accepted Chinese titles and become an "outer subject" to the Chinese Son of Heaven. In contrast, "to visit" depicted intercourse between Chinese princes who had no monarch-subject relations with one another.[269]

When the authority of the Zhou court declined and regional Chinese states often waged wars for hegemony during the Spring and Autumn period (770–476 B.C.), the meaning of the two verbs also evolved with the changed situation. A "lesser state" now paid tribute to a "greater state." But the most frequently conducted diplomatic activity of the time was the visit by an ambassador to the court of a peer state.[270] "To pay tribute" and "to visit" thus portrayed bilateral relations of totally different natures.

The Japanese usage of these two verbs also underlined their fundamental difference in meaning. "Paying tribute," an annotation to the codified law explains, "means a court visit by a foreign ruler; 'visiting' refers to sending a minister on a friendly mission."[271] In Japanese primary sources, a Japanese ambassador did not "pay tribute" to the Tang court. Instead, he "visited" *(toburafu)* China.[272] And when the Chinese verb *chaogong* was occasionally employed to describe a Japanese diplomat's visit to China, the reading assigned to the verb was *kayō*,[273] which means to "reach" China.

The *kundoku* method could also have a concentrating effect on a Chinese word. This effect was achieved by reading a Chinese word in Japanese, thereby revising its original meaning and converting it to an honorific. Discussions among Japanese scholars who delivered lectures on the *Chronicles of Japan* to court officials show how they used the *kundoku* method to achieve this concentrating effect on a Chinese verb. The discussions centered on the proper way of reading the Chinese verb *jie ju* (to live separately), which appeared in the Sui state letter to Japan in 608: "Now we learn that Your Majesty [the Japanese emperor], living separately beyond the sea, bestows the blessing of peace on your

subject."[274] A doctor suggested: "We may follow the word's Chinese meaning and read it *yoriite*.[275] But all words concerning the Heavenly Emperor
must be tabooed, even when they appear in a letter from the Chinese
Son of Heaven. How about reading the word *mashimashite*?"[276]

A gerund, *mashimashite* is a Japanese honorific that means "to live."[277]
This honorific concentrated the meaning of the Chinese verb *ju* and
solved the problem of the Chinese verb's not showing due respect to the
Japanese emperor.

The *kundoku* method enabled Japanese officials to write state letters
that conformed to Chinese verbal requirements for foreign correspondence while protecting the dignity of their master. Subjecting the
wording of their letter to Japanese interpretation, they transformed
diplomatic correspondence into a means of deliberately causing misunderstanding on the part of the Chinese. And this was exactly the function that the Japanese court desired its state letter to perform: to open
the channel of official contact with China in order to bring about substantive economic and cultural benefits to Japan while offering no real
political submission to the Tang emperor.

Paradoxically, accepting such a Japanese state letter also benefited the
Tang court, albeit in a very different way. To the court, the practice was
in line with its "loose rein" policy toward countries insignificant in the
Chinese world: stay in touch but refrain from full-scale sovereign-vassal
relations with them in order to avoid the burden of fulfilling the obligations expected of a suzerain state. Moreover, a foreign state letter, no
matter whether it actually or only ostensibly complied with the Chinese
verbal requirements, was a symbolic acknowledgment of China's centrality. Accepting such a letter projected the image of China as the
suzerain. The real message in the letter was of secondary importance.

Both Japan and China thus perceived benefits in presenting and
accepting state letters in a fixed format. The sophisticated and resource-
ful Japanese courtiers never intended their state letter to announce
Japan's political independence. Neither did they use it to fight for
"equal footing" with Tang China nor did they cease using it to avoid possible controversy over its wording. Rather, they invented the *kundoku*
method to handle the wording of their diplomatic correspondence to
China.

The way in which China and Japan conducted diplomatic communication is a reminder that their bilateral relations were sovereign-vassal

only in appearance, not in substance. The complex motives of the two countries in establishing their official relations and their sophisticated ways of maintaining them are clearly beyond the explanatory capacity of both the Chinese "investiture system" and the Japanese theory of "equality." Only the concept of reciprocity is equal to the task.

8 Information Gathering

Gathering information was a crucial task for a Japanese ambassador dispatched to China. For centuries, Japan's overseas intelligence work focused on volatile situations in Korea and on China's intention toward the region. An active player in Korea, Japan maintained a foothold in Mimana, had a close ally in Paekche, and considered southern Korea its sphere of influence. Furthermore, China and Korea were sources for Confucian learning, Chinese political institutions, and the advanced technology that Japan needed for nation building. Japan's intelligence work with regard to its East Asian neighbors thus comprised gathering political and military intelligence, on the one hand, and information on cultural and technological developments, on the other.

The Changing Focus of Japan's Intelligence Work

The relative importance of these two aspects of Japan's intelligence activities changed in the 660s, when competing Chinese and Japanese interests in Korea brought the two countries to military confrontation. Japan tried to maintain its influence over southern Korea, but China saw this attempt as a menace to its effort to control the Korean peninsula. This conflict of interest intensified after a joint force of Tang and Silla defeated Paekche, and Paekche loyalists appealed to Japan for help to restore their kingdom. Japan responded to the request in 663 by sending a fleet to Korea, where it clashed with the Tang forces at the Hakusonkō River and was completely destroyed.[1]

Defeat at the Hakusonkō River prompted Japan to revise its Korea policy from one of direct involvement to one of noninterference. In the meantime, Silla forsook its alliance with China and waged a prolonged military campaign against the Tang occupying forces in order to establish its own rule in Korea. Eventually, in 676, China decided to relocate the seat of its protectorate in Korea from Pyongyang back to southern Manchuria. The Tang court had lost its dominance over Korea and never regained control of the region.

The new power relationship in Northeast Asia removed Korea as a source of tension between China and Japan. It also caused a reorientation of Japan's intelligence activities. The Japanese court remained keenly interested in developments in China, but this interest was no longer the product of a concern over possible Chinese military operations in Korea. Instead the court now needed the information so as to time the dispatch of its ambassadors to China. It was considered desirable for its ambassadors to arrive in the Middle Kingdom during a time of peace and prosperity so as to better perform the task of transplanting Chinese cultural perceptions and concepts to Japan.

Information on China, though of crucial importance to Japan, had always been difficult to obtain because of the geographic isolation of Japan from the Asian continent. Although a Chinese metaphor describes China and Japan as "two neighboring countries separated by only a strip of water *(yi yidai shui),*"[2] the two countries are in fact divided by the Sea of Japan, the Yellow Sea, and the East China Sea. These formidable natural barriers hindered the flow of information. Consequently, the Japanese court and its diplomats were often ill informed of the situation in China. Awada no Ason Mahito was a diplomat who suffered such a lack of information.

Mahito arrived in China in 701 unaware that Wu Zetian (r. 684–705) had become the first female ruler of China by establishing the Zhou dynasty in 684. When a local official informed him that he had come ashore at Yancheng county, Chuzhou prefecture (present-day Huaian, Jiangsu province), the Great Zhou, Mahito was apparently puzzled. "Great Zhou?" asked he. "Formerly this country was called Great Tang. Why is it now called Great Zhou?" His ignorance must have startled the Chinese official, who could hardly believe that an ambassador did not even know the proper name of his host country. "In the second year of the Yongchun reign period [682]," the official patiently explained, "the emperor died. The empress dowager succeeded him...and called the country Great Zhou."[3]

When the news of the new Chinese dynasty reached Japan, the courtiers must have been terribly embarrassed by their lack of current information about China, as they improved their information gathering procedures and included in their codified law a clause stating that "news of the frontier," along with information on military campaigns, surprise attacks, bandits, and rescues, was to be treated as an "urgent military matter" and something that must be reported promptly to the court.[4]

Information Gathering:
The Indirect and Direct Means

To obtain information on China, the Japanese court resorted to both indirect and direct means. Dispatching ambassadors to Parhae, which bordered China in Manchuria, was an indirect means.

Japanese ambassadors returning from Parhae and other East Asian countries were supposed to include "news on Tang" (*Tang xiaoxi*) in their reports to the court.[5] In 758, for example, a Japanese ambassador returning from Parhae used 434 words—an extensive amount—in his report to describe the An Lushan rebellion of 755, an incident that had badly shaken the Tang empire and marked the beginning of its decline. An Lushan, the military commissioner of Fanyang (present-day Zhuo-xian, Hebei province) rebelled and proclaimed himself emperor of the Great Yan. He then marched a crack troop of two hundred thousand soldiers south to Luoyang, where he established the offices of his own government. The Tang emperor, Xuanzong, responded by ordering Geshu Han to lead a force of three hundred thousand soldiers to defend the Tong Garrison and Feng Changqing to encircle Luoyang. The garrison, however, fell. Emperor Xuanzong abdicated in Jiannan (present-day Chengdu, Sichuan province) in the sixth month of 756. One month later, Emperor Suzong ascended the Tang throne. In addition to this information, the Japanese ambassador's report portrayed the reactions to the incident by officials in Youzhou (present-day Beijing): some dispatched ambassadors to Parhae, asking for military support to suppress the rebellion, while others secretly communicated with An Lushan, hoping to take advantage of the incident to enlarge their own power. This report of a China in political turmoil concerned the Japanese court so deeply that the court instructed the Dazai Headquarters in northern Kyūshū to take precautionary measures against any eventuality.[6]

Ambassadors from Silla and Koguryŏ were another indirect source of information on China. In 763, a Koguryŏ ambassador informed his host of the death of Emperor Suzong and the ascendence of Daizong to the throne. He also reported that a widespread famine in China forced peo-

ple to resort to cannibalism for survival and that the unruly general Shi
Chaoyi, having occupied Dengzhou (present-day Dengxian, Henan
province) and Xiangyang (present-day Xiangyang, Hubei province),
had proclaimed himself Emperor Shengwu.[7] In 764, an ambassador
from Silla offered news of the whereabouts of a Japanese monk who had
been dispatched to China earlier.[8] And in 770, another ambassador
from Silla was rewarded by the Japanese court for having conveyed
"news on Tang" and for having brought over a letter from a visiting
Japanese ambassador in China.[9]

The most reliable way of acquiring information on China was to dispatch an ambassador to the Middle Kingdom. This direct means was,
however, both costly and dangerous. Furthermore, the Japanese court
could employ it only spasmodically. In their "news on Tang," Japanese
ambassadors described, among other things, successions to the throne.
"The current Son of Heaven [Emperor Daizong] used to be Prince of
Guangping," a report made in 778 reads. "His name is Di,[10] and he is
fifty-three years old. The crown prince is Prince of Yong, whose name is
Shi."[11] Another ambassador reported in 805 on the same matter in
greater detail: "The tabooed name for the current Son of Heaven is
Yong. He is the only son of the recently deceased emperor [Dezong].
Forty-five years of age, he has more than forty sons and daughters. The
crown prince is Chun, who is Prince of Guangling and is twenty-eight
years old. Mrs. Wang is the empress dowager, mother of the current
emperor, and wife of the deceased emperor."[12]

The complex power relationship between the court and some of the
independent-minded local magnates after the death of Emperor Dezong
also found entry into the report made in 805: Li Shigu, military commissioner of Ziqing (present-day Yidu, Shandong province), commanded a
force of over five hundred thousand soldiers. In the name of paying condolences to the late emperor, he led a troop of one hundred thousand
soldiers to attack Zhengzhou (present-day Zhengzhou, Henan province).
The situation was not brought under control until the neighboring prefectural authorities interfered and the court sent a high-ranking eunuch
to comfort Li.[13] Wu Shaocheng, military commissioner of Caizhou
(present-day Runan, Henan province), was another powerful local figure who had been seeking opportunities to enlarge his military forces
and augment his power.[14]

Even relations between Tang and Tibet, which bore no direct relevance to Japan, received attention from Japanese diplomats. The report of 805 described the intricate politics of dynastic marriage between the two countries and offered an acute observation of the situation in China: "Located northwest of Changan, Tibet has several times invaded China. The city of Changan is now merely five hundred *li* away from the Tibetan borders. Internally, the court distrusts the military commissioners; and externally, it is at enmity with Tibet. People in the capital are nervous and do not have a moment of peace."[15]

Everyone on a mission to China, diplomat, student, or monk, had the obligation to collect information on China and to report it to the Japanese court. While traveling in China from 838 to 848, the monk Ennin recorded in his diary a wide range of information, which he referred to as "news on Tang,"[16] the same term that Japanese ambassadors used in their reports to the court.

Collected in this diary of more than eighty thousand words are pieces of information on the jurisdiction of the military commissioner at Yangzhou, the size of the city, the distance between the city and Changan, the number of soldiers deployed in Yangzhou and in seven other prefectures under the control of the military commissioner, and the total number of circuits and prefectures in the Tang empire.[17]

Ennin's diary vividly describes Tang administrative practices: "In handling administrative matters, officials hold hearings twice a day, one in the morning, another in the evening. They wait for the drumbeats before entering the office and sitting down for the hearing. All visitors, official or private, must wait for this moment before they can see the officials."[18]

The diary also records the death of Emperor Wenzong and the empress dowager,[19] the palace intrigues that resulted in the mysterious death of the crown prince—the Prince of Yong—and the purge of his associates,[20] rice prices in Shandong province,[21] the military confrontation between Tang and the Uighurs,[22] and recent events in Silla and Parhae.[23]

Ennin admitted that he made conscious efforts to acquire the relevant information by talking to a registrar at the office of the army-supervising commissioner in Yangzhou.[24] This conduct by Ennin was incompatible with his stated purpose of "searching for the Buddhist law" in China. It is plausible that he gathered the information under instructions from the Japanese court.[25]

Siphoning Knowledge from China

Information comprises both news and knowledge. For Japanese diplomats sent to China, obtaining knowledge of Chinese culture was as
important a task as collecting news in the host country.[26] In 716, Tajihi
expressed the wish to study Chinese classics under a Tang scholar. His
request was quickly granted. During a ceremony held at the Court for
State Ceremonial, Tajihi presented a piece of wide cloth as a token of
the tuition fee to Zhao Xuanmo, thus formally becoming a student of
Zhao, who was an instructor from one of the four schools of the
Directorate of Education.[27]

The interest of Tajihi in the Chinese classics coincided with the Tang
policy of seeking to edify foreigners with Chinese culture. The court
sought to foster an interest among foreign diplomats in a proper understanding of the Chinese world order based on Confucian moral teachings. It hoped that these diplomats would bring their understanding
home and persuade their rulers to adopt a pro-China stance. In consequence of this wishful thinking, the court decreed in 715 that all foreign ambassadors be brought to the State University to observe how
Confucian ethical codes were being taught.[28] And in 752, Emperor
Xuanzong granted Fujiwara no Kiyokawa a special imperial favor: a tour
of the Confucian, Buddhist, and Daoist worship halls in the inner
palace that served members of the imperial family exclusively and were
in principle closed to outsiders.[29]

A diplomat's stay in China was often too short for him to pursue a
branch of Chinese learning systematically. The task of acquiring in-depth
knowledge of China therefore fell to Japanese students and monks, who
lived in China for an extended period of time and took Chinese masters
as their teachers. To avail more Japanese of the rare opportunity to study
in China, the Japanese court attached as members of its delegation to
Tang China not only students and monks, but also musicians,[30] translators, physicians, painters, and diviners.[31] Abe no Nakamaro (698–770)
and Kūkai (774–835) were two such members.

Born into an aristocratic family in Yamato (present-day Nara prefecture), Nakamaro had been a bright and diligent pupil since childhood.
At nineteen, he traveled to China as a student of the Japanese delegation of 716. At the Tang capital, Changan, Nakamaro, like hundreds of

other foreign students, received a stipend from the court and enrolled in the State University. He devoted the next ten years to the study of Chinese culture,[32] and he excelled in the civil service examination in 727. He became the first and the only Japanese to hold the "Presented Scholar" degree. Obtaining the degree was a considerable achievement, for the degree was granted only to a select few who exhibited an upright character, had mastered Confucian classics, and had demonstrated resourcefulness in handling policy issues. The degree also opened the door to promising court positions for its holders.

The first appointment for Nakamaro was editing clerk *(jiaoshu)* at the heir apparent's library. He conducted textual research on books and accompanied the heir as study mate. He had access to a wide range of books as well as the opportunity to associate himself with other scholar-officials. His talent soon became known to some literary giants of the time. Wang Wei, Li Bai, and Chu Guangxi presented poems to Nakamaro and became his friends.[33]

After a short period at the heir apparent's library, Nakamaro became Left Reminder (Zuo Shiyi). On recommendation of the metropolitan governor, he was promoted in 731 to Left Rectifier of Omissions (Zuo Buque).[34] Nakamaro was now a member of the inner circle at the court. He checked draft decrees and remonstrated with the emperor about deviations from traditions and laws in the emperor's conduct. His talent impressed Emperor Xuanzong, who granted him the Chinese name Chao Heng as a special imperial favor.

Although a rising star at the Tang court, Nakamaro yearned to return home to serve his native land. In the name of taking care of his aging parents, he memorialized the court in 734 for permission to leave China.[35] To his disappointment, the request was rejected. In frustration Nakamaro wrote a poem:

Admiring righteousness is merely an empty reputation.
 Offering loyalty prevents me from fulfilling filial piety.
The day of dedicating service to my country does not yet exist.
When will it be time to return home?[36]

Nakamaro had to wait eighteen years before the time eventually came in 752. That year, a Japanese delegation arrived in China, and Nakamaro was put in charge of receiving the diplomats. He soon learned that Kibi no Makibi, who had traveled with him to Tang as a fellow student in 716, was now vice-ambassador of the delegation. The successful career of Makibi must have motivated Nakamaro to ask the court once again that he be allowed to leave China. Knowing that Nakamaro had been away from home for thirty-six years, the sympathetic Emperor Xuanzong granted his request. As a token of appreciation for his long service to China, the emperor promoted Nakamaro to Director of the Palace Library (Mishu Jian), holding concurrently the title Chief Minister of the Court of the Imperial Regalia (Weiwei Qing). He also entrusted Nakamaro with the task of escorting the Japanese diplomats home.

Aboard the first ship with the ambassador, Nakamaro left China in the eleventh month of 753. The fleet, however, encountered a storm. Whereas the other three ships managed to sail back to Japan, the ship that Nakamaro boarded failed to return. Friends in both China and Japan soon learned about the incident. They assumed that Nakamaro had died in the storm.[37] Saddened by the news, Li Bai wrote a moving poem to mourn his Japanese friend.[38]

Nakamaro, in fact, survived the incident. Although his ship had been blown off course, it had not sunk. Drifting southwest, the ship eventually reached the Vietnamese coast. After much hardship, Nakamaro returned to Changan in the sixth month of 755. Exhausted and scared, he never attempted to sail home again. During the last fifteen years of his life, Nakamaro served Emperor Suzong as Left Cavalier Attendant-in-Ordinary (Zuo Sanqi Changshi) and then as protector-general of Annan (present-day Hanoi, Vietnam) in 761. In 766, during Emperor Daizong's reign, local tribes in present-day Yunnan province rebelled. As protector-general, Nakamaro led a force and pacified them.[39] Upon finishing his tenure at Annan, Nakamaro returned to the capital to receive the title Dynasty-Founding Duke of Beihai Prefecture.[40] He died in 770 at the advanced age of seventy-three, leaving behind him the unfulfilled dream of serving Japan with his formidable knowledge and administrative expertise. The Tang court honored Nakamaro by posthumously appointing him area commander in chief of Luzhou (in Shanxi province) and buried him in Changan.[41]

In 774, four years after the death of Nakamaro, a boy was born into the aristocratic Saeki family at Byōbugaura (present-day Zentsūji, Kagawa prefecture). Years later, he took the Buddhist vows to become Kūkai

(Sea of Void)[42] and followed in Nakamaro's footsteps by traveling to China. Unlike Nakamaro, however, Kūkai was able to return home, eventually becoming a Japanese cultural hero.[43]

Unfortunately, the life story of Kūkai has been obscured by legends and historical records compiled after his death.[44] We do not know much about his childhood,[45] except that he was the fifth child in his family and that he had an early exposure to Buddhism through his father, who was a Buddhist and who once sponsored the building of a local clan temple. In 788, at the tender age of fifteen, the boy left home for Nagaoka (located in the southwestern suburbs of Kyoto). There he studied Confucian classics and poetry under his maternal uncle Ato no Ōtari,[46] a man of erudition who had served Crown Prince Iyo as instructor of Confucian teachings during the reign of Emperor Kammu (r. 781–806). In 791, he enrolled in the State University and received extensive training in the Chinese classics.

Like most of his classmates in the university, Kūkai aspired to be a court official after graduation. His future career, however, became uncertain when his family was implicated in the murder of a prominent courtier, Fujiwara no Tanetsugu (737–785).[47] This setback of the Saeki clan in court politics must have prompted Kūkai to reconsider his career and to reorient his intellectual pursuits. He developed an interest in Esoteric Buddhism after the monk Gonzō, of the Iwabuchi temple in Kyoto, showed him a copy of a sutra. He was told that reciting the formula prescribed in the sutra one million times would enable him to memorize the texts and to understand the meaning of any scripture.[48] He eventually left the university in 793 to become a wandering hermit. "I climbed Mount Tairyū in Awa and meditated at Muroto Cape in Tosa," Kūkai vividly recalled years later. "The valley reverberated to the sound of my voice as I recited, and the planet Venus appeared in the sky."[49] Between travels to remote mountainous regions for self-cultivation, Kūkai engaged himself in a comparative study of Buddhism, Daoism, and Confucianism. In 797, he completed the *Indication of the Goals of the Tree Teachings (Sangō shiiki)*, in which he asserted the superiority of Buddhism over the other two schools of thought.[50] The next year, he underwent ordination at the Great Eastern Temple (Tōdaiji) in Nara.

The scholarly Kūkai soon realized that proper understanding of Esoteric Buddhism required a knowledge of Sanskrit and private instruction on the methods of meditation. He decided to seek advice from masters in China.[51]

The opportunity came in 804. Kūkai was chosen, probably on the recommendation of the monk Gonzō, to travel to China with a Japanese delegation. After several weeks at sea, he came ashore at the Chian Garrison, Changxi county (present-day Xiapu county, Fujian province), in the eighth month of 804. The Japanese delegation was, however, accorded a cold welcome by local officials, who had never received a delegation from Japan and were unsure of the proper way to handle the matter. To obtain much-needed help and permission to travel in China, Kūkai, on behalf of the ambassador, drafted a letter to the surveillance commissioner at Fuzhou.[52] In a separate letter to the same commissioner, he also expressed the wish to stay in China for twenty years to study Buddhism.[53] The two letters, written in elegant parallel prose, apparently impressed the commissioner, who made the necessary arrangements for the delegation to journey to the capital.[54] By the end of the year, Kūkai was in Changan.

In early 805, Kūkai received court permission to study in Changan and to stay at the Ximing Temple. What happened to Kūkai in the following months was a miracle. He met with Huiguo (746–805), patriarch of Esoteric Buddhism. "I have been waiting for you for a long time," the master told him. "Why did you come so late?" Kūkai was deeply touched by Huiguo's kindness. He did not immediately realize that the master had, on sight, chosen him as his successor. Kūkai thereafter received systematic instruction on Esoteric Buddhism: meditation on the pictorial representations of the immanence of the Great Sun Buddha (Mahāvairocana) in the universe (mandala), the ritual hand gestures and the body postures (*mudra*s), and the mystic phrases (*mantra*s), all of which were means to help a believer realize that he could attain Buddhahood in his very body. Kūkai also studied the two basic scriptures of Esoteric Buddhism: the *Diamond Element (Jingang jie)* and the *Womb Treasury (Taizang jie)*, as well as the Sanskrit formulas for the Womb Mandala, and more than one hundred other sutras.[55] Only a few months after his first meeting with Huiguo, Kūkai became an ordained master of Esoteric Buddhism in the early eighth month of 805. To further his knowledge of the Esoteric teachings, he studied Sanskrit and Sanskrit hymns. He also called on Masters Muniśrī and Prajñā from India and

Kashmir respectively. From Prajñā, he received the original Sanskrit versions as well as the Chinese translations of two sutras.[56]

Kūkai had a versatile mind and entertained broad interests in Chinese culture. While in China, he studied and acquired the works of such famous calligraphers as Wang Xizhi, Ouyang Xun, and Yan Zhenqing. He also learned the "flying white" *(feibai)*, a cursive style of calligraphy done with a dry brush, showing hollow lines.[57] Tang poet Hu Bochong compared him to Zhang Zhi, the Eastern Han dynasty "Sage of the Cursive Script." In a poem, Hu wrote of Kūkai:

Heaven has bestowed on my master many talents,
of which his cursive script is most unconventional and free.
Hard to come by,
Hard to come by![58]

Together with Emperor Saga (r. 809–823) and Tachibana no Hayanari,[59] Kūkai was later recognized as one of the three most celebrated calligraphers in Japan, whom their contemporaries fondly referred to as the "Three Brushes."[60] According to a Japanese legend, while in China, Kūkai had been invited by Emperor Shunzong (r. 805) to amend a piece of calligraphy written on a palace wall by Wang Xizhi, which had faded away over the years. He is said to have demonstrated the amazing ability to inscribe simultaneously five lines of words, by using one brush in his mouth, one in each of his hands, and one in each of his feet. And the repaired work is said to have been exactly the same as the original. For this ability, Kūkai received from the emperor the title "Monk of the Five Brushes."[61]

Kūkai was a gifted poet and parallel prose writer, whose literary attainments were the admiration of Tang officials, scholars, and monks. Wang Changling presented Kūkai with his work on poetry.[62] In the preface to his poem, Zhu Qiancheng called Kūkai a "sage" and marveled at his mastery of Sanskrit, calligraphy, the *Treasury of Analysis of the Law (Abhidharmakośa Sutra)*, and the Three Vehicles.[63] In the poem Zhu wrote, "His writings surpass those of all Confucian scholars."[64] Ma Zong, administrative aide at Quanzhou and a gifted scholar, once read a poem by Kūkai for a Chinese monk.[65] This poem was written in the "split and join" style *(lihe shi)*, which required the poet to split the first word of a sentence into two segments, each of which should stand as an individual character, and to use them as the first and last words in the following sentence. Kūkai's grasp of this difficult poetic style impressed Ma, who commented, "Among the native [Chinese], hardly anyone is as ingenious as you are."[66] Zheng Ren also called Kūkai a "rare talent." He predicted that "in the future, when the history of Buddhist monks is being compiled, there will be one more account of a sage [i.e., Kūkai]."[67]

Kūkai had intended to stay in China for twenty years. After only two years, however, he decided to curtail his stay in order to fulfill the wish of Huiguo, who wanted him to spread Esoteric Buddhism to Japan.

To prepare Kūkai for the task, Huiguo entrusted him with ritual implements and objects, including Buddhist relics and a Buddhist sculpture made of white sandalwood. Huiguo also arranged to have a number of mandalas printed and sutras transcribed. Shortly after the preparations were completed, in the last month of 805, Huiguo died.

Huiguo's death signaled to Kūkai that the time had come for him to leave China. He contacted a visiting Japanese ambassador and obtained court permission to return home. Before leaving Changan, he bid farewell to Yicao of Qinglong Temple:

Studying the same doctrine
Under one master [Huiguo],
You and I are friends.
See yonder white mists
Floating in the air
On the way back to the peaks.
This parting may be our last meeting in this life.
Not just in a dream.
But in our deep thought,
Let us meet again
Hereafter.[68]

Kūkai then headed for the port of departure. There, by permission of the military governor at Yuezhou (present-day Shaoxing, Zhejiang province), he acquired a wide range of books on Buddhism, Daoism, Confucianism, poetry, prose, stone inscriptions, music, divination, and medicine.[69] In the tenth month of 806, Kūkai was back in Japan.

"Watching the bamboo and observing the flowers, I think of spring in my country."[70] Kūkai wrote this sentence in China, using the bamboo and the flowers as metaphors for the accomplishments of Chinese high culture. Now back at home, he would play an active role in engendering a cultural spring in Japan.

Among Kūkai's contributions to Japan were the large number of books, sutras, and other precious cultural objects that he brought home. In a list of these items, Kūkai recorded 140 "newly translated sutras"; forty-two works written in Sanskrit; thirty-two works including commentaries and works on treaties and other matters; three Womb Mandalas; two Diamond Mandalas; portraits of Jingangzhi (Vajabodhi), Shanwuwei (Śubhākarasimha), Bukong, Huiguo, and Yixing; three Sanskrit manuscripts; and the ritual implements and objects that Huiguo had entrusted to him.[71] These items helped Kūkai establish the Shingon (True Word) sect of Esoteric Buddhism centered in Kyoto.[72]

Kūkai was a pioneer in education for common people. In 828 in Kyoto he opened the School of Arts and Sciences (Shugei Shuchi In)— the first private institution that admitted students irrespective of their family backgrounds and financial means—and offered a curriculum with a wide variety of subjects that included Buddhism, Confucianism, Daoism, law, logic, philosophy, grammar and composition, arts, mathematics, and medicine.[73]

For the educated Japanese, Kūkai compiled the *Secret Treasure House of the Mirrors of Poetry (Bunkyō hifu ron)* in 820.[74] A study of the Chinese poetics and prosody from the Six Dynasties to the Tang, this work helped Japanese improve their writing skills in classical Chinese.

Kūkai was also credited, albeit doubtfully, with the invention of the two Japanese *kana* syllabaries. Based on elements borrowed from Chinese characters,[75] the syllabaries enabled men and women to express themselves in writing in the vernacular, thus paving the way for Japanese literature to bloom during the Heian period.

Kūkai died in 835. To commemorate his contributions to Japan, the Japanese court granted him in 921 the posthumous title "Kōbō Daishi" (Grand Master for the Propagation of the Buddhist Law). Japanese today memorialize Master Kōbō as a mythical sage, still alive, who wanders in the mountains and renders help to the needy. The popularity of Master Kōbō among ordinary people is perhaps best implied by the Japanese proverb "Even Kōbō makes mistakes with his brush" *(Kōbō nimo fude no ayamari).*

Acquiring Books

A reservoir of knowledge, books provided access to Chinese culture. Books circulated in East Asia before the invention of woodblock printing technology toward the end of the Tang dynasty took the form of handwritten copies *(xieben)*.[76] Acquiring books of Chinese learning played a crucial part in the grand strategy of Japan to transform itself into a regional power.

Japan's need for Chinese books was apparent when examined in terms of the relative strength of the country vis-à-vis its East Asian neighbors. Owing to its geographic distance from China, Japan had been slower than Korean states in acquiring Chinese learning and technology. The result was an underdeveloped economy and a primitive political system based on a loose confederation of tribal principalities. This situation was incompatible with the ambitions of the third-century Yamato rulers with regard to Korea. They realized that they must first create a hierarchical political order at home, transform Japan into a centralized state, and elevate themselves to sovereign rulers before they could be players in affairs in southern Korea. In their efforts to achieve these goals, the Yamato rulers found Confucianism inspiring and useful. The Confucian ideal of a universe under the rule of a single ruler offered them both political wisdom and practical ways of governance. Obtaining books on Confucian learning and books on philology that would facilitate the mastery of the Chinese language thus became a task of both cultural and political significance.

KOREAN STATES AS SOURCES OF BOOKS

The principal channel by which Japan could obtain books was from Paekche, a state located conveniently in the southwest of the Korean peninsula that had maintained friendly relations with Japan. In Japanese legend, the *Confucian Analects (Lun yu)* and the *Thousand-Character Text (Qianzi wen)* were the first two books that a Paekche ambassador presented to the Wo ruler in 286.[77]

The *Confucian Analects,* in twenty chapters, was a collection of discussions on contemporary moral and social issues between Confucius and his disciples, both of whom contributed to the writing of the work. Having assumed its final form at the end of the Spring and Autumn period (770–476 B.C.), the work had become a classic for educated Chinese during the Western Han dynasty (206–8 B.C.), when Confucianism was established as the state orthodoxy.

The *Thousand-Character Text* was compiled by the fifth-century writer

Zhou Xingsi (470?–520). The circumstances under which the work was introduced to Japan remain dubious. The work in question certainly could not have been brought to Japan in 286, when it was not yet compiled. However, it is plausible that Wanikishi, the ambassador from Paekche, did bring some kind of character primer to Japan. Books of this nature introduced their readers to everyday characters for basic vocabulary, arranged in groups, and dealt with such topics as history, moral teachings, society, natural phenomena, and education. They were usually written in the style of a jingle, with the last word of each sentence rhyming.[78]

With the deepening of domestic political reforms on the Chinese model, the Yamato court needed and acquired more books dealing with Confucianism, philology, and other branches of Chinese learning. This was evident in the "Twelve-Cap Ranks" promulgated in 603. This new system used "virtue," "humanity," "decorum," "faith," "righteousness," and "knowledge" as the names for new court ranks. And the "Seventeen-Article Constitution" of 604 employed terminology from a wide variety of Chinese classics including the *Book of Historical Documents (Shang shu)*, the *Classic of Poetry (Shi jing)*, the *Book of Rites (Li ji)*, the *Chunqiu with Zuo Commentaries (Chunqiu Zuoshi zhuan)*, the *Confucian Analects*, the *Classic of Filial Piety (Xiao jing)*, the *Guanzi*, the *Hanfei zi*, the *Mozi*, and the *Laozi* to stress the importance of loyalty, harmony, dedication, and ability in government affairs.[79]

BOOKS ACQUIRED FROM CHINA

Buddhist sutras, which were first introduced to Japan in the sixth century,[80] were added to the list of books desired by the Japanese court in the seventh century, when the Yamato rulers used Buddhism to promote political unification. They identified themselves with the Buddha and portrayed the Buddha as occupying a plane higher than that of the native Japanese deities, thus elevating themselves above other clan chieftains. When they had achieved political unification, the Yamato rulers advocated Buddhism as a protecting force for the nation and at times looked to Buddhism for ideological support. Such was the historical context in which court nobles and powerful provincial families developed a strong attachment to Buddhism. They enthusiastically supported efforts to acquire Buddhist sutras from China.

A bibliography compiled by Enchin in 854. It includes 458 *juan* of Buddhist and other works that Enchin had collected in Fuzhou, Wenzhou, and Taizhou, China. (Reproduced from the catalog for *Documents Relating to Enchin (Enchin kankei bunsho),* a special exhibition of national treasures organized by the Nara National Museum, July 6 to August 1, 1982)

It was in 607 that a Japanese ambassador stepped onto Chinese soil and informed the Sui court that his master had dispatched him and several monks to China because "to the west of the ocean, a Bodhisattva of the Sovereign [i.e., the Sui emperor] reveres and promotes Buddhism."[81] This ambassador acquired a copy of the *Lotus Sutra (Fahua jing)* and became the first Japanese diplomat to obtain books in China. His acquisition was of symbolic importance: Japan had transformed itself from a passive receiver of limited Chinese cultural influence through Korean states to an active "shopper" who introduced works to Japan in a selective manner according to its own needs.[82]

The imported Buddhist works helped Prince Shōtoku complete his commentaries on the *Sutra of Queen Srīmārā (Shengman jing)*, the *Lotus Sutra,* and the *Vimalakīrti Sutra (Weimo jing)* in about 615. Admittedly, both the authorship and the time of completion of these commentaries require further research. They could well have been the outcome of a collective effort by the prince and the Korean monks under whom he studied.[83] There is, however, no doubt that the Buddhist works to which the prince referred in the commentaries were already available in Japan.

Buddhist sutras and works, referred to collectively as "inner works" *(neidian)* by Buddhists, added a new dimension to the spiritual life of the educated Japanese. These works were brought to Japan mainly by monks who traveled to China with Japanese delegations, as has been mentioned. Genbō was one of them. He stayed in China for almost twenty years before returning home in 735 with more than 5,000 *juan* of Buddhist works.[84] Other Japanese monks, such as the "Eight Masters" of the ninth century, were also eager to obtain Buddhist sutras in China. Altogether they brought back some 5,400 *juan* of Buddhist works.[85]

During the Tang dynasty, the Japanese court wanted Chinese books mainly to nourish native Japanese culture. Acquiring books and other cultural objects through official tributary arrangements or from the market was now the major task for Japanese ambassadors dispatched to China. They were rewarded according to the amount of such items that they managed to bring home. In 654, the court generously rewarded Kishi no Nagani with a higher rank, a family name, and two hundred households for his "having obtained numerous Chinese books and precious objects."[86] In 701, Awada no Ason Mahito was sent to China with the task of "obtaining books."[87] When Japanese diplomats in China received permission to shop at marketplaces, books were often at the top of their shopping list.[88] Tajihi no Mahito Agatamori was reported to have used all the grants from the Tang court to purchase books in 716.[89]

The Tang court, however, denied foreigners and its own people full access to the Chinese cultural heritage out of concern for geopolitics and internal security. Except for authorized persons, Tang codified law forbade possession or study of maps of the heavens; *The Six Strategies of the Great Duke; The Three Plans of the Yellow Stone Duke;* books dealing with the calendar, the sun, the moon, and the five stars; and books on methods of predicting good and evil. The court feared that unrestricted access to these books might avail plotters of information and methods necessary to organize insurrections against the government.[90] As a measure to control the circulation of books outside China, the court subjected foreign ambassadors' requests for books to official approval. While Chinese classics were relatively easy to acquire, access to certain historical, philosophical, and military works was carefully guarded to prevent China's hostile neighbors from using them to their own advantage.

In 686, Empress Wu rejected the request of a Silla ambassador for the *Book of Rites (Li ji)* and other works. Instead, she commissioned a work for Silla. This work of fifty *juan* included ceremonial and funeral rites, selected imperial edicts, and articles and poems on moral persuasion transcribed from an early Tang collectanea.[91]

In the viewpoint of some Tang officials, indiscriminate granting of books to foreigners exposed China to potential danger. Xue Deng, minister of justice, pointed out: "Should they be able to read our language, they would understand our laws and regulations, and the fundamental principles and practices that we use to govern China. Should they become literate in Chinese, they would learn from our successes and defeats, which have been fully recorded in our dynastic histories. Should they have access to geographic works, they would gain knowledge of our strategic places. With knowledge of China, they would be able to help their rulers work out strategic plans and military maneuvers against us, causing trouble for China."[92]

Xue's concern was typical of Tang officials, who believed that foreigners were hostile to China. Allowing them access to books was therefore a self-defeating practice. The same concern surfaced again in 730, when a Tibetan ambassador requested, in the name of a Tang princess married to the Tibetan ruler, the bestowal of the *Classic of Poetry*, the *Book of Rites*, the *Chunqiu with Zuo Commentaries (Zuo zhuan)*, and the *Selections of Refined Literature (Wen xuan)*. The court initially decided to grant his request and ordered the Palace Library to transcribe the books for him. However, Yu Xiulie (692–772), a proofreader of the library, disputed the decision. In his memorial to the throne, Yu urged the court to exercise vigilance in handling the ambassador's request. In his opinion, these books contained information on China's military strategies toward foreign countries. Allowing the Tibetans access to the books was therefore potentially disadvantageous to China. More specifically,

Yu pointed out that the *Book of Historical Documents* recorded the traditional Chinese way of war. *The Classic of Poetry* contained poetic descriptions of a grand Chinese expedition against the tribes in southern China, which revealed such Chinese military tactics as using carriages and maneuvering troops.[93] The "monthly instructions" *(yueling)* in the *Book of Rites* listed month by month the suitable activities, including military operations, for an emperor to perform to ensure that his actions were in harmony with nature and would achieve the desired goals.[94] The *Chunqiu with Zuo Commentaries* described the tactics that Chinese generals employed in maneuvering troops. To Yu, the bestowal of the last work on the Tibetans was particularly objectionable, since it treated the most volatile period in Chinese history, during which the legitimate Zhou king was losing control over his empire and the local warlords were resorting to despicable tricks against each other in attempts to establish themselves as the paramount leader in China. "If this book is granted to the Tibetans," Yu concluded, "it will definitely be a disaster to China."[95] He even wanted the court to deny the Tibetan ambassador access to general works on history and philosophy because they too contained discussions of military matters. To Yu, allowing "barbarians" access to Chinese books was as suicidal as sending soldiers to the camp of one's enemy or providing bandits with provisions.

Yu's memorial was referred to the Secretariat-Chancellery (Zhongshu Menxia) for discussion. While they could not rule out the possibility of "barbarians" learning dirty tricks from Chinese books, officials there emphasized that the same books also preached such values as loyalty, faith, and righteousness, which might reform the "barbarians" for the better. Emperor Xuanzong compromised. He bestowed Chinese classics on the Tibetan ambassador but rejected his request for other books.[96]

If the Tang court was selective in granting foreigners access to the Chinese cultural heritage, so was its Japanese counterpart in adopting this heritage. Interest of the Japanese court in all branches of Chinese learning did not lead to a policy of wholesale cultural importation from China. The court rejected "Confucianization," and the Japanese people resisted a pervasive intrusion of Confucianism into their way of life and values.[97] This mentality is best revealed in a ninth-century bibliographical work: *A Catalog of Books Currently Extant in Japan (Nihonkoku genzaisho mokuroku).*[98]

THE CATALOG OF BOOKS EXTANT
IN NINTH-CENTURY JAPAN

The catalog was compiled in about 891 on imperial order by Fuji-wara no Sukeyo (?–897).[99] It employs the traditional four-category classification of classics, history, philosophy, and collections of literary works, and contains bibliographical entries for more than 1,800 books in the imperial collection of the Japanese court.[100] These books, whose authors include both Chinese and Japanese, are further classified into forty subcategories, totaling more than 18,000 *juan*.[101]

This catalog was a testimony to the successful efforts of the Japanese in acquiring Chinese books. During a period of three centuries, they built an imperial library whose holdings of 18,000 *juan* equaled more than one-third of the Tang court collection.[102] Moreover, books at the Japanese imperial library are also qualitatively impressive, covering all forty subcategories used in the bibliographic section of the *Dynastic History of the Sui*.

A quantitative analysis of the catalog in question indicates that books in the category of "philosophy" are the highest in number, amounting to 937 titles.[103] Besides such philosophical works as the *Dao de jing*, a copy of which Fujiwara no Kiyokawa acquired in China in 752,[104] books on agriculture, astronomy, astrology, the five elements, and medicine also fall into this category. This is a convincing piece of evidence for the pragmatism the Japanese exhibited in absorbing Chinese culture. A similar mentality is present in Japanese codified law. The "Statute on Learning" prescribed mathematical arts as one of the subjects for students in the state and the provincial universities.[105] The "Statute on Medical Service and Management" required students to learn medicine and acupuncture. To raise the level of professionalism and to stop the corrupt practice of obtaining the title of "Doctor of Medicine" through bribery, in 757 the court issued a list of Chinese books as the required textbooks for examinations on medicine, astrology, astronomy, and the calendar.[106]

Books in the category of "classics" number 396 titles. More than half of the books in this category deal with Confucianism, including the *Book of Changes*, the *Book of Historical Documents*, the *Classic of Poetry*, the *Book of Rites*, the *Chunqiu with Zuo Commentaries*, the *Classic of Filial Piety*, and the *Confucian Analects*. This is hardly surprising, since the "Statute on Learning" made Confucianism a major subject for students in the state and provincial universities.[107] A "Doctor in Chinese Classics" (Myōgyō Hakase), usually of the senior sixth rank, lower grade, enjoyed a status higher than that of doctors in other specialties.[108] Moreover, for a Doctor in Chinese Classics to pass the merit examination for promotion, he was required to update his knowledge of Confucian learning.[109] Imperial family members and court nobles were also interested in Confucianism. They studied, among other things, the *Classic of Changes* and the *Book of Rites* under learned Japanese scholars. Lectures on Chinese classics and other works were regularly conducted at the court.[110]

Another 158 books that are referred to as "philological works" *(xiao xue)*, are also listed under the category of "classics."[111] These works, however, do not all deal with philology; many touch on phonetics and critical interpretation of texts, and include model essays, poems, and calligraphy—works used by the Japanese as essential references.

Only 260 works are listed under the category of "history." Significantly, the majority of these works are treatments of the Chinese legal and institutional systems, and of the geography of some coastal prefectures. They helped the Japanese develop their own legal system.[112] They also benefited Japanese diplomats dispatched to China, who often came ashore in these prefectures. The Japanese were apparently less interested in the Chinese dynastic histories, lineage records of the imperial house and influential local families, or records of the daily activities of the Chinese emperors. The dynastic histories, for example, amount to only 35 titles—a lower number than the number of works on law and geography.

The lowest number of books in any category, 239, are in the category "collections of literary works." This is, however, not an indication that the Japanese lacked interest in classical Chinese literature. In fact, Tang literary geniuses and their works enjoyed great popularity among educated Japanese. Zhang Zhuo was one of these geniuses.

Zhang first demonstrated his literary talent during the civil service examination. In the test on current topics *(duice)*, over which Empress Wu personally presided, he staged such an impressive performance that copies of Zhang's answers were made available on imperial order for court officials and foreign ambassadors to study.[113] Zhang's talent won him the name of "Bronze Scholar," whose articles enjoyed a popularity as durable as bronze cash of the highest quality.[114] Zhang Zhuo's fame spread far beyond the boundaries of China. Ambassadors from Silla, Japan, and other East Asian countries offered high prices for his works.[115] He became known even to the Turkic ruler Mochuo Qaghan. Upon receiving the news that the Tang court had recently deprived Zhang Zhuo of his title censor, the Qapaghan remarked, "China has a genius—Zhang Zhuo. But he is not entrusted with power. This incident alone shows sufficiently how incompetent the Chinese court is!"[116]

Appreciation of Chinese literature became increasingly fashionable among eighth-century Japanese nobles, and in 728 the State University offered courses on Chinese literature to its students. Japanese writers also started writing articles, poems, and prose in classical Chinese. They soon demonstrated considerable mastery of Chinese literary styles and rhetoric, and their works formed an important part of the Japanese cultural tradition.[117]

The 84 titles that appear under the subcategory of "general collections" *(zongji)* also indicate a strong interest in Chinese literature among the Japanese. Totaling 2,646 *juan,* they include the writings of famed Chinese literary figures and serve as a window to the vast richness of Chinese literature. For easy comprehension and appreciation, the texts are carefully edited and are supplemented with textual studies, annotations to words and sentences, and research into the sources of allusions used in the texts. These "general collections" provided Japanese scholars and court officials with model writings of all styles that they could consult when writing or polishing their own works.[118] Their usefulness made the "general collections" highly desirable among the Japanese.

This quantitative analysis of *A Catalog of Books Currently Extant in Japan* exhibits the Japanese pattern of assimilation of Chinese culture: although all important branches of Chinese learning were of interest, the emphasis was on such practical knowledge as philology, medicine, astrology, and matters relating to the calendar.

Acquiring Foreign Talent

Information in books contributes to a country's development only when people absorb it and use it to serve their needs. Often capable people are more efficient than books for transmitting information, knowledge, and skills from one country to another. Although the Wo rulers of third-century Japan aspired to be the overlords of Korean states, they realized that these states were economically, culturally, and politically more advanced than Japan and that to accomplish their objectives Japan's domestic development would have to be accelerated by importing talented foreigners. To achieve this, successive Wo rulers resorted to both peaceful and violent means. Sending ambassadors to neighboring countries to obtain talented people was one of the peaceful means.

Invited Foreign Talent, Migrants, and Prisoners of War

The process of inviting talented foreigners to Japan had begun as early as 284, when three high-ranking Wo officials traveled to Paekche to invite Wang Ren to serve as tutor for the heir apparent. Once in Japan, Wang instructed the heir apparent on various Chinese works and became famous for his erudition. The Japanese praised him as a scholar who thoroughly understood Chinese culture and later commemorated him as "the first ancestor of chiefs of writing."[1] At the request of the Wo court, Paekche also presented as tribute scholars who were authorities on the "five classics"[2] as well as specialists in medicine, divination, calendrical matters, and music.[3] These scholars and specialists were expected to serve the court for an extended period of time.

Along with the aforementioned scholars and specialists, Wo ambassadors brought back a variety of skilled laborers for employment in Japan. Seamstresses were imported from Paekche and the state of Wu in 283 and 306, and weavers, also from the state of Southern Wu, in 310 and 470.[4] A physician from Silla who treated Emperor Ingyō was brought in 414,[5] and such "skilled hands" as tanners were brought in from Koguryŏ in 493.[6]

Chinese migrants also became a source of skilled workers for Wo. When warfare between competing Chinese states ravaged the Middle Kingdom during the third to six centuries, a large number of Chinese fled to Korea. Among these Chinese refugees were many blacksmiths, potters, saddlers, brocade weavers, painters, interpreters, irrigation workers, sericulture workers, and carpenters. Together with some Koreans, a number migrated further to Japan.[7] One example of this migration was the Chinese clan headed by Gongyue.

Gongyue arrived in Japan from Paekche in 283 and reported to the Wo court that he "was coming to offer allegiance with 120 districts of the people of his own land, when the men of Silla prevented them, and they were all forced to remain in the land of Kara." The Wo court immediately responded to this report by sending an ambassador to bring Gongyue's clansmen held by Silla to Japan. By three years after his departure, however, the ambassador still had not returned home. To ensure safe passage to Japan for the Chinese migrants, the Wo court then dispatched two other ambassadors accompanied by a crack troop to Kara. Upon receiving news of this, the king of Kara quickly released all of Gongyue's followers.[8]

Prisoners of war provided another source of skilled laborers for Japan. The primary target of Wo military action was southern Korea, where Chinese migrants congregated. In 205, a Wo expeditionary force attacked Tatara, a center of metal smelting in southern Silla, for the purpose of seizing local and Chinese metal workers.[9] In 407, Wo forces brought back a hundred or so captives from southern Silla.[10] In 462, Wo troops again captured some thousand people from Silla.[11] And in 463, the Wo court launched a military campaign for the sole purpose of forcing Paekche to offer Wo "skilled men." This imminent Wo attack so intimidated the king of Paekche that he handed over to Japan a large number of potters, saddlers, painters, brocade weavers, and interpreters.[12]

Educated Chinese were also sometimes among the prisoners of war. Xu Shouyan and Sa Hongke were two examples. They were presented as prisoners of war to Japan by the Paekche court in 661.[13] At first they worked as agricultural workers. When their expertise in Chinese phonetics became known to the court, they were asked to teach the subject in the capital. In 691, both of them were appointed "Doctor of Chinese Phonetics" and were rewarded with rice, silver, and paddy fields for their services.[14]

The number of Chinese in Japan thus grew steadily. A registration conducted by the court in 540 indicated that the Hata (Qin) clan alone, which was one of the major Chinese migrant groups in Japan, amounted to 7,053 households.[15]

Talented People from Tang

In the seventh century, the Japanese court prioritized its policies. Domestic reforms now replaced involvement in south Korea to become the major concern for the court. This new orientation made importation of foreign talent an even more important task for the court. Prisoners of war remained a source by which Japan obtained skilled laborers, although now they were captured and presented to Japan by Koguryŏ and Paekche, rather than obtained by Japanese expeditionary forces dispatched to Korea.[16] Some Chinese arrived in Japan on their own, some with the returning Japanese delegations. We read about Japanese diplomats coming home with "Tang people,"[17] some of whom became famed for their expertise. Wang Yuanzhong, for instance, was a craftsman who built a fast boat for the Japanese emperor and was granted a junior fifth rank, lower grade, in 722.[18] Huangfu Dongchao and Huangfu Shengnü were both accomplished musicians. They were promoted from the junior sixth rank, upper grade, to the junior fifth rank, lower grade, in 766 after they performed Tang court music during a Buddhist assembly held at the Fahua Temple in the capital.[19] Li Yuanhuan was a textile expert. He was granted a senior sixth rank, upper grade, in 750. Then, in 761, the emperor honored him by granting him a first name. Two years later, he was appointed director of the Weaving Office, concurrently holding the post of assistant governor of Izumo (in present-day Shimane prefecture).[20] Numerous other "Tang people" also received official ranks and names from the court as recognition for their contributions to Japanese society.[21]

XIAO YINGSHI AND YUAN JINQING

Compared to skilled workers, the most highly talented Chinese were more difficult to come by, owing to objections from the Tang court. Xiao Yingshi (717–768) is a case in point.

Xiao was a born literary genius. He learned composition at the tender age of four and was admitted to the National University at ten. A Chinese legend says that Xiao once dreamed of reams of paper, flowers, and brocade; and these three objects spurred the flow of literary thoughts and ideas in his writing.[22]

Xiao had a photographic memory. He once traveled with two friends to the Longmen Grottoes (near present-day Luoyang). As they proceeded toward the grottoes, they stopped to read the inscriptions on stone tablets that lined the road. Xiao impressed his friends by memorizing the inscriptions after reading them only once. His friends, in contrast, had to read the inscriptions two or three times in order to memorize them.

Xiao took the civil service examination in 735 when he was nineteen. He excelled in the oral test on current topics and became a "Presented Scholar." In his early twenties, Xiao had mastered the Confucian, Buddhist, and Daoist classics. He was equally well versed in genealogy, chronology, and philology. His literary talents earned him respect from ranking officials and a job at the Palace Library as proofreader in 742.

Unfortunately, Xiao was also a conceited and irritable man. For no good reason, he would flog the servant who had been serving him for years. Once recovered from the incident, however, the servant would again serve him wholeheartedly as if nothing had happened. "You are just a servant," a friend advised him, "why don't you choose a better master for yourself?" "Don't you think I also know that?" the servant replied. "But I admire his great and profound scholarship. And that makes me very unwilling to leave him."[23]

Xiao was fond of roaming the suburbs of the capital with a bottle of wine in hand. One day, after a visit to a local scenic spot, he rested at an inn and opened the bottle. As he was drinking and singing, clouds gathered and suddenly there was a downpour. An old man dressed in purple rushed in with a boy to seek shelter from the rain. Mistaking the man for someone insignificant, Xiao wantonly bullied him. Before long, the wind died down and the sky cleared. A string of horses and carriages arrived at the inn. With many attendants crowding around, the old man mounted a horse and galloped away. Xiao was stunned. He rushed out of the inn to find out who the man was. "That is Mr. Wang, vice-minister of personnel," one of the attendants told him.

Back in the capital, Xiao called at Wang's residence, but Wang refused to receive him. The next day, Xiao wrote Wang a long letter of apology.

When Xiao eventually met with Wang, the vice-minister scolded him: "It is regrettable that we are not related. Otherwise I would have given you some parental instruction!" After a pause, Wang continued: "Although you are renowned for your literary talents, you remain such a supercilious person! Did you really stop improving yourself once you received your degree?"[24]

Xiao, however, refused to change. He turned down an invitation from Li Linfu, a powerful chief minister, on grounds of observing mourning for his father. After Xiao had performed the ritual of removing the mourning dress to signify the end of the mourning period, Li conveyed a message through a friend of Xiao that he would like to arrange a gathering at a Buddhist temple. This time, Xiao accepted the invitation. As chief minister, Li expected Xiao to show due respect by greeting him outside the temple when he dismounted from his horse. When Li arrived at the temple, however, Xiao was nowhere to be seen. He was inside the temple, weeping for his late father. Li was deeply offended. He had no choice but walk into the temple to offer condolences to Xiao, an action that made Li look like a peer of Xiao, not his superior.[25]

Ironically, Xiao's temperament only enhanced his reputation as an eccentric literary genius. Anecdotes about Xiao found entry in a number of Tang and Song works,[26] and his fame extended even to Silla and Japan. As a result, a Japanese ambassador memorialized the Tang court that his countrymen wished Xiao to be their teacher. His request, however, was rejected because a Secretariat drafter and other officials voiced strong objections.[27]

Although Japanese diplomats were unsuccessful in persuading the Tang court to allow established Chinese scholars to leave for Japan, they did succeed in bringing some educated young Chinese back home. Yuan Jinqing was one such person.

Yuan went to Japan in 735 with a returning Japanese delegation when he was eighteen. Although a teenager, Yuan had already gained a thorough understanding of the *Examples of Refined Usage (Er ya)*, a third-century lexicographic work, and of the *Selections of Refined Literature* that had been compiled in the sixth century. He was appointed Doctor of Chinese Phonetics at the Great Learning Bureau and was entrusted with the task of teaching the "Tang dynasty pronunciation" (Tōon), which was based on the northern dialects. Yuan's task was important, for the court wanted to keep up with the developments in high Chinese culture, developments that had been centered in northern China. The Japanese, however, had been under the cultural influence of successive southern Chinese dynasties so that when reading Chinese characters, for example, many still used the "Wu dynasty pronunciation" (Goon) that was based on southern dialects.

Yuan stayed at this job for thirty-four years. As a recognition of his considerable contribution to standardizing the pronunciation of Chinese characters, he was appointed director of the Great Learning Bureau in 778. And fifty years after his arrival in Japan, in 785, Yuan was made governor of Hyūga (in present-day Miyazaki prefecture).[28]

JIANZHEN

The efforts of generations of Japanese diplomats to bring top Tang talents home eventually came to fruition in 754, when the vice-ambassador of a Japanese delegation returned home with the monk Jianzhen and a number of his disciples.[29]

The future Jianzhen was born into the Chunyu family of Yangzhou in 688. His father was a Buddhist who had taken monastic vows and had studied Zen Buddhism. The boy was brought to a local temple when he was thirteen. The visit changed his life. The statue of a kind and benevolent Buddha so moved him that he told his father that he wanted to be a monk. The boy's wish was granted, and he became an acolyte. In 705, the child monk came under the tutelage of Daoan, who administered the vow of bodhisattvas for him and gave him the Buddhist name Jianzhen. In 707, Jianzhen embarked on a study tour, first to Luoyang, then to Changan. There he underwent full ordination through Master Hongjing and became an officially certified monk with the qualifications to preach Buddhist teaching. That year, Jianzhen was only twenty-one years old. He returned to Yangzhou in 713 and devoted himself to the spread of Buddhism. He lectured on Buddhist sutras, supervised construction of temples and Buddhist statues, held assemblies, donated cassocks, and had a phonetic work on Buddhist sutras transcribed. As many as forty thousand people underwent the ceremonies held by Jianzhen to join the clergy by having their hair tonsured. He became famous not only in his hometown, Yangzhou, but throughout central China.

In 742, two Japanese visited Jianzhen. They prostrated themselves before him, touching his feet with their foreheads as an expression of respect. "Although in its eastward flow the Buddha's law has reached Japan," they told him, "nobody there can teach it. Prince Shōtoku of our country once said, 'Two hundred years from now, the holy teaching will flourish in Japan.' Now that heaven has bestowed this destiny on Japan, we wish you could travel east to promote Buddhism."

These two visitors were the monks Yōei and Fushō, who had been dispatched to China by the Japanese court in 733 to invite senior Chinese monks to Japan to promote Buddhism and to administer ordinations.

Jianzhen replied:

> I have heard that after Sage Huisi of South Mountain died [in 577], he was reincarnated as a Japanese prince to promote Buddhism and save the masses. I have also heard that Prince Nagaya of Japan revered the Buddha's law. He once donated one thousand cassocks to the senior and the ordinary monks of our country. Four sentences are said to have been embroidered to each of the cassocks:
>
> > Though our mountains and rivers are located elsewhere,
> > the same sky holds the winds and the moon.
> > I offer these cassocks to you Buddhists,
> > to form a relationship in our future lives.[30]
>
> Judging from these events, Japan is indeed a country where the Buddha's law is flourishing and a country that is bound with China by karma.

Jianzhen then looked at his disciples and asked, "My fellow believers, would any of you accept this invitation from a remote country and spread the law to Japan?" His audience remained silent. No one responded. Finally, one monk stepped forward and told Jianzhen: "Japan is too far away. One would have to risk his life to cross the vast blue sea. Of a hundred attempts to reach Japan, none has been successful. Besides, it is a rare fortune to be born a human being in China. Our efforts to improve ourselves and to follow the Buddhist regulations are incomplete. And we have not yet reached the state of nirvana. For these reasons, my fellow monks have all kept silent and not answered your question."

"We do this for the sake of spreading the law. Why should we cherish our body and life?" Jianzhen retorted. "If none of you will go, I shall go by myself." His determination moved his disciples. Twenty-one of them agreed to travel with him to Japan.

A dry lacquer statue of Master Jianzhen (Ganji). Collection of Tōshōdaiji, Nara, Japan. (Sherman E. Lee, *A History of Far Eastern Art*, 5th edn. [New York: Harry N. Abrams, 1994, p. 180)

Compared to making the decision to leave for Japan, executing the plan to do so was much more difficult. Neither Jianzhen nor his disciples had any idea that it would take them five frustrated attempts before they eventually reached Japan. The difficulty came mainly from Tang codified law, which strictly forbade Chinese to leave the country without official permission.

According to Tang law, Chinese and foreigners, except for diplomats on official business, were "not permitted to leave or enter the country's borders."[31] The Tang court maintained tight border control and made illegally passing through a customs barrier by both persons and animals, climbing over the boundary gates, and falsifying a name and passing through the boundary gates criminal offenses punishable by one year of penal servitude.[32] The prohibition applied to both commoners and the clergy, but the experience of the monk Xuanzang (600–664) provided a precedent for Jianzhen.

More than one century previous, in 626, Xuanzang and a few fellow monks had memorialized the court for permission to travel to the "Western Region" to study Buddhism. But the court rejected their request. While the other monks abandoned the plan, Xuanzang decided to go ahead without the court's permission. He went to Liangzhou (in present-day Gansu province), the gateway to Central Asia, where he was questioned by local officials about his intentions. As soon as the local governor-general learned that Xuanzang wanted to "travel to the West to search for law," he ordered the monk to return to the capital.

Xuanzang, however, eventually managed to leave China illegally. Almost twenty years later, in 645, he came back with a voluminous number of Buddhist sutras. His courageous journey to India made him a cultural hero. Emperor Taizong honored him with an audience, during which he asked, "Master, why didn't you inform me when you left China?" The question apparently embarrassed Xuanzang. He replied, "Before my departure, I repeatedly memorialized the court. But my sincere wish was too insignificant to be granted. My immense admiration for the Buddha's law urged me to take the liberty of leaving China. Thinking back, I cannot but feel deeply ashamed about such an offense." The emperor pardoned him: "Master, you have taken the Buddhist oaths and are very much different from commoners. I commend your efforts and your risk of life to search for the law in order to benefit ordinary people. There is no need to feel ashamed."[33]

The experience of Xuanzang might have convinced Jianzhen not to inform the court of his plan. However, preparations for a voyage to Japan involved, among other things, shipbuilding and purchasing a large amount of dried foodstuffs, none of which could be carried out in total secrecy. To avoid trouble, Jianzhen claimed that he was preparing for a trip to the Guoqing Temple at Mt. Tiantai (in present-day Zhejiang province) to make donations. Unfortunately, an internal dispute ruined his plan.

Among the twenty-one disciples of Jianzhen who decided to follow their master to Japan was Ruhai, a Korean. He was outraged when fellow monk Daohang criticized him for lacking both the character and the knowledge necessary for preaching the monastic regulations and the Buddhist law. "He should not travel to Japan with us," suggested Daohang. Covering his head with a piece of cloth to disguise his identity, the angry Ruhai went to the prefectural capital and reported Daohang to the investigation commissioner. "Do you know, my commissioner, monk Daohang has had a ship built, recruited quite a number of people, and stored food in order to collude with pirates. Moreover, several hundred pirates are already in the Jiji Temple, Kaiyuan Temple, and Daming Temple in the city."

This accusation could not have been made at a worse time. The coasts of Taizhou, Wenzhou, and Mingzhou had recently been devastated by pirate attacks led by Wu Lingguang. They had cut off transportation lines, disrupting both official and private travelers.[34]

Ruhai's report stunned the commissioner. He ordered the imprisonment and interrogation of Ruhai and dispatched soldiers to search the temples. There they confiscated the foodstuffs and arrested four Japanese monks. Daohang tried to hide himself with a local family but to no avail. He denied any involvement with pirates and revealed that he was a domestic monk of Linzong, brother of the powerful chief minister Li Linfu. Having verified his identity, the authorities released Daohang and warned him not to try to cross the sea again.

Yōei and Fushō were less fortunate than Daohang. They spent more than four months in prison. After being released, they said to each other: "Our wish is to invite monks of great virtue to teach the monastic regulations and the law in Japan. Now an imperial edict orders the authorities at Yangzhou to send us four Japanese monks home. Our trip will be worthless if we obey the order and return home without Tang masters." They decided to approach Jianzhen again. "Don't you worry," the master comforted them. "If you proceed according to the situation, your wish will definitely come true."

Preparations for the second attempt to leave China started by the end of 743. Jianzhen and his followers bought a military ship, hired eighteen boatmen, and purchased a large amount of foodstuffs. Loaded onto the ship were also medicines, lacquerware, Buddhist statues, sutras, and utensils, various kinds of incense and spices, copper coins, and clothes. Besides the seventeen monks, a number of jade workers, painters, and people skilled in carving, encasing, and casting also decided to travel to Japan with Jianzhen. In the twelfth month of 743, a total of eighty-five people left Yangzhou. This time no internal dispute erupted among the travelers. The weather, however, worked against them. Soon after they cleared the mouth of the Yangzi River, they ran into a hurricane whose mountainous waves broke their ship apart, abruptly ending their second attempt.

When the ship was repaired, Jianzhen tried a third time to set sail for Japan, but the ship foundered on rocks. After local fishermen rescued them, the prefect of Mingzhou, not knowing Jianzhen's real intention, settled him at a local temple. Jianzhen spent most of the following year resting at the temple and seeking an opportunity to leave China. He sometimes accepted invitations and traveled to temples in the adjacent prefectures to lecture on Buddhist sutras or to administer ordination for local monks. Unfortunately, Jianzhen revealed his intention to a monk from Yuezhou, and the monk reported Jianzhen's plan to the local authorities. Yōei was immediately arrested, yoked, and escorted back to the capital. On the way to Changan, he fell seriously ill at Hangzhou and consequently received permission to remain there for treatment. That ended Jianzhen's third attempt to reach Japan.

Hardship, however, dampened the spirits of neither Yōei nor Fushō. They were as determined as ever to bring Jianzhen home. Deeply moved by their resolution, Jianzhen decided in 744 to send a disciple to Fuzhou to prepare for a fourth attempt. He then left Ningbo with some thirty people, using the same pretext he had formerly used: that the trip was for making donations to Guoqing Temple at Mt. Tiantai. However, Jianzhen received an official communication from the investigation commissioner while on his way to Fuzhou, urging him to abandon the trip and to return to Yangzhou. At the time, he was unaware that back in Yangzhou his disciple Lingyou and monks of other temples had reported his travels to the local authorities. The risk that Jianzhen would face when sailing abroad deeply concerned these monks, and they wanted the authorities to stop him. A report from Yangzhou soon reached the investigation commissioner of the Jiangdong Circuit. In consequence, he ordered the relevant prefectural authorities to detain and question the senior monks in their respective jurisdictions who might have hosted Jianzhen on his way to Fuzhou. These interrogations quickly yielded clues to Jianzhen's whereabouts. He was located and detained and, guarded by ten rings of soldiers, sent back to Yangzhou.

Monks and commoners in Yangzhou were delighted to see their beloved master back. Jianzhen, however, was depressed. He scolded Lingyou and thereafter viewed him with dismay. To cheer his master up, Lingyou asked Jianzhen to pardon him. In a gesture of apology, Lingyou stood in the yard every night and remained standing there until dawn. Sixty days later, Jianzhen finally forgave him.

In the spring of 748, Yōei and Fushō again visited Jianzhen in Yangzhou. A few months later, preparations for the fifth attempt were in place. Jianzhen and an entourage of thirty-five people left Yangzhou in the sixth month for the Zhoushan archipelagos southeast of the mouth of the Yangzi River. They stayed there for a few months, waiting for a following wind.

In the middle of the tenth month, Jianzhen told his followers: "Last night I had a dream. Three officials, one in red and the other two in green, bid me farewell. They must be deities of the nation who came to say good-bye. If we make a move now, we should be able to cross the sea."

As soon as they left Zhoushan, however, they faced a strong head wind. Instead of sailing toward Japan, their ship drifted aimlessly for two weeks before reaching Zhenzhou (present-day Sanya, Hainan Island) in south China. This narrow escape from disaster on the high seas offered Jianzhen only temporary relief. He was soon devastated by two tragedies. On their way from Hainan Island to Yangzhou, Yōei, who had assisted Jianzhen since his first attempt to reach Japan eight years previously, died of disease at Duanzhou (present-day Zhaoqing city in Guangdong province). Grief over Yōei's death coupled with anxiety over the future so stressed Jianzhen that his resistance was apparently lowered. Subsequently, he developed an eye infection, and inappropriate treatment eventually caused him to lose his eyesight. To make matters worse, Xiangyan, one of his favorite disciples, also died of disease soon after. Jianzhen was now a blind and old man; nevertheless he refused to abandon his hope of spreading the Buddha's law to Japan.

Late in the tenth month of 753, the ambassador, the vice-ambassador, and other ranking officials of the eleventh Japanese delegation to China visited Jianzhen ostensibly to pay him their respects. During their visit, however, they told him that while in Changan they had requested, but failed to receive, the court's permission to bring him to Japan. They nonetheless urged him: "Master, we wish you would make a decision at your earliest convenience about going to Japan anyway. It will not be difficult for you to accompany us should you decide to leave for Japan, as our four ships are fully prepared for the voyage." Jianzhen, although at the advanced age of sixty-six, accepted their invitation without hesitation.

The visit by the Japanese diplomats soon spawned a rumor among the commoners and monks in Yangzhou that their beloved master was again going to attempt to leave for Japan. Alerted, local authorities put Jianzhen's home temple under surveillance. Fortunately, however, a Zen monk had already prepared a boat for Jianzhen, and on the nineteenth day of the month, the master secretly left his temple. As he was about to board the boat, twenty-four child monks from the temple rushed to his side. With tears in their eyes, they begged him: "You are about to sail east and we will have no chance to see you again. Please leave us something for the future to remember you by!" As a manner of granting their request, Jianzhen took time to administer the ceremony of ordination for them. Having done so, he set sail for Suzhou, where some twenty-four more followers awaited him.

On the twentieth day of the month, the Japanese ambassador had Jianzhen and his entourage board the vice-ambassador's ship. A number of treasures that Jianzhen brought with him were also loaded aboard. These included eight statues of Sakyamuni and the Goddess of Mercy, seven types of Buddhist ceremonial equipment, sutras of various kinds amounting to more than three hundred *juan,* and three pieces of invaluable calligraphy by the famous fourth-century calligraphers Wang Xizhi and Wang Xianzhi.

The ambassador's decision, however, worried other members of the Japanese delegation. "Authorities of Guangling prefecture have already learned about the master's plan to go with us. They are about to search our ships," they said to each other. "If they find the master on board, our ambassador will suffer. Moreover, we'll also be implicated if we [sail off with the master but] are forced back to China by headwinds." As a result, the ambassador decided that Jianzhen and his followers should disembark. During the subsequent two weeks, Jianzhen's attempt to reach Japan again seemed in danger of failure. Fortunately, however, the sympathetic vice-ambassador took the liberty of smuggling the Tang monks back aboard his ship. On the fifteenth day of the eleventh month, 753, in faint moonlight, the four Japanese ships weighed anchor for home. The voyage was not easy, but after two months of hardship on the high seas, Jianzhen finally set foot on Japanese soil during the first month of 754. Twelve long years had passed since his first attempt to reach Japan in 742.

The Multipolar Nature of the International System in Asia

Chinese rulers saw the whole world as coming under their jurisdiction. "Under the wide heaven," one Chinese saying goes, "all is the King's land. Within the sea-boundaries of the land, all are the King's servants."[1] This world was unipolar, with China at the center and the neighboring countries at the peripheries. When they wanted to contact China, they did so by entering the tributary system of the Middle Kingdom.

The Tributary System Reassessed

Originating during the Western Zhou dynasty (eleventh century–771 B.C.), the tributary system institutionalized relations between the Zhou king and his Chinese and foreign subjects. Geographic distance between a subject and the Zhou king defined the relations between them. A subject was put in one of five classes in a graded system of "five submissions" (*wufu*),[2] in which each classification stipulated the appropriate symbolic actions he had to perform in order to acknowledge his political subordination to the crown and to fulfill economic obligations to the Zhou court. He or his ambassador was required to visit the court on a regular basis at specified time intervals.[3] He was to offer local products in a given amount and of certain types as tribute to the Zhou king. Through the bestowal by the Zhou and acceptance on his part of Chinese civil and military titles and royal seals, a sovereign-vassal relationship was established between the involved parties, which required the vassal to respond promptly to instructions from the Zhou court. The court in return would grant the vassal moral and military support at his request.[4]

Many traditional Chinese scholars regarded foreign countries as negligible to China. They paid attention to these countries only when their rulers or ambassadors glorified China by "paying tribute" to the Son of Heaven. In their works, the centrality of China in the tributary system was axiomatic. A court visit by a foreign ruler or his ambassador was perceived as a token of conformity to the Chinese world order and a public acknowledgment of subordination to the Son of Heaven. The Chinese wishfully and universally described the purpose of many foreign missions as "coming to pay tribute" *(laichao)*,[5] "asking to become (China's) subject" *(qingli)*,[6] or "returning to tribute-offering status" *(guixian)*.[7]

The Chinese primary sources compiled by these scholars are the basis on which a rich body of modern scholarship on the diplomatic history of China has developed.[8] Among them, works by Japanese scholars deserve attention. Some examine the relations among China, Japan, Koguryŏ, Silla, and Paekche in terms of an "oriental history."[9] They treat these "oriental" countries and the relations among them as one entity because they shared similarities in political institutions, culture, and economy. They consider the history of China's external relations as a process in which Chinese culture spread to the world outside China, and China's neighbors responded to that cultural expansion. They compare this process to the formation of a concentric circle, with China proper at the center, annexing its neighbors or bringing them to varying degrees into the Chinese political orbit through tributary arrangements.

As a theoretical framework, "oriental history" is both credible and helpful in terms of its treatment of the aforementioned guiding principles of China's diplomacy. This framework is also a welcome departure from the Europe-centered research methods popular with many late-nineteenth-century Japanese historians.[10]

Other Japanese historians use the "investiture system" *(sakuhō taisei)* to study the diplomatic history of East Asian countries. Similar to the "oriental history" approach, the investiture theory emphasizes the homogeneity of East Asian countries. This homogeneity is evident in that they shared a culture based on the Chinese written language, they patronized Buddhism and Confucianism, they built economic ties with each other through tributary arrangements, and they all had a Chinese-style statute and code system. They thus formed a "historical civilization zone" or an "East Asian world."[11]

Countries in the "East Asian world" used the "investiture system" as a general medium for conducting diplomacy. Through the bestowal and acceptance of Chinese titles, this system created a political hierarchy between China and its neighbors[12] that was an extension of the Chinese domestic social order, known as the "status system."[13]

Focusing on the bestowal and acceptance of Chinese titles, the investiture theory is more specific than the "oriental history" approach in its treatment of China's official relations with East Asian countries.[14] The theory emphasizes change in the investiture system, thus distinguishing itself from the method of those scholars who use the Roman Empire as a model for their perception of East Asian history and who study China and its diplomacy during the Qin-Han period in terms of the development of an "empire."[15]

The tributary system was based on an assumption of China's centrality in world affairs. It was a "schematic design" for China's foreign relations.[16] Political submission brought about by military conquest or by cultural influence was the cornerstone of the system.[17] Indeed, China at times did beat some neighbors into submission. The degree of submission, however, could not be properly defined merely by a country's geographic distance from China. In theory, the tributary system was centered on China with neighboring countries as its vassals. But in reality, participants in the system were not homogeneous, and the system was open to countries of dubious political inclinations. Moreover, for the Middle Kingdom, which was not always militarily superior to its neighbors, military conquest was not a routine way of handling external affairs. Even when an advanced Chinese culture attracted a foreign ambassador to "pay tribute" to China, the contact did not always result in a formal sovereign-vassal relation. There were times as well when China refused to play the role of a suzerain in order to avoid being burdened by obligations to a vassal state. China deliberately rejected requests by some foreign rulers to become "outer subjects" in order to leave them out of the Chinese world. In short, the creation of actual "tributary relations" was a consequence of historical circumstances and not necessarily the norm for all of China's external relations.

Nor was China always the centrally dominant party in relations with other countries.[18] This had been the case since the Zhou court lost control of the regional Chinese lords in the Spring and Autumn period. These lords waged wars against one another and allied themselves with "barbarian" groups for hegemony or survival.[19] Alliance with "barbarians" had since become a strategy for Chinese rulers.

Han Wudi (r. 140–187 B.C.) adopted the policy of "allying with one barbarian group to check the other" *(lianyĭ yi zhiyi)*. He befriended the Yuezhi (in the Amu Darya River Valley) in order to check the Xiongnu.[20] In this relationship, Han China in fact played the role of a tribute-paying country to the Xiongnu.[21] Li Yuan, founding father of the Tang, turned to the Eastern Turks for support before revolting against the Sui. He became a nominal vassal of the Turkic ruler and received from his master soldiers and horses.[22] Later, the Uighurs became indispensable partners of the Tang court in the court's campaigns to subdue internal rebels and fend off Tibetan attacks.[23] In these cases, China treated these neighbors as peers or even as superiors. Traditional Chinese historians, however, were often too proud openly to admit that such situations had obtained. In consequence, little about them has survived in Chinese records.[24]

Nevertheless, some traditional Chinese scholars acknowledged that there was a gap between the publicly preferred "tributary relations" and the extent to which such relations actually existed in China's external relations. They realized that diplomatic matters could not be viewed merely through the lens of China's centrality.

Sima Qian (145–186 B.C.), the great Han dynasty historian, disagreed with the idea that the best policy to follow with respect to the Xiongnu was that they should "become China's subject or face war." Ban Gu (39–62), another famous Han dynasty scholar, argued for a stable pattern for China's external relations but did not reassert the doctrine of "tributary relations." Fan Ye (398–446) and Shen Yue (441–513) both openly doubted the usefulness of the tributary system.[25]

In many respects, the tributary system was not a static structure centered on China but a delicate equilibrium, sensitive to needs and changes in conditions of all involved parties.[26] As time passed, "tributary relations" between China and some neighbors would degenerate into a mere form of official contact, which preserved the centrality of China only at the ceremonial level. The Chinese court sometimes acted to reimpose the tributary pattern on its neighbors, thus destabilizing them. With a few exceptions, however, the pattern in question could be sustained only spasmodically.[27] "Tributary relations" came to embrace a wide spectrum of China's external affairs, ranging from "total subjugation to virtual de facto equality."[28] The great variety of China's power relations with its neighbors therefore cannot be portrayed simply as "tributary relations."

The neighbors of China were not passive objects of China's foreign policy. The ruler of a vassal state was often a dynamic player of international politics. He decided the timing for establishing or stopping contacts with China.[29] He sought Chinese military and civil titles to strengthen his position at home and support his claims abroad. Even when he followed a directive from China, he did so not so much to fulfill his political obligation to China as a vassal as to use the Chinese directive to his advantage.[30] He would often ignore any instruction from China deemed unfavorable to the interests of his country. He could and would stop paying tribute to or even clash with China when substantial conflicts of interest occurred in the bilateral relations.[31] Generally, his country was neither a political nor a military satellite of China.[32] If we must identify a general "medium" for international relations among Asian countries, it would be "official contacts" of heterogenous natures. And these relations must be examined in the light of the individual motives of the involved countries.[33]

Self-Interest and Mutual Self-Interest in International Politics

Self-interest was the foundation for each country's external behavior. It motivated a country to secure its existence and development in international society by trying to create an international environment conducive to its own domestic development and external expansion. The self-interest, the strength, and the international position of a country configured its international relations and determined whether a country's external relations took the form of peaceful contacts with its neighbors, of war against other countries, of mutually beneficial economic exchange, or of carefully calculated political maneuvers.[34]

An understanding of the role of national self-interest in international politics had always been a part of the political wisdom of Chinese rulers, and the Chinese policy of luring foreign rulers with valuables and satisfying their needs for Chinese goods was based on such an understanding. The perception of the value and the use of this policy started during the Xin dynasty (9–25)[35] and continued throughout the Eastern Han dynasty.[36] The Sui court also adopted this policy. In 607, Emperor Yang displayed a great quantity of valuables during a gala held for foreign rulers from the Western Region. Impressed, the Turkic ruler expressed his wish to become a subject of the Sui emperor. During the same year, Sui ambassadors visited other countries in the region, persuading their rulers by generous Chinese gifts to offer loyalty to China.[37]

The Tang emperor also demonstrated a good understanding of self-interest as the driving force in diplomacy. Emperor Gaozu once observed, "In my view, the Turks, both ruler and subjects, are intent on nothing but money and valuables."[38] The Turks, and the Qidan as well, "would act [to invade China] whenever they see some benefit [in doing so]."[39] It was believed to be the greedy and ferocious nature of the "barbarians" that motivated them to wage war against China.[40] On occasion they sought peace and accorded the Chinese court political eulogies. These actions, however, were often due not to the moral influence of any Tang emperor but to a fear of Chinese military action against them when pervasive natural disasters and pestilence had ravaged their countries. They needed breathing space for recuperation in times of difficulty.[41]

Considerations of self-interest quite obviously conditioned the stance of a country toward others. The ruler of Nanzhao had once allied himself with the Turks. In the mid-eighth century, however, he decided to switch loyalty to Tang China. "The Chinese court," he explained, "acts on rites and righteousness, and seldom makes demands on its neighbors. Unlike the Chinese, the Turks are insatiably avaricious. We shall now give up the alliance with the Turks and offer loyalty again to Tang. This action will free us from the duty of sending soldiers far away to defend the Turks. Nothing will benefit Nanzhao more than this decision."[42]

When chieftains of various Wo tribes contacted authorities at Lelang, a Chinese commandery established in northern Korea in 108 B.C. by the Western Han court, they sought to benefit themselves by initiating contact.[43] In A.D. 57, the first Wo ambassador arrived at the capital of the Eastern Han court (25–220);[44] the second came in 107.[45]

Wo diplomats, however, never called on China on a regular basis. A chronology of Japan-China relations from the first to the ninth centuries reveals this irregularity in the visits of Japanese ambassadors to China. There were periods of frequent contacts as well as of lengthy intervals between contacts. This irregularity clearly indicated that, in its diplomacy with China, Japan set its own agenda and acted on self-interest to satisfy its own needs.

No Wo ambassador, for example, came to China during the second century. This interval continued well past the third century. Then within merely nine years, the female Wo ruler Himiko sent four ambassadors to the Wei court (220–265) in 238, 243, 245, and 247 respectively.[46] After the death of Himiko, diplomatic contacts with China slowed. Iyo, the female successor to Himiko, contacted the Wei court only once.[47] The fourth century was another quiet period in China-Wo relations except for the Wo delegation dispatched to the Western Jin court (265–316) in 306.[48] With the arrival of a Wo ambassador at the Eastern Jin court (317–420) in 413, a new age of frequent diplomatic contacts with China began.[49] Over the next sixty years, ten Wo ambassadors called on the Southern Song court (420–479),[50] and a Wo delegation also visited the Southern Qi court (479–502) in 479.[51] The sixth century, however, saw only one Wo ambassador pay respect to the Southern Liang court (502–557) in 502.[52] When these ambassadors arrived in China, they acquired official titles, bronze mirrors, and military banners, which their masters could use to bolster their claims to political supremacy, to build a military system, and to exert influence on southern Korea.

Starting from the seventh century, a profound change occurred in Japan-China relations. Five Japanese ambassadors called on the Sui court within the short period of fourteen years from 600 to 614.[53] None of them, however, requested Chinese titles from the court. These titles were now useless since Japan had achieved political unity in the sixth century and no longer needed Chinese titles as a ploy in establishing superiority in domestic politics. Japanese ambassadors to the Sui and later on to the Tang were mainly diplomats seeking cultural and economic benefits from China for their country.

During the Tang dynasty, sixteen Japanese ambassadors visited the capital, Changan.[54] The ambassadors took advantage of their official relations with China to acquire knowledge of Chinese institutions and culture as well as to obtain fine Chinese products. Japan needed the information and used such items to consolidate its political order and to nourish its own culture. After the first ambassador visited the Tang in 630, an interlude of more than twenty years followed that lasted until 653. From 653 to 701, however, as many as seven Japanese delegations contacted Tang central and local authorities. During the eighth century, the interval between the various Japanese delegations sent to China averaged about ten years. In the ninth century, however, the interval between visits lengthened to thirty years. These changes in the length of the interval between missions seem to suggest that the Japanese court was determining the timing for its ambassadors to call on China according to its own needs.

Ma Duanlin (1254–1323), a Southern Song scholar, seems to have well surmised the motive foreign rulers had in contacting China in his comments "Barbarians from various islands come to pay tribute. Is it not true that they merely wish to benefit themselves from trade and gifts [from the Chinese court] rather than that they truly admire the right-eousness [of the Chinese emperor]?"[55]

Not only was self-interest the guiding principle of the nations that had relationships with China, it also guided Chinese diplomacy. China's public endorsement of virtue *(de)* and righteousness *(yi)* as the basis for state conduct[56] meant in actuality that these moral principles were the means and justifications China used to realize its own self-interest.[57] This is obvious in Chinese political thinking since benefit to the country and its people was considered the yardstick of all moral principles.[58] The character *de* did not only represent an abstract moral concept; it also stood for the concrete way by which a specific issue was handled appropriately according to the circumstances.[59] *De* is therefore also trans-lated as "efficacy."[60] "What *de* means," a Han dynasty etymological work explains, "is achieving proper arrangements for things."[61] A capable ruler should "order his affairs so that they express righteousness"[62] and "handle things and make decisions in accordance with the very nature of the related matters."[63] In this definition of "virtue" and "righteous-ness," the "appropriateness" of an action to be taken depends on its pro-duction of results desirable to the parties involved.[64]

Appropriate actions based on righteousness and virtue thus would produce benefits. This explains why strategists and thinkers of the War-ring States period advocated "righteousness." "Beneficialness is the consequence of all righteousness," one observed.[65] "Righteousness con-tributes to the advantage of the state," another concluded.[66] Since "right-eousness is the root of gain," yet another suggested, "a nation should consider righteousness, not self-interest, as that which is to its advan-tage."[67] Some strategists compared "righteousness" and "virtue" to "weapons to gain benefit for the state," making the utilitarian nature of these moral principles quite explicit.[68] Self-interest thus was apparently the fundamental motive of both China and its neighbors in establishing relations with each other.

When a country initiates contact with another country, it raises demands on its counterpart to take certain actions. Thus, the initiating country is a "demander." If the other country acts according to the demander's requests, the responding country then becomes a "supplier." However, for a supplier to act in a way that allows the demander to fulfill its own self-interest, the supplier must believe that its action would first benefit itself. Under no circumstances would a supplier act as a passive, altruistic provider of services to a selfish demander. The supplier also acts from self-interest and sees its deeds as a way of actively seeking its own national interests. For countries to enter a bilateral relationship, therefore, there must be some overlap of their respective interests, even though the national interest of one might not be identical with that of the other. Were this not the case, a relationship would not be established in the first place. The concept of "mutual self-interest" is thus necessary for understanding a functional bilateral relationship. "Mutual self-interest" refers to a win-win situation for the parties involved in a bilateral relationship that enables each to realize its own self-interest by interacting with the other according to a set of mutually accepted rules.[69]

Mozi (470–391 B.C.?), a philosopher of the Warring States period, was the first to use the term "mutual self-interest" *(jiao xiang li)*.[70] Courtiers of the Jin (eleventh to fourth centuries B.C.), a regional Chinese state (located in southern Shanxi province), elaborated why a harmonious relationship with the Rong and the Di (nomads in western and northern China respectively) would work for both parties.

> The *Rong* and the *Di* are continually changing their residence, and are fond of exchanging land for goods. Their lands can be purchased; this is the first advantage. Our borders will not be kept in apprehension. The people can labor on their fields, and the husbandmen complete their toils; this is the second. When the *Rong* and the *Di* serve Jin, our neighbors all round will be terrified, and the states will be awed and cherish our friendship; this is the third. Tranquilizing the *Rong* by our goodness, our armies will not be toiled, and weapons will not be broken; this is the fourth. Using only measures of virtue, the remote will come to us, and the near will be at rest; this is the fifth.[71]

Living at peace with barbarians was a nonmilitary approach to external affairs. It developed into a "loose rein" *(jimi)* policy during the Han dynasty expressed in a simile to the effect that China should handle "barbarians" like a farmer trying to control his horse with a halter *(ji)* and his ox by a bridle *(mi)*.[72]

The "loose rein" policy was a low-key foreign policy that required a minimum use of force for control in bilateral relations. It stressed the importance of keeping in touch with foreign countries without establishing substantive political relationships with them. And the gist of this policy was that "all courtesies must be returned" *(jimi zhi yi li wu buda)* if foreign ambassadors complied with the court ceremonial when visiting China.[73]

Tang courtiers demonstrated that they understood this policy well. Although they supported repulsing military assaults on Chinese borders and keeping Chinese troops on alert so as to provide justifiable responses to threats, they opposed attempts to conquer neighboring countries.[74] As far as they were concerned, China would gain nothing from using force to annex neighboring countries, nor would China sustain any loss by losing control of them.[75] This was because most foreign lands were as barren as "stony fields," and their people were unlikely to be reformed in the light of Chinese customs.[76] The best way of dealing with these countries was to live at peace with them, providing they did not raid Chinese borders.[77] Nor did the court believe that China should accept them as vassal states.[78] They were convinced that keeping at a political distance from them freed China from the obligations that a suzerain owed to its subjects.

China's neighbors benefited from the "loose rein" policy as well. This policy allowed foreign ambassadors access to both Chinese culture and the exquisite commodities China produced without burdening them with the obligations expected of a vassal state.

China-Japan relations before the eleventh century also embodied the spirit of mutual self-interest. The sovereign-vassal relations between the two countries from the third to the sixth centuries were instrumental in strengthening the position of various Wo rulers at home and in extending their influence over southern Korea. Chinese regional states welcomed these relations since they created the image of a suzerain for the rulers of these states and enhanced their claim to be the legitimate sovereign of China. The ruler of the Song was so eager to take advantage of the system that he announced in 420 the bestowal of titles on a Wo ruler without a Wo ambassador being present at his court.[79]

During the Sui-Tang period, official ties with China were the channel through which Japan kept up with cultural and political developments in China. Japanese ambassadors managed to return home "loaded with Chinese gifts" without offering political submission to China.[80] They did so by paying lip service to the China-centered world order.[81] Observing Tang court protocol, they presented state letters and gifts to Tang emperors and accepted Chinese honorific titles that they had never requested. Japan's political allegiance to China thus seemed to have continued undisturbed on the ceremonial level.

The Tang court was aware of the changes in its relations with Japan. But it chose not to reimpose the sovereign-vassal pattern on the country since Japan was marginal to the geopolitics of Tang China in East Asia. Except for the military confrontation at the Hakusonkō River in 663, Japan was neither an ally nor a foe of China. Maintaining loose official ties with Japan was in China's interest. Regarding the visits by Japanese ambassadors as reflecting the far-reaching moral influence of Tang emperors in foreign countries, the Tang court happily received them.

The Multipolar International System in Asia

No country played a fixed role in Asian international politics. A country could be a "demander" on one occasion but a "supplier" on another. The international system in Asia operated by means of several poles and was multipolar in nature.[82]

China had long been the leading player in the system owing to its political, economic, and cultural advantages over neighboring peoples. These peoples, although mostly nomadic and illiterate, tried to use the system to their best advantage by deciding on the time and the terms for contacting China and on which elements of Chinese culture they wished to adopt. They too were active players.

From the mid-third century onward, "barbarians" north of the Great Wall became formidable forces in international politics. They established regional regimes and waged wars against China. Eventually, in 316, they destroyed the unified China that had existed under the Western Jin court to become masters of the vast area north of the Yangzi River during the next two centuries.

The Sui court managed to bring areas south of the Great Wall back under Chinese control but was unable to reassert the centrality of China vis-à-vis neighboring countries. China faced a new international environment, which would continue to evolve despite China's wishes.

During the Tang dynasty, China's neighbors to the northeast (Parhae, Koguryŏ, Paekche, Silla, and Japan) and to the southwest (Tibet and Nanzhao) became stable agrarian or semi-agrarian states one after another. Their societies became better organized. A literary culture developed in these countries as well. In the meantime, the countries north and northwest of the Great Wall (the Turks and the Uighurs) became militarily stronger than China.[83] Inspired by China's political cosmology, many Asian rulers also developed a political ideology of their own. They claimed the existence of a hierarchy in which they themselves were the center. They thus challenged the unipolar assumption of Chinese foreign policy that viewed China as the Asian epicenter.

Asian rulers practiced this new political ideology in different manners. Chieftains of the Turks, the Uighurs, and the Tibetans requested privileged treatment by the Tang court, and the court was compelled to deal with them as peers. Rulers of Koguryŏ, Silla and Paekche, in contrast, maintained their sovereign-vassal relations with China. They wanted to gain Chinese support for their individual ambitions to unify the Korean peninsula, a goal none of them could achieve by their own strength.[84] They did, however, reject instructions from China that they deemed contradictory to their self-interest.[85] As a group, they ignored, even if they did not overtly repudiate, China's supremacy.

The Japanese sovereigns, too, quietly disengaged themselves from sovereign-vassal relations with China. They instructed their courtiers to phrase state letters to China in such a way that these letters rejected, but did not openly challenge, China's suzerainty. In 648, the court also initiated an indirect official contact with China in order to dilute the political overtones of their bilateral relations by entrusting the ambassador of Silla with a memorial to be delivered to the Tang emperor.[86] And, in 654, Japan turned a deaf ear to a Tang instruction to attack Paekche, Japan's ally in Korea.[87] Thus Japan maintained official relations with China in order to achieve economic and cultural gains without compromising its independent political stance.

The multipolar nature of the international system in Asia became apparent when Asian countries made it clear that relations with China were only one aspect of their diplomacy. Many of them had equally important relations with other neighboring peoples.[88] In the ninth century, for example, Silla, Parhae, and Japan maintained regular diplomatic contacts among themselves. Some continued to send embassies to

Changan, while they were in a formal vassal relationship to another powerful patron state.[89]

By its utilitarian and flexible character, the multipolar international system in Asia allowed its participants to relate to and benefit one another through their official contacts. However, the multipolar nature of the system and the unitary means of official contact by which the system functioned resulted in a tension. This tension did not manifest itself as long as China's neighbors sought to use Chinese court audiences as occasions to indicate their respective international standing, to confirm or adjust their mutual relationships, and to reap cultural and economic benefits from the Middle Kingdom. Asian rulers, however, would change their minds when overland and maritime trading activities of private merchants replaced official contacts to become a major medium for cultural and economic exchanges with China. The first Tang merchant, for example, arrived in Japan in 819. From then until the collapse of the Tang in 907, every two to three years, on average, a Tang ship sailed to or returned from Japan. Altogether there were thirty-nine of these trading voyages.[90]

With this development of commercial ventures in international relations, the importance of official contact with China as a means for economic and cultural exchange diminished. Official contact became an embodiment mainly of the power relations between China and a group of peer states. In the meantime, private trade facilitated the economic and cultural ties among them. The multipolar nature of the international system in Asia could now properly manifest itself in the various ways in which the system functioned.

Appendix I

A Chronology of China-Japan Relations
from the First to the Ninth Centuries

THE EASTERN HAN (25–220)

57   An ambassador from Nuguo arrives at the Eastern Han capital, Luoyang. He receives a golden seal with an inscription consisting of six characters cut in intaglio, "The King of Nuguo, [appointed by] Han."

107   Suishō, the ambassador of Yamatai, and other petty warlords from Wo visit the Chinese commandery at Lelang. They ask for a court audience with the Han emperor at the capital.

THE WEI (220–265)

238   Himiko, the female ruler of Yamatai, sends Nashōme and Toji Gori to the Chinese commandery at Daifang. Expecting a coalition with Yamatai in its struggle against Wu, the Wei court allows the Wo diplomats to proceed to the capital, Luoyang. There they receive the titles "Pro-Wei Queen of Wo" for Himiko, and "Shuaishan Colonel" and "Shuaishan Commandant" for themselves.

240   Ti Jun, the Wei ambassador sent to Wo, informs Himiko that she has been downgraded from "Pro-Wei Queen of Wo" to "Caretaker of Wo."

240–247   Himiko sends ambassadors to the Wei court in 240, 243, 245, and 247. They request military banners, bronze mirrors, and swords. Iyo, the female successor to Himiko, also sends a representative to contact the Wei.

THE WESTERN JIN (265–316)

306   A Wo delegation visits the Western Jin court.

THE EASTERN JIN (317–420)

413   A Wo ambassador pays respects to the Eastern Jin court.

THE STATE OF SOUTHERN SONG (420–479)

421   A Wo ambassador receives titles for his master from the Song court.

425 and 430   A Wo ambassador presents a memorial and local products to the Song court.

438   A Wo ambassador informs the Southern Song court that Hanzei, the ruler of Wo, has granted himself the title "King of Wo, Area Commander in Chief Commissioned with Extraordinary Powers, Supervising the Military Affairs of Wo, Paekche, Silla, Mimana, Qinhan, and Muhan, General in Chief for Pacification in the East." The ambassador requests Song approval of this and other military titles for Wo officials.

443　A Wo ambassador requests the title "Area Commander in Chief
Commissioned with Extraordinary Powers" for Ingyō, ruler of Wo. The Song
court rejects his request.

451　Ingyō eventually acquires the title "King of Wo, Area Commander in
Chief Commissioned with Extraordinary Powers, Supervising the Military
Affairs of Wo, Silla, Mimana, Jialuo, Qinhan, Muhan, General for
Pacification in the East."

460　A Wo ambassador presents local products to the Song court.

462　Ankō, the ruler of Wo, receives from the Song court a title that is the
same as that for Ingyō.

477　Yūryaku, the ruler of Wo, dispatches an ambassador to the Song court.

478　The Song court grants Yūryaku the title "General in Chief," making him
a peer of the king of Paekche.

THE STATE OF SOUTHERN QI (479–502)

479　The Qi court promotes Yūryaku to "General in Chief for Defense in the
East" and reappoints him "Area Commander in Chief Commissioned with
Extraordinary Powers."

THE STATE OF SOUTHERN LIANG (502–557)

502　The Liang court promotes Yūryaku to "General in Chief for
Expedition in the East" but refuses to let him interfere with military
affairs in Paekche.

THE SUI (581–618)

600　A Wo ambassador visits the Sui court. Not only does he not request any
official Chinese titles, he presents to the court a state letter that omits the
title "King of Wo," the term "subject," and the first name that the previous
Wo state letters used as references to the Wo ruler. To express the Wo
ruler's authority and dignity, the letter uses his native designation "Ōkimi
Ametarashihiko" and its pronunciation transliterated into Chinese
characters, *abei jimi amei duolisibigu.*

607　The flourishing of Buddhism in China prompts the Wo court to send
Ono no Imoko and several monks to Sui China. Imoko acquires a copy of
the *Lotus Sutra,* thus becoming the first Wo diplomat to obtain books
directly from China. Furthermore, he presents the Sui court with a state
letter that addresses the Japanese ruler as "the Son of Heaven in the land
of the rising sun" and the Sui emperor as "the Son of Heaven in the land of
the setting sun."

608　Displeased by the wording of the Wo state letter, Emperor Yang
dispatches Pei Shiqing to Japan to "investigate local customs."

610　A Wo ambassador presents local products to the Sui court.

614　Inukami no Mitasuki and others visit Sui China.

THE TANG (618–906)

630   Inukami no Mitsuki and Yakushi Enichi lead the first Japanese mission
      to Tang. They come back to report: "The Great Tang is a country whose
      laws and ordinances are complete and fixed. We should maintain regular
      contacts with it."

631   Gao Biaoren, a Tang ambassador, arrives in Japan. Owing to a dispute
      over the ceremonial arrangements for his reception, Gao decides not to
      deliver the Tang edict to the Japanese court.

648   On behalf of the Japanese court, an ambassador of Silla delivers a
      Japanese memorial to the Tang emperor to wish him good health.

653   Kishi no Nagani and Takada no Nemaro are appointed ambassadors to
      China. Upon his return home, Nagani receives generous rewards from the
      court for "having obtained numerous Chinese books and precious objects."

654   Takamukō no Genri is appointed "supervising ambassador" and Kawabe
      no Maro ambassador to China. They present the Tang court with large
      pieces of amber and agate as gifts. In the same year, the Japanese court
      ignores a Tang instruction to attack its ally, Paekche, in Korea.

659   Sakaibe no Ishinuno and Tsumori no Kiza are dispatched to China. Kiza
      presents one male and one female of the Emishi people to the Tang court.
      The court, however, detains members of the Japanese delegation for fear
      that they may leak to Paekche the information of an impending Tang mili-
      tary campaign against Paekche.

663   A battle between Tang and Japanese forces breaks out at the Hakusonkō
      River.

664–671   The commander in chief of the Tang forces stationed at Paekche
      sends five ambassadors to contact the Japanese court in 664, 665, 667, 669,
      and 671 respectively. In 664, the commander brings with him prisoners of
      war from Japan, Silla, Paekche, and Tamna to attend a ceremony during
      which Emperor Gaozong performs the ritual of worshiping Mt. Tai
      (Taishan).

670   A Japanese ambassador congratulates Emperor Gaozong on the Tang
      military conquest of Koguryŏ.

701   Awada no Ason Mahito, as "Ambassador Carrying the Ensign," visits
      China. One of his tasks is to obtain books. The Tang court arranges for the
      Japanese diplomats to shop at markets. While in China, Awada accepts the
      honorific Chinese title "Vice-Director of the Court of Imperial
      Entertainment."

716   Tajihi no Mahito Agatamori visits China as "supervising ambassador."
      While in Tang, he and other Japanese diplomats study the Chinese classics
      under the guidance of the Tang scholar Zhao Xuanmo. They use all the
      grants received from the Tang court to purchase books.

732   Tajihi no Mahito Hironari travels to Tang as ambassador. Nakatomi no

Ason Nashiro, the vice-ambassador, requests copies of the *Dao de jing* and portraits of Laozi from the Tang court.

750   As ambassador to China, Fujiwara no Kiyokawa impresses Emperor Xuanzong during a court audience. The emperor orders portraits of Kiyokawa and his two deputies to be made and stored in the palace. Kiyokawa accepts the title "Lord Specially Advanced" and his two vice-ambassadors, "Overseer for the Grand Master of Imperial Entertainments with Silver Seal and Blue Ribbon." Kiyokawa is also granted two special imperial favors before he leaves China—a tour of the worship halls for Confucianism, Buddhism, and Daoism in the inner palace and a poem written by Emperor Xuanzong.

759   Kō Gentaku is dispatched to China to fetch another Japanese ambassador who was sent to China earlier. Emperor Suzong sends Shen Weiyue to accompany Kō Gentaku back home.

761   Having appointed Naka no Mahito Ihatomo ambassador to China, the Japanese court decides, for the first time, to cancel a planned mission to China.

762   The court appoints Nakatomi no Takanushi ambassador to China but again cancels the voyage after the ships built for the delegation are damaged before leaving Japanese shores.

775   Saeki no Imaemishi, the ambassador to China, refuses to leave Japan, claiming he is sick. The delegation eventually leaves for China without an ambassador. The Tang emperor sends Zhao Baoying, Sun Xingjin, Qin Yanqi, Gao Helin, and others to accompany the Japanese diplomats back home.

778   As "Escorting Ambassador," Fuse no Ason Kiyonao, accompanies the Tang ambassador, Zhao Baoying, and others back home.

801   Fujiwara no Kuzunomaro, as "Ambassador Carrying the Ensign," pays respects to the Tang court. He receives from the court an "appointment order" with no specific position.

834   Fujiwara no Tsunetsugu travels to China as ambassador. His deputy Ono no Takamura, however, refuses to leave Japan and is consequently punished by banishment. Tsunetsugu receives from the Tang court the honorific title "General of the Cloudlike Flags of Great Tang, Acting Chamberlain for Ceremonial, and Concurrent Left General of the Imperial Insignia Guards."

894   The Japanese court appoints Sugawara no Michizane as ambassador to China. The chaotic situation in China, however, delays his departure, and the court eventually abandons the plan to send him.

Appendix 2

The Letter to the Surveillance Commissioner
at Fuzhou Drafted for the Ambassador

Kanō[1] writes *(qi):*[2]

Great mountains are calm, but beasts do not complain about the hardships, running to dwell on them. Deep waters are silent, but fishes and dragons do not mind the pains, rushing to live there. For the same reason, the western barbarians (Xiqiang)[3] can scale perilous peaks to pay tribute to the virtuous [Chinese] emperor *(chuiyi jun),*[4] while the southern tribesmen (Nanyi)[5] can cross deep oceans to present [gifts to] the enlightened [Chinese] ruler *(xing cuo di).*[6] Knowing well that the trip to China is so difficult and dangerous as to end in their death, still they disregard their own lives. This is indeed due to the far-reaching moral influence [of the Chinese emperor].

Humbly I think that the Great Tang is under sage rule, where frost and dew come seasonably, the Son of Heaven lives in fine palaces, one brilliant ruler follows the trail of his predecessor, and one sage emperor succeeds another. [His virtue] has spread everywhere to cover over the nine parts of the sky *(jiuye)*[7] and to encompass the eight corners *(bahong)* of the world.[8] Therefore, in my country, Japan, gentle breezes and timely rain come suitably, and we know for certain that there is a sage emperor in China. Cutting big trees on great peaks, [we build boats]; sending brilliant blossoms *(huanghua)*[9] to the vermilion court, [we dispatch ambassadors]. Holding jewels from Penglai[10] [and] offering jade of Kunyue,[11] [the Japanese ambassadors present tributary gifts to China]. [This practice] originated in high antiquity and continues until today. It has been observed [by successive Japanese emperors] without interruption.

[Out of his] consideration of the plan handed down by the ancestors and his admiration for the moral influence of the present Chinese emperor, the master of our land *(guozhu)*[12] thus now respectfully dispatches his ambassador, Fujiwara no Ason Kanō, Right Major Councillor of the State Council, senior third rank, and concurrent acting Grand Governor of Echizen,[13] and others to proffer national offerings and special gifts.

Irrespective of the peril to ourselves, Kanō and his fellows carried out this command and, at the risk of death, ventured upon the sea. After departing our native shores, en route to China we encountered a severe storm [in which] violent rains ripped the sails and murderous winds damaged the rudder. Great waves surged high as if they would reach the sky, tossing our small boats. In the morning, a south wind began to blow, making us afraid of being driven toward the island of Tamna,[14] whose people are as cruel as wolves. In the evening, a north

234 : APPENDIX 2

wind rose, and we dreaded being blown to the land of Ryūkyū, where the tribes-men have the nature of tigers. Our faces were contorted with fear because we anticipated being buried in the mouth of some giant turtle. We knitted our brows with dread because we feared we would find ourselves the occupants of a whale's belly. Our boats rose and fell with the waves and were blown north and south by the wind. All we could see was the blue color of sky and sea. How could we catch sight of white mist hanging over the mountains and valleys? We drifted with the waves for more than two months. Our water was exhausted, our crew worn out. The ocean was so vast, and the land so far away. [We were as helpless] as [birds] wanting to fly over the sky with wounded wings or [fish] wishing to swim across the sea with injured fins. How could we fully describe [the hardships we suffered]?

In the early eighth month, we suddenly saw a peak in the clouds. We were over-whelmed with joy even greater than that of an infant being brought to his mother or of withered sprouts being drenched with rain. That Kanō and his fellowmen ventured many times upon the deadly waves and have the chance to live again has been brought about by the virtuous power [of the Chinese emperor]. It was some-thing we [would have been] unable to achieve by our own strength.

Moreover, as for the treatment that the Great Tang accords the Japanese ambassadors, whereas they are compared to [ambassadors from] the eight [north-ern] tribesmen *(badi)* and the seven (western) barbarians *(qirong)* who gather like clouds and mist [in the Chinese capital], moving forward on their knees in the imperial palace and kowtowing at the Chinese court, [the Tang emperor in fact often] grants Japanese ambassadors special favor *(shusi)*[15] to help them complete their missions *(qucheng)*.[16] They are treated as distinguished guests *(shangke)*.[17]

Facing the dragon countenance, they receive his edicts in person. His auspi-cious inquiries and glorious favors shown toward them are far beyond their expectations. How can the Japanese ambassadors be mentioned in the same breath with those from insignificant barbarian [countries]?

Furthermore, bamboo and bronze tallies *(zhufu,*[18] *tongqi)*[19] were originally used as protection against fraud *(zhufu tongqi ben bei jianzha)*.[20] When [as in Japan] cus-toms are unaffected and the people straightforward, what is the use of such doc-uments? Thus, since our country has always been honest in serving its friendly neighbor [China], no list of gifts *(yinshu)* has ever been used when offering pres-ents [to Tang China], and none of our ambassadors has been treacherous. For generations, this has been the practice, which is still observed nowadays. Besides, ambassadors dispatched [to China] must be chosen from trusted subjects [of the Japanese Tennō]. As the appointees are all trusted servants, what further need is there for using a list? Is not this why Chinese works state, "To the east [of China], there is a country [Japan] where people are sincere and straightforward, and this is the land of propriety and the country of gentlemen"?[21]

But this time, officials from the [Fuzhou] prefecture blamed [the Japanese ambassador] for [not carrying] the document *(wenshu),* and they were suspicious of our trustworthiness. They inspected the ships and listed both the private and official goods on them. What they did complies with [the relevant Chinese] laws, and their actions are reasonable. This is surely the way conscientious officials should perform their duty. However, even though we had just arrived from a remote place, we were deeply troubled by this humiliating situation (chutu).[22] The weariness resulting from the hardships we suffered at the sea is still heavy on our hearts, and our hearts and bellies are not yet satiated with the flavor of the virtuous liquor [of the Chinese emperor]. Suddenly, new restrictions are imposed on us, making us feel completely at a loss.

Before the Jianzhong era [780–784], the ships of [Japanese] tributary missions arrived directly at Yangzhou and Suzhou. [Members of the missions] never suffered the anguish of being tossed adrift at sea. They were accorded solicitous hospitality by the officials from both prefectures and counties. The ambassadors were allowed to go about [their business] freely, and the goods on their ships were never inspected. However, what the officials [from Fuzhou prefecture] have now done to us is different from the precedent, and the reception given us is far from our anticipation. Humble and insignificant as we are, our hearts are filled with surprise and resentment.

Humbly I beg you [the surveillance commissioner at Fuzhou] to grant the grace of treating gently people from afar and to give due regard to the righteous value of befriending neighbors. If [you] could be tolerant of their customs and not consider their practices as outlandish, small streams of various barbarians will flow into Shun's sea,[23] and the hollyhocks of myriad [outer] subjects will raise their heads toward Yao's sun.[24] People drawn by the moral influence [of the Chinese emperor] will gladly [gather at the Chinese court] like spokes coming together at the hub of a wheel and like ants attracted to pungent meat,[25] happily forming lines to come. I humbly beg to be treated in the usual way by earnestly writing this letter, in which I have not expressed myself as well as I might have. Earnestly [I] write (jinqi).[26]

Appendix 3

Components of Japanese State Letters

1 Opening Sentence	3 Comment on Recent Weather	5 Regards to the Addressee	6 Account of the Sender's Situation	8 Ending Words	Source
大蕃國云 天皇敬問 小蕃國云 天皇問					Fujiwara no Tokihara, *Engi shiki,* 12, p. 359
東天皇敬 白西皇帝	季秋薄冷	尊如何， 想清愈	此如常	謹白不具	Toneri Shinnō, *Nihon shoki,* 22, p. 151, 608/9/11
天皇敬問 新羅 (國)王	春首猶寒	國境之內， 當並平安	比無恙也	指宜往意， 並寄土物 如別	Sugano no Mamichi, et al., *Shoku Nihongi,* 3, p. 24, 706/1/12
天皇敬問 新羅國王	寒氣嚴切	比如何也		指宜往意， 更不多及	*Shoku Nihongi,* 3, p. 27, 706/11/3
天皇敬問 渤海郡王	漸熱	想平安好			*Shoku Nihongi,* 10, p. 113, 728/4/16
天皇敬問 渤海國王	季夏甚熱		比無恙也	指宜往意	*Shoku Nihongi,* 19, p. 218, 753/6/8

1 Opening Sentence	3 Comment on Recent Weather	5 Regards to the Addressee	6 Account of the Sender's Situation	8 Ending Words	Source
天皇敬問 高麗國王	餘寒未退	想王如常		遣書指不 多及	*Shoku Nihongi*, 22, pp. 259–260, 759/2/1
天皇敬問 高麗國王	春景漸和	想王佳也		指此示懷	*Shoku Nihongi*, 32, p. 401, 772/2/28
天皇敬問 渤海國王	夏景炎熱	想王安和			*Shoku Nihongi*, 34, pp. 434–435, 777/5/23
天皇敬問 新羅國王	春景韶和	想王佳也		遣書指不 多及	*Shoku Nihongi*, 36, p. 457, 780/2/15
天皇敬問 渤海王	春寒	惟王平安		指此遣書， 旨不多及	Fujiwara no Otsugu et al., *Nihon kōki*, 21, p.96, 811/1/22
天皇敬問 渤海王	春首餘寒	王及首領 百姓并 平安好		略此還報， 一二無悉	*Nihon kōki*, 24, p. 131, 815/1/22

Abbreviations

BS	*Bei shi*
CFYG	*Cefu yuangui*
DTKYL	*Da Tang kaiyuan li*
HHS	*Hou Han shu*
HJAS	*Harvard Journal of Asiatic Studies*
HS	*Han shu*
JAOS	*Journal of the American Oriental Society*
JAS	*The Journal of Asian Studies*
JS	*Jin shu*
JTS	*Jiu Tang shu*
LS	*Liang shu*
NQS	*Nan Qi shu*
NS	*Nan shi*
QTW	*Quan Tang wen*
SBBY	*Sibu beiyao*
SBCK	*Sibu congkan*
SGZ	*San guo zhi*
SJ	*Shi ji*
SS	*Song shu*
SSJZS	*Shisan jing zhushu*
TD	*Tong dian*
TDZLJ	*Tang dazhaoling ji*
THY	*Tang huiyao*
TLD	*Tang liudian*
TPYL	*Taiping yulan*
WS	*Wei shu*
WYYH	*Wenyuan yinghua*
XTS	*Xin Tang shu*
ZZTJ	*Zizhi tongjian*

Notes

CHAPTER 1: THE ISLANDS OF IMMORTALS

1. Xiao Yi, *Jin louzi*, 5, p. 5; Ren Fan, *Shuyi ji*, a, p. 19a. See also Edward H. Schafer, "Fusang and Beyond," pp. 379–380.
2. Zhang Junfang, *Yunji qiqian* (*SBCK* edn.), 100, pp. 5a–b.
3. Wang Jia, *Shiyi ji*, 10, pp. 5a–5b; Ren Fan, *Shuyi ji*, a, p. 15a.
4. Sima Qian, *Shi ji* (hereafter *SJ*), 6, p. 247; 28, p. 1369.
5. Li Fang, *Taiping guangji*, 4, p. 26; Luo Jun, *Baoqing siming zhi*, 12, p. 17a.
6. Scholars have identified Xu Fu (255 B.C.–?) as a native of Qi, one of the Warring States. His ancestor was the lord of a principality in eastern China during the Western Zhou dynasty. The exact birthplace of Xu Fu is still debated by scholars. See Wang Jinlin, *Han Tang wenhua yu gudai Riben wenhua*, pp. 52–53.
7. *SJ*, 118, p. 3086; Fan Ye, *Hou Han Shu* (hereafter *HHS*), 85, p. 2822; Chen Shou, *San guo zhi* (hereafter *SGZ*), 47, p. 1136; Liu Xu et al., comps., *Jiu Tang shu* (hereafter *JTS*), 2, p. 33; Li Fang, *Taiping yulan* (hereafter *TPYL*), 782, p. 6a.
8. Wang Yucheng, *Xiaochu ji* (*SBCK* edn.), 14, pp. 6a–b.
9. Wang Chong, *Lun heng* (*SBCK* edn.), 5, p. 5a; 8, p. 8a; 19, p. 9b. See also Hashikawa Tokio, "Wajin ga chōsō o mitsuida koto," in *Ishihama sensei koki kinen Tōyōgaku ronsō*, ed. Ishihama Sensei Koki Kinenkai, pp. 449–458. In this book, representatives sent to China by various tribal leaders in Japan before its political unification in the fifth century are called "messengers." In contrast, the head of a diplomatic mission and his deputy representing a unified Japan under the Yamato court from the fifth century onward are referred to as "ambassador" and "vice-ambassador" respectively.
10. Li Yanshou, *Nan shi* (hereafter *NS*), 10, p. 307.
11. Pronunciation for this term is specified in Ban Gu, *Han shu* (hereafter *HS*), 28b, p. 1659; Chen Pengnian, *Guang yun* (*SBBY* edn.), 2, p. 17b. Gao You's annotation to the *Huainan zi* (*SBCK* edn.), 2, p. 10b, suggests that the Chinese were knowledgeable of the Wo language in the Eastern Han dynasty. "Wo" is used throughout this book to refer to tribal units on the Japanese archipelagos before the fifth century. When quoting Japanese sources on these tribal units, however, I use the Japanese transliteration "Wa." In contrast, the term "Japan" is employed to refer to the unified state after the fifth century. Japanese scholars generally believe that the term "Japan" (Yamato) came into use during the reign of Suiko Tennō (593–628). Chinese records, however, suggest that it was not until Empress Wu Zetian's time (r. 685–704) that the term in question came into use. See *JTS*, 199a, p. 5340.

12. See examples in *HHS*, 85, p.2818; *SGZ*, 30, p. 849; Shen Yue, *Song shu*, 97, p. 2394. For further discussions of the Wo, see Mark Hudson, "Ethnicity in East Asia: Approaches to the Wa," pp. 51–63; see also his *Ruins of Identity: Ethnogenesis in the Japanese Islands*, pp. 175–205; Uchida Ginpū, "Gishi Wajinden naka no nettaiteki shokiji ni tsuite," in *Tōhōgaku ronshū*, ed. Ono Katsutoshi Hakase Shōju Kinenkai, pp. 51–57; Miki Tarō, *Wajinden no yōgo no kenkyū*, p. 276; and Kōmei Sasaki, "The Wa People and Their Culture in Ancient Japan: The Cultures of Swidden Cultivation and Padi-Rice Cultivation," pp. 24–46. Masako Nakagawa, however, seems to believe that the term "Wo" in Chinese records refers specifically to ancient Japan. See her "The *Shan-hai ching* and *Wo:* A Japanese Connection."

13. Xu Shen, *Shuowen jiezi*, 8, p. 162; Gu Yewang, *Yu pian* (*SBBY* edn.), 3, p. 19.

14. *HS*, 28b, p. 1658.

15. *HHS*, 1b, p. 84.

16. *SGZ*, 30, p. 857. For discussions of Chinese opinions of Japan and the "Eastern Barbarians," see Inoue Hideo, "Go Kanjo no Tōikan," in *Ono Katsutoshi hakase shōju kinen tōhōgaku ronshū*, ed. Ono Katsutoshi Hakase Shōju Kinenkai, pp. 33–56. See also his "Sangokushi no Tōi ōshakan."

17. English translations of these accounts are in L. C. Goodrich and R. Tsunoda, *Japan in the Chinese Dynastic Histories*, pp. 14–59. Unless indicated otherwise, the following discussion of ancient Japan is based on records from *HHS*, 85, pp. 2820–2822; and *SGZ*, 30, pp. 854–856.

18. For discussions of archaeological findings in Japan, see Richard Pearson, "The Contribution of Archaeology to Japanese Studies"; Anazawa Wakou and Manome Tun'ichi, "Two Inscribed Swords from Japanese Tumul," in *Windows on the Japanese Past: Studies in Archaeology*, ed. Richard Pearson, Gina L. Barnes, and K. Hutterer, pp. 375–395; Kiyotari Tsuboi, "Issues in Japanese Archaeology"; Jonathan Edward Kidder Jr., "The Earliest Societies in Japan," in *Ancient Japan*, ed. Delmer M. Brown, vol. 1 of *The Cambridge History of Japan*, ed. John W. Hall et al., pp. 48–107; and Gina Barnes, *Protohistoric Yamato: Archaeology of the First Japanese State*. For contacts between Japan and the Asian continent, see Takashi Okazaki, "Japan and the Continent," in *Ancient Japan*, ed. Delmer M. Brown, vol. 1 of *The Cambridge History of Japan*, ed. John W. Hall et al., pp. 268–316.

19. Wang Qinruo, *Cefu Yuangui* (hereafter *CFYG*), 959, p. 15b; Makoto Sahara, "Rice Cultivation and the Japanese."

20. *CFYG*, 959, p. 15b.

21. Wei Zheng et al., comps., *Sui shu*, 81, p. 1827; Akazawa Takeru, "Maritime Adaptation of Prehistoric Hunter-Gatherers and Their Transition to Agriculture in Japan"; A. Okikawa and S. Koyama, "A Jomon Shellmound Database," pp. 187–200; C. Melvin Aikens and Akazawa Takeru, "Fishing and Farming in Early Japan: Jomon Littoral Tradition Carried into Yayoi Times

at the Miura Caves on Tokyo Bay," in *Pacific Northeast Asia in Prehistory: Hunter-Fisher-Gatherers, Farmers, and Sociopolitical Elites,* ed. C. Melvin Aikens and Song Nai Rhee, pp. 75–82; Mori Kōichi, *Kōkogaku to kodai Nihon,* pp. 52–60.

22. For a discussion of the Japanese diet, see Masao Minagawa and Takeru Akazawa, "Dietary Patterns of Japanese Jomon Hunter-Gatherers: Stable Nitrogen and Carbon Isotope Analysis of Human Bones," in *Pacific Northeast Asia in Prehistory,* ed. C. Melvin Aikens and Song Nai Rhee, pp. 59–68.

23. The loom parts were found in Toro, Shizuoka city, and the bronze bell in Kagawa county, Shikoku prefecture. See Nunome Junrō, "Dōtakumen no kōjikei kigu o motta jimbutsu gazō ni tsuite," pp. 25–31; Mark Hudson, "From Toro to Yoshinogari: Changing Perspectives on Yayoi Period Archaeology," in *Bibliographic Reviews of Far Eastern Archaeology: Hoabinhinan, Jōmon, Yayoi, Early Korean States,* ed. Gina L. Barnes, pp. 63–112.

24. Michiko Y. Aoki, *Records of Wind and Earth: A Translation of Fudoki with Introduction and Commentaries,* pp. 38, 51, 69, 70, 101, 114, 128, 192, 239, 245, and 254.

25. *TPYL,* 814, p. 4a.

26. *NS,* 76, p. 1976; Yao Silian, *Liang Shu* (hereafter *LS*), 54, p. 808.

27. Ō no Yasumaro, *Kojiki,* C, p. 323.

28. *TPYL,* 820, pp. 6b–7a.

29. For a discussion of tattooing in ancient Japan, see Robert van Gulik, *Irezumi: The Pattern of Dematography in Japan,* p. 247.

30. For blackened teeth, see Yuan Ke, *Shanhai jing jiaozhu,* pp. 259 and 348, translated in Anne Birrell, *The Classic of Mountains and Seas,* pp. 128 and 160. See also Liu An, *Huainan zi* (*SBCK* edn.), 4, p. 8a; Xiao Tong, *Wen xuan* (*SBCK* edn.), 5, p. 23a; and 12, p. 6b; and William H. and Helen Craig McCullough, *A Tale of Flowering Fortunes,* vol. 2, pp. 589 and 647.

31. Higuchi Kiyoyuki, "Yon-roku seiki no i shoku jū," in *Zemināru Nihon kodaishi(ge),* ed. Ueda Masaaki et al., pp. 553–562.

32. Yamao Yukihisa, *Gishi Wajinden,* p. 158. For the beliefs concerning death, see Gary L. Ebersole, *Ritual Poetry and the Politics of Death in Early Japan,* pp. 79–86.

33. This custom is also recorded in Japanese sources. See Basil Hall Chamberlain, trans., *The Kojiki: Records of Ancient Matters,* p. 116; W. G. Aston, trans., *Nihongi: Chronicles of Japan from the Earliest Time to A.D. 697,* p. 326. According to Chen Jianxian, the custom might have originated from south China. See his "Jing Chu wufeng yu Riben gusu," in *Zhong Ri minsu de yitong he jiaoliu,* ed. Jia Huixuan and Shen Renan, p. 200.

34. Li Yanshou, *Bei shi* (hereafter *BS*), 94, p. 3136. This practice is known as *kugatachi,* which the Wo court still used from the third to the six centuries. See Toneri Shinnō et al., comps., *Nihon shoki* (*Shintei zōho kokushi taikei* edn.),

10, p. 273, 278/4; 13, p. 340, 415/9; and 17, p. 31, 530/9. (Subsequent *Nihon shoki* citations are to this edition unless otherwise specified.) In these records, a person's innocence was tested by the court "giving orders to ask the Gods of Heaven and Earth (to answer by means of) the ordeal by boiling water," or "calling the Gods to witness (when they) plunge their hands in boiling water," or "setting (the caldrons for) the ordeal by boiling water." The English translations are from Aston, *Nihongi*, vol. 1, pp. 258 and 316; and vol. 2, p. 22.

35. Gina L. Barnes, *China, Korea, and Japan: The Rise of Civilization in East Asia*, p. 218.

36. Takemoto Toru suggests "Yamai" was the name of this state. See his "The Kyūshū Dynasty: Furuta's Theory on Ancient Japan."

37. The top and the bottom of this tower are depicted on the shards of a jar discovered at the Karakokagi site, Nara. See *Mainichi Shimbun*, 1992.5.21.

38. Jonathan Edward Kidder Jr., "Yoshinogari and the Yamatai Problem"; Sahara Makoto, "Yoshinogari, the World of the Wei Dynasty Annals," in *Ancient Japan*, ed. Richard J. Pearson, pp. 154–157; Imamura Keiji, *Prehistoric Japan: New Perspective on Insular East Asia*, pp. 182–185; Mark Hudson and Gina Barnes, "Yoshinogari: A Yayoi Settlement in Northern Kyūshū."

39. Barnes, *China, Korea, and Japan*, p. 221; Makoto Sahara, "Once There Was a War: Changes in Stone Projectile Points."

40. According to Yamao Yukihisa, "Himiko" is an abbreviation for "Fimemiko," meaning "a female who was close to and served the god." This term refers to someone who possessed mystical power and is therefore not a personal name but a title. See his *Gishi Wajinden*, p. 201.

41. In Korea, for example, after sowing in the spring and the harvest in autumn, sacrifices were offered to ghosts and deities. During the ceremony people drank and danced day and night. *HHS*, 85, pp. 2810 and 2813.

42. Yamao Yukihisa, *Gishi Wajinden*, pp. 207–211. Himiko's "Way of Spirits" might already have been a primitive creed similar to proto-Daoism in China. See Ueda Masaaki, *Wakoku no sekai*, pp. 77–80. As late as the Heian period, the court still appointed "imperial shamans who knew the way of ghosts and deities." See Kiyohara no Natsuno et al., *Ryō no gigei*, 2, pp. 31–32. The term *guidao* also appears in *SGZ*, 8, p. 263.

43. These Japanese principalities were "secondary states," the formation of which took place through close contact with an already extant and operating state. See Barbara J. Price, "Secondary State Formation: An Explanatory Note," in *Origins of the State*, ed. Ronald Cohen and Elman R. Service, pp. 161–184; and Song Nai Rhee, "Secondary State Formation: The Case of Koguryŏ," in *Pacific Northeast Asia in Prehistory*, pp. 191–196.

44. *HHS*, 1b, p. 84; 5, p. 208; and 85, p. 2821.

45. They came to China in 238, 243, 245, and 247. The time of the visit by Iyo's envoy, however, is not specified. See *SGZ*, 30, pp. 857–858.
46. *JS*, 3, pp. 55 and 72–74; Toneri Shinnō et al., *Nihon shoki*, 10, p. 282.
47. *JS*, 10, p. 264.
48. Ten to the Southern Song court (420–479) in 421, 425, 430, 438, 443, 451, 460, 462, 477, and 478; one to the Southern Qi court (479–502) in 479; and another to the Southern Liang court (502–557) in 502. See Shen Yue, *Song shu* (hereafter *SS*), 97, pp. 2394–2395; Xiao Zixian, *Nan Qi shu* (hereafter *NQS*), 58, p. 1012; *NS*, 6, p. 185; and 79, p. 1975; and *LS*, 2, p. 36; 54, p. 807.
49. They arrived in China in 600, 607, 608, 610, and 614. See Wei Zheng et al., *Sui shu*, 81, pp. 1826–1827; and Toneri Shinnō et al., *Nihon shoki*, 22, pp. 148, 151, and 157.
50. They were appointed in 630, 653, 654, 659, 665, 669, 701, 716, 732, 750, 759, 761, 762, 775, 778, 801, 834, and 849. Those appointed in 761, 762, and 894 did not, in the end, go to China. For a chart with more information about these envoys, see Mori Katsumi, *Ken Tō shi*, pp. 25–27. A brief English description of the Japanese envoys dispatched to Sui and Tang appears in Edwin O. Reischauer, *Ennin's Travels in T'ang China*, pp. 42–47.

CHAPTER 2: CHINESE INSIGNIA
IN EAST ASIAN POLITICS

1. Imamura Keiji, *Prehistoric Japan: New Perspective on Insular East Asia*, pp. 185–186 and 223; Mori Kōichi, *Kokōgaku to kodai Nihon*, pp. 87–104.
2. *JS*, 97, p. 2536. This may be a mistake for 239. A quotation of the *Wei zhi* in the *Nihon shoki* attaches this event to the third year of the Jingchu period, i.e., 239. See Toneri Shinnō et al., *Nihon shoki*, 9, pp. 257 and 239. For easy location of information on events recorded in official Japanese chronicles, the year, month, and date (if available) of an event are indicated by numbers following the page reference. An intercalary month in the lunar calendar is indicated by an asterisk.
3. This tribe used to inhabit northwestern China but moved farther west early in Han Wendi's reign (179–157 B.C.). In about 139 B.C., it eventually settled down along the Amu Darya River, whose course forms part of the Kazakhstan-Afghanistan border.
4. *SGZ*, 3, p. 97; Ōba Osamu, "'Himiko o Shin Gi Waō to suru seisho' o meguru mondai," in *Suenaga sensei koki kinen kodaigaku ronsō*, ed. Suenaga Sensei Koki Kinenkai, p. 182. Charlotte von Verschuer has translated the title for Himiko "Qin Wei Wowang" into "Queen of Wo, Friend of the Wei Dynasty" *(reine de Wo, amie de la dynaste des Wei)*. See her *Les relations officielles du Japon avec la Chine aux VIIIe et IXe siècles*, p. xiv. This translation, however, obscures the overlord-vassal nature of the relations between Wei and Wo.

5. *HHS,* 28, p. 3632; *SGZ,* 30, pp. 833–835 and 837.

6. *SGZ,* 30, p. 857; Takeda Sachiko, *Kodai kokka no keisei to ifukusei,* pp. 221–222.

7. Xu Shen, *Shuowen jiezi,* 7b, p. 23b; *HS,* 76, p. 3215; Liu Xi, *Shi ming (SBCK* edn.), 7, p. 54b.

8. *HHS,* 47, p. 1578.

9. *SGZ,* 60, p. 1390; *JTS,* 194a, p. 5164; 194b, p. 5185; 198, p. 5300; and 199b, p. 5344.

10. Wei Zheng et al., *Sui shu,* 84, p.1871.

11. *SGZ,* 30, pp. 857–858. The Wo messengers visited the Wei court in 240, 243, 245, and 247 respectively. For a discussion of Wei-Wo relations, see Martin Collcutt, Marius Jansen, and Isao Kumakura, *Cultural Atlas of Japan,* pp. 45–46.

12. Yu Shinan, *Beitang shuchao,* 63, p. 1a; Xu Jian, *Chuxue ji,* 12, p. 304; *TPYL,* 241, p. 3a. See also Ōba Osamu, "Kan no chūrōshō kōi to Gi no sozzen chūrōshō sozzen kōi."

13. *SGZ,* 30, p. 850. This official was from the state of Chenhan in southeastern Korea.

14. Gari Ledyard, "Yin and Yang in the China-Manchuria-Korea Triangle," in *China among Equals,* ed. Morris Rossabi, p. 334.

15. Ouyang Xiu, *Xin Tang shu* (hereafter *XTS*), 219, p. 6183.

16. *SS,* 14, p. 345.

17. Sakamoto Yoshitane, *Kodai Higashi Ajia no Nihon to Chōsen,* p. 327. See also Ikeuchi Hiroshi, "Kōson shi no Taihōgun setchi to Sō Gi no Rakurō Taihō nigun," in *Man-Senshi kenkyū (jōsei),* vol. 1, pp. 237–250; Nishijima Sadao, "Shin Gi Waō sakuhō ni itaru Higashi Ajia no jōsei," in *Kodaishi rōnsō,* ed. Inoue Mitsusada Hakase Kanreki Kinenkai, pp. 1–48; and Mori Kōichi, *Kokōgaku to kodai Nihon,* pp. 80–86.

18. *SGZ,* 8, p. 254; K. H. J. Gardiner, "The Kung-sun Warriors of Liao-tung (189–293)."

19. *SGZ,* 30, p. 849.

20. Ibid., 4, p. 121; 30, p. 851.

21. Fang Xuanling et al., comps., *Jin Shu* (hereafter *JS*), 97, p. 2533.

22. The provisional nature of any titles that a foreign ruler granted to himself is evident in the use of the term *jia* to describe his action in Chinese sources. See Lü Buwei, *Lüshi chunqiu (SBCK* edn.), 17, p. 4a. When used as a verb, *jia* implies that the action of granting a title, position, or instruments was itself a temporary measure. Examples are found in *HHS,* 47, p. 1577; *SGZ,* 30, p. 851; and *XTS,* 198, p. 5647. In particular, the connotation of the verb *jia* constitutes a contrast with that of *wei, chu,* and *shou,* use of which delivers the message that a title was formally granted to someone. Wei Shou, *Wei Shu* (hereafter *WS*), 30, pp. 728–729; and 74, pp. 1643–1645.

23. Hirano Kunio, "Nichi-Chō-Chū sangoku kankei ron ni tsuite no oboegaki," pp. 58 and 60.

24. The Wei edict announced the formal bestowal of "Pro-Wei Queen of Wo" using the sentence pattern "appoint someone as something" *(yi . . . wei . . .),* a practice from the beginning of the Han dynasty. See *HHS,* 5, p. 3121; and Ōba Osamu, "'Himiko o Shin Gi Waō to suru seisho' o meguru mondai," p. 179.

25. *SGZ,* 30, p. 857. Here *jia* is used as an adjective and attached to a title or a position, indicating that both the title and the position were created on special occasions and were revocable later on. The following are some examples: "acting grand protector" *(jiashou)* in *SJ,* 95, p. 3847; "concurrent subofficial functionary" *(jiali)* in *HS,* 54, p. 2460; "temporary rank" *(jiapin)* and "temporary title" *(jiajue)* in *WS,* 113, p. 2975; and "acting chief minister of the Court for State Ceremonial" *(jia Honglu qing)* in *JTS,* 47, p. 1577; *CFYG,* 997, p. 12b.

26. Sakamoto Yoshitane, *Kodai Higashi Ajia no Nihon to Chōsen,* pp. 278–280. For the term *jiashou,* see also a record in *JS,* 1, p. 6.

27. *JTS,* 198, pp. 5294–5295.

28. Sima Guang, *Zizhi tongjian* (hereafter *ZZTJ*), 195, p. 6146.

29. *XTS,* 220, p. 6204.

30. *JTS,* 197, p. 5283.

31. Cornelius J. Kiley, "State and Dynasty in Archaic Yamato"; Imamura, *Prehistoric Japan,* p. 224.

32. *JS,* 10, p. 264; Ikeda On, "Giki kyūnen Wakoku kenhōbutsu o megutte," in *Egami Namio Kyōju koki kinen ronshū,* ed. Egami Namio Kyōju Koki Kinen Jigyōkai, p. 27. See also Kurihara Tomonobu, "Shichishitō no meimon yori mita Nihon to Kudara Tōshin no kankei"; and Murayama Shichiro and Roy A. Miller, "The Inariyama Tumulus Sword Inscription."

33. *SS,* 97, pp. 2392 and 2393–2394.

34. Koguryŏ dispatched its first delegation to Song in 423; Paekche followed suit in 424. See *SS,* 97, pp. 2392 and 2394.

35. Hirano Kunio, "Nichi-Chō-Chū sangoku kankei ron ni tsuite no oboegaki," pp. 60–61; Sakamoto Yoshitane, *Kodai Higashi Ajia no Nihon to Chōsen,* pp. 26–27, 65–67, 121, and 197.

36. *SS,* 97, p. 2394.

37. Ibid. See also *SS,* 5, p. 85.

38. "Hanzei" is probably a mistake for "Ingyō" since the former had already stepped down in 410. However, positive identification of this Wo ruler has been difficult since Japanese sovereigns prior to 539 were mostly legendary, and Chinese records about them also are not always accurate. For a discussion of Chinese official titles granted to Wo rulers during the fifth century, see Sakamoto Yoshitane, *Wa no goō,* pp. 146–217.

39. Ōba Osamu, "Zen Kan no shōgun," in his *Shin Kan hōseishi no kenkyū,* pp.

357–362. *Jiangjun* first appears in Gongyang Gao, *Chunqiu Gongyang zhuan* (*SSJZS* edn.), 16, p. 2285.

40. Paekche and Silla were located in southwest and southeast Korea respectively; Qinhan was to the east of the Naktong River, and Muhan, also known as Mahan, occupied modern Kyŏnggi, Ch'ungch'ŏng, and Chŏlla provinces. For a discussion of relations between Japan and Korean states, see Hirano Kunio, "The Yamato State and Korea in the Fourth and the Fifth Centuries."

41. Charles O. Hucker, *A Dictionary of Official Titles in Imperial China,* s.v. "Shih ch'ih-chieh."

42. Sakamoto Yoshitane, *Kodai Higashi Ajia no Nihon to Chōsen,* pp. 268 and 288.

43. *NQS,* 58, p. 1012; *NS,* 79, p. 1975.

44. Takeda Yukio, "Heisei shōgun Wazui no kaishaku," p. 5.

45. *SS,* 97, pp. 2392 and 2394.

46. Sakamoto Yoshitane, *Kodai Higashi Ajia no Nihon to Chōsen,* p. 291. Other member states of the ring included Rouran in the north and Tuyuhun, Wudu Wang, Hexi Wang, and Dangchang Wang in the west.

47. *SS,* 97, p. 2395; and 5, p. 100; *NS,* 2, p. 53.

48. *SS,* 6, p. 129; *NS,* 2, p. 65. That a Chinese court sometimes bestowed titles on an abdicated foreign ruler was not an unusual act when means of communication were primitive and information on foreign events could reach the Chinese court long after they had occurred.

49. *SS,* 10, p. 197; and 97, pp. 2395–2396; *NS,* 3, p. 91. For a discussion of the situation in East Asia, and the relations between Japan and various Chinese and Korean States, see Nishijima Sadao, "Yon–roku seiki no Higashi Ajia to Nihon," in *Zemināru Nihon Kodaishi (ge),* ed. Ueda Masaaki et al., pp. 599–606.

50. *NQS,* 58, p. 1012; *NS,* 79, p. 1975.

51. *LS,* 2, p. 36; *NS,* 6, p. 185; and 79, p. 1975. See also Sakamoto Yoshitane, "Wa no goō no shakugō mondai," in *Zemināru Nihon kodaishi (2),* ed. Ueda Masaaki et al., pp. 381–392.

52. *LS,* 2, p. 36; *NS,* 6, p. 185.

53. *LS,* 54, p. 801.

54. Miyazaki Ichisada, *Nazo no shichishitō,* p. 192. See also his "Shichishitō meimon shishaku."

55. Takeda Yukio, "Heisei shōgun Wazui no kaishaku," p. 5.

56. Ibid., p. 21.

57. Ibid., pp. 29–31.

58. *SS,* 97, p. 2395. For a discussion of the state letter that Yūryaku presented to the Song court, see Yokoyama Sadahiro, "Waō Bu no jōhyōbun ni tsuite."

59. Hucker, *A Dictionary of Official Titles,* s.v. "K'ai-fu yi-t'ung san-ssu."

60. Du You, *Tong dian* (hereafter *TD*), 185, p. 989; Wang Pu, *Tang huiyao* (hereafter *THY*), 100, p. 1792.

61. Hucker, *A Dictionary of Official Titles*, s.v. "T'e-chin": "a supplementary title, in early use apparently only as an honorific."

62. Situo, *Enryaku sōroku*, in *Tōdaiji yōroku*, ed. Tsutsui Eishun, vol. 1, p. 21.

63. Fujiwara no Otsugu et al., comps., *Nihon kōki*, 12, p. 42, 805/6/8. For discussions of "appointment order," see Ōba Osamu, "Tō kokushin no kobungakuteki kenkyū," in *Seiiki bunka kenkyū*, ed. Seiiki Bunka Kenkyūkai, vol. 3, pp. 281–368.

64. Hucker, *A Dictionary of Official Titles*, s.v. "Yün-hui chiang-chün": "Merit title for military officers of rank 3b1."

65. Ibid., s.v. "Chien-chiao t'ai-ch'ang-ch'ing": "An honorary status without any real authority."

66. Ennin, *Nittō guhō junrei kōki*, 1, p. 20.

67. Howard J. Wechsler, "T'ai-tsung (reign 626–649) the Consolidator," in *Sui and T'ang China, 589–906*, ed. Denis C. Twitchett, vol. 3, part 1 of *The Cambridge History of China*, ed. John K. Fairbank and Denis C. Twitchett, pp. 231–235.

68. Ise Sentarō, *Chūgoku seiiki keieishi no kenkyū*, pp. 326–328 and 337–341. See also Kaneko Shūichi, "Tōdai sakuhōsei ippan," in *Higashi Ajia shi ni okeru kokka to nōmin*, ed. Nishijima Sadao Hakase Kanreki Kinenkai, pp. 311–312.

69. *HHS*, 89, p. 2946.

70. Song Minqiu, *Tang dazhaoling ji* (hereafter *TDZLJ*), 128, p. 2725. See also Wang Zhenping, "Act on Appropriateness and Mutual Self-Interest: Early T'ang Diplomatic Thinking, 618–649."

71. Tezuka Takayoshi, "Shin Gi Waō kō," p. 26.

CHAPTER 3: THE MESSENGER OF THE EMPEROR

1. Jia Changchao, *Qunjing yinbian* (*SBCK* edn.), 6, p. 5b.

2. James Legge, *The Chinese Classics*, vol. 5, p. 360.

3. Bai Juyi, *Baishi liutie shilei ji*, 10, p. 35b.

4. *ZZTJ*, 192, p. 6039.

5. Ichikawa Seinei, *Quan Tang shi yi*, in *Quan Tang shi*, a, p. 10173.

6. Qian Qi, *Qian Kaogong ji* (*SBCK* edn.), 5, p. 6b; Huangfu Zeng, *Tang Huangfu Zeng shiji* (*SBCK* edn.), 1, p. 68a; Peng Dingqiu, *Quan Tang shi*, 779, p. 8813; 787, p. 8875; 813, p. 9157. For the role that members of Japanese missions to China played in assimilating Chinese culture, see Verschuer, *Relations officielles*, pp. 187–230.

7. *ZZTJ*, 196, p. 6169.

8. *JTS*, 12, p. 356.

9. *SGZ*, 57, pp. 1332–1333.

10. Xing Bing, *Lun yu zhushu* (*SSJZS* edn.), 13, p.2507.

11. *THY*, 59, p. 1028; *CFYG*, 999, p. 20b.

12. Xu Shizeng, *Wenti mingbian xushuo*, p. 166.

13. Xing Bing, *Lun yu zhushu*, 13, p. 2507; *HS*, 72, p. 3066.

14. Kong Yingda, *Mao shi zhengyi* (*SSJZS* edn.), 3, p. 316. Wang Jun, a scholar in the reign of Han Zhaodi (r. 86–74 B.C.), was recommended to hold an official post for his mastery of this skill. See *HS*, 72, p. 3066. For other records concerning the *zhuandui*, see *HS*, 99b, pp. 4139–4140; *HHS*, 24, p. 852; and *SGZ*, 59, p. 1365. For *zhuandui* in Tang and Song sources, see Quan Deyu, *Quan Zaizhi wenji* (*SBCK* edn.), 36, pp. 3b and 4a; Zhou Shaoliang, *Tangdai muzhiming huibian*, b, p. 1887; and Dugu Ji, *Piling ji* (*SBCK* edn.), 15, p. 8b; and 16, p. 5b.

15. Xing Bing, *Lun yu zhushu*, 13, p. 2507; Legge, *The Chinese Classics*, vol. 1, p. 129.

16. Xing Bing, *Lun yu zhushu*, 13, p. 2508.

17. Wang Liqi, *Yanshi jiaxun jijie*, vol. 4, pp. 290–291; Wei Zheng et al., *Sui shu*, 51, p. 1337.

18. Xu Yin, *Xu gong Diaoji wenji* (*SBCK* edn.), 1, p. 6a.

19. Yuan Zhen, *Yuan Zhen ji*, vol. 46, p. 497.

20. *CFYG*, 664, p. 3502. For a discussion of Gao's visit to Japan, see Takigawa Masajirō, "Shichi seiki no Tōa henkyoku to Nihon shoki," in *Nihon shoki kenkyū*, ed. Yokoda Kenichi, vol. 6, pp. 208–220.

21. Xiang Zonglu, ed., *Shuoyuan jiaozheng*, vol. 12, p. 293; Bai Juyi, *Baishi liutie shilei ji*, 10, p. 35b.

22. *SJ*, 110, p. 2913.

23. Wei Zheng et al., *Sui shu*, 51, p. 1332.

24. Kong Yingda, *Li ji zhengyi* (*SSJZS* edn.), 11, p. 1327. During the Zhou dynasty, grand master was the designation of the second highest category of officials below minister. See Hucker, *A Dictionary of Official Titles*, s.v. "Ta-fu."

25. Wei Zheng et al., *Sui shu*, 81, p. 1827. Toneri Shinnō, *Nihon shoki*, 22, p. 150, 608/8/12, identifies Pei as a steward (*zhangke*) in the Office of State Visitors (Dianke Shu), which was a unit of the Court of State Ceremonial (Honglu Si), a position that was also of the ninth rank. See Wei Zheng et al., *Sui shu*, 28, p. 776.

26. Wang Wei, *Wang Youcheng ji* (*SBCK* edn.), 12, p. 2b.

27. For a discussion of Gao Biaoren, see Ikeda On, "Hai Seisei to Kō Byōjin."

28. *HS*, 94a, pp. 3773–3774.

29. *JTS*, 199a, p. 5332.

30. Ibid., 130, p. 3629; Peng Dingqiu, *Quan Tang shi*, 271, p. 3033. This was also the practice of the Song dynasty when sending ambassadors to the Qidan, its main adversary in the north. See Yue Ke, *Kui tan lu* (*SBCK* edn.), 6, p. 13b.

31. *THY*, 67, 1183; 97, p. 1737.

32. Liu Xi, *Shi ming*, 6, p. 45b.

33. Zhangsun Wuji, *Gu Tanglü shuyi*, 25, p. 454.

34. *THY*, 99, p. 1769; *TD*, 185, p. 989; *CFYG*, 662, p. 3495; and 664, p. 3502;

ZZTJ, 193, p. 6090; *TPYL*, 782, p. 5a. Tang ambassadors sent to other countries also carried *jie*; see *JTS*, 196a, p. 5236; and *THY*, 100, p. 1785. For a detailed discussion of *jie*, see Edwin Pulleyblank, *The Background of the Rebellion of An Lu-shan*, p. 149, note 32. See also Robert des Rotours, "Les insignes en deux parties (fou) sous la dynastie des T'ang," pp. 92–93.

35. Zheng Xuan et al., *Zhou li zhushu* (*SSJZS* edn.), 15, p. 739; Liu Xi, *Shi ming*, 6, p. 45b.

36. *HHS*, 26, p. 3599; Zhangsun Wuji, *Gu Tanglü shuyi*, 10, p. 213.

37. Zhangsun Wuji, *Gu Tanglü shuyi*, 10, pp. 203–204; Wallace Johnson, *The T'ang Code*, vol. 2, pp. 87–88.

38. *ZZTJ*, 194, p. 6117.

39. Zhangsun Wuji, *Gu Tanglü shuyi*, 10, p. 213; Johnson, *The T'ang Code*, vol. 2, pp. 98–99.

40. *JTS*, 112, p. 3336; *THY*, 67, p. 1183.

41. *XTS*, 197, p. 5629; *CFYG*, 160, p. 9b. For a discussion of this issue, see Li Jinxiu, *Tangdai caizhengshi gao (xia)*, vol. b, p. 787.

42. *JTS*, 149, p. 4016; *CFYG*, 654, pp. 18a–b; Zhou Xunchu, ed., *Tang yulin jiaozheng*, 3, p. 235.

43. *JTS*, 98, p. 3076; *THY*, 62, p. 1083.

44. *JTS*, 98, p. 3076.

45. Ibid., 75, p. 2629; and 130, p. 3629.

46. Ibid., 96, p. 3025.

47. *THY*, 79, p. 1452.

48. Sugano no Mamichi et al., comps., *Shoku Nihongi*, 24, p. 285, 762/1/6, p. 288, 762/8/9, and p. 292, 763/1/17; 36, p. 464, 780/11/26, p. 465, 780/12/4; 38, p. 500, 784/6/2, and p. 521, 786/8/22. Xu Gongqing and Lu Rujin, for example, received the family names of Kiyokawa and Sakiyama respectively.

49. Ibid., 24, p. 287.

50. Zhu Qingyu, *Zhu Qingyu shiji* (*SBCK* edn.), pp. 4a and 7a; Peng Dingqiu, *Quan Tang shi*, 787, p. 8875. See also Sugano no Mamichi et al., *Shoku Nihongi*, 35, p. 448, 779/4/19.

51. *JTS*, 62, p. 2380.

52. Wei Zheng et al., *Sui shu*, 81, p. 1817; *JTS*, 2, p. 30; 3, p. 44; 194a, pp. 5155 and 5157; *XTS*, 86, p. 3709; *ZZTJ*, 187, pp. 5840 and 5855; and 196, pp. 6177 and 6179.

53. *JTS*, 62, p. 2379.

54. *ZZTJ*, 197, p. 6212.

55. *JTS*, 55, pp. 2255–2256.

56. *XTS*, 216b, p. 6100.

57. Zhangsun Wuji, *Gu Tanglü shuyi*, 10, pp. 203–204; Fujiwara no Fuhito et al., comps., *Ritsu*, 3, pp. 42–43.

58. *JTS*, 69, p. 2523.
59. Yao Xuan, *Tang wencui*, 15, p. 9b.
60. *JTS*, 92, p. 2967; *THY*, 6, pp. 75–76.
61. *JTS*, 92, p. 2967; *THY*, 6, p. 75–76.
62. *JTS*, 135, p. 3714.
63. Fujiwara no Yoshifusa et al., comps., *Shoku Nihon kōki*, 3, p. 21, 834/1/7.
64. Yoshimine no Yusyo, Shigeno no Sadanushi, *Keikokushū* (*Gunsho ruijū* edn.), 13, p. 554.
65. The Japanese ranking system consisted of nine major ranks, each of which was subdivided into senior and junior ranks, which were again divided into upper and lower grades.
66. Toneri Shinnō et al., *Nihon shoki*, 25, p. 253, 653/5/12. See Verschuer, *Relations officielles*, pp. 24–29, for discussion of the composition of Japanese missions; and pp. 261–391 for French translations of records in Japanese official chronicles on Japanese missions to China from 701 to 884.
67. The mission of 750 had only one ambassador but two vice-ambassadors. The mission of 775 had as many as three vice-ambassadors but no ambassador, since the appointed ambassador was too sick to travel to China. See Sugano no Mamichi et al., *Shoku Nihongi*, 18, p. 211, 750/9/24; 33, p. 421, 729/6/19; and 34, p. 430, 776/10/14.
68. Toneri Shinnō et al., *Nihon shoki*, 25, p. 253, 653/5/12.
69. Ibid., 25, p. 255, 653/2; Sugano no Mamichi et al., *Shoku Nihongi*, 7, p. 66, 725/8/20.
70. Sugano no Mamichi et al., *Shoku Nihongi*, 2, p. 9, 701/1/23.
71. Ibid., 22, p. 260, 759/2/1. For use of "single ambassador," see also Toneri Shinnō et al., *Nihon shoki*, 19, p. 84, 554/12.
72. Toneri Shinnō et al., *Nihon shoki*, 27, p. 296, 669.
73. Ibid., 27, p. 290, 665, and p. 292, 667/11/13.
74. Sugano no Mamichi et al., *Shoku Nihongi*, 7, p. 67, 716/8/20, 716/9/4. The vice-ambassador of the mission to China in 776 was dismissed, and two new vice-ambassadors were appointed. See ibid., 34, p. 430, 776/12/14.
75. Ibid., 23, p. 281, 761/10/22; and 24, p. 286, 762/3/1. For the possible reason for the vice-ambassador's dismissal, see Sugano no Mamichi et al., comps., *Shoku Nihongi*, ed. Aoki Kazuo et al., vol. 3, p. 404, note 1.
76. In 748, Jianzhen (Ganjin 688–763), the famous Tang monk who risked his life five times to reach Japan, had fifty-three people on board his ship. Among them, eighteen were sailors. And in 761, a Japanese ambassador came home accompanied by thirty-nine people. Of them, thirty were sailors. See Sugano no Mamichi et al., *Shoku Nihongi*, 23, p. 280, 761/8/12; and Oumi no Mifune, *Tō Daiwajō tōsei den*, p. 62.
77. Hata no Ōmaro was one such specialist. Upon returning from China, he compiled a six-volume work containing his questions and the answers provided

him by the Tang legal experts. See Sugano no Mamichi et al., *Shoku Nihongi*, 12, p. 137, 735/5/7; and ibid., ed. Aoki Kazuo et al., vol. 2, p. 289, note 31.

78. Sugano no Mamichi et al., *Shoku Nihongi*, 30, p. 372, 769/10/29.

79. Ibid., 29, p. 357, 768/7/30.

80. Toneri Shinnō et al., *Nihon shoki*, 19, p. 89, 560/9.

81. Fujiwara no Yoshifusa et al., *Shoku Nihon kōki*, 9, p. 101, 840/4/23.

82. *Honchō monzui*, 2, p. 139. For the selection of diplomats to China, see Robert Borgen, "The Japanese Mission to China (801–806)," pp. 3–4.

83. Sugano no Mamichi et al., *Shoku Nihongi*, 34, p. 435, 777/6/1.

84. Toneri Shinnō et al., *Nihon shoki*, 26, p. 271, 659/7/3; Aston, *Nihongi*, vol. 2, p. 262.

85. Sugano no Mamichi et al., *Shoku Nihongi*, 3, p. 21, 704/7/1. The English translation is from J. B. Snellen, trans., "Shoku Nihongi," pp. 216–217.

86. *TD*, 185, p. 989; *THY*, 100, p. 1792. This office, the Sishan Si, was known as the Guanglu Si before 684, and after 705 it resumed its previous name.

87. *JTS*, 199a, p. 5341; *XTS*, 220, p. 6208. The English translation is from L. C. Goodrich and Tsunoda Ryusaku, *Japan in the Chinese Dynastic Histories*, pp. 45–46. Some Japanese scholars, however, question the reliability of the records in *JTS* and *XTS*. See Masumura Hiroshi, "Kyūshin ryō Tōsho Nihonden no kentō," in *Tōyōshi ronshū*, ed. Uchida Ginpū Hakase Shōju Kinenkai, pp. 471–498. Not surprisingly, in 796 the Tang court rejected a goodwill Tibetan ambassador whom they considered untrustworthy. See *XTS*, 216b, p. 6099.

88. Ichikawa Seinei, *Quan Tang shi yi*, a, p. 101173; Situo, *Enryaku sōroku*, p. 21. I am grateful to Denis C. Twitchett, who kindly allowed me to use his English translation of the poem.

89. Bai Juyi, *Bai Kong liutie*, 79, p. 24b. Chinese sources record him as Xingneng, "Xingneng" being the transliteration of his name "Kiyonao." But Xingneng might have also been the name of another Japanese diplomat, Kamunabi no Mahito Kiyono, who was one of the administrative officers on the same mission to China in 778. Note the similarity of the two names Kiyonao and Kiyono. Sugano no Mamichi et al., *Shoku Nihongi*, ed. Aoki Kazuo et al., vol. 5, p. 539, note 41.

90. *CFYG*, 997, p. 4a; Tao Gu, *Qing yi lu*, b, p. 32b.

91. See the *Kaifūsō*, nos. 115–118; the *Man'yōshū*, 3, p. 182, no. 368, p. 184, no. 374; and Yoshimine no Yasuyo, Shigeno no Sadanushi, *Keikokushū*, 1, p. 143; and 10, p. 155.

92. *Kaifūsō*, p. 177.

93. Sugano no Mamichi et al., *Shoku Nihongi*, 9, p. 100, 724/2/22, p. 102, 724/11/23; 11, p. 128, 732/1/20, p. 130, 732/9/5; 12, p. 140, 736/1/21, p. 147, 737/9/28; and 13, p. 151, 738/1/13.

94. Umakai has six poems in the *Kaifūsō*, nos. 88–93. One piece of prose in the

Keikokushū, 1, p. 144 was entitled "The (Chinese) Dates." He also has six poems in the *Man'yōshū,* 1, p. 45, no. 72; 3, p. 167, no. 312; 8, p. 317, no. 1535; and 9, p. 380, nos. 1729–1731. For an English translation of poem no. 72, see Edwin A. Cranston, *A Waka Anthology,* vol. 1, p. 496. He might also have facilitated the compilation of the *Topographies (Hitachi fudoki)* in 713–726.

95. For a discussion of the smallpox epidemic that devastated Japan in the Tempyō period (729–749), see William W. Farris, *Population, Disease and Land in Early Japan 645–900,* pp. 53–59.

96. Dazai Headquarters was the headquarters of the governor-general located in Fukuoka, Kyūshū. It governed nine provinces and the islands of Iki and Tsushima.

97. Sugano no Mamichi et al., *Shoku Nihongi,* 9, pp. 100–101, 724/4/7, p. 106, 726/10/26; and 12, p. 146, 737/8/5.

98. Ibid., 13, p. 155, 739/3/26.

99. Fujiwara no Fuhito et al., *Ritsu,* p. 13, p. 158.

100. Sugano no Mamichi et al., *Shoku Nihongi,* 28, p. 348, 767/10/18; 29, p. 359, 768/10/15; 32, p. 399, 772/1/10; 34, p. 425, 776/1/7; and 36, p. 461, 780/6/26.

101. *Man'yōshū,* 6, p. 176, no. 1019. The English translation is from Konishi Jin'ichi, *A History of Japanese Literature,* vol. 1, p. 400.

102. *Man'yōshū,* 6, p. 176, no. 1021. The English translation is from Konishi Jin'ichi, *A History of Japanese Literature,* vol. 1, p. 401.

103. *Man'yōshū,* 6, p. 176, no.1022. The English translation is from Konishi Jin'ichi, *A History of Japanese Literature,* vol. 1, p. 401.

104. *Man'yōshū,* 6, p. 178, no. 1023. The English translation is from Konishi Jin'ichi, *A History of Japanese Literature,* vol. 1, p. 402.

105. Sugano no Mamichi et al., *Shoku Nihongi,* 13, p. 158, 740/6/15.

106. *Kaifūsō,* p. 177.

107. Sugano no Mamichi et al., *Shoku Nihongi,* 15, p. 173, 743/5/3, p. 178, 744/9/15; 16, p. 185, 746/3/7, p. 186, 746/4/1, p. 188, 746/9/20; 17, p. 198, 749/4/1, p. 203, 749/7/2; and 18, p. 210, 750/9/1.

108. Fujiwara no Yoshifusa et al., *Shoku Nihon kōki,* 3, p. 23, 834/1/19.

109. Six of Takamura's poems appear in Ki no Tsurayuki et al., comps., *Kokin waka shū:* 6, p. 166, no. 335; 9, pp. 184–185, no. 407; 16, p. 265, no. 829, and p. 269, no. 845; and 18, p. 291, no. 936, and p. 296, no. 961. For English translations of these poems, see Laurel Rasplica Rodd and Mary Catherine Henkenius, *Kokinshū: A Collection of Poems Ancient and Modern,* pp. 142, 164, 287, 291, 319, and 325. Another two are in Yoshimine no Yasuyo, Shigeno no Sadanushi, *Keikokushū:* 13, p. 166; and 14, p. 172. For a discussion of a late Heian period novel based on Takamura's life, see Ward Geddes, "Takamura Monogatari." The novel is in vol. 7 of *Nihon koten bungaku taikei.*

110. *Kaifūsō*, p. 41.

111. Toneri Shinnō et al., *Nihon shoki*, 22, p. 157, 614/6/13; and 23, p. 180, 630/8/5.

112. Ibid., 22, p. 161, 623/7; 23, p. 180, 630/8/5; Sugano no Mamichi et al., *Shoku Nihongi*, 20, p. 246, 758/4/28.

113. Toneri Shinnō et al., *Nihon shoki*, 25, p. 255, 654/2.

114. *Kaifūsō*, pp. 96–97.

115. Sugano no Mamichi et al., *Shoku Nihongi*, 27, p. 333, 766/7/26. See also ibid., ed. Aoki Kazuo et al., vol. 4, pp. 505–506, note 30.

116. He had one piece of prose in the *Keikokushū*, 10, p. 155.

117. Fujiwara no Yoshifusa et al., *Shoku Nihon kōki*, 9, p. 101, 840/4/23. Other "aristocratic families of diplomacy" included the Sakaibe and the Nakatomi families. Ishinuno and Iwatsumi from the Sakaibe family served the mission to China in 659 and 665 respectively with unspecified titles, and Ōkida was the vice-ambassador of the mission of 701. Nakatomi no Ason Nashiro was the vice-ambassador to China in 732, and his son, Takanushi, was made the ambassador in 762. See Sugano no Mamichi et al., *Shoku Nihongi*, 24, p. 288, 762/7. For a discussion of Japanese diplomatic families, see Verschuer, *Relations officielles*, pp. 30–31.

118. Fujiwara no Yoshifusa et al., *Shoku Nihon kōki*, 1, p. 9, 833/3/13; Fujiwara no Mototsune et al., comps., *Nihon Montoku Tennō jitsuroku*, 4, p. 43, 852/12/22.

119. Fujiwara no Mototsune et al., *Nihon Montoku Tennō jitsuroku*, 4, p. 44, 852/12/22.

120. Sugano no Mamichi et al., *Shoku Nihongi*, 36, p. 474, 781/6/24. But he was later replaced by Fujiwara no Tamaro, and the mission was eventually abandoned. Yakatsugu's poems have been included in the *Keikokushū*, 1 and 10.

121. Fujiwara no Mototsune et al., *Nihon Montoku Tennō jitsuroku*, 7, p. 71, 855/1/22.

122. Ibid., 4, p. 41, 852/11/7.

123. Ibid., 9, pp. 101–102, 857/9/3.

124. Fujiwara no Yoshifusa et al., *Shoku Nihon kōki*, 4, p. 42, 835/10/19.

125. Fujiwara no Mototsune et al., *Nihon Montoku Tennō jitsuroku*, 5, p. 53, 853/6/2.

126. Sugano no Mamichi et al., *Shoku Nihongi*, 3, p. 32, 707/8/16; 18, p. 213, 751/3*/9; 19, p. 220, 754/7/13.

127. Ibid., 34, p. 430, 777/1/3. In 777, the court appointed Ono no Iwane, vice-ambassador to China, as the concurrent governor of Harima.

128. The practice started in 776, when the State Council issued an instruction to explain the necessity of rendering support to members of the China mission. In the early ninth century, the practice was still in use. And in 834, the court again followed the practice. See *Ruijū sandai kyaku*, 6, p. 271. See also Kiyohara no Natsuno et al., comps., *Ryō no gige*, 17, p. 197.

129. Fujiwara no Yoshifusa et al., *Shoku Nihon kōki*, 2, p. 17, 833/11/18.

130. Ibid., 3, p. 22, 834/1/12.

131. Ibid., 3, p. 26, 834/5/13. The administrative officer was made concurrent deputy governor of Yamashiro, and, in 835, the associate administrative officer was made concurrent deputy governor of Mimasaka. See ibid., 4, p. 40, 835/5/13; and Fujiwara no Mototsune et al., *Nihon Montoku Tennō jitsuroku*, 7, p. 71, 855/1/22; and 9, pp. 101–102, 857/9/3.

132. Fujiwara no Yoshifusa et al., *Shoku Nihon kōki*, 3, p. 26, 834/5/13, p. 27, 834/7/1; and 4, p. 44, 835/12/25.

133. Ibid., 1, p. 9, 833/3/13, 833/3/24; and 5, p. 47, 836/1/17.

134. Ibid., 4, p. 36, 835/1/11.

135. Ibid., 4, p. 43, 835/12/2. That the senior fourth rank, upper grade, was only lent to Takamura was obvious since he was officially granted senior fifth rank, lower grade, in 836. See ibid., 4, p. 43, 852/12/22.

136. Koremune no Naomoto, *Ryō no shūge*, 29, p. 739.

137. Sugano no Mamichi et al., *Shoku Nihongi*, 34, p. 435, 777/6/1.

138. Fujiwara no Tokihira, *Engi shiki*, 18, p. 490.

139. Ibid., 18, p. 490; 28, p. 704.

140. Sugano no Mamichi et al., *Shoku Nihongi*, 18, p. 212, 751/2/17.

141. Fujiwara no Yoshifusa et al., *Shoku Nihon kōki*, 4, p. 42, 835/10/16, p. 43, 835/10/27, 835/11/20.

142. Adachi Kiroku and Shioiri Ryōdō, eds., *Nittō guhō junrei kōki*, 1, p. 9. In 838, for example, Ishikawa no Ason Michimasa, a vice-ambassador to China, was promoted to the fourth rank after he died in China.

143. Fujiwara no Tokihira, *Engi shiki*, 18, p. 490; Fujiwara no Yoshifusa et al., *Shoku Nihon kōki*, 5, pp. 51–52, 836/5/10; Kiyohara no Natsuno et al., *Ryō no gige*, 4, pp. 144 and 145–146.

144. Sugano no Mamichi et al., *Shoku Nihongi*, 20, p. 244, 757/12/9. Family members of Sakaibe no Ishinuno, head of the mission to China in 659, in 757 received "merit rice fields" almost one century after his death. For the grant of such fields, see also Kiyohara no Natsuno et al., *Ryō no gige*, 3, p. 108; and Koremune no Naomoto, *Ryō no shūge*, 12, pp. 350–352.

145. Sugano no Mamichi et al., *Shoku Nihongi*, 36, p. 476, 781/9/22. Fuse no Ason Kiyonao, the ambassador, was a holder of junior fifth rank, lower grade, when he left for China in 778. He was granted a senior fifth rank, lower grade, when he returned to Japan in 781. His two administrative officers were both promoted from the junior sixth rank, lower grade, to junior fifth rank, lower grade.

146. Ibid., 3, p. 22, 705/8/11; 12, p. 137, 735/4/23, p. 141, 736/1/21; and 19, p. 220, 754/4/7, 754/7/13.

147. Koremune no Naomoto, *Ryō no shūgei*, 13, p. 410; Sugano no Mamichi et al., *Shoku Nihongi*, 7, p. 70, 717/11/8. The preferential treatment was, how-

ever, extended to the immediate family of a mission member only, not to his relatives.

148. Sugano no Mamichi et al., *Shoku Nihongi*, 3, p. 32, 707/8/16.

149. Koremune no Naomoto, *Ryō no shūge*, 13, p. 408.

150. Sugano no Mamichi et al., *Shoku Nihongi*, 12, p. 140, 736/2/7.

151. Ibid., 27, p. 329, 766/2/8.

152. Ibid., 22, p. 270, 760/2/20; and 24, p. 291, 763/1/9.

153. Ibid., 33, p. 421, 775/4/10.

154. Fujiwara no Mototsune et al., *Nihon Montoku Tennō jitsuroku*, 7, p. 71, 855/1/22.

155. For an English translation of the novel, see Edwin A. Cranston, "Atemiya: A Translation from the Utsubo Monogatari." A discussion of the novel can be found in Donald Keene, *Seeds in the Heart: Japanese Literature from Earliest Times to the Late Sixteenth Century*, pp. 441–446.

156. Oumi no Mifune, *Tō Daiwajō tōsei den*, pp. 63–66.

157. For recent studies of Xuanzang, see Sally H. Wriggins, *Xuanzang: A Buddhist Pilgrim on the Silk Road;* and Kahar Barat, *The Uygur-Turkic Biography of the Seventh-Century Buddhist Pilgrim Xuanzang: Ninth and Tenth Chapters.*

158. A term used during the Tang to refer to the vast area west of the Jade Gate Cross (Yumen Guan, located to the northwest of present-day Dunhuang, Gansu province) that covered Central and Western Asia, the Indian peninsula, Eastern Europe, and North Africa.

159. Sugano no Mamichi et al., *Shoku Nihongi*, 1, pp. 5–6, 700/3/10; Shiban, *Honchō kōsō den*, 1, pp. 6–9.

160. Sugano no Mamichi et al., *Shoku Nihongi*, 24, pp. 295–296, 763/10/6.

161. Ibid., 13, p. 156, 739/11/3. Primary sources vary in terms of the place where Hironari was captured. *Shoku Nihongi* suggests the "Kunlun Kingdom," a loosely used term that refers to the vast area south of the Indo-China peninsula, including the Malay and Indonesian islands. A record in the *Wenyuan yinghua* is more specific, pointing to the "Linyi Kingdom," which was located in the central coastal part of modern Vietnam, around Hue. See Li Fang, *Wenyuan yinghua* (hereafter *WYYH*), 471, p. 2410. For a detailed study of Japanese ambassadors dispatched to Tang China, see Masumura Hiroshi, *Ken Tō shi no kenkyū.*

CHAPTER 4: THE VOYAGE TO CHINA

1. Fujiwara no Yoshifusa et al., *Shoku Nihon kōki*, 3, p. 24, 834/2/1, p. 26, 834/5/13, p. 28, 834/8/4, p. 29, 834/8/10; and 7, p. 81, 838/12/15. See also Sugano no Mamichi et al., *Shoku Nihongi*, 23, p. 281, 761/9/10; and 31, p. 395, 771/11/1.

2. Fujiwara no Yoshifusa et al., *Shoku Nihon kōki*, 3, p. 29, 834/8/14.

3. Ennin, *Nittō guhō junrei kōki*, 1, p. 1.

4. Fujiwara no Yoshifusa et al., *Shoku Nihon kōki*, 5, p. 58, 836/8/20; Sugano no Mamichi et al., *Shoku Nihongi*, 35, p. 445, 778/11/13. The side walkway or track, referred to as a *funadana*, was a feature of oceangoing ships. In contrast, a smaller boat fit only for coastal sailing is referred to as "a boat with no sidetrack." See *Man'yōshū*, 1, p. 15, no. 58; and 17, p. 436, no. 3956. Ian H. Levy translates this feature as a "gunwale." But these sidetracks were much wider than the gunwales of a small boat. See his *Ten Thousand Leaves*, vol. 1, p. 69. Cranston's translation is simply "the tiny open boat." See his *Waka Anthology*, p. 260.

5. Mozai Torao, "Ken Tō shi gaikan," in Mozai Torao et al., eds., *Ken Tō shi kenkyū to shiryō*, pp. 26–27.

6. Sugano no Mamichi et al., *Shoku Nihongi*, 8, p. 75, 719/1/1, refers to the small boats as *dokutei sen*, that is, "boats whose bottoms are made of one piece of wood." Toneri Shinnō et al., *Nihon shoki*, 24, p. 193, 642/8/6, refers to such a boat as a *moroki fune*. For a discussion of the boat, see Mori Katsumi, *Ken Tō shi*, p. 33.

7. Sugano no Mamichi et al., *Shoku Nihongi*, 11, pp. 129–130, 732/9/4.

8. Ibid., 11, p. 130, 732/9/4 and p. 131, 733/4/3. See also *Man'yōshū*, 19, p. 377, no. 4265.

9. Sugano no Mamichi et al., *Shoku Nihongi*, 3, p. 25, 706/2/22; and 20, p. 246, 758/3/16; Fujiwara no Yoshifusa et al., *Shoku Nihon kōki*, 6, p. 67, 837/4/5. The practice of naming a ship according to its performance could be traced back to 274, when a ship that floated lightly and sailed as fast as a racer was named *Karano*. See Toneri Shinnō et al., *Nihon shoki*, 10, pp. 271–272, 274/10.

10. Sugano no Mamichi et al., *Shoku Nihongi*, 20, p. 246, 758/3/16; and 24, p. 294, 763/8/12.

11. Ibid., 7, p. 67, 717/2/1; 18, p. 212, 751/4/4; and 34, p. 432, 777/2/6. Fujiwara no Tokihira, *Engi shiki*, 8, p. 176, preserves a prayer titled "Presenting Offerings on Dispatching an Ambassador to China." Its content, however, seems to have been more suitable for the occasion of opening a new seaport in Osaka than that of praying for the safety of a mission to China. The two occasions, however, were indeed related to each other. See Donald L. Philippi's comment on and his translation of the prayer in his *Norito, a Translation of the Ancient Japanese Ritual Prayers*, pp. 12 and 71. The prayer reads:

> By the solemn command of the Sovereign Grandchild,
> I humbly speak for you,
> The deities whose praises are fulfilled in Sumi-no-e:
> Because there was no suitable port
> For dispatching ambassadors to China,

[The Emperor] was considering
Having to board ship from the land of Harima.
Just then, a divine command came, instructing and teaching:
  "I will build a port,"
Exactly in accordance with this instruction and teaching,
A port was built.
Whereupon [the Emperor] was glad and rejoiced
And as tokens of reverence
Had [me] bring and present to you these offerings. Thus I humbly
  speak.

12. Fujiwara no Yoshifusa et al., *Shoku Nihon kōki*, 7, p. 81, 838/12/15.
13. Ibid.
14. Koremune no Naomoto, *Ryō no shūge*, 35, p. 876.
15. Fujiwara no Tokihira, *Engi shiki*, 30, p. 737; Verschuer, *Relations officielles*, pp. 43–47.
16. Fujiwara no Tokihira, *Engi shiki*, 30, p. 738.
17. Fujiwara no Yoshifusa et al., *Shoku Nihon kōki*, 4, p. 37, 835/3/12.
18. Fujiwara no Tokihira, *Engi shiki*, 37, pp. 824–825.
19. Fujiwara no Yoshifusa et al., *Shoku Nihon kōki*, 3, p. 24, 834/2/2.
20. Ibid., 5, p. 48, 836/2/7; Verschuer, *Relations officielles*, pp. 47–52.
21. Fujiwara no Yoshifusa et al., *Shoku Nihon Kōki*, 5, p. 48, 836/2/17.
22. Ibid., 5, pp. 49–50, 836/4/10.
23. Sugano no Mamichi et al., *Shoku Nihongi*, 2, p. 9, 701/1/23. For a discussion of the life and poems of Okura, see Keene, *Seeds in the Heart*, pp. 138–146.
24. *Man'yōshū*, 5, p. 103, no. 894. The English translation is from Inoue Yasushi, *The Roof Tile of Tempyō*, trans. James T. Araki, p. 8. Cranston also has an English translation of this poem. See his *Waka Anthology*, pp. 364–366.
25. In Japanese, the word "pine" *(matsu)* is a pun on "wait." The "pine grove" therefore is intended to mean "the grove of waiting."
26. *Man'yōshū*, 5, p. 103, nos. 895 and 896. The English translation is from Inoue, *Roof Tile of Tempyō*, pp. 8–9. Cranston also has an English translation of poem no. 896. See his *Waka Anthology*, p. 366.
27. *Man'yōshū*, 8, p. 293, no. 1454. The English translation is from Inoue, *Roof Tile of Tempyō*, p. 11.
28. *Man'yōshū*, 9, p. 408, no. 1791. The English translation is taken from Inoue, *Roof Tile of Tempyō*, p. 11.
29. Wayne P. Lammers, *The Tale of Matsura: Fujiwara Teika's Experiment in Fiction*, pp. 70–71. Another fictional tale, part of which also describes the Japanese delegations to Tang, is *The Tale of the Hollow Tree (Utsubo monogatari)*. This work is believed to have been completed in the second half of the tenth century and has been traditionally attributed to Minamoto no Shitagō

(911–983). For a brief discussion and partial translation of the work, see Cranston, "Atemiya." See also Keene, *Seeds in the Heart,* pp. 441–446.

30. *Man'yōshū,* 9, p. 404, no. 1784. The English translation is from Heihachirō Honda, *The Manyoshu: A New and Complete Translation,* p. 147.

31. Fujiwara no Yoshifusa et al., *Shoku Nihon kōki,* 5, p. 50, 836/4/24. See also a record on page 48, 836/1/25, concerning the increase in the production of placer gold in Mutsu.

32. Ibid., 5, p. 50, 836/4/24.

33. Sugano no Mamichi et al., *Shoku Nihongi,* 11, p. 131, 732/3*/26. The ensign used to be made of yak's tail. It was later replaced by a sword, and thus the term "sword of authority" was derived. See Kiyohara no Natsuno et al., *Ryō no gige,* 5, p. 187. See also Verschuer, *Relations officielles,* pp. 53–54, for a discussion of *settō.*

34. Edwin O. Reischauer, *Ennin's Diary,* p. 88, note 381; Ennin, *Nittō guhō junrei kōki,* 1, p. 20. Apart from ambassadors to China, the "sword of authority" was granted to Japanese officials on other missions, such as a punitive expedition. See Sugano no Mamichi et al., *Shoku Nihongi,* 13, p. 158, 740/9/3.

35. Sugano no Mamichi et al., *Shoku Nihongi,* 34, p. 434, 777/4/22.

36. Fujiwara no Yoshifusa et al., *Shoku Nihon kōki,* 5, pp. 52–53, 836/5/13.

37. Sugano no Mamichi et al., *Shoku Nihongi,* 34, p. 429, 776/11/15, p. 430, 776/12/14, p. 434, 777/4/21, p. 435, 777/6/1.

38. Ibid., 8, p. 75, 718/12/15; Sugano no Mamichi et al., *Shoku Nihongi,* 12, p. 137, 735/3/10.

39. Fujiwara no Fuhito et al., *Ritsu,* 3, p. 47.

40. Fujiwara no Yoshifusa et al., *Shoku Nihon kōki,* 5, pp. 50–51, 836/4/29. A similar edict was also issued to the China mission in 776. See Sugano no Mamichi et al., *Shoku Nihongi,* 34, pp. 427–428, 776/4/15. For a general discussion of court edicts, see G. B. Sansom, "The Imperial Edicts in the Shoku Nihongi (700–790)."

41. Koremune no Naomoto, *Ryō no shūge,* 36, p. 901.

42. Fujiwara no Yoshifusa et al., *Shoku Nihon kōki,* 5, p. 51, 836/4/30.

43. Ibid., 5, p. 52, 836/5/12.

44. Ibid., 5, p. 53, 836/5/18.

45. Ibid.

46. Ibid., 5, p. 54, 836/5*/8.

47. Sugano no Mamichi et al., *Shoku Nihongi,* 30, p. 374, 770/3/4; and 33, p. 414, 774/3/4.

48. Ibid., 35, p. 447, 779/2/13, p. 450, 779/7/10; and 36, p. 455, 780/1/5.

49. Fujiwara no Otsugu et al., comps., *Nihon kōki,* 12, p. 35, 804/9/18.

50. Fujiwara no Yoshifusa et al., *Shoku Nihon kōki,* 5, pp. 54–55, 836/5*/13.

51. Ibid., 5, p. 59, 836/12/3.

52. Kiyohara no Natsuno et al., *Ryō no gige*, 6, p. 214. Green was the color of the court robe for officials of the sixth and seventh ranks.

53. Fujiwara no Yoshifusa et al., *Shoku Nihon kōki*, 5, pp. 59–60, 836/12/3.

54. Ibid., 5, p. 60, 836/12/3.

55. Ibid., 5, p. 56, 836/7/15.

56. Ibid., 5, p. 56, 836/7/17.

57. Ibid., 5, p. 58, 836/8/20.

58. *Man'yōshū*, 9, p. 495, no. 4264.

59. Mozai Torao, "Ken Tō shi gaikan," pp. 32–40.

60. Mori Katsumi, *Ken Tō shi*, p. 37. See also Nakamura Taichi, "Kodai suijō kōtsū ni kansuru kisoteki kōsa," in *Nihon kodai no kokka to saigi*, ed. Hayashi Rokurō and Suzuki Yasutami, pp. 629–634, for detailed discussions of the dimensions, building materials, and structural features of ships excavated from the Kinki and Kantō areas. See also Ōba Osamu, "Qian Tang shi chuan de xingtai," in *Gudai Zhong Han Ri guanxi yanjiu*, ed. Lin Tianwei and Huang Yuese, pp. 47–31.

61. Sugano no Mamichi et al., *Shoku Nihongi*, 24, p. 287, 762/4/17.

62. Ibid., 35, p. 444, 778/11/13; Ennin, *Nittō guhō junrei kōki*, 1, pp. 1–2; Fujiwara no Mototsune et al., *Nihon Montoku Tennō jitsuroku*, 5, p. 53, 853/6/2.

63. Fujiwara no Yoshifusa et al., *Shoku Nihon kōki*, 8, p. 90, 839/8/20, p. 93, 839/10/9; 13, p. 163, 843/12/9; and 18, p. 209, 848/3/26.

64. Ibid., 8, p. 89, 839/7/17.

65. Ennin, *Nittō guhō junrei kōki*, 1, p. 1. Fujiwara no Otsugu et al., *Nihon kōki*, 12, pp. 41–42, 805/6/8. For a discussion of the ocean navigation skills of the Japanese, see Mozai Torao, *Kodai Nihon no kōkai jutsu*, pp. 180–211.

66. Wei Zheng et al., *Sui shu*, 81, p. 1827, records this route starting from the Chinese side: "Going by way of Paekche, Pei Shiqing [the Sui ambassador to Japan in 608] reached the island of Chiku; then, after sighting Tara in the south, he passed Tsushima and sailed far out into the great ocean. [Then] going eastward, he reached Suō.... [Then] he had to pass through more than ten countries before he reached the seacoasts." The English translation is from Goodrich and Tsunoda, *Japan in the Chinese Dynastic Histories*, p. 36. This route was traveled by Xu Fu as early as the Qin dynasty; it had been the major sea route linking China with the Korean states and Japan. See Sun Guangqi, "Xu Fu dongdu hanglu yanjiu," in *Quanguo shoujie Xu Fu taolunhui lunwenji*, ed. Zhongguo Hanghai Xuehui et al., pp. 171–193. A record in the *Nihon shoki* describes the first half of this route, taken by the China mission of 659: "They started from the Bay of Mitsu in Naniwa.... They left the Bay of Ōtsu in Tsukushi.... They arrived at an island on the southern border of Paekche. The name of the island is not known." This route was also known as the "Silla Route," which the mission of 654 took:

"They proceeded by way of Silla and anchored at Laizhou [a major seaport in the Shandong peninsula]." Toneri Shinnō et al., *Nihon shoki*, 25, p. 255, 654/2; and 26, p. 270, 659/7/3; Aston, *Nihongi*, vol. 2, pp. 246 and 260.

67. Sugano no Mamichi et al., *Shoku Nihongi*, 1, pp. 2–3, 697/4/13, p. 4, 698/7/19, p. 5, 698/11/4.

68. Edwin O. Reischauer, "Notes on T'ang Dynasty Sea Routes"; Robert Borgen, "The Japanese Mission to China (801–806)"; Verschuer, *Relations officielles*, pp. 55–57; Sun Guangqi, "Zhong Ri shuidao zhilu de hanghai xue bianxi," in *Zhong Ri guanxishi guoji xueshu taolunhui lunwen*, ed. Zhongguo Zhong Ri Guanxishi Yanjiuhui, pp. 79–84.

69. Fujiwara no Yoshifusa et al., *Shoku Nihon kōki*, 6, p. 65, 837/3/15.

70. Ibid., 6, p. 67, 837/4/5.

71. Ibid., 6, p. 68, 837/7/22.

72. Ibid., 7, p. 75, 838/3/27, p. 76, 838/4/5.

73. Ibid., 7, p. 76, 838/6/28.

74. Ibid., 7, p. 76, 838/5/3.

75. Sugano no Mamichi et al., *Shoku Nihongi*, 34, p. 433, 777/4/17, p. 434, 777/4/22.

76. Fujiwara no Yoshifusa et al., *Shoku Nihon kōki*, 7, p. 77, 838/6/22.

77. Fujiwara no Mototsune et al., *Nihon Montoku Tennō jitsuroku*, 4, p. 43, 852/12/22.

78. Fujiwara no Fuhito et al., *Ritsu*, 1, p. 3; 3, p. 44. See also the related Tang code in Zhangsun Wuji, *Gu Tanglü shuyi*, 10, pp. 203 and 207. The English translation is based on Wallace Johnson, *The T'ang Code*, vol. 2, p. 92.

79. Fujiwara no Yoshifusa et al., *Shoku Nihon kōki*, 7, p. 81, 838/12/15.

80. Ki no Tsurayuki et al., *Kokin waka shū*, no. 407. The English translation is from Steven D. Carter, *Traditional Japanese Poetry: An Anthology*, pp. 208–209. Rodd and Henkenius also have an English translation of this poem. See their *Kokinshū*, p. 164.

81. Fujiwara no Yoshifusa et al., *Shoku Nihon kōki*, 8, p. 86, 839/3/16.

82. Fujiwara no Otsugu et al., *Nihon kōki*, 13, p. 45, 805/7/16.

83. Fujiwara no Yoshifusa et al., *Shoku Nihon kōki*, 9, p. 98, 840/2/14, p. 106, 840/6/17; 10, p. 123, 841/9*/19, p. 124, 841/10/15; 12, p. 142, 842/8/4; 16, p. 186, 846/5/23; 17, p. 195, 847/1/12, p. 198, 847/4/23; 18, p. 206, 848/1/13, p. 207, 848/2/3; and 19, p. 226, 849/5/12; Fujiwara no Mototsune et al., *Nihon Montoku Tennō jitsuroku*, 1, p. 8, 850/4/17; and 4, p. 44, 852/12/22.

CHAPTER 5: THE JOURNEY TO CHANGAN

1. The Chinese transliteration *zhuan* was given by the Tang scholar Yan Shigu in one of his notes to *HS*, 7, p. 228. In another note, he pointed out that the major characteristic of *zhuan* was the use of carts in transportation. See *HS*,

1b, pp. 57–58. For discussions of the Tang transportation system, see Aoyama Sadao, *Tō Sō jidai no kōtsū to chishi chizu no kenkyū.*

2.   Dong Gao, *Quan Tang wen* (hereafter *QTW*), 357, p. 1628.

3.   Relay stations in the metropolitan districts of Changan and Luoyang numbered ten and eight respectively. See Yan Gengwang, "Tang liangjing chengfang kao," in his *Tangshi yanjiu conggao*, pp. 258–303.

4.   Song Minqiu, *Changan zhi*, 11, pp. 3a–b; *TD*, 33, p. 192; Li Linfu, *Tang liudian* (hereafter *TLD*), 5, p. 32b–37a; Wang Yinglin, *Yu hai*, 172, p. 32b; *THY*, 61, p. 1061; *XTS*, 46, p. 1198. For poems describing stations at the water's edge, see Peng Dingqiu, *Quan Tang shi*, 200, pp. 2073 and 2076; 299, p. 3391; 356, p. 4008; and 540, p. 6205. See also Kiyohara no Natsuno et al., *Ryō no gige*, 8, pp. 274 and 275. Japan also had a transportation system modeled on that in Tang China. Relevant records in Japanese primary sources will therefore be used in discussions of its Tang counterpart.

5.   *THY*, 61, p. 1064; Peng Dingqiu, *Quan Tang shi*, 532, p. 5978.

6.   For trees outside stations, see Peng Dingqiu, *Quan Tang shi*, 341, p. 3824; and 363, p. 4097. For storied buildings, see ibid., 189, p. 2034; 199, pp. 2052 and 2059; 232, p. 2560; 356, p. 3999; 357, p. 4018; 524, pp. 6003 and 6005; 534, pp. 6093 and 6099; 535, p. 6104; 540, p. 6201; and 541, p. 6229. For pavilions, see *QTW*, 773, p. 3615; *JTS*, 120, p. 3452; and 195, p. 5199; Peng Dingqiu, *Quan Tang shi*, 344, pp. 3856–3857; *THY*, 61, p. 1059; Liu Yuxi, *Liu Mengde wenji*, 26, pp. 7a–8a; Liu Zongyuan, *Liu Hedong ji*, 29, pp. 8a–b; Bai Juyi, *Baishi changqing ji* (*SBCK* edn.), 15, pp. 18b–19a; and Li Zhao, *Tang guoshi bu*, b, p. 65. For ponds in stations, see Peng Dingqiu, *Quan Tang shi*, 354, p. 3973; 363, p. 4097; and 533, p. 6089.

7.   *THY*, 61, p. 1059. In both Changan and Luoyang, there might have been two Duting stations to handle the extremely busy official transportation requirements there. See Yan Gengwang, "Tang liangjing chengfang kao," pp. 286–287 and 298. Xin Deyong, however, disagrees and suggests that there was only one station in Changan. See his "Tang Changan Duting yi kaobian," in his *Gudai jiaotong yu dili wenxian yanjiu*, pp. 113–116.

8.   *THY*, 61, p. 1060.

9.   Ennin, *Nittō guhō junrei kōki*, 2, p. 47; Peng Dingqiu, *Quan Tang shi*, 341, p. 3824.

10.   Zhang Zhuo, *Chaoye qianzai* (*Tang Wudai biji xiaoshuo daguan* edn.), 1, p. 16.

11.   A good example would be Yang Yan, who was denounced by the emperor and immediately sent off from the capital without a chance to bid farewell to his wife. When he arrived at the Lantian station, Yang managed to persuade the stationmaster to allow him to remain in the station so that his wife could come to meet him. The stationmaster got permission for Yang's extended stay from the metropolitan prefecture on the pretext that the station was short of horses. Li Fang, *Taiping guangji*, 153, p. 1098.

12. *THY*, 61, p. 1061. Many private inns lined the major roads. They provided accommodations, meals, and donkeys for travelers. See *TD*, 7, p. 41; and Peng Dingqiu, *Quan Tang shi*, 200, p. 2068.

13. Peng Dingqiu, *Quan Tang shi*, 297, p. 3366. For travelers' early departure from relay stations, see also ibid., 344, p. 3863.

14. Xu Song, *Tang liangjing chengfang kao*, 5, p. 16; *Henan zhi*, 1, p. 23b.

15. Kiyohara no Natsuno et al., *Ryō no gige*, 8, p. 275; Koremune no Naomoto, *Ryō no shūge*, 38, p. 931; *XTS*, 46, p. 1198. For relay boats, see Peng Dingqiu, *Quan Tang shi*, 200, pp. 2076 and 2087; 201, p. 2098; and Bai Juyi, *Baishi changqing ji*, 17, p. 25b.

16. *TLD*, 5, pp. 33a–b, 34a. After 740, however, some of the stations along the waterways in south China were abandoned. The court believed that it was a waste to have these stations running in parallel with overland stations; furthermore, they enabled some officials to travel at a leisurely pace that resulted in delays in carrying out their duties. Some, however, remained in operation as late as the 850s. See *THY*, 61, pp. 1060 and 1066.

17. For discussions of breeding grounds during the Tang, see Ma Junmin and Wang Shiping, *Tangdai mazheng*, pp. 33–44.

18. *TLD*, 17, p. 28b; and 30, p. 12b.

19. Ibid., 5, p. 32b; and 8, pp. 14a–b.

20. *QTW*, 684, p. 3134. This was also the practice in Japan. These families were referred to as "relay station households," and they were supposed to provide their service until they were too old, sick, or poor to carry on the duty. See Kiyohara no Natsuno et al., *Ryō no gige*, 8, p. 274; and Fujiwara no Tokihira, *Engi shiki*, 28, pp. 705 and 717.

21. *TD*, 33, p. 192; *JTS*, 60, p. 2352; *XTS*, 92, p. 3809; Peng Dingqiu, *Quan Tang shi*, 483, p. 5493; and 541, p. 6220. The master was also referred to as *yizhang* or *yiguan*. See *JTS*, 191, p. 5105; Zhangsun Wuji, *Gu Tanglü shuyi*, 15, p. 287; *TLD*, 5, p. 33a; and *XTS*, 46, p. 1198; and 156, p. 4901.

22. *TLD*, 5, pp. 33b–34a. To each batch of travelers, a serviceman (*yizi*) would be assigned, whose duty was to ride a horse and lead the travelers. See Zhangsun Wuji, *Gu Tanglü shuyi*, 10, p. 210; *THY*, 61, p. 1060; and Kiyohara no Natsuno et al., *Ryō no gige*, 7, p. 253.

23. *THY*, 61, pp. 1059–1060 and 1062; *JTS*, 171, p. 4446; and 186b, p. 4861.

24. Zhangsun Wuji, *Gu Tanglü shuyi*, 15, p. 278.

25. Ibid., 15, p. 287.

26. *WYYH*, 624, pp. 3236–3237.

27. *XTS*, 46, p. 1198.

28. *TLD*, 3, p. 37a; *CFYG*, 484, pp. 14a–b. For a discussion of the funding of relay stations, see Li Jinxiu, *Tangdai caizheng shi gao*, vol. a (part 3), pp. 983–1007.

29. The lands allocated to a relay horse were known as "relay station fields"

(yitian). The size of such fields for each horse would be reduced to 5.8 acres if a relay station was near a pasture. See *TD*, 2, p. 16. For "relay station fields," see also Han Yu, *Changli xiansheng ji* (*SBCK* edn.), 25, p. 3a.

30. *CFYG*, 484, p. 5b.

31. Ibid., 484, pp. 17b and 18a.

32. Zhangsun Wuji, *Gu Tanglü shuyi*, 25, p. 470; Johnson, *T'ang Code*, vol. 2, p. 446.

33. *THY*, 61, p. 1059; Liu Su, *Sui Tang jiahua* (*Shuofu san zhong* edn.), p. 17b.

34. Zhangsun Wuji, *Gu Tanglü shuyi*, 10, p. 209; Johnson, *T'ang Code*, vol. 2, p. 94.

35. Zhangsun Wuji, *Gu Tanglü shuyi*, 10, p. 209; Johnson, *T'ang Code*, vol. 2, p. 94.

36. *THY*, 61, p. 1062.

37. Zhangsun Wuji, *Gu Tanglü shuyi*, 26, p. 492; Johnson, *T'ang Code*, vol. 2, pp. 472–473: "All cases of wrongful entry of a post relay station are punished by forty blows with the light stick. If anything is improperly taken, the punishment is one hundred blows with the heavy stick. If the value of the illicit goods would be punished more heavily, the punishment is to be comparable to [the punishment for] robbery. If entry of a post relay station is permitted and anything is taken that should not be, the punishment is the same."

38. Zhangsun Wuji, *Gu Tanglü shuyi*, 25, p. 470; Johnson, *T'ang Code*, vol. 2, p. 446: "All cases of the use of post horses under false pretenses are punished by life exile with added labor. If officials at the post relay station or customs barrier know the circumstances, they receive the same punishment."

39. Zhangsun Wuji, *Gu Tanglü shuyi*, 10, p. 210; Johnson, *T'ang Code*, vol. 2, p. 95: "All cases of riders taking an excessive number of post horses are punished by one year of penal servitude for the first one and increased by a degree for each further horse. (Where post donkeys are required yet the rider uses a horse, the punishment is reduced one degree.) If the officer in charge knows the circumstances, he receives the same punishment."

40. Zhangsun Wuji, *Gu Tanglü shuyi*, 10, p. 211; Johnson, *T'ang Code*, vol. 2, pp. 96–97: "All cases of improperly taking the wrong route while riding a post horse are punished by one hundred blows with the heavy stick for the first *li*, increased by one degree for each further five *li*, and with a maximum punishment of two years' penal servitude. If the rider goes beyond the proper destination to another place, the punishment is increased one degree in each case. . . . If the rider passes a post relay station without changing horses, the punishment is eighty blows with the heavy stick."

41. Zhangsun Wuji, *Gu Tanglü shuyi*, 10, p. 212; Johnson, *T'ang Code*, vol. 2, p. 97: "All cases of carrying private articles while riding post horses are punished by eighty blows with the heavy stick for the first *jin* of weight." However, an official traveler was allowed to use relay horse to carry his personal belongings not exceeding ten *jin* in weight. See Zhangsun Wuji, *Gu*

Tanglü shuyi, 15, p. 279; and Johnson, *T'ang Code*, vol. 2, p. 184. A similar regulation governed users of the relay boats: "In all cases, those who are traveling on government ships are permitted to carry two hundred *jin* of clothing and grain. If this limit is exceeded and more is secretly carried, both the person who accepts the exceeding clothing and grain and the person who entrusts it are punished by fifty blows with the light stick." See Zhangsun Wuji, *Gu Tanglü shuyi*, 27, p. 506–507; and Johnson, *T'ang Code*, vol. 2, p. 490.

42. Zhangsun Wuji, *Gu Tanglü shuyi*, 15, p. 287; Johnson, *T'ang Code*, vol. 2, p. 196: "If post horses are borrowed or lent, the punishment is one hundred blows with the heavy stick. For five days, the punishment is one year of penal servitude. If a postal relay stationmaster illegally borrows men, horses, or donkeys, the punishment is reduced one degree in each case."

43. *THY*, 61, p. 1059.

44. Ibid., 61, p. 1062; Peng Dingqiu, *Quan Tang shi*, 344, p. 3962; *ZZTJ*, 215, p. 6872.

45. *TLD*, 5, p. 32b; and 8, pp. 14a–b.

46. Ibid., 8, pp. 14a–b; and 30, pp. 24a–25b.

47. *THY*, 61, p. 1059; *XTS*, 46, p. 1196. In Japan, an official on an urgent mission was supposed to pass more than ten stations a day and did not need to dismount to pay respects to ranking officials he encountered on the road. See Kiyohara no Natsuno et al., *Ryō no gige*, 7, p. 253; and Fujiwara no Tokihira, *Engi shiki*, 50, p. 996.

48. Zhangsun Wuji, *Gu Tanglü shuyi*, 10, p. 208; Johnson, *T'ang Code*, vol. 2, p. 93: "All cases of postal relay couriers who fall behind schedule are punished by eighty blows with the heavy stick for the first day, increased one degree for each further two days, and with a maximum punishment of two years of penal servitude." Some demoted officials and criminals who were sent into exile were ordered to pass at least ten relay stations a day. This hectic travel schedule caused some to die on the road. See *ZZTJ*, 215, p. 6872.

49. *TLD*, 5, pp. 33b–34a; *THY*, 61, pp. 1060 and 1061.

50. Zhangsun Wuji, *Gu Tanglü shuyi*, 10, p. 210.

51. *THY*, 61, p. 1061. A record in the *Ryō no gige* states that a courier would be provided with official goods at each station "according to [his] ranking" (Kiyohara no Natsuno et al., *Ryō no gige*, 8, pp. 276–277). See also Koremune no Naomoto, *Ryō no shūge*, 38, p. 935.

52. Zhangsun Wuji, *Gu Tanglü shuyi*, 10, p. 210; *THY* 61, p. 1060; Johnson, *T'ang Code*, vol. 2, p. 96.

53. *TLD*, 8, p. 14b.

54. Zhangsun Wuji, *Gu Tanglü shuyi*, 10, p. 210.

55. *TLD*, 30, pp. 24b–25a.

56. Carts had been widely used for travel and in battles before the Tang. See,

for example, *SJ,* 124, p. 3184; and *JS,* 25, pp. 762–763. For Tang officials riding in carriages on business trips, see Peng Dingqiu, *Quan Tang shi,* 199, p. 2052.

57. *TLD,* 17, p. 28b; *THY,* 61, p. 1060; Kiyohara no Natsuno et al., *Ryō no gige,* 8, pp. 275 and 276; Fujiwara no Tokihira, *Engi shiki,* 28, pp. 709 and 717. Wallace Johnson, however, does not seem to differentiate the *yima* from the *zhuanma.* He renders both as "post relay horses." See *T'ang Code,* vol. 2, p. 471. W. G. Aston is more discriminating. His English translations for *yima* and *zhuanma* are "special post horse" and "ordinary horse" respectively. See his *Nihongi,* vol. 2, p. 207.

58. It is, however, unclear whether the "transportation horses" were still kept at county seats or allocated to relay stations. In Japan, some relay stations received both transportation and relay horses. See Kiyohara no Natsuno et al., *Ryō no gige,* 8, p. 275; and Fujiwara no Tokihira, *Engi shiki,* 28, pp. 711–717. These horses were managed by the district *(gun)* authorities. Some stations received three to five horses and left them in care of the "transportation households" *(denko).* See Kiyohara no Natsuno et al., *Ryō no gige,* 8, p. 275; and Fujiwara no Tokihira, *Engi shiki,* 28, p. 717.

59. Zhangsun Wuji, *Gu Tanglü shuyi,* 15, p. 278; Johnson, *T'ang Code,* vol. 2, p. 182; Kiyohara no Natsuno et al., *Ryō no gige,* 8, p. 276.

60. *XTS,* 46, p. 1198.

61. Zhangsun Wuji, *Gu Tanglü shuyi,* 8, p. 172; Johnson, *T'ang Code,* vol. 2, p. 46. This exchange document was also referred to as *zhuandie.* See *THY,* 61, p. 1061.

62. *THY,* 61, pp. 1059–1060.

63. *TD,* 33, p. 192.

64. Li Jinxiu, *Tangdai zhidu shi lüelun gao,* pp. 343–353.

65. *TLD,* 3, p. 17b. Riding animals also included camels, mules, and donkeys. See *ZZTJ,* 216, p. 6919; and Li Fang, *Taiping guangji,* 153, p. 1098.

66. *TLD,* 3, pp. 44a–b. For horse riders, the daily travel distance was twenty-three miles (seventy *li*); for ox and donkey riders, seventeen miles (fifty *li*); and for cart riders, ten miles (thirty *li*).

67. *JTS,* 45, pp. 1949–1950. Riding horses also became popular among the Tang court ladies. See the case of Yang Guifei in Zheng Chuhui, *Minghuang zalu,* b, p. 52.

68. For records of ninth-century officials riding transportation horses on business trips, see Peng Dingqiu, *Quan Tang shi,* 337, p. 3780; and 357, p. 4013.

69. *THY,* 61, p. 1060. But in Japan, use of "transportation horses" to travel was still strictly regulated. Only newly appointed provincial governors were permitted to do so when assuming office in provincial capitals. See Fujiwara no Tokihira, *Engi shiki,* 50, p. 996.

70. Zhangsun Wuji, *Gu Tanglü shuyi,* 26, p. 491; *XTS,* 46, p. 1198; Johnson,

T'ang Code, vol. 2, p. 471: "According to the *Statues on Public Stables and Pasture:* 'Officials and the nobles of the first rank should be provided with eight horses, hereditary princes, princes of commanderies, and officials of the second rank and above with six horses, officials of the third rank and lower should each have a graduated entitlement.'"

71. *THY*, 61, p. 1059; *XTS*, 46, p. 1196. In Japan, official travelers who were not on urgent business were not supposed to pass more than eight stations a day. See Kiyohara no Natsuno et al., *Ryō no gige*, 7, p. 253.

72. It is worth noting that there were still people who rode in carts on business or private trips in the late eighth and early ninth centuries. See Peng Dingqiu, *Quan Tang shi*, 199, p. 2053; 357, p. 4014; 539, p. 6161; and 541, p. 6240; and Tian Tao and Guo Chengwei, eds., *Longjin fengsui pan jiaozhu*, vol. 4, p. 133. A court regulation also stated: "If a person uses a cart, [the private possessions carried] must not exceed thirty *jin*." See Zhangsun Wuji, *Gu Tanglü shuyi*, 15, p. 279; and Johnson, *T'ang Code*, vol. 2, p. 184.

73. The appointment of a censor in 737 to supervise the "lodges and stations" in the two metropolitan areas perhaps signaled the beginning of this integration. In 758, a "commissioner for (supervision) of relay stations and lodges" in various prefects was selected, who performed his duty until 780. And the Chancellery requested in 779 that two censors be chosen and posted as "commissioner for (supervision) of relay stations and lodges" to Changan and Luoyang respectively. See *THY*, 61, p. 1059. This integration was also evident in the way the Tang official transportation system was referred to in Chinese. Before the 730s, the system was mentioned as *yizhuan;* later, as *guanyi*.

74. Peng Dingqiu, *Quan Tang shi*, 198, pp. 2024–2025.

75. Li Jifu, *Yuanhe junxian tuzhi*, 2, p. 44. A record in *ZZTJ*, 197, p. 6212, indicates that in 644 the commander of a Tang expedition force dispatched a courier to send the news of a victory over the Karashahr (Yanqi) back to the capital. He reached the capital in a month, covering some 2,409 miles (7,300 *li*) in a month, or 80 miles a day.

76. Han Yu, *Changli xiansheng wenji*, 10, p. 14a.

77. Peng Dingqiu, *Quan Tang shi*, 355, p. 3979.

78. Ibid., 526, p. 6020.

79. Ibid., 692, p. 7951.

80. *QTW*, 675, p. 3095.

81. Du Mu, *Fanchuan wenji* (*SBCK* edn.), 2, p. 6b. The English translation is based on Edward H. Schafer, *The Golden Peaches of Samarkand*, p. 37.

82. *XTS*, 76, p. 3494; *ZZTJ*, 215, p. 6872.

83. *JTS*, 41, p. 1664. Other records suggest that Consort Yang preferred lychees from Guangzhou prefecture for their better taste. See *ZZTJ*, 215, p. 6872; Yue Shi, *Yang Taizhen waizhuan*, in *Kaiyuan Tianbao yishi shizhong*, b, p. 139; Li Zhao, *Tang guoshi bu*, a, p. 19; and Zheng Chuhui, *Minghuang zalu*, p. 57.

For her to enjoy fresh lychees from Guangzhou, they had to be transported much faster since the distance between Changan and Guangzhou was 1,798 miles (5,447 *li*). See *JTS*, 41, p. 1712.

84. Zhangsun Wuji, *Gu Tanglü shuyi*, 26, p. 492; Johnson, *T'ang Code*, vol. 2, pp. 472–473.

85. *THY*, 61, pp. 1064–1065.

86. *CFYG*, 63, p. 2a.

87. *THY*, 61, p. 1066.

88. *JTS*, 165, p. 4303; *THY*, 61, p. 1064.

89. *THY*, 61, p. 1063.

90. Zhou Xunchu, ed., *Tang yulin jiaozheng*, p. 92.

91. *JTS*, 166, p. 4331; Li Zhao, *Tang guoshi bu*, p. 52.

92. *THY*, 61, p. 1066.

93. Yuan Zhen, *Yuan Zhen ji*, 38, p. 432.

94. Zhou Xunchu, ed., *Tang yulin jiaozheng*, p. 576.

95. Li Fang, *Taiping guangji*, 251, p. 1949.

96. Yuan Zhen, *Yuan Zhen ji*, 38, pp. 431–432; *THY*, 61, p. 1062.

97. *ZZTJ*, 255, p. 8306.

98. Sun Qiao, *Sun Qiao ji* (*SBCK* edn.), 3, pp. 8b–9a.

99. Han Yu, *Changli xiansheng ji waiji* (*SBCK* edn.), 4, p. 5a.

100. Sun Qiao, *Sun Qiao ji*, 3, pp. 8a–b.

101. Duan Chengshi, *Youyang zazu (xuji)* (*SBCK* edn.), 1, p. 4b.

102. *QTW*, 745, p. 2463. A shortage of horses in fact occurred much earlier. See, for example, the memorial to the court in 821 in *THY*, 61, p. 1064.

103. For a detailed study based on a field trip to the landing place of this Japanese mission, see Xu Chen, "Ennin no nittō guhō keiro kō—Chūgoku Kōsoshō Nantsu, Jūkō ni okeru jōrikuchi to keiro," trans. Suzuki Yasutami, in *Nihon kodai kokkai to saigi*, ed. Hayashi Rokurō and Suzuki Yasutami, pp. 661–682. Southern Jiangsu was also where the fifteenth Japanese mission that reached China in 777 landed. See Sugano no Mamichi et al., *Shoku Nihongi*, 35, p. 443, 778/9/23. A Japanese mission taking the "northern route" to sail to Tang China would arrive at Dengzhou or Laizhou in modern Shandong province. For a discussion of such a mission's overland journey from Dengzhou to the capital, see Zhu Yafei, "Cong 'Ru Tang qiufa xunli xingji' kan Tangdai Shandong de duiwai jiaowang." Dengzhou and Laizhou during the Tang were China's window to the Korean States and Japan. See Chen Shangsheng, "Tangdai de Xinluo qiaominqu," and Chen Wenjing, "Tangdai Xinluo qiaomin de huodong," in *Gudai Zhong Han Ri guanxi yanjiu*, ed. Lin Tianwei and Joseph Wong, pp. 27–38.

104. Fujiwara no Otsugu et al., *Nihon kōki*, 12, p. 41, 805/6/8.

105. Li Fang, *Taiping guangji*, 243, p. 1882. This story should be treated with caution. The ambassador might not have been Japanese since the alleged inci-

dent occurred in the early 740s, which was around ten years after 733, when the tenth Japanese mission had arrived in Tang. But the story can still be a reliable indication of how some foreign diplomats suffered at the hands of corrupt Tang officials and criminals, for Li Yong, the prefect in the story, was a historical figure. He once headed Beihai prefecture (in eastern Shandong province), and his misdeed came to light in 746. See *JTS*, 190b, p. 5043.

106. These provisions were uncooked foodstuffs *(shengliao)*. The term *shengliao* was used in contrast to the term *shouliao* (cooked foodstuffs). See Ono Katsutoshi, *Nittō guhō junrei kōki no kenkyū*, vol. 1, p. 140.

107. Ennin, *Nittō guhō junrei kōki*, 1, pp. 3, 4, and 5; Fujiwara no Otsugu et al., *Nihon kōki*, 12, p. 41, 805/6/8; Kūkai, *Seireishū*, 5, p. 269.

108. Ennin, *Nittō guhō junrei kōki*, 1, p. 8. For a study on the physical size of Yangzhou, see Li Tingxian, *Tangdai Yangzhou shi kao*, pp. 337–345.

109. Peng Dingqiu, *Quan Tang shi*, 548, p. 6335.

110. *JTS*, 110, p. 3313; 124, p. 3533; *ZZTJ*, 221, p. 7102. For a study of the foreign community in the Tang, see Fan Bangjin, "Tangdai fanfang kaolüe."

111. *XTS*, 34, p. 886.

112. Peng Dingqiu, *Quan Tang shi*, 279, p. 3137.

113. Ibid., 131, p. 1335.

114. Ennin, *Nittō guhō junrei kōki*, 1, p. 5; *THY*, 86, p. 1582; *QTW*, 612, p. 2775. For a discussion of the importance of the Grand Canal to the Tang court, see Quan Hansheng, "Tang Song diguo yu yunhe," in his *Zhongguo jingji shi yanjiu (shang)*, pp. 269–282.

115. *JTS*, 88, p. 2878; Li Fang, *Taiping guangji*, 402, pp. 3241–3242.

116. Hong Mai, *Rongzhai suibi* (*SBCK* edn.), 9, p. 11a; *XTS*, 91, pp. 3790–3791.

117. Peng Dingqiu, *Quan Tang shi*, 301, p. 3430; 474, p. 5377; 498, p. 5666; and 511, p. 5846. Wang Zhongmin, Sun Wang, and Tong Yangnian, eds., *Quan Tang shi waibian*, a, p. 160; Li Fang, *Taiping guangji*, 273, p. 2151.

118. Zhangsun Wuji, *Gu Tanglü shuyi*, 8, p. 178. The English translation is based on Johnson, *T'ang Code*, vol. 2, p. 56. But his rendering of the first sentence is "When foreigners enter China and are on the road, it is not allowed to trade with them." This might be a misreading of the term *jiaoza*. For a similar regulation by the Japanese court, see Kiyohara no Natsuno et al., *Ryō no gige*, 10, p. 339.

119. Ennin, *Nittō guhō junrei kōki*, 1, p. 6.

120. Ibid., 1, p. 17.

121. *THY*, 86, p. 1581.

122. Ennin, *Nittō guhō junrei kōki*, 1, pp. 19 and 21.

123. *XTS*, 46, p. 1196.

124. Ennin, *Nittō guhō junrei kōki*, 1, p. 7; "Zuda shinnō nittō ryakki," in *Dai Nihon bukkyō zensho*, vol. 68, p. 162; Kūkai, *Seireishū*, 5, p. 269.

125. Ennin, *Nittō guhō junrei kōki*, 1, pp. 7 and 26; Ono Katsutoshi, *Nittō guhō junrei kōki no kenkyū*, vol. 1, p. 176.

126. Sugano no Mamichi et al., *Shoku Nihongi*, 35, p. 444, 778/11/13. In principle, only half of an ambassador's companions were permitted to travel to the capital. *XTS*, 48, pp. 1257–1258. For a discussion of the Tang court's reception of foreign ambassadors, see Wang Zhenping, "Act on Appropriateness and Mutual Self-Interest."

127. Sugano no Mamichi et al., *Shoku Nihongi*, 35, p. 443, 778/9/23. In 804, the prefect in Fuzhou adopted the same practice when receiving the seventeenth Japanese mission to China. See Fujiwara no Otsugu et al., *Nihon kōki*, 12, p. 41, 805/6/8.

128. Toneri Shinnō et al., *Nihon shoki*, 26, p. 270, 659/7/3; Ennin, *Nittō guhō junrei kōki*, 1, p. 5.

129. Fujiwara no Otsugu et al., *Nihon kōki*, 12, p. 41, 805/6/8; Ennin, *Nittō guhō junrei kōki*, 4, p. 104.

130. Ennin, *Nittō guhō junrei kōki*, 1, pp. 4, 6, 20; and 2, p. 34.

131. Ibid., 1, pp. 9–10; Ono Katsutoshi, *Nittō guhō junrei kōki no kenkyū*, vol. 1, p. 397, note 2. For a short description of a Japanese mission's travel from the port of landing to the capital of Tang China, see Verschuer, *Relations officielles*, pp. 60–62.

CHAPTER 6: DIPLOMACY IN THE TANG CAPITAL

1. Sugano no Mamichi et al., *Shoku Nihongi*, 35, p. 448, 779/4/21; Fujiwara no Otsugu et al., *Nihon kōki*, 12, p. 42, 805/6/8; Song Minqiu, *Changan zhi*, 11, pp. 3a–b.

2. *JTS*, 120, p. 3452; and 195, p. 5199; *QTW*, 571, p. 2593; 603, p. 2735; and 773, p. 3615; Li Shangyin, *Li Yishan wenji* (*SBCK* edn.), 2, p. 3b; *THY*, 98, p. 1744; Yan Gengwang, "Tang liangjing chengfang kao," pp. 288–289.

3. Fujiwara no Otsugu et al., *Nihon kōki*, 12, p. 42, 805/6/8. The Japanese mission of 804 arrived at the Changle relay station on the twenty-first day of the twelfth month, and the ceremony was held on the twenty-third day.

4. Zheng Xuan et al., *Zhou li zhushu* (*SSJZS* edn.), 37, p. 893. The welcome ceremony in the suburbs was to show respect to a visitor. The successive Chinese courts used this ceremony to welcome distinguished guests and foreign ambassadors. See *Chunqiu Zuoshi zhuan* (*SSJZS* edn.), 17, p. 1833; *Guo yu* (*SBCK* edn.), 1, p. 17b; *SJ*, 69, p. 2262; *HS*, 57b, p. 2581; Yuan Zhen, *Yuanshi changqing ji* (*SBCK* edn.), 51, p. 7b; and *THY*, 99, p. 1763.

5. Fujiwara no Otsugu et al., *Nihon kōki*, 12, p. 42, 805/6/8.

6. Ibid.

7. Sugano no Mamichi et al., *Shoku Nihongi*, 35, p. 445, 778/11/13; Fujiwara no Otsugu et al., *Nihon kōki*, 12, p. 42, 805/6/8. The Japanese court had a similar practice. See Toneri Shinnō et al., *Nihon shoki*, 22, p. 153, 610/10/9;

and Sugano no Mamichi et al., *Shoku Nihongi*, 35, p. 448, 779/4/21. For "flying dragon horses," see Peng Dingqiu, *Quan Tang shi*, 427, p. 4705.

8. Minamoto no Tsunenori, *Daishi go gyōjō shūki*, in *Zoku gunshō ruijū*, vol. 206, p. 499.

9. Wei Zheng et al., *Sui shu*, 1, pp. 17–18; Arthur F. Wright, "The Sui Dynasty (581–617)," in *Sui and T'ang China, 589–906*, ed. Denis C. Twitchett, vol. 3, part 1 of *The Cambridge History of China*, ed. John K. Fairbank and Denis C. Twitchett, pp. 78–81.

10. Yang Kuan, *Zhongguo gudai ducheng zhidushi yanjiu*, pp. 169–184; Nancy Steinhardt, *Chinese Imperial City Planning*, pp. 94–96; Heng Chye Kiang, *Cities of Aristocrats and Bureaucrats: The Development of Medieval Chinese City-scapes*, pp. 1–29; Wang Tao, "A City with Many Faces: Urban Development in Pre-modern China," in *Exploring China's Past*, trans. and ed. Roderick Whitfield and Wang Tao, pp. 117–121; Xin Deyong, "Tang Changancheng jianzhi congkao."

11. *XTS*, 49a, pp. 1284–1285.

12. *JTS*, 140, p. 3831.

13. *XTS*, 49a, pp. 1285–1286.

14. *JTS*, 74, p. 2619. For the sunset drumroll, see Bai Xingjian, *Li wa zhuan* (*Tangren xiaoshuo* edn.), p. 120.

15. Zhangsun Wuji, *Gu Tanglü shuyi*, 26, pp. 489–490; Johnson, *T'ang Code*, vol. 2, pp. 469–470. From 757 onward, blows with the light stick as punishment for a violation of the curfew did not apply to officials. Their cases would be referred to court for decision. Dou Yi et al., *Song xingtong*, 26, p. 16a. For the drumbeats at sunset, see Schafer, *Golden Peaches of Samarkand*, p. 282, note 73.

16. *TLD*, 25, p. 25b; *XTS*, 49a, pp. 1285–1286.

17. Tian Tao and Guo Chengwei, eds., *Longjin fengsui pan jiaozhu*, vol. 3, p. 99. Two kinds of judgments *(pan)* are preserved in primary sources: those with real names of the involved parties and those using "A" and "B" as names for the involved parties. The former were judgments for real cases, and the latter were answers to examination questions by candidates for official positions. See Xu Shizeng, *Wenti mingbian xushuo*, pp. 127–128; and Nunome Chōfu and Ōno Hitoshi, "Haku Kyoi hyakudōhan shakugi."

18. Li Fang, *Taiping guangji*, 452, pp. 3692–3693; and 484, pp. 3985–3986; Shen Jiji, *Renshi zhuan* (*Tangren xiaoshuo* edn.), pp. 52–58. For English translations of these two stories, see Yang Xianyi and Gladys Yang, *Tang Dynasty Stories*, pp. 13–25 and 70–86.

19. *THY*, 86, p. 1576.

20. Zhangsun Wuji, *Gu Tanglü shuyi*, 8, p. 172; 26, pp. 489–490; Johnson, *T'ang Code*, vol. 2, pp. 46 and 469–470.

21. Peng Dingqiu, *Quan Tang shi*, 65, p. 753; and 584, p. 6321.

22. *THY*, 86, p. 1583.

23. Song Minqiu, *Changan zhi*, 8, p. 2b.

24. *QTW*, 549, p. 2469.

25. For discussions of the two markets in Changan, see Denis Twitchett, "The T'ang Market System."

26. Ennin, *Nittō guhō junrei kōki*, 4, p. 92. For stores in alleyways, see Cheng Hongzhao, *Tang liangjing chengfang kao jiaobu ji*, 3, p. 201.

27. *THY*, 86, p. 1581; Schafer, *Golden Peaches of Samarkand*, p. 282, note 73.

28. Yan Wenru and Yan Wanjun, *Liangjing chengfang kao bu*, pp. 560–562 and 567.

29. Twitchett, "The T'ang Market System," p. 208.

30. Luoyang, the capital of the Northern Wei, began this practice. Zhou Zumo, *Luoyang qielan ji jiaoshi*, vol. 4, pp. 151–161, describes this:

> On the south side of the Imperial Drive and four *li* outside the Xianyang Gate was the main marketplace of Luoyang, which was eight *li* in circumference.... To the east of the marketplace were the two wards Tongshang (Ward of Conducting Trade) and Dahuo (Ward of Shipping Merchandise). All residents were shrewd, making a living as butchers or tradesmen.... To the south of the marketplace were the two wards Tiaoyin (Ward of Musical Tones) and Yuelü (Ward of Musical Notes), the residents of which were [mostly] musicians and singers. The most skillful [performing] artists of the empire came from here.... To the west of the marketplace were the two wards Yangu (Wine-buyers' Ward) and Zhishang (Wine-servers' Ward), the residents of which were mostly in the business of making wine.... To the north of the marketplace were the two wards Cixiao (Ward of Motherly Love and Filial Devotion) and Fengzhong (Ward of Homage to the Deceased), the residents of which were sellers of inner and outer coffins and handlers of hearse rentals.... In addition, there were the two wards: Fucai (Ward of the Wealthy) and Jinsi (Ward of Gold Stores), where rich men lived. Within a stretch of ten *li*, residents for the most part were artisans, merchants, and tradesmen.

The English translation is from Yi-t'ung Wang, *A Record of Buddhist Monasteries in Luoyang*, pp. 181–188. See Yang Kuan, *Zhongguo gudai ducheng zhidushi yanjiu*, pp. 148–150, for further discussion of this issue.

31. Duan Anjie, *Yuefu zalu*, p. 11b; Song Minqiu, *Changan zhi*, 8, p. 2b.

32. Sun Qi, *Beili zhi*, p. 16a.

33. Ibid., pp. 12a–b.

34. Li Fang, *Taiping guangji*, 417, p. 3400.

35. Ibid., 452, pp. 3692–3693; Peng Dingqiu, *Quan Tang shi*, 441, p. 4918.

36. Zhou Xunchu, ed., *Tang yulin jiaozheng*, p. 739; Duan Chengshi, *Youyang zazu (qianji)* (*SBCK* edn.), 7, pp. 6a–b; *Youyang zazu (xuji)* (*SBCK* edn.), 1, pp. 5a–b.

37. Li Fang, *Taiping guangji*, 84, p. 542.

38. *ZZTJ*, 225, p. 7265. For discussions of foreigners in Changan, see Xiang Da, *Tangdai Changan yu Xiyu wenming*, pp. 4–33.

39. *CFYG*, 159, p. 9a; *TD*, 146, p. 764; *JTS*, 29, p. 1073; *XTS*, 3, p. 57; *THY*, 34, p. 628; *QTW*, 12, p. 58; and 770, p. 3600.

40. Ennin, *Nittō guhō junrei kōki*, 3, p. 83.

41. *JTS*, 7, pp. 141 and149; *THY*, 34, p. 628; Ma Duanlin, *Wenxian tongkao*, 148, p. 1294. The court eventually banned the game in Changan and Luoyang in 715. See *THY*, 34, p. 629. See also Edward H. Schafer, "Ritual Exposure in Ancient China."

42. Peng Dingqiu, *Quan Tang shi*, 419, p. 4617. The English translation is from Schafer, *Golden Peaches of Samarkand*, p. 28.

43. For a discussion of Tang dynasty wine, see K. C. Chang, ed., *Food in Chinese Culture*, pp. 119–124. See also Françoise Sabban, "The History and Culture of Food and Drink in Asia: China," trans. Elborg Forsters, in *The Cambridge World History of Food*, ed. Kenneth F. Kiple and Kriemhild C. Ornelas, pp. 1171–1172; and Li Bincheng et al., *Sui Tang Wudai shehui shenghuo shi*, pp. 74–79.

44. Wang Renyu, *Kaiyuan Tianbao yishi*, p. 93.

45. For wine shops in the Eastern market in Changan, see Cheng Hongzhao, *Tang Liangjing chengfang kao jiaobu ji*, 3, p. 201. In the Xuanyang ward south of the Eastern market, there were also wine shops. See Peng Dingqiu, *Quan Tang shi*, 192, p. 1973.

46. Peng Dingqiu, *Quan Tang shi*, 176, p. 1797. The English translation is from Schafer, *Golden Peaches of Samarkand*, p. 21.

47. Peng Dingqiu, *Quan Tang shi*, 162, p. 1686. The English translation is from Schafer, *Golden Peaches of Samarkand*, p. 21. For Li Bai's other poems about the western ladies, see Peng Dingqiu, *Quan Tang shi*, 165, p. 1709; and 171, p. 1758. See also the poems on the same theme by other Tang poets in *Quan Tang shi*, 18, p. 200; 165, p. 1709; 199, p. 2052; and 333, p. 3718.

48. This office managed the funerals of Chinese officials, foreign diplomats, and their companions. See *THY*, 66, p. 1151; and *XTS*, 46, p. 1194.

49. Established in 731, this office handled relations with the Uighurs, the Tibetans, and other tribes in the Western Region. It was originally situated in the Chongren ward east of the "imperial city" but was shifted southwest to the Changxing ward in 810. See *JTS*, 15, p. 450; *THY*, 6, p. 70; and 66, p. 1152; Xu Song, *Tang liangjing chengfang kao*, 2, p. 42; and 3, p. 53; and Song Minqiu, *Changan zhi*, 7, p. 11a. The office became a subordinate office in the Court of State Ceremonial in 754 and was responsible primarily for hosting banquets for foreign visitors. The Tibetan ambassador, for example, was granted a banquet at the Libin Yuan in 768. See *CFYG*, 110, p. 14a; *XTS*, 170, p. 5169; *THY*, 66, p. 1151; and *ZZTJ*, 240, p. 7758. The Libin Yuan was abolished in 825.

50. *TLD*, 4, pp. 28b–29a; 18, pp. 8b–9a and 10b–11a; *JTS*, 43, p. 1832; and 44, p. 1885; *XTS*, 48, p. 1258; *THY*, 59, p. 1028.

51. *XTS*, 48, p. 1258.

52. *THY*, 66, p. 1511. This was a practice in line with the *Tang Code*, which stipulated that "those who are allowed to enter the imperial palace, the imperial audience hall, or the various offices in the capital are all listed on name registers. Those who are not listed on the name register but yet are permitted to enter are all escorted in." See Zhangsun Wuji, *Gu Tanglü shuyi*, 7, pp. 152–153. The English translation is from Johnson, *T'ang Code*, vol. 2, p. 21. The register for persons holding official status included their titles and names, and that for people without official status recorded their age and physical features. See *JTS*, 128, p. 3593; and *ZZTJ*, 224, p. 7189.

53. *JTS*, 96, p. 3025.

54. Zhangsun Wuji, *Gu Tanglü shuyi*, 9, p. 195; Johnson, *T'ang Code*, vol. 2, p. 77.

55. Zhangsun Wuji, *Gu Tanglü shuyi*, 9, p. 195; Johnson, *T'ang Code*, vol. 2, p. 77; *TLD*, 10, pp. 65b–66a.

56. Zhangsun Wuji, *Gu Tanglü shuyi*, 9, p. 195; Johnson, *T'ang Code*, vol. 2, p. 76; Fujiwara no Fuhito et al., *Ritsu*, 3, p. 39. For the case of Wang Xiu, a secretary from the Secretariat who was sentenced to strangulation for divulging secrets, see Tian Tao and Guo Chengwei, *Longjin fengsui pan jiaozhu*, vol. 1, p. 1.

57. Kiyohara no Natsuno et al., *Ryō no gige*, 36, pp. 894–895.

58. *ZZTJ*, 224, pp. 7218–7219 and 7228.

59. Zhou Shaoliang, ed., *Tangdai muzhiming huibian*, vol. b, pp. 1886–1887.

60. *THY*, 66, p. 1152; Song Minqiu, *Changan zhi*, 7, p. 5a.

61. Tian Tao and Guo Chengwei, *Longjin fengsui pan jiaozhu*, vol. 2, p. 60.

62. *CFYG*, 974, p. 18a. There are also ordinances that regulated trading with foreigners along the Chinese borders. See Bai Juyi, *Baishi liutie shilei ji*, 22, p. 73a; and 24, p. 92b.

63. Ennin, *Nittō guhō junrei kōki*, 1, p. 21.

64. *THY*, 86, p. 1581. *XTS*, 46, p. 1196, records that a marketplace was set up particularly for the Turkic ambassadors. When they requested permission for trading, their goods would be listed and reported to the court, and the value of each item would be assessed. An aide from the Court of the Imperial Treasury would supervise the trading activities.

65. Zhangsun Wuji, *Gu Tanglü shuyi*, 8, p. 177; Johnson, *T'ang Code*, vol. 2, p. 55. See also p. 54 for the usual punishments for this offense: "For illegal trade with foreigners, those who take or give goods worth one *chi* of silk are punished by two and one-half years of penal servitude. One degree of punishment is added for goods worth each further three *pi* of silk, and for goods worth fifteen *pi*, the punishment is life exile with added labour." Illegal trade with foreigners had been treated as a more serious offense before the

Tang, when offenders were sometimes sentenced to death. See Wei Zheng et al., *Sui shu*, 85, p. 1892.

66. Ennin, *Nittō guhō junrei kōki*, 1, p. 19.

67. Toneri Shinnō et al., *Nihon shoki*, 26, p. 271, 659/7/3. Aston, *Nihongi*, vol. 2, p. 262, relates: "Kawachi no Aya no Ōmaro, a servant of Han Zhixing, slandered our visitors, who were found guilty by the Court of Tang, and were already condemned to banishment.... Among the visitors was one Yuki no Muraji Hakatoko, who made representations to the Emperor in consequence of which their punishment was remitted."

68. Toneri Shinnō et al., *Nihon shoki*, 26, p. 271, 659/7/3; Aston, *Nihongi*, vol. 2, pp. 262–263.

69. *ZZTJ*, 226, p. 7267.

70. *THY*, 100, p. 1798; Lu Xinyuan, *Tang wen shiyi*, 8, p. 4697; Situo, *Enryaku sōroku*, p. 22; Sugano no Mamichi et al., *Shoku Nihongi*, 35, p. 443, 778/10/23.

71. *TLD*, 18, p. 17a; 19, p. 19b; *XTS*, 48, p. 1160. In the case of the Japanese mission to China in 834, each member also received an official salary *(lu)* of five bolts of silk. See Ennin, *Nittō guhō junrei kōki*, 1, p. 19.

72. *XTS*, 48, p. 1250. Provisions and daily necessities for members of a Japanese mission might have been deficient. See Ennin, *Nittō guhō junrei kōki*, 1, p. 6. Kūkai, a Japanese student monk who traveled with the mission of 801 to China, complained that the provisions and cloth that he received from the Tang court could barely support him and that there was no surplus that he could use to pay for his tuition. See Kūkai, *Seireishū*, 71, p. 281.

73. *TLD*, 18, p. 17a; *XTS*, 46, p. 1196.

74. *TLD*, 4, p. 28a.

75. Ibid., 4, p. 27b. For a discussion of the *chang shiliao*, see Kiyokoba Azuma, "Tō ritsuryōsei jidai no jōshokuryōsei ni tsuite," in *Ritsuryōsei*, ed. Tōshi Kenkyūkai, pp. 305–331.

76. *TLD*, 18, p. 17a.

77. *THY*, 24, p. 463. They were supposed to attend the court meeting every four days.

78. *TLD*, 4, p. 28a; *XTS*, 46, p. 1196. For a discussion of the supply of foodstuffs to foreign visitors, see Li Jinxiu, *Tangdai caizheng shi gao (shang)*, pp. 956–959.

79. *TLD*, 4, pp. 27b–28a. The Office of Fine Wine (Liangyun Shu) and the Offices of Delicacies (Zhenxiu Shu) and of the Winery (Zhangyun Shu), all under the Court of Imperial Entertainments (Guanglu Si), provided wine, fish, and soy paste. See *TLD*, 15, pp. 7a–b, 8a, and 9a. The Shayuan Directorate and the Office of Imperial Parks Products (Goudun Shu) under the Court of the National Granaries (Sinong Si) supplied mutton, pork, and charcoal; and the court itself provided grain and oil. For a discussion of

food production and supply, see K. C. Chang, *Food in Chinese Culture*, pp. 87–118; and E. N. Anderson, *The Food of China*, pp. 53–56.

80. Bai Juyi, *Baishi liutie shilei ji*, 11, p. 42a; *XTS*, 48, p. 1257.

81. Tian Tao and Guo Chengwei, *Longjin fengsui pan jiaozhu*, vol. 2, p. 83.

82. Zheng Xuan et al., *Zhou li zhushu*, 83, p. 897; *TPYL* (*SBCK* edn.), 232, pp. 1a–b: "*Hong* means grand ceremony, and *lu*, to display order." Another interpretation of the term in question is found in *HS*, 19a, p. 730. It suggests that "*honglu* means to pass on [the words of the emperor] in a loud voice."

83. *Er ya* (*SSJZS* edn.), 3, p. 2581.

84. *QTW*, 412, p. 1894.

85. Ibid., 312, p. 1420.

86. *XTS*, 221b, pp. 6264–6265, lists eight "fence countries" and refers to them as "eight barbarian countries" *(bafan)*. The term *ba* (eight) means "many." Therefore the term *bafan* and a similar term *baman*, refer to "barbarian countries" in general. See *HHS*, 88, p. 2911; and *THY*, 100, p. 1798.

87. Bai Juyi, *Baishi liutie shilei ji*, 16, p. 65b; *THY*, 100, p. 1798; Niida Noboru, ed., *Tōryō shūi*, p. 852.

88. Niida Noboru, *Chūgoku hōseishi kenkyū (4)*, vol. 1, pp. 15–17; Kaneko Shūichi, "Tōdai sakuhōsei ippan," in *Higashi Ajiashi ni okeru kokka to nōmin*, ed. Nishijima Sadao Hakase Kanreki Kinenkai, p. 315.

89. *ZZTJ*, 193, p. 609.

90. *TLD*, 18, pp. 8b–9a, 10b–11a; *JTS*, 43, p. 1832; and 44, p. 1885; *XTS*, 48, p. 1257.

91. Xiao Song et al., comps., *Da Tang Kaiyuan li* (hereafter *DTKYL*), 79, p. 4a.

92. *TD*, 123, p. 644; *XTS*, 19, p. 425; and 48, p. 1257.

93. *XTS*, 46, p. 1196. The arrangement of musical entertainment and the deployment of guards of honor for such a banquet were also determined by the status of a diplomat. The court used such categories as "bigger barbarian country" *(dafan)*, "medium barbarian country" *(zhongfan)*, or "smaller barbarian country" *(cifan)* to differentiate their ambassadors from each other. *TD*, 131, p. 686; *DTKYL*, 79, p. 6b; and 80, p. 5a.

94. *TLD*, 4, p. 28a; 18, pp. 10b–11a and 17a; and 19, p. 19b.

95. Wang Wei, *Wang youcheng ji*, 12, p. 2b.

96. *JTS*, 194a, p. 5164.

97. The Western Turks surrendered to the Tang some twenty years later, in 659. See *ZZTJ*, 195, pp. 6148–6149.

98. *JTS*, 199a, p. 5321.

99. This was also the practice of the Northern Wei court (A.D. 386–534). See *NQS*, 58, p. 1009.

100. *Sanfu huangtu* (*SBCK* edn.), 6, p. 7a; *HS*, 9, p. 295; 70, p. 3015; 99b, pp. 4155–4156; Xiao Tong, *Wen xuan*, 43, p. 26a; *JTS*, 194a, p. 5172; and 198, p. 5317; Peng Dingqiu, *Quan Tang shi*, 781, p. 8833.

101. *JTS*, 10, p. 251; 169, p. 4405; *XTS*, 94, p. 3829.

102. For usage of the phrase *manyi zhidi* in Tang sources, see *QTW*, 172, p. 784; and Wang Wei, *Wang youcheng ji*, 12, pp. 2a–3b.

103. Adachi Kiroku and Shioiri Ryōdō, eds., *Nittō guhō junrei kōki*, vol. 1, p. 88, note 11.

104. *JTS*, 194a, p. 5159. In 788, a large Uighur delegation came to China to make wedding arrangements for their leader and a Tang princess. Some of the members were lodged at the Directorate for the Palace Buildings (Jiangzuo Jian). See *THY*, 6, p. 77.

105. Wang Wei, *Wang youcheng ji*, 12, p. 2b; Sugano no Mamichi et al., *Shoku Nihongi*, 35, pp. 443 and 445; Fujiwara no Otsugu et al., *Nihon kōki*, 12, p. 42.

106. Ennin, *Nittō guhō junrei kōki*, 1, p. 18.

107. Ichikawa Seinei, *Quan Tang shi yi*, a, p. 10173.

108. *TDZLJ*, 128, p. 2726.

109. Liu Su, *Da Tang xinyu*, 8, p. 127.

110. Situo, *Enryaku sōroku*, p. 21.

111. *TLD*, 18, pp. 11a and 17a; *JTS*, 44, p. 1885; *XTS*, 48, 1258.

112. An abbreviation for *jiubin li*. The Chinese court classified Chinese lords and foreign rulers into nine groups *(jiufu)* according to the distance of their places from the capital and accorded them different receptions when they visited the Chinese court. The *jiufu* are *houfu, dianfu, nanfu, caifu, weifu, manfu, yifu, zhenfu,* and *fanfu*. See Zheng Xuan et al., *Zhou li zhushu*, 33, p. 863. For *jiubin li*, see also *SJ*, 81, p. 2441.

113. *TLD*, 4, p. 6b. For the presentation of gifts from "barbarian" countries, see also Bai Juyi, *Baishi liutie shilei ji*, 22, p. 73a; and 24, p. 92b.

114. *Er ya*, 1, p. 2569; Gu Yewang, *Yu pian* (*SBBY* edn.), b, p. 48a; *SJ*, 177, p. 3044; *Guo yu*, 17, p. 1a; Bai Juyi, *Bai Juyi ji*, 55, p. 1044; Li Deyu, *Li Wenrao wenji* (*SBCK* edn.), 2, p. 9a.

115. *SJ*, 1, p. 3; *ZZTJ*, 1, p. 29.

116. *Guo yu*, 1, p. 2b; Liu An, *Huainan zi* (*SBCK* edn.), 1, p. 6a; *SJ*, 6, pp. 242–243; *JTS*, 196a, p. 5220; 197, p. 5272; and 199b, p. 5346.

117. Wei Zheng et al., *Sui shu*, 73, p. 1676; *JTS*, 195, p. 5196; Han Yu, *Han Changli quanji* (*SBBY* edn.), 16, p. 6b; Xu Yin, *Xu gong Diaoji wenji* (*SBCK* edn.), 8, p. 10b; Peng Dingqiu, *Quan Tang shi*, 720, p. 8261.

118. *Guo yu*, 17, p. 1a; *JS*, 114, p. 2911; *JTS*, 194a, p. 5170; 195, p. 5214; and 219, p. 6183; Cui Zhiyuan, *Guiyuan bigeng ji* (*SBCK* edn.), 16, p. 8b; *THY*, 62, p. 1078; Peng Dingqiu, *Quan Tang shi*, 23, p. 300; Yao Xuan, *Tang wencui*, 19a, p. 3a.

119. *Er ya*, 1, p. 2569; Gu Yewang, *Yu pian*, b, p. 48a.

120. *TLD*, 18, p. 9a; *TD*, 74, p. 403.

121. *XTS*, 48, p. 1258.

122. *DTKYL*, 79, pp. 1a–2b. For a graphic explanation of the protocol held at the

guest house, see Iwami Kiyohiro, "Tō no kokusho juyo reigi ni tsuite," pp. 56–57.

123. This practice originated from Confucius' time, when a messenger, on behalf of the Son of Heaven, conferred on a marquis an additional degree of distinction by allowing him not to descend and do obeisance before announcing an edict. See *Chunqiu Zuoshi zhuan*, 13, p. 1800; and Legge, *The Chinese Classics*, vol. 5, p. 154.

124. For a description of the proper way to kowtow, see Jia Changchao, *Qunjing yinbian* (*SBCK* edn.), 2, p. 12a.

125. *DTKYL*, 79, pp. 1b–2a.

126. *JTS*, 21, p. 815.

127. Zheng Xuan et al., *Zhou li zhushu*, 18, p. 759; Zheng Yuan and Jia Gongyan, eds., *Yi li zhushu* (*SSJZS* edn.), 26b, p. 1087.

128. Zheng Xuan et al., *Zhou li zhushu*, 18, p. 760; and 33, p. 860. *TD*, 74, p. 403, elaborates that *bin* refers to the various feudal lords whose domains were within two thousand *li* from the capital.

129. Zheng Xuan et al., *Zhou li zhushu*, 18, pp. 759 and 760. A Han dynasty work further explains that "close and attached" mean "[foreigners] would give up their customs, surrender to the virtue and righteousness [of the Chinese emperor], attach themselves to the Chinese way of life, and be on good terms [with China]." Shi You, *Ji jiu pian* (*SBCK* edn.), p. 34b.

130. *TD*, 74, p. 403.

131. *CFYG*, 972, p. 10b.

132. *WYYH*, 508, pp. 2b–3a.

133. Ibid., 551, p. 7a.

134. Ibid., 508, p. 2a; Kōbō Daishi Zenshū Henshū Iinkai, *Kōbō daishi zenshū*, vol. 15, pp. 399–403.

135. *TLD*, 4, p. 10b; Fujiwara no Tokihira, *Engi shiki*, 21, p. 527. "The sea has become calm" was also used as the title of a Tang poem. See Peng Dingqiu, *Quan Tang shi*, 780, p. 8820.

136. *CFYG*, 972, p. 10b; Wang Yinglin, *Yu hai*, 108, p. 12a. This Japanese prince was probably a member of the previous Japanese mission of 835, who remained in China and later presented valuables and pieces of music to the court in the name of a prince. This was a common practice that some foreigners used to secure a court audience for themselves.

137. *QTW*, 406, p. 1865; *WYYH*, 508, pp. 2b–3a. This ambassador, however, might have been a Korean, for writers of later periods sometimes mixed up "Riben" (Japan) and "Ridong" (Korea) when editing Tang dynasty works. See Cao Xun, "Tangren shiti zhong de 'Ridong' houshi you ewei 'Riben' zhe," p. 198.

138. This music was known as *mei* in Chinese, which consisted of music from Koryŏ and Paekche. The music of the southern, western, and northern

"barbarians" was referred to as *ren, zhuli,* and *jin* respectively. See Cai Yong, *Du duan* (*SBCK* edn.), a, p. 16b.

139. *WYYH,* 508, pp. 2a–3a; *QTW,* 406, p. 1865.

140. *JTS,* 28, p. 1039.

141. *WYYH,* 551, p. 7a.

142. See his annotation to Zheng Xuan et al., *Zhou li zhushu,* 24, p. 802.

143. *JTS,* 198, p. 5316.

144. *TLD,* 7, pp. 4a–b. For festivals during the Tang, see Zhang Zexian, "Tangdai de jieri." Other important events unrelated to the "guest protocol" were also conducted at the "outer court." Examples are the announcement of an amnesty, a military parade, and the presentation of a title to the emperor.

145. *JTS,* 4, pp. 84–85.

146. *TLD,* 7, pp. 5a–b. For a poetic description of the Hanyuan Hall, see Li Hua's prose in Wang Yinglin, *Yu hai,* 159, pp. 41b–42a. See also Yang Kuan, *Zhongguo gudai ducheng zhidushi yanjiu,* pp. 173–176; Steinhardt, *Chinese Imperial City Planning,* pp. 101–102; and Fu Xinian, "Tang Changan Daminggong Hanyuandian yuanzhuang de tantao."

147. Wang Dang, *Tang yulin,* 8, pp. 279–280; Wang Yinglin, *Yu hai,* 159, pp. 41a–b.

148. For the "early audience," see Wang Wei, *Wang youcheng ji,* 6, p. 11b; Qian Qi, *Qian Kaogong ji* (*SBCK* edn.), 8, p. 7a; Lü Wen, *Lü Heshu wenji* (*SBCK* edn.), 1, p. 5b; Huangfu Zeng, *Tang Huangfu Zeng shiji* (*SBCK* edn.), 1, p. 69b; and Peng Dingqiu, *Quan Tang shi,* 738, p. 8415.

149. Qian Qi, *Qian Kaogong ji,* 8, p. 6b.

150. Zhou Xunchu, ed., *Tangren yishi huibian,* vol. 17, p. 807.

151. *CFYG,* 516, pp. 8b–9a.

152. Zhangsun Wuji, *Gu Tanglü shuyi,* 9, p. 189; *XTS,* 46, p. 1194; Johnson, *T'ang Code,* vol. 2, p. 70.

153. Zheng Xuan et al., *Zhou li zhushu,* 23, p. 795; Yu Shinan, *Beitang shuchao,* 105, p. 4b; *JTS,* 29, p. 1079.

154. For the composition of the Huanghui Guards of Honor, see *XTS,* 23a, pp. 483–484.

155. *JTS,* 28, p. 1041; and 30, pp. 1090 and 1097.

156. *XTS,* 21, p. 464.

157. *JTS,* 28, pp. 1041, 1042, and 1044.

158. *TD,* 131, p. 685; *DTKYL,* 79, pp. 5a–7a. For a discussion of this event and the related protocol, see Iwami Kiyohiro, *Tō no hoppō mondai to kokusai chitsujo,* pp. 360–365; and see Verschuer, *Relations officielles,* p. 67, for an illustration of the movements and the standing positions of participants in this event.

159. *DTKYL,* 80, pp. 5a–7b. For a discussion of food in ceremonies and on special occasions, see Chang, *Food in Chinese Culture,* pp. 132–136.

160. *TLD*, 3, p. 6a; Xu Jian, *Chuxue ji*, 8, p. 142; Li Tai, *Guadi zhi*, a, p. 11a. For a discussion of the political importance of foreign goods to the Chinese court, see Robert Ford Campany, *Strange Writing: Anomaly Accounts in Early Medieval China*, pp. 113–116. In return Japanese ambassadors received gifts from the Tang court. These gifts and the goods that Japanese diplomats purchased from markets included, among other things, ceramics, glasses, lacquerware, books, and Buddhist statues. For a detailed archaeological study of Chinese ceramics in Japan, see Chang Lan, *Qi-shisi shiji Zhong Ri wenhua jiaoliu de kaoguxue yanjiu*, pp. 14–106. For discussions of exchange of goods through tributary arrangement between China and Japan during the seventh and the ninth centuries, see Charlotte von Verschuer, *Le commerce extérieur du Japon des origines au XVIe siècle*, pp. 9–16 and 19–24; and Tōno Haruyuki, *Ken Tō shi to shōsōin*.

161. *XTS*, 48, p. 1258.

162. Ibid.

163. Ibid., p. 1257.

164. Ibid., p. 1258.

165. *TLD*, 18, p. 10b.

166. *XTS*, 16, p. 383. For records concerning the presentation of gifts on other occasions, see *TLD*, 4, pp. 8b–9a; *DTKYL*, 97, pp. 4a–5a; and *XTS*, 19, p. 427.

167. *DTKYL*, 97, p. 3b.

168. Ibid., 79, p. 4a; Kong Yingda, *Li ji zhengyi* (*SSJZS* edn.), 11, p. 1323; *XTS*, 19, p. 425. See also Verschuer, *Relations officielles*, pp. 10–12, for discussion of the standing position of the Japanese ambassador during a Tang court audience.

169. *Chunqiu Zuoshi zhuan*, 4, p. 1735; Legge, *The Chinese Classics*, vol. 5, pp. 30–32.

170. *NQS*, 58, pp. 1009–1010.

171. *JTS*, 194, pp. 5191–5193; *ZZTJ*, 213, p. 6792.

172. *JTS*, 10, p. 252; and 195, p. 5200. A similar dispute on precedence between Silla and Parhae also occurred at the Tang court in the late ninth century. For a discussion, see Hamada Kōsaku, "Tōchō ni okeru Bokkai to Shiragi no sōchō jiken ni tsuite," in *Kodai Higashi Ajiashi ronshū (2)*, ed. Suematsu Yasukazu Hakase Koki Kinenkai, vol. b, pp. 341–358.

173. Sugano no Mamichi et al., *Shoku Nihongi*, 19, pp. 219–220, 754/1/17. Modern scholars disagree on the authenticity of this record. Yamao Yukihisa suggests the record is a fabrication. See his "Kudara sansho to Nihon shoki," in *Chōsenshi Kenkyūkai rombunshū*, ed. Chōsenshi Kenkyūkai, vol. 15, pp. 32–33. See also Pyŏn In-sŏk, "A Study of Disputes among Foreign Ambassadors over Seating Order at the Court of the T'ang Dynasty," pp. 129–148. Wang Xiaofu is of the same opinion. See his "Tangchao yu Xinluo guanxi shi lun," pp. 164–167. Ishii Masatoshi, however, disagrees. He points out

that the Tang general Wu Huaishi appeared in both Japanese and Chinese sources and was probably a historical figure, not a fabrication. See his "Tō no shōgun Go Kaijitsu ni tsuite," pp. 24–29. See also his "Ōtomo no Furumaro sōgen ni tsuite," pp. 29–34. Sakayori Masashi also argues for the truthfulness of the incident. He refers to a record in the *Samguk sagi* as indirect evidence (Kim Pu-sik, *Samguk sagi*, 9, p. 5a). It reports that a Japanese ambassador visited the Silla court in autumn, in the eighth month, 753, but was denied a court audience because of his arrogance. Sakayori believes that this event was probably the aftermath of the dispute on precedence at the Tang court in early January. See his "Shichi hachi seiki no Dazaifu," p. 40. Ikeda On takes a compromise position. He believes that the dispute indeed happened but that the account of the dispute in the *Shoku Nihongi* needs further study. See his "Tenhō kōki no Tō, Ragi, Nichi kankei o megutte," in *Shunshi Ben Rinseki kyōju kanreki kinen Tōshi ronsō*, pp. 208–251. My opinion is that the inaccuracies in the account in question are not sufficient to prove that Furumaro never raised the issue of the seating arrangement with the Tang court.

174. For a detailed study of Abe no Nakamaro, see Sugimoto Naojirō, *Abe no Nakamaro den kenkyū*.

175. Wang Wei, *Wang youcheng ji*, 12, pp. 2a–3b.

176. Situo, *Enryaku sōroku*, p. 21.

177. Ichikawa Seinei, *Quan Tang shi yi*, a, p. 10173.

178. Kūkai, *Seireishū*, 5, p. 268; Borgen, "Japanese Mission to China," p. 27.

179. *JTS*, 10, p. 252; *ZZTJ*, 213, p. 882.

180. *SJ*, 100, p. 2732; and 107, p. 2847; *JTS*, 197, p. 5280; *THY*, 99, p. 1763.

181. Wei Zheng et al., *Sui shu*, 3, p. 76. Other similar practices include "preferential treatment" *(youli)*, "generous reception" *(lishu youwo)*, and "lavish reward" *(youlao)*. See *JTS*, 196a, p. 5266; and 199a, pp. 5321, 5336, and 5352.

182. *CFYG*, 997, p. 11b.

183. Sugano no Mamichi et al., *Shoku Nihongi*, 35, p. 443, 778/10/23; Fujiwara no Otsugu et al., *Nihon kōki*, 12, p. 42, 805/6/8; Ennin, *Nittō guhō junrei kōki*, 1, p. 20. See also Ono Katsutoshi, *Nittō guhō junrei kōki no kenkyū*, vol. 1, p. 424.

184. Minamoto no Tsunenori, *Daishi go gyōjō shūki*, p. 499.

185. Inoue Mitsusada, "Kani jūnikai to sono shiteki igi," in his *Nihon kodai kokka no kenkyū*, p. 300.

186. Ennin, *Nittō guhō junrei kōki*, 1, p. 20.

187. The author is grateful to Professor Denis Twitchett for having brought to his attention the existence of the interstate dependence system in other parts of Asia and Central Asia.

188. Hirano Takuji, "Ritsuryō ikaisei to shoban," in *Nihon kodai no seiji to seido*, ed. Hayashi Rokurō Sensei Kanreki Kinenkai, p. 108.

189. Alternative expressions of the concept include *ka*, *kaka*, and *kado*. For exam-

ples of usage, see Sugano no Mamichi et al., *Shoku Nihongi*, 1, p. 4, 698/7/19; 6, pp. 60–61, 770/9/2; 9, p. 92, 722/4*/25; and 40, p. 546, 790/5/5; Koremune no Naomoto, *Ryō no shūge*, 34, p. 865; Kūkai, *Shūi zatsushū*, in *Kōbō daishi Kūkai zenshū*, vol. 7, pp. 186–187; and Nishijima Sadao, "Ken Tō shi to kokusho," in *Ken Tō shi kenkyū to shiryō*, ed. Nishijima Sadao et al., p. 66.

190. For a definition of *i*, see Koremune no Naomoto, *Ryō no shūge*, 13, p. 403.

191. Ibid., 13, p. 404: "For all the remote provinces where there are various kinds of barbarians, tax and corvée [levied on them] have to be decided on according to the local situation. They need not be the same as these levied on the *kaka*." An annotation to the text reads: "*Kaka* means Chūgoku."

192. Hirano Takuji, "Ritsuryō ikaisei to shoban," p. 102.

193. Toneri Shinnō et al., *Nihon shoki*, 14, p. 371, 463/8: "The land of Silla was refractory and given to vain talk, and did not send presents, therefore they feared the intentions of the Central Land [Japan]." The English translation is from Aston, *Nihongi*, vol. 1, p. 351.

194. However, only independent states, not tribes such as the Hayato people and the hairy people living in Hokkaidō, were qualified as "barbarian countries." See Koremune no Naomoto, *Ryō no shūge*, 13, pp. 408–409.

195. Ibid., 13, p. 410.

196. *Nihon kiryaku*, 13, pp. 268–269, 795/7/16, and 272, 798/6/20; Kōbō Daishi Zenshū Henshū Iinkai, *Kōbō daishi zenshū*, vol. 15, p. 423. See also Hirano Kunio, "Kiki ritsuryō ni okeru 'kikai' 'gaiban' no gainen to sono yōrei," p. 124.

197. Koremune no Naomoto, *Ryō no shūge*, 4, p. 91. A question was quoted in the annotation to the text: "What is the difference between guests from barbarian countries *(ban)* and barbarians *(i)*?" The answer was: "Those who are called *ban* are the barbarians in the capital who came to pay tribute [to the Japanese court]. As for those foreigners who do not belong to any tribute-paying mission, they are labeled *i*." See ibid., 19, pp. 568–569. The concepts of *ban* and *i* are also discussed in Verschuer, *Relations officielles*, pp. 2–3, and in Paku Sekisen, "Nihon kodai kokka no tai ban ninshiki."

198. Sugano no Mamichi et al., *Shoku Nihongi*, 18, p. 214, 752/6/14; 19, p. 218, 753/5/10; 22, p. 259, 759/1/3; and 36, p. 455, 780/1/5.

199. Wei Zheng et al., *Sui shu*, 81, p. 1827; Wang Wei, *Wang youcheng ji*, 12, p. 2b.

200. For discussions of Japanese court protocol, see Nabeta Hajime, "Roku shichi seiki no hinrei ni kansuru oboegaki," in *Ritsuryōsei no shomondai*, ed. Takigawa Masajirō Hakase Beiju Kinenkai, pp. 399–426; Tajima Isao, "Nihon no ritsuryō kokka no 'hinrei'"; and Tokoro Isao, "Chōga gishikibun no seiritsu," in *Nihon kodaishi ron'en*, ed. Endō Motoo Sensei Shōju Kinenkai, pp. 571–610.

201. *JTS*, 99, p. 5340.

CHAPTER 7: WEIGHT AND
NUANCES IN STATE LETTERS

1. Historically the term "Japan" (Riben) did not come into use until Empress
    Wu's reign (r. 684–704). See *SJ*, 2, p. 60, for the commentary by Zhang
    Shoujie in 736. Japanese scholars have different opinions on this issue. See,
    for example, Honiden Kikushi, "Zui Tō kōshō to Nihon kokugō no seiritsu."
    However, to avoid confusion, "Japan" is used throughout this chapter. Only
    when quoting Chinese and Japanese sources will "Wo" and "Wa" be used in
    reference to Japan.

2. Wei Zheng et al., *Sui shu*, 3, p. 71; *CFYG*, 970, p. 2b. Some scholars locate
    Jialuoshe in Burma or in the Malaysian peninsula. For a study of Emperor
    Yang, see Arthur Wright, "Sui Yang-ti: Personality and Stereotype," in *The
    Confucian Persuasion*, ed. Arthur Wright, pp. 47–76.

3. For discussion of Sui foreign policies, see Arthur Wright, "The Sui Dynasty,"
    pp. 138–147; Pan Yihong, *Son of Heaven and Heavenly Qaghan*, pp. 112–118;
    Liu Jianming, *Suidai zhengzhi yu duiwai zhengce*, pp. 197–330; and Wu Yugui,
    Tujue hanguo yu Sui Tang guanxi shi yanjiu, pp. 81–146.

4. Wei Zheng et al., *Sui shu*, 83, p. 1841.

5. Ibid., 3, p. 70.

6. Ibid., 31, p. 886; *ZZTJ*, 190, p. 5965.

7. Wei Zheng et al., *Sui shu*, 81, p. 1825.

8. Ibid., 81, p. 1827; *CFYG*, 997, p. 11b; Zuikei Shūhō, *Zenrin kokuhōki*, a,
    p. 11.

9. Masumura Hiroshi, "Nisshutsu tokoro tenshi to nichibotsu tokoro tenshi,"
    pp. 30–35. Masumura points out that Emperor Yang was not angry, as some
    scholars have suggested. The Chinese word to indicate anger was *nu*. See *SJ*,
    100, p. 2730; *HS*, 37, p. 1976; and 94a, p. 3755; Wei Zheng et al., *Sui shu*,
    84, p. 1866; and *JTS*, 199b, p. 5343.

10. For this practice, see Ō no Yasumaro *Kojiki*, b, pp. 336–337; Toneri Shinnō
    et al., *Nihon shoki*, 23, p. 182, 636/7/1; and 25, p. 240, 647. "All persons
    holding official rank must draw up in lines to right and left outside the
    south gate at the hour of the tiger (3–5 a.m.), and wait there until the first
    appearance of the sun.... Those who come late will not be permitted to
    enter and take up their attendance." The English translation is from Aston,
    Nihongi, vol. 2, p. 227.

11. Wei Zheng et al., *Sui shu*, 81, p. 1826. There is good authority for the
    authenticity of this Chinese record. See Koremune no Naomoto, *Ryō no
    shūge*, 24, p. 677; and 35, p. 875; and Kiyohara no Natsuno et al., *Ryō no gige*,
    6, p. 206.

12. The importance of "investigating local traditions" (*guan fengsu*) is discussed in
    HS, 30, p. 1756; and 72, p. 3063. See also Wang Liqi, *Fengsu tongyi jiaozhu*, p. 8.

13. Wei Zheng et al., *Sui shu*, 81, p. 1826; Zuikei Shūhō, *Zenrin kokuhōki*, a, p. 11. In the *Sui shu*, 81, p. 1827, the character *shi* was missing from Pei's name. This is not necessarily owing to the taboo on using the character *shi*, which was part of the first name of Emperor Li Shimin (r. 627–649), during whose reign the *Sui shu* was compiled. An edict of 626 stipulated that courtiers and ordinary people could use the characters *shi* and *min* as long as they did not appear together. See *JTS*, 2, pp. 29–30. For a discussion of Pei Shiqing, see Ikeda On, "Hai Seisei to Kō Byōjin," pp. 8–12.

14. *JTS*, 196a, p. 5222; *THY*, 97, p. 1730.

15. *JTS*, 199a, p. 5329.

16. *QTW*, 999, pp. 4643–4644 and 4644–4647; and 1000, pp. 4650–4651 and 4652–4654. State letters in Chinese from such Central Asian countries as Kangguo (Samarkand), Chean Guo (Kharghan), Tuhuoluo (Tokhara), and Xieyu Guo (Jakuda) were, however, not written by the locals. They were translations by Tang officials. See *QTW*, 999, pp. 4647–4649. In 719, a Tang court decree authorized prefectural authorities on the western frontiers to open and translate foreign state letters and to seal them up and present them to the court. See *THY*, 26, p. 505.

17. Kurihara Tomonobu, *Jōdai Nihon taigai kankei no kenkyū*, pp. 241–242.

18. Wang Gung-wu classifies China's diplomatic rhetoric into five groups: (1) language that was largely moral and cosmological and expressed inclusiveness, (2) rhetoric dealing with tribute, (3) derogatory language justifying the use of force, (4) routine communication stressing realism and flexibility, and (5) rhetoric of contractual relations. See his "The Rhetoric of a Lesser Empire," in *China among Equals*, ed. Morris Rossabi, p. 48.

19. *HS*, 78, p. 3282; Wei Zheng et al., *Sui shu*, 84, pp. 1870 and 1875; Xu Jingzong, *Wenguan cilin*, 664, pp. 6a–b.

20. A "memorial" was used by an inferior to report matters to a superior. See Cai Yong, *Du duan*, a, p. 4b; *TLD*, 8, pp. 5a–b; and *THY*, 26, p. 504.

21. Wei Zheng et al., *Sui shu*, 84, p. 1869. For discussion of the form of address used in correspondence between China and other countries, see Kurihara Tomonobu, *Jōdai Nihon taigai kankei no kenkyū*, pp. 185–186; and Hirano Kunio, "Nichi-Chō-Chū sangoku kankeiron ni tsuite no oboegaki," p. 57.

22. See the case of Rouran, a dominant tribe in Mongolia, in *WS*, 130, p. 2303. The practice was also used in domestic politics when a new dynasty had been established through the abdication of the previous emperor. The new emperor, showing a degree of courtesy, usually allowed the abdicated emperor and his family members to address themselves by personal name, thus not openly calling them "subjects" of the new regime. See *SGZ*, 2, p. 76; and 13, p. 415; and *JS*, 3, p. 52.

23. *SGZ*, 30, p. 857. The English translation is based on Goodrich and Tsunoda, *Japan in the Chinese Dynastic Histories*, pp. 16–17.

24. Kurihara Tomonobu, "Gishi Wajinden ni mieru Yamataikoku o meguru kokusai kankei no ichimen," " p. 6.

25. Xu Shizeng, *Wenti mingbian xushuo*, p. 114.

26. Liu Xi, *Shi ming*, 6, p. 46a; Wang Liqi, *Wenxin diaolong jiaozheng*, p. 134; Xu Shizeng, *Wenti mingbian xushuo*, pp. 115–116. For the use of conferment to grant the title "prince" *(wang)*, see *SJ*, 60, pp. 2111, 2113, and 2114; and *SGZ*, 1, p. 36. For an English translation of the passage from *Wenxin diaolong jiaozheng*, see Wong Siu-kit, Allan Chung-hang, and Kwong-tai Lam, *The Book of Literary Design*, p. 71.

27. Ōba Osamu, "Himiko o Shin Gi Waō to suru seisho o meguru mondai," p. 180.

28. *SS*, 97, p. 2394.

29. Ibid., 5, p. 85. Emperor Hanzei is called "Wowang Zhen." The term "Zhen" stands for his first name "Mizuhawake."

30. Ibid., 5, p. 100. This record refers to Emperor Ingyō as "Andong Jiangjun Wowang Woji." The term *ji* is an abbreviation for the emperor's first name "Ōasa Tsumawakuko no Sukune." See also *NS*, 2, p. 53.

31. *SS*, 6, p. 129; and 97, p. 2395. Emperor Ankō is referred to as "Wowang Shizi Xing." The term "Xing" stands for his first name "Anaho." See also *NS*, 2, p. 65.

32. *SS*, 10, p. 197; *NS*, 3, p. 91. In the edicts issued in 478, 479, and 502, Emperor Yūryaku was called "Wu," an abbreviation for his first name "Ōhatsuse no wakatakeru."

33. *NQS*, 58, p. 1012; *NS*, 79, p. 1975.

34. *LS*, 2, p. 36; *NS*, 6, p. 185; and 79, p. 1975. In 451 and 502, titles were granted to the Japanese rulers. As it was a common practice of the Chinese court to use edicts to announce the bestowal of Chinese titles on foreign rulers, edicts must have been issued to Japan, even though the Chinese sources do not record them. The forms of address used in these edicts should have been the same as those that appear in other relevant records.

35. Cai Yong, *Du duan*, a, p. 4b. Other official dispatches used by Chinese officials are the illuminative memorial *(zhang)*, the report to the throne *(zou)*, and the debate *(boyi)*.

36. Liu Xi, *Shi ming*, 6, p. 46b; Xiao Tong, *Wen xuan*, 37, p. 1a.

37. *SGZ*, 30, p. 857.

38. For memorials from Japan to China during this time, see *SS*, 97, p. 2394 and 2395; and *NS*, 79, p. 1974. The Japanese ambassadors to China in 238, 413, and 438 may also have brought memorials to China even though there is no record of these memorials. See *JS*, 97, p. 2536; and 10, p. 264; and *SS*, 5, p. 85.

39. *SS*, 97, p. 2395; *NS*, 79, p. 1974.

40. For more discussion on this topic, see Karl Friday, "Pushing beyond the Pale: The Yamato Conquest of the Emishi and Northern Japan."

41. The Chinese translators of the *Scripture of the Lotus of the Fine Dharma (Miaofa lianhua jing)* were perhaps the first to use Chinese characters as phonetic marks to render Sanskrit terms in 406. The Koreans then learned this method and spread it to Japan. See Jin'ichi Konishi, *A History of Japanese Literature,* vol. 1, pp. 332–336. Abé Ryūichi demonstrates that the use of Chinese characters as phonetic marks was a means to "deprive the hiero-glyphic characters of their inherent and necessary identities with external objects." Bleached of their Chinese cultural and political connotations, these Chinese characters became tools for the ninth-century Japanese cler-gy headed by Kūkai to challenge the "Confucian state ideology grounded on the principle of the rectification of names" and to redefine the relationship between the state and the Buddhist establishment. See his *The Weaving of Mantra,* pp. 388–395. I would further argue that this peculiar way of using Chinese characters was itself a practice of "rectification of names." Compilers of Japanese state letters to China during the Sui and the Tang dynasties used Chinese characters to transliterate the native title for the Japanese ruler, thus redefining his relationship with China according to a Japan-centered ideology. For futher discussion of this issue, see "Recon-structing a Japanese State Letter to Tang China" in this chapter.

42. Similarly, the ruler of Nanzhao gave up the title "Emperor of the East" that the Tibetan ruler had granted to him before offering loyalty to Tang China. See *JTS,* 197, p. 5283.

43. Wei Zheng et al., *Sui shu,* 81, p. 1826. For the compilation of the *Sui shu,* see Denis C. Twitchett, *The Writing of Official History under the T'ang,* pp. 22 and 87. See also his "The Problem of Sources," in *Sui and T'ang China, 589–906,* ed. Denis Twitchett, vol. 3, part 1 of *The Cambridge History of China,* ed. John K. Fairbank and Denis C. Twitchett, pp. 38–47.

44. Miki Tarō, *Wajinden no yōgo no kenkyū,* pp. 233–237.

45. The names of the aforementioned Japanese rulers are: "Ōtarashihiko-oshirowake," "Wakatarashihiko," and "Tarashinakatsuhiko" respectively.

46. Mori Kimiyuki, "Tennō gō no seiritsu o megutte," p. 18. He points out that *ametarashihiko* can also be interpreted as *amakutararetaokata,* meaning "the son born by (coming from) heaven." In any case, *ametarashihiko* is a Japanese designation equivalent to the Chinese title "emperor" *(huangdi).*

47. Zhang Chujin, *Hanyuan,* p. 27b.

48. Wei Zheng et al., *Sui shu,* 3, pp. 71 and 74; and 81, p. 1828; Toneri Shinnō et al., *Nihon shoki,* 22, p. 151, 608/9/11, p. 157, 614/6/13.

49. *SJ,* 110, p. 2897; *HS,* 95, p. 3849; Wei Zheng et al., *Sui shu,* 84, p. 1868. Similar terms that China's rivals used when sending a letter to China

include *yishu, qianshu,* and *baoshu.* For a discussion of these terms, see Kuri-hara Tomonobu, "Nichi Zui kōshō no ichisokumen," in his *Jōdai Nihon taigai kankei no kenkyū,* pp. 213–215.

50. *SJ,* 110, pp. 2896 and 2899; Wei Zheng et al., *Sui shu,* 84, p. 1868; *JTS,* 194b, pp. 5190–5191; 196a, pp. 5222 and 5230; and 197, p. 5282; *THY,* 94, p. 1687; Wang Zhenping, "Speaking with a Forked Tongue: Diplomatic Corre-spondence between China and Japan: 238–608."

51. Toneri Shinnō et al., *Nihon shoki,* 22, p. 150, 608/8/3. The English transla-tion is from Aston, *Nihongi,* vol. 2, pp. 137–138. See also Zuikei Shūhō, *Zen-rin kokuhōki,* a, pp. 10 and 22.

52. Zuikei Shūhō, *Zenrin kokuhōki,* a, p. 10. For Tang edicts using "greet," see Li Yong, *Li Beihai quanshu,* 7, p. 5b; and Wang Chang, *Jinshi cuibian,* 68, p. 13a. See also an edict to the Silla ruler in Xu Jingzong, *Wenguan cilin,* 646, pp. 261 and 263.

53. Zuikei Shūhō, *Zenrin kokuhōki,* a, p. 10.

54. *Keiseki kōdenki,* quoted in Zuikei Shūhō, *Zenrin kokuhōki,* a, p. 11. A work by an unknown author with an unknown date of completion, the *Keiseki kōdenki* might be an alternative title for the *Juten,* which is included in the thirteenth-century bibliographical work *Honchō shojaku mokuroku.* See Sakamoto Tarō, *Shōtoku Taishi,* pp. 122–123.

55. Some modern Japan scholars suggest that the original Sui letter used the expression "Wowang," and the compilers of the *Nihon shoki* faithfully cited this letter, but Japanese courtiers of later times changed the word *wang* to *huang.* See Toneri Shinnō, *Nihon shoki* (*Nihon koten bungaku taikei* edn.), 22, p. 191, note 21; and Sakamoto Tarō, *Shōtoku Taishi,* p. 122.

56. *Shu* was an abbreviation for *xishu* (a letter bearing the imperial seal) or *cishu* (a letter granted by the emperor). See Xu Shizeng, *Wenti mingbian xushuo,* pp. 113–114. See also Nakamura Hiroichi, "Tōdai no jisho ni tsuite."

57. Other official correspondence included *fachi,* an edict to announce the establishment and abolition of prefectures and counties, to add or cut the number of governmental officials, to dispatch troops, to dismiss officials, to deprive them of the titles, and to appoint officials of the sixth rank and above; *chizhi,* a decree to handle matters that the established rules and reg-ulations did not deal with; and *chidie,* an edict to deal with routine matters according to existing rules and practices. For samples and the functions of Tang decrees, see Hong Zun, *Hanyuan qunshu* (*Zhibuzuzhai congshu* edn.), 5, pp. 2b–3a; *TLD,* 9, p. 5a; *JTS,* 43, p. 1849; and *XTS,* 47, p. 1210. See also Nakamura Hiroichi, "Tōdai no choku ni tsuite."

58. The same was also used to crown the empress, to appoint the crown prince, to grant titles to princes, to convey the special kindness and respect of the emperor to especially distinguished men, and to confer honors upon his subjects.

59. Nakamura Hiroichi, "Tōdai no seishoshiki ni tsuite."
60. Nakamura Hiroichi, "Tōdai no irō seisho ni tsuite," in *Ritsuryōsei*, ed. Tōshi Kenkyūkai, pp. 333–358.
61. *TLD*, 9, p. 5a.
62. State letters composed by Zhang Jiuling, Bai Juyi, Lu Zhi, and Feng Ao are examples in point. Zhang was famous for his conviction of China's cultural superiority. A number of state letters that he composed showed indignation at the insolence of China's "vassal states." See *QTW*, 285, pp. 1295–1306; 464, pp. 2128–2129; 665, p. 3038; and 728, p. 3369. See also P. A. Herbert, *Under the Brilliant Emperor,* pp. 14 and 21.
63. Wang Gung-wu, "The Rhetoric of a Lesser Empire," p. 47.
64. These regulations were similar to the "written codes of conduct" *(shuyi)* that the educated Chinese followed when drafting private letters. A record in the *Nittō guhō junrei* shows Tang monks exchanging felicitations according to such codes (Ennin, *Nittō guhō junrei kōki,* 3, p. 83). See also Patricia Ebrey, "T'ang Guides to Verbal Etiquette." For a detailed study of Chinese official correspondence in successive dynasties, see Xu Tongxin, *Gongduxue shi.*
65. This was a work by Yang Ju, a "Hanlin probationer" *(Hanlin daizhao)* at the Editorial Office (Daizhao Yuan) in the 890s who had the rare opportunity of reading memorials to the court and drafting imperial decrees in response. See *JTS*, 177, p. 4600; and *XTS*, 46, p. 1183; and 189, p. 5394. Some of the edicts that Yang drafted are preserved in *QTW*, 819, p. 3872. For a brief discussion of Yang's work, which was edited later by the Song scholar Hong Zun, see Chen Zhensun, *Zhizhai shulu jieti,* 6, p. 175.
66. The Tang court stamped its decree with one of the six imperial seals. A decree in reply to a foreign ruler used the *Tianzi xingbao;* one that expressed the kindness of the Chinese emperor to a foreign ruler used the *Tianzi zhibao.* When requesting foreign military assistance, a decree used the *Tianzi xinbao. TLD*, 8, pp. 16b–17b; *XTS*, 220, p. 6208.
67. Fang Risheng, *Gujin yunhui juyao xiaobu* (1606 edn.), 8, p. 54a; Zhao Yi, *Gaiyu congkao* (1852 edn.), 36, p. 8a.
68. Zhang Ji, *Zhang Siye shiji* (*SBCK* edn.), 2, p. 9a.
69. Li Zhao, *Hanlin zhi* (*Baichuan xuehai* edn.), p. 4a. This whitish paper scroll was sometimes made of hemp.
70. Ibid., p. 4b; *XTS*, 46, pp. 1183–1184; Ma Duanlin, *Wenxian tongkao*, 54, p. 490; Peng Dingqiu, *Quan Tang shi*, 427, p. 4704; Huangfu Zeng, *Tang Huangfu Zeng shiji* 1, pp. 68a–b.
71. *JTS*, 5, p. 101; *THY*, 54, p. 927; Peng Dingqiu, *Quan Tang shi,* 271, p. 3052.
72. Li Zhao, *Hanlin zhi*, pp. 4a–b.
73. Wang Wei, *Wang youcheng ji*, 2, p. 8b; Peng Dingqiu, *Quan Tang shi,* 50, p. 616; 271, p. 3032; and 482, p. 5493.
74. Gao Cheng, *Shiwu jiyuan,* 10, pp. 27a–b.

75. Li Zhao, *Hanlin zhi*, pp. 4a–b; *XTS*, 221a, p. 6236. This regulation was in effect from 806 to 820. For the use of the letter case in China and Japan, see *THY*, 54, p. 926; Ennin, *Nittō guhō junrei kōki*, 3, p. 90; and 4, p. 110. For a translation of the *Hanlin zhi*, see F. A. Bischoff, *La forêt des princeaux: Étude sur l'Académie du Han-lin sous la dynastie des T'ang, et traduction du Han-lin tche*, vol. 18.

76. Li Zhao, *Hanlin zhi*, pp. 4a–b. Japan and Parhae also used a letter case in diplomatic communication. See Zuikei Shūhō, *Zenrin kokuhōki*, a, p. 13; and Sugano no Mamichi, *Shoku Nihongi*, 32, p. 410, 773/6/24.

77. Such as "Summer days are getting hot," "Mid-summer is very hot," "The early autumn is still hot," "Recently, the autumn days are rather cool," and "The middle of the winter is very cold." See Zhang Jiuling, *Tang chengxiang Qujiang Zhang xiansheng wenji* (*SBCK* edn.), 7, pp. 11b–13a; Liu Dabin *Maoshan zhi*, 1, pp. 20a, 21b, and 22b; and *QTW*, 100, p. 457.

78. *Jiu* refers to the father-in-law and *sheng*, to the son-in-law. See Kong Yingda, *Li ji zhengyi* (*SSJZS* edn.), 51, p. 1622–1623; Zhao Qi and Sun Bi, eds., *Mengzi zhushu* (*SSJZS* edn.), 10a, p. 2742; *SGZ*, 32, p. 875; and Fang Risheng, *Gujin yun hui juyao xiaobu*, 8, p. 88b.

79. For discussions of these dynastic marriages, see Pan Yihong, "Marriage Alliances and Chinese Princesses in International Politics from Han through Tang."

80. Tibet also used marriage as a means to control the king of Bolor (Xiao Bolü, located in the Yasin valley, eastern Pakistan). See *JTS*, 104, p. 3203.

81. Kinship terms became diplomatic rhetoric during the Han dynasty. The court used them when communicating with China's military rivals. See Wang Gung-wu, "The Rhetoric of a Lesser Empire," p. 57.

82. Zhang Jiuling, *Tang chengxiang Qujiang Zhang xiansheng wenji*, 11, pp. 2b–3a, 3a–b, 9a, 10a, and 12b; Lu Zhi, *Tang Lu Xuangong hanyuan ji* (*SBCK* edn.), 10, p. 4a.

83. *THY*, 6, p. 75; *ZZTJ*, 196, p. 6164.

84. *JTS*, 122, p. 3506; *CFYG*, 997, p. 8a; Li Deyu, *Li Wenrao wenji*, 5, pp. 7a–b; *ZZTJ*, 220, p. 7059; and 246, p. 7965.

85. See the case of Wang Xizhi's letters in Yan Kejun, *Quan Jin wen* (*Quan Shanggu Sandai Qin Han Sanguo Liuchao wen* edn.), pp. 1585, 1587, and 1592.

86. When enthroned as Emperor Chengdi of the Eastern Jin at a young age, Sima Yan bowed to his chief minister Wang Dao when the two met. In his edicts to Wang Dao, Sima Yan always used the expression *jingwen*. See *JS*, 65, p. 1751.

87. See Li Feng's epitaph in Shaanxisheng Bowuguan Fupingxian Wenhuaguan, "Tang Li Feng mu fajue jianbao," pp. 325–326. Emperor Gaozong used the phrase *jingwen* in his edict to Li Feng, who was the fifteenth son of Li Yuan. The same phrase was also used in letters of Chinese Buddhist emperors to

Buddhist masters. See Shamen Guangding, *Guoqing bailu* (*Taishō Tripitaka* edn.), 2, pp. 802 and 806; 3, p. 815; and 4, p. 816; and Liu Dabin, *Maoshan zhi*, 1, p. 21b.

88. See the letters exchanged between the Han and Xiongnu rulers, and between the Tang emperor and the ruler of the Kirghiz. *SJ*, 110, pp. 2896, 2897, and 2899; Li Deyu, *Li Wenrao wenji*, 6, p. 1b.

89. Xu Jingzong, *Wenguan cilin*, 646, pp. 261 and 263; Li Yong, *Li Beihai quanshu*, 7, p. 5b; Wang Chang, *Jinshi cuibian*, 68, p. 13a.

90. *CFYG*, 974, p. 17b.

91. Ibid., 975, p. 12a. For discussions of the connotations of *jingwen* and *wen*, see Yamada Hideo, "Nichi, Tō, Ragi, Bōtsu aida no kokusho ni tsuite," in *Nihon kōkogaku kodaishi ronshū*, ed. Itō Nobuo Kyōju Kanreki Kinenkai, pp. 346–347. See also Kaneko Shūichi, "Tōdai no kokusai bunsho keishiki ni tsuite," pp. 29–30.

92. For Abaoji, see *XTS*, 219, p. 6173; and Tuotuo et al., *Liao shi*, 1, p. 1. He later became the first ruler of Liao (916–1125).

93. The commentary in parentheses is by Hong Zun, the Song scholar who edited *Hanyuan qunshu*, into which the *Hanlin xueshiyuan jiugui* was incorporated.

94. A Chinese emperor used this style when sending a letter to his subject. If an inferior used the same style in a letter to his superior, he would be deemed as having challenged the authority of his boss. See Xu Ling, *Xu Xiaomu ji* (*SBCK* edn.), 4, p. 1a; and *JTS*, 107, p. 3265.

95. Abaoji adopted the title "emperor" in 916 after he had annexed the land of the Turks into his regime. Tuotuo et al., *Liao shi*, 1, p. 10.

96. "Biaoxin" was the native title of Hequan, the Nanzhao chieftain to whom the Tang court granted the tile "Ruler of Nanzhao" in 809. See *JTS*, 197, p. 5284; and *XTS*, 222b, p. 6281.

97. In contrast, a Tang letter to the generals and ministers of Nanzhao used jute paper. See Li Zhao, *Hanlin zhi*, p. 4b.

98. Yang Ju, *Hanlin xueshiyuan jiugui*, in *Hanyuan qunshu* (*Zhibuzuzhai congshu* edn.), pp. 33a–b. For a discussion of these regulations, see Kaneko Shūichi, "Tōdai kokusai kankei ni okeru Nihon no ichi ni kansuru ichi shiron," pp. 19–21.

99. Wang Pu, *Wudai huiyao*, 13, p. 174.

100. Zhou Xunchu, *Tang yulin jiaozheng*, vol. 1, p. 28; Li Fang, *Taiping guangji*, 493, p. 4048. For a definition of *xiang*, see Xu Shen, *Shuowen jiezi*, 5b, pp. 4a–b; and Zhang Yi, *Guangya shuzheng*, 3a, p. 14a.

101. The origin of the verb was "giving things to an inferior." See Kong Yingda, *Li ji zhengyi*, 35, p. 1514.

102. For a definition of *gong*, see Zhang Yi, *Guangya shuzheng*, 1b, p. 12a. For sample uses of the term, see *CFYG*, 975, p. 4a; and *JTS*, 195, pp. 5206 and 5215; and 196b, p. 5254.

103. Xiao Tong, *Wen xuan*, pp. 2a–b; Zhang Jiuling, *Tang chengxiang qujiang Zhang xiansheng wenji*, 8, p. 5b; Li Qunyu, *Li Qunyu shiji*, p. 2a. But usage of *lingqu* was inconsistent. Records contradicting my interpretation exist. For example, a Tang letter to the ruler of the Turks in 717 used *lingqu*, even though the Turks were far from submissive to the Tang court at the time. See *CFYG*, 974, p. 17b.

104. *JTS*, 196b, p. 5246; *CFYG*, 997, p. 17a; *THY*, 97, p. 1734.

105. Xu Shen, *Shuowen jiezi*, 6b, p. 4b; Zhu Junsheng, *Shuowen tongxun dingsheng*, 16, p. 21a; Ding Du, *Ji yun*, 7, p. 540.

106. *JTS*, 195, pp. 5206 and 5215; 196b, p. 5254; and 198, p. 5316; *ZZTJ*, 181, p. 5642.

107. *NS*, 59, p. 1451.

108. The two Tang decrees to the Tibetan chief minister from 783 to 796, Shang-jiezan (Zhang rGyal tshan), also used *lingzhi*. They read: "Now such and such *(mouwu)* gifts are granted to you, my chamberlain. You should receive them when they arrive." See Lu zhi, *Tang Lu Xuangong hanyuan ji*, 10, pp. 7a and 10a–b. In the second decree, "receive them" appears as *lingye* in Chinese. Other Tang dynasty records also show that the use of *lingzhi* and *lingye* indicate that the gift recipient enjoyed an especially close relationship with the sender: Princess Jincheng, Zhang Yue, and the king of Silla. See Zhang Juling, *Tang chengxiang Qujiang Zhang xiansheng wenji*, 11, p. 3b; Liu su, *Da Tang xinyu*, p. 129; Bai Juyi, *Baishi changqing ji*, 39, p. 37a; and *CFYG*, 975, p. 11449. Japanese state letters to Parhae in 777 and 872 also employed *lingzhi*. See Sugano no Mamichi et al., *Shoku Nihongi*, 34, pp. 434–435, 777/5/23; and Fujiwara no Tokihara et al., *Nihon Sandai jitsuroku*, 21, pp. 308–309, 872/5/25.

109. Sugano no Mamichi et al., *Shoku Nihongi*, 35, p. 443, 778/9/23; Fujiwara no Otsugu et al., *Nihon kōki*, 12, p. 42, 805/6/8.

110. Toneri Shinnō et al., *Nihon shoki*, 27, p. 288, 664/5/17, p. 290, 665/9/23; and 28, pp. 308–309, 672/3/21; Sugano no Mamichi et al., *Shoku Nihongi*, 35, p. 448, 779/5/3.

111. Sugano no Mamichi et al., *Shoku Nihongi*, 33, p. 414.

112. Ibid., 13, p. 156; and 32, p. 410. Korean scholars of the twelfth century also chose "present" in their records about gift exchange between peer countries. See Kim Pu-sik, *Samguk sagi*, 3, p. 2a; and 11, p. 11b.

113. Sugano no Mamichi et al., *Shoku Nihongi*, 34, pp. 434–435, 777/5/23; Fujiwara no Otsugu et al., *Nihon kōki*, 21, p. 96, 811/1/22; Fujiwara no Tokihara et al., *Nihon Sandai jitsuroku*, 21, pp. 308–309, 872/5/25.

114. Kōbō Daishi Zenshū Henshū Iinkai, *Kōbō daishi zenshū*, 15, pp. 357–358. For examples of using *tianshu* to refer to Tang state letters, see Li Bai, *Li Taibai shi* (*SBCK* edn.), 9, p. 28a; Wang Wei, *Wang youcheng ji*, 6, p. 12b; Liu Chang-

qing, *Liu Suizhou shiji* (*SBCK* edn.), 8, p. 3b; and Peng Dingqiu, *Quan Tang shi*, 813, p. 9145.

115. Fujiwara no Yoshifusa et al., *Shoku Nihon kōki*, 8, pp. 91–92, 839/9/17; Zuikei Shūhō, *Zenrin kokuhōki*, a, p. 22.

116. Sugano no Mamichi et al., *Shoku Nihongi*, 11, p. 129, 732/8/17. For a discussion of Tang state letters, see also Kaneko Shūichi, "T'ang International Relations and Diplomatic Correspondence."

117. Sugano no Mamichi et al., *Shoku Nihongi*, 11, p. 129, 732/8/17; and 13, p. 156, 739/11/3.

118. Ibid., 13, p. 156; and 32, p. 410, has two records of Parhae sending state letters to inform Japan of the whereabouts of the Japanese ambassadors.

119. The administrative center of this prefecture was in modern Shaoxing, Zhejiang province.

120. Sugano no Mamichi et al., *Shoku Nihongi*, 13, p. 156, 739/11/3. Heguri no Ason Hironari eventually came back to Japan and reported to the court that their ship, with 115 people on board, had drifted to the Kunlun state (located in southern Burma). There local bandits encircled and captured them. In captivity, ninety of them died of malaria. Some were killed, and some were missing. Only Hironari and three others survived.

121. The headquarters of this protectorate was located at modern Hanoi, Vietnam.

122. Zhang Juling, *Tang chengxiang Qujiang Zhang xiansheng wenji*, 12, pp. 9b–10b.

123. Wang Wei, *Wang youcheng ji*, 12, p. 3b.

124. The battle was fought at the river mouth of Baicun Jiang (Japanese: Hakusonkō). See *JTS*, 199a, pp. 5332–5334; *XTS*, 3, p. 63; *ZZTJ*, 201, p. 6337; and 286, Toneri Shinnō et al., *Nihon shoki*, 27, p. 286, 663/8/17, 27. See also Kitō Kiyoaki, *Hakusonkō*.

125. Toneri Shinnō et al., *Nihon shoki*, 27, p. 289, 665/8.

126. Ibid., 27, p. 288, 664/5/17, p. 298, 671/1/13, and p. 301, 671/11/10.

127. Yamada Hideo suggests that during the Sui and the Tang, Chinese state letters to Japan had three types of beginning: "respectfully greet," "greet," and no greeting. See his "Nichi, Tō, Ragi, Bōtsu aida no kokusho ni tsuite," pp. 361–362.

128. Segments of these Tang letters are found in the *Zenrin kokuhōki*, a, p. 22. Zuikei Shūhō compiled this work in 1470. He probably consulted the Tang letters when writing his book, since the Japanese court had palace secretaries (*naiki*) in charge of the preservation of Tang state letters to Japan, and some of them might have survived into Shūhō's time. See Fujiwara no Yoshifusa et al., *Shoku Nihon kōki*, 8, p. 92, 839/9/17. But Shūhō's discussion of the Tang letters is self-contradictory in places. He reports that the Tang state letter of 671 used "the Heavenly Emperor (Tianhuang) of the State of Japan" to address the Japanese ruler, but he also records that the Tang letter of 673 used the title "the ruler of Wo."

129. Zuikei Shūhō, *Zenrin kokuhōki*, a, p. 13. In fact it was the Japanese court that issued the certificate to Guo in the name of the local authorities. The court also issued specific instructions to the Dazai Headquarters on how to handle Guo's visit. See Toneri Shinnō et al., *Nihon shoki*, 27, p. 288, 664/10/4.

130. Among traditional scholars, Zuikei Shūhō strongly advocated the assertion. See *Zenrin kokuhōki*, b, p. 65. Motoori Norinaga was another traditional scholar holding the same opinion. See his *Gyojū gaigen*, in *Motoori Norinaga zenshū*, pp. 61–62. Even the famous Qing dynasty scholar Huang Zunxian held the same opinion. See his *Ribenguo zhi*, 4, p. 12b. For modern scholars who support the assertion, see Mori Katsumi, *Ken Tō shi*, p. 76; Naitō Konan, *Nihon bunkashi kenkyū*, p. 75; Kimiya Yasuhiko, *Nisshi kōtsushi*, vol. a, p. 178; Robert Borgen, "The Japanese Mission to China," p. 11; and Verschuer, *Relations officielles*, pp. 8–9.

131. Itazawa Takeo, "Nittō tsūkō ni okeru kokusho mondai ni tsuite"; Nishijima Sadao, "Ken Tō shi to kokusho"; Yuasa Yukihiko, "Ken Tō shi kōben nisoku." Nakamura Hidetaka, although failing to reach a specific conclusion, agrees that it is plausible that Japan sent state letters to China. See his *Nihon to Chōsen*, p. 39. See also Hori Toshikazu, "Nihon to Zui, Tō ryōkoku tono aida ni kawasareta kokusho," in his *Ritsuryō sei to Higashi Ajia sekai: Wadashi no Chūgoku shigaku (2)*, pp. 175–201; and Mori Kimiyuki, *Kodai Nihon no taigai ninshiki to tsūkō*, pp. 51–57.

132. Kūkai, *Seireishū*, 5, pp. 266–271. See also an English translation of this letter by Robert Borgen in the appendix of his "The Japanese Mission to China," pp. 26–28. Itazawa Takeo raises questions about the authenticity of Kūkai's letter. He suggests that the letter was not a genuine work of Kūkai but a fabrication of his disciples. See his "Nittō tsūkō ni okeru kokusho mondai ni tsuite," p. 10. Records in other primary Japanese sources indicate that Kūkai did not arrive at Fuzhou at all. See Minamoto no Tsunenori, *Daishi go gyōjō shūki*, in *Zoku gunsho ruijū*, 206, pp. 498–499.

133. Mori Katsumi gives the reading of his name as Fujiwara no Kuzunomaro. See his *Ken Tō shi*, p. 224. For an account of Fujiwara Kadonomaro's mission to China, see Fujiwara no Otsugu et al., *Nihon kōki*, 12, p. 31, 804/3/25 and pp. 41–42, 805/6/8.

134. For Yan Jimei, see *JTS*, 185, p. 4832; Han Yu, *Shunzong shilu (Haishan xianguan congshu* edn.), 3, pp. 3a–b; and Ji Yougong, *Tang shi jishi*, 36, pp. 1a–2b. See also Cen Zhongmian, *Langguan shizhu timing xin kaoding*, p. 182; and Yu Xianhao, *Tang cishi kao quanbian*, pp. 87, 2008, 2065, and 2160.

135. The administrative center of Fuzhou prefecture was located in modern Fuzhou city, Fujian province.

136. Fujiwara no Otsugu et al., *Nihon kōki*, 12, p. 42, 805/6/8.

137. *THY*, 54, p. 926; Lu Xinyuan, *Tang wen shiyi*, 8, p. 4697. See also Bai Juyi, *Baishi changqing ji*, 39, p. 37a.

138. Kurihara Tomonobu, *Jōdai Nihon taigai kankei no kenkyū*, p. 246.
139. Fujiwara no Otsugu et al., *Nihon kōki*, 24, p. 131, 815/1/22. Using a separate list of gifts was also common among ordinary people; see Kōbō Daishi Kūkai Zenshū Henshū Iinkai, *Kōbō daishi zenshū*, 15, p. 392.
140. For the use of *biegong*, see also Fujiwara no Tokihira, *Engi shiki*, 23, p. 586. The term refers to the special gifts presented to the Tang court by the Japanese ambassador. In contrast, *guoxin* refers to the ordinary Japanese "tributary offerings," which contain specific goods in a fixed amount that was specified in the *Engi shiki*, 30, p. 738. For explanations of the meaning of *biegong* and *guoxin*, see also Kūkai, *Seireishū*, 5, p. 267, notes 39 and 40.
141. *Zuda shinnō nittō ryakki*, p. 162.
142. The permit also specified the traveler's name, his status, and the destination of his trip. Depending on the status of a traveler, he would receive a permit of a specific type. Court officials used the *fuquan*, couriers carried the *didie*, soldiers held the *zongli* and others, the *guosuo*. See Zhangsun Wuji, *Gu Tanglü shuyi*, 8, p. 172; Ennin, *Nittō guhō junrei kōki*, 2, p. 38; and 4, p. 101. For a study of the *guosuo*, see Cheng Xilin, *Tangdai guosuo yanjiu*, especially pp. 142–156.
143. Zuikei Shūhō, *Zenrin kokuhōki*, a, pp. 12–13.
144. A record in the *THY*, 26, p. 505, shows that, in 719, a decree was issued to the prefectural authorities in the West, ordering them to open and to translate foreign state letters, and then to seal them up and present them to the central court. However, since state letters from Japan and other East Asian countries were written in Chinese, it does not seem likely that this practice was also applied to state letters from these countries.
145. Ennin, *Nittō guhō junrei kōki*, 4, p. 110. The English translation is from Reischauer, *Ennin's Diary*, p. 393.
146. Ibid. 1, p. 9. The English translation is from Reischauer, *Ennin's Diary*, p. 40.
147. Kujō no Kanezane, *Gyokuyō*, 10, p. 226.
148. This is also the opinion of Ono Katsutoshi. See his *Nittō guhō junrei kōki no kenkyū*, vol. 1, p. 222, note 2.
149. A record in Xu Shizeng, *Wenti mingbian xushuo*, p. 119, points out that state letter is "indispensable for any country" *(nai youguo zhi buke fei zhe)*. The Song court rejected Japanese officials from the Dazai Headquarters for not carrying state letters with them. See Tuotuo et al., *Song shi*, 491, p. 14136. *Gao huangdi yuzhi wenji*, a Ming dynasty work published during the Jiajing period (1522–1566), confirms the use of state letters between Tang and Japan (16, p. 29a).
150. Sugano no Mamichi et al., *Shoku Nihongi*, 18, pp. 214–215, 752/6/17.
151. Ibid., 35, p. 452, 779/10/9; and 36, p. 457, 780/2/15.
152. Ibid., 36, p. 457, 780/2/15.

153. *JTS*, 199a, p. 5340; *XTS*, 220, p. 6208. *Tong qiju* means "a junior sending greetings to a senior." See *HS*, 11, p. 333; Liu Yiqing, *Shishuo xinyu* (*SBCK* edn.), 1a, pp. 31a–b; and Fang Bao, *Fang Wangxi quanji*, 9, p. 117. A memorial from the Japanese ruler was therefore taken by the Tang court as an indication of his loyalty and respect to the Son of Heaven. In the Japanese sources, *biao* also refers to foreign courts' state letters to Japan. See, for example, Sugano no Mamichi et al., *Shoku Nihongi*, 32, p. 410, 773/6/24. However, *biao* was sometimes used in a broader sense, referring to any documents, official or private, handed to the Chinese court. In 735, for example, Nakatomi no Ason Nashiro presented a *biao*, asking for copies of the *Laozi*. This *biao* was certainly not a state letter. See *CFYG*, 99, p. 18b.

154. *CFYG*, 970, pp. 16a–b; Wang Yinglin, *Yu hai*, 153, p. 12b.

155. *CFYG*, 970, pp. 16a and 18a; 971, pp. 10a and 19b; 972, pp. 3b, 4a, and 10a; and 997, p. 4a; *JTS*, 6, p. 131; 12, p. 325; and 17b, p. 576; Wang Yinglin, *Yu hai*, 153, p. 12b; and 154, pp. 17a–b; *TPYL*, 782, p. 5b.

156. Koremune no Naomoto, *Ryō no shūge*, 31, pp. 773–774.

157. Nishijima Sadao, "Ken Tō shi to kokusho," pp. 46–53 and 71.

158. In contrast, "edict" *(choku)* was employed to handle routine administrative affairs. See Koremune no Naomoto, *Ryō no shūge*, 31, p. 773. See also Nakano Takayuki, "Irō shōsho to tai banshi shō no kankei ni tsuite."

159. *Shin gishiki*, in *Gunsho ruijū*, 80, pp. 4 and 46; *Chūshi shō*, in *Gunshō ruijū*, 106, p. 1173. There were two palace secretaries *(dainaiki)*, two associate palace secretaries *(chūnaiki)*, and two assistant palace secretaries *(shōnaiki)*.

160. Koremune no Naomoto, *Ryō no shūge*, 36, p. 891; Fujiwara no Mototsune, *Nihon Montoku Tennō jitsuroku*, 5, p. 50, 853/3/28; Fujiwara no Tokihira, *Engi shiki*, 12, p. 362; *Ryōshō*, in *Gunsho ruijū*, 78, p. 228.

161. *Dairi shiki*, in *Zōho kojitsu sōsho*, b, pp. 57–58. For the handling of imperial decrees, see Koremune no Naomoto, *Ryō no shūge*, 31, pp. 777–785.

162. Sugawara no Michizane, *Ruijū kokushi*, 194, p. 1285, 824/5/9. For a discussion of the use of Japanese imperial seals, see Ogino Minahiko, "Inshō shijō no Nihon to Chūgoku," in *Taigai kankei to shakai keizai*, ed. Mori Katsumi Hakase Kanreki Kinenkai, p. 74.

163. Fujiwara no Tokihira, *Engi shiki*, 12, p. 368.

164. Ibid., 12, p. 367; *Chūshi shō*, p. 1712. See also Nakano Takayuki, "Irō shōsho ni kansuru kisoteki kōsa."

165. This opening sentence reads *"Aramikami to Ame no shita shirasu Hinomoto no subera ga ohomugotorama"* in Japanese or *"Mingshen yuyu Riben tianhuang zhaozhi"* in Chinese. See Fujiwara no Fuhito et al., *Ritsuryō*, 8, p. 366.

166. Koremune no Naomoto, *Ryō no shūge*, 31, p. 774.

167. Toneri Shinnō et al., *Nihon shoki*, 29, pp. 333–334, p. 674/8/3; Sugano no Mamichi et al., *Shoku Nihongi*, 11, p. 127, 731/12/21; and 36, p. 455, 779/1/2.

168. This action was known as *semmyō* in Japanese. See Fujiwara no Fuhito et al.,

Ritsuryō, vol. 3, p. 638, additional notes, 1c. For discussions of the word *sen*, see Yokota Ken'ichi, "'Nihon shoki' to 'Jingiryō', 'Kōshikiryō,'" in *Ritsuryō-sei no shomondai*, ed. Takigawa Masajirō Hakase Beiju Kinenkai, pp. 577–587; Inaoka Kōji, "Shoku Nihongi ni okeru semmyō," in Sugano no Mamichi et al., *Shoku Nihongi* (*Shin Nihon koten bungaku taikei* edn.), ed. Aoki Kazuo et al., vol. 2, pp. 663–703; and Yoshikawa Shinji, "Nara jidai no sen." G. B. Sansom points out: "The strict interpretation of *'semmyō'* is: the proclamation by an official of the Emperor's commands." See his "Imperial Edicts in the *Shoku Nihongi*," pp. 8–9. Cranston further points out that these proclamations are "characterized by a grandiloquent oratorical quality." See his *Waka Anthology*, pp. 154–155.

169. The Japanese worked out the format for the *irō shōsho* in the early eighth century. The actual use of the *irō shōsho* began as late as the Hōki period (770–780). It became a major vehicle for diplomatic communication in the Tenchō period (824–834). See Nakano Takayuki, "Irō shōsho ni kansuru kisoteki kōsa," p. 63. See also his "Irō shōsho to tai banshi shō no kankei ni tsuite," p. 74. But he fails to note that the Japanese court used written documents much earlier in contacting China.

170. Fujiwara no Tokihira, *Engi shiki*, 12, p. 350. According to Koremune no Naomoto, *Ryō no shūge*, 31, p. 774, "barbarian country" refers to Silla. But the court had not specified which state was a "greater country" and which, a "lesser country."

171. Sugano no Mamichi et al., *Shoku Nihongi*, 3, p. 24, 706/1/12, p. 27, 706/11/3; 10, p. 113, 728/4/16; 19, p. 218, 753/6/8; 32, p. 401, 772/2/28; 34, p. 434, 777/5/23; and 36, p. 457, 780/2/15; Fujiwara no Otsugu et al., *Nihon kōki*, 21, p. 96, 811/1/22.

172. Nishijima Sadao, "Ken Tō shi to kokusho," p. 83. But a "decree to a barbarian ambassador" could begin with any of the five opening lines, which vary considerably from one another depending on the occasion. See Fujiwara no Fuhito et al., *Ritsuryō*, 3, p. 637, additional notes 1a. It is therefore uncertain that the opening line that Nishijima Sadao chose had actually been used in a state letter to Tang China.

173. Koremune no Naomoto, *Ryō no shūge*, 31, p. 774.

174. Morohashi Tetsuji, *Dai Kan Wa jiten*, revised edn., s.v. *meishin*. For examples of the term *akitsukami* being written in the Chinese characters *mingshen*, see *Man'yōshū*, 6, p. 188, no. 1050; and Koremune no Naomoto, *Ryō no shūge*, 34, p. 850.

175. For sample usage of the term *mingshen* in Chinese sources, see *Chunqiu Zuoshi zhuan*, 10, p. 1783; and 31, p. 1950; Zheng Xuan et al., *Zhou li Zhushu* (*SSJZS* edn.), 36, p. 881; *Guo yu*, "Zhou yu," a, p. 10a; Kong Yingda, *Mao shi zhengyi*, 18-2, p. 562; *SJ*, 33, p. 1528; and Peng Dingqiu, *Quan Tang shi*, 50, p. 617.

176. *THY*, 1, pp. 1–12; and 2, pp. 13–22.

177. The meaning of this expression in the Japanese context was evident in some Japanese imperial decrees that replaced the expression by "country of the eight islands" *(Ōyashima no kuni)*. See Toneri Shinnō et al., *Nihon shoki*, 1, p. 6; and Ō no Yasumaro, *Kojiki*, pp. 20–22. The term *ya* often means "many"; thus *yashima* refers to the various Japanese islands. See *Kojiki*, a, p. 90; and *Man'yōshū*, 6, p. 188, no. 1050. In such Chinese terms as *baman, badi,* and *bafan, ba* also means "many." They refer to all the barbarians. See Zheng Xuan et al., *Zhou li Zhushu*, 33, p. 861; *Er ya*, 7, p. 2616; and Xiao Tong, *Wen xuan*, 6, p. 26a.

178. For sample usage of the term *yuyu* in Japanese sources, see *Man'yōshū*, 1, p. 8, nos. 1 and 2. Sometimes, the term *ame no shita shirasu* is also written in Chinese characters as *linxuan*. See *Hitachi no kuni fudoki* (*Nihon koten bungaku taike* edn.), p. 34. G. B. Sansom translates *ame no shita* as "realm under heaven." But he correctly points out, "It should not be supposed that he thus claims to rule all the known world." See his "Imperial Edicts in the *Shoku Nihongi*," p. 11.

179. Joseph R. Levenson, "T'ien-hsia and Kuo and the Trans-valuation of Values."

180. For records using the term *yuyu*, see *JS*, 3, p. 81; Wang Liqi, *Wenxin diaolong jiaozheng*, vol. 4, p. 134; Xiao Tong, *Wen xuan*, 22, p.30a; Shamen Guanding, *Guoqing bailu*, 2, p. 802; Liu Su, *Da Tang xinyu*, p. 148; Peng Dingqiu, *Quan Tang shi*, 483, p. 5493; and Saichō, *Kenkairon engi*, in Itō Shō, *Rinkō chōsho*, 2, p. 102.

181. Nishijima Sadao suggests that *zhu ming le mei yu de* was used to modify "Japan," and thus the whole title means "Japan, which is in the universe ruled by the shining God." He further suggests that the sentence in Emperor Xuanzong's letter, which reads, "Japan, the land of ritual and Confucian teachings, is protected by God," indicates that *mingshen yuyu* indeed appeared in the Japanese state letter presented to him earlier. See his "Ken Tō shi to kokusho," p. 82.

182. Fujiwara no Tokihira, *Engi shiki*, 12, p. 350.

183. Cai Yong, *Du duan*, a, p. 1b. See also Nishijima Sadao, *Chūgoku kodai kokka to Higashi Ajia shakai*, p. 51.

184. *JTS*, 55, pp. 2249–2250; *XTS*, 86, p. 3709; *THY*, 94, p. 1698; *ZZTJ*, 186, p. 5820; and 187, p. 5840.

185. The other two were the "Earthly Emperor" (Dihuang) and the "Grand Emperor" (Taihuang). See *SJ*, 6, p. 236; and Sima Zhen, *Bu shi ji*, pp. 3a–b. Both Liang Wudi (r. 502–548) and Sui Wendi (r. 581–604) worshiped the "Heavenly Emperor." See Wei Zheng et al., *Sui shu*, 6, p. 111; and 69, pp. 1606–1607. Zhu Ci, a rebellious Tang general, used "Heavenly Emperor" as the title of his reign in 784. See *JTS*, 200b, p. 5389; and *XTS*, 225b, p. 6446. For a discussion of this term, see Fukunaga Mitsuji, "Kōten Jōtei to Tennō Taitei to Genshi Tenson."

186. Yuan Kang, *Yue jue shu*, 10, p. 89a. Yuan Kang used the title "Tianhuang" to refer to Gou Jian, the ruler of the Yue, whom Yuan thought should be the Son of Heaven.

187. *JTS*, 5, p. 99; and 6, p. 115; *XTS*, 3, p. 71; and 9, p. 81; and *THY*, 1, p. 3. See also Liang Zhangju, *Chengwei lu*, in *Ming Qing suyu cishu jicheng*, 9, p. 5a. But it mistakenly attaches this event to 675.

188. *JTS*, 5, p. 112; *XTS*, 3, p. 79; *THY*, 1, p. 3. For the use of the term, see also *Weicheng dianxun*, a Tang work commonly believed to have been completed during Wu Zetian's reign. Part of it has been preserved in the form of quotations in Fujiwara no Takanori, *Meibunshō* (*Zoku gunsho ruijū* edn.), 1, pp. 113–114.

189. Tonami Mamoru, *Tōdai seiji shakaishi kenkyū*, pp. 420 and 442–443. He quotes two Buddhist scriptures and thirteen inscriptions that contain the term *tianhuang* in the Stein collection. For another five inscriptions containing this term, see Nagahiro Toshio and Mizuno Seiichi, *Kanan Rakuyō Ryūmon sekkutsu no kenkyū*, pp. 250, 259, 264, 270, and 350.

190. Tōno Haruyuki, "Tennōgō no seiritsu nendai ni tsuite," in his *Shōsōin monjo to mokkan no kenkyū*, p. 401.

191. Sugano no Mamichi et al., *Shoku Nihongi*, 3, p. 21, 704/7/1.

192. The other six titles are Tenshi (Chinese: Tianzi) to be used in sacrificial ceremonies, Kōtei (Chinese: Huangdi) in proclamations to the Japanese as well as the "barbarians," Heika (Chinese: Bixia) in memorials from Japanese courtiers to their emperor, Daijō Tennō (Chinese: Taishang Tianhuang) for an abdicated emperor, Jōyo (Chinese: Chengyu) to refer to an emperor in action, and Kyoga (Chinese: Chejia) to refer to an emperor traveling by carriage. See Koremune no Naomoto, *Ryō no shūge*, 28, pp. 701–702. See also Cai Yong, *Du duan*, a, p. 2b; and *HS*, 1b, p. 58, for the relevant Chinese records with regard to the explanations of these terms.

193. The other three groups of Chinese characters are *huang yu sun ming, xu mai mi ma nai mei ji deng*, and *xu mai liang mei ji zhi*. See Koremune no Naomoto, *Ryō no shūge*, 28, p. 701; and 40, p. 971.

194. Nishijima Sadao, "Ken Tō shi to kokusho," p. 85. The title "Tennō" (or Sumeramikoto), however, does not, as Verschuer has suggested, mean that the Japanese ruler was a sovereign "who reigns over the universe." See her translation of this title in *Relations officielles*, p. 8. Discussion of the term *ame no shita shirasu* in this chapter reveals that the title in question should mean "a sovereign who rules Japan."

195. Zhang Jiuling, *Tang chengxiang qujiang Zhang xiansheng wenji*, 12, p. 9b.

196. Nishijima Sadao, "Ken Tō shi to kokusho," p. 78.

197. Ibid., p. 83.

198. Verschuer, however, misunderstands the primary source. She suggests that the Tang court interpreted *zhu ming le mei yu de* as the title for "a local sov-

ereign like the Qaghan of the Turks and the Uighurs, and the kings of the numerous other tributary states." See her *Relations officielles,* p. 8. For a discussion of the use of *zhu ming le mei yu de,* see also Furuse Natsuko, *Ken Tō shi no mita Chūgoku,* pp. 119–122.

199. *Nihon shoki,* 22, p. 151, 608/9/11.

200. Ibid.

201. Ibid.

202. Nishijima Sadao was the first to reconstruct the second half of this opening sentence, *"jingbai Da Tang huangdi."* See his "Ken Tō shi to kokusho," p. 83.

203. Gu Yewang, *Yu pian,* b, p. 67b: *"bai* is to inform *(gao).*" A quotation from the "Zishu" preserved in Xu Shizeng, *Wenti mingbian xushuo,* p. 115, further explains that *"gao* is to inform a superior." For examples of an inferior using *bai* to inform his superior, see *HHS,* 62, p. 2064. This term was used in the same manner as late as the Qing dynasty. See Liang Zhangju, *Langji xutan,* 1, p. 247.

204. For records using *jingbai,* see Shamen Guanding, *Guoqing bailu,* 2, p. 805; and 3, pp. 808 and 809, for correspondence between the monks of the Guoqing Temple at Mt. Tiantai, Sui royal family members who patronized the temple, and the local prefectural authorities, and for a letter by the monk Kūkai. See also Keiō, *Kōbō daishi shō,* in *Tendai kahyō* (*Dai Nihon bukkyō zensho* edn.), 1, p. 195; and Nishijima Sadao, "Ken Zui shi to kokusho mondai," pp. 43–44. The eleventh-century Japanese still used *jingbai.* See Miyoshi no Tameyasu, *Chōya gunsai* (*Kokushi taikei* edn.), 2, pp. 33–34.

205. See the discussion of the ending of Japanese state letters by Nakano Takayuki, in "Irō shōsho no ketsugo no hensen ni tsuite." For samples of the usage of these components in Japanese state letters, see my Appendix 3.

206. Toneri Shinnō et al., *Nihon shoki,* 22, p. 151, 608/9/11. The English translation is from Aston, *Nihongi,* vol. 2, p. 139.

207. Sugano no Mamichi et al., *Shoku Nihongi,* 3, p. 27, 706/11/3. The English translation is from J. B. Snellen, trans., "Shoku Nihongi," pp. 233–234. Japanese state letters to Parhae used the same format. See *Shoku Nihongi,* 34, pp. 434–435, 777/5/19.

208. Tōno Haruyuki, "Tennōgō no seiritsu nendai ni tsuite," p. 415. The exact time that the title "Tianhuang" came into use in Japan remains an open question. For other opinions on this issue, see Miyazaki Ichisada, "Tennō naru shōgo no yurai ni tsuite"; and Honiden Kikushi, "Kodai Nihon no kunshugō to Chūgoku no kunshugō."

209. For letters written by Wang Xizhi, see Yan Kejun, *Quan Jin wen,* pp. 1580–1617. Most of their letters are preserved in the form of their own calligraphy. For a list of works containing these letters, see Xu Xianyao, *Er Wang chidu yu Riben shuji suozai guoshu zhi yanjiu,* pp. 4–9.

210. Yan Kejun, *Quan Jin wen,* pp. 1587, 1589, and 1592.

211. Xu Xianyao, *Er Wang chidu yu Riben shuji suozai guoshu zhi yanjiu*, pp. 16–22.

212. For further discussion of *shuyi*, see Yamada Hideō, "Shogi ni tsuite," in *Taigai kankei to shakai keizai*, ed. Mori Katsumi Hakase Kanreki Kinenkai, pp. 29–44; Patricia Ebrey, "Tang Guides to Verbal Etiquette"; and Zhou Yiliang and Zhao Heping. *Tang Wudai shuyi yanjiu*, pp. 53–93.

213. *JTS*, 199a, p. 5341; Xu Xianyao, *Er Wang chidu yu Riben shuji suozai guoshu zhi yanjiu*, p. 124. Entries in the *Nihonkoku genzaisho mokuroku*, a Japanese bibliographic work compiled in 891, confirm the spread of Chinese works on the *shuyi* to Japan, among them the works by the Two Wangs.

214. Sakamoto Tarō, *Nihon no shūshi to shigaku*, p. 15.

215. Wei Zheng et al., *Sui shu*, 81, p. 1828. The English translation is from Goodrich and Tsunoda, *Japan in the Chinese Dynastic Histories*, pp. 42–43.

216. For a detailed study on how the Japanese consulted Chinese works while compiling the *Nihon shoki*, see Kojima Noriyuki, *Jōdai Nihon bungaku to Chūgoku bungaku (jō)*, pp. 20–50. See also G. W. Robinson, "Early Japanese Chronicles: The Six National Histories," in *Historians of China and Japan*, ed. W. G. Beasley and E. G. Pulleyblank, pp. 213–228.

217. Kin Bunkyo, "Kanji bunkaken no kundoku genshō," in *Wa Kan hikaku bungaku kenkyū no sho mondai*, ed. Wa Kan Hikaku Bungaku Kai, p. 175.

218. Komatsu Shigemi, *Kana*, pp. 22–23.

219. Tsukishima Hiroshi, *Heian jidaigo shinron*, p. 25.

220. Kobayashi Yoshinori, "Nihon shoki kokun to kanseki no ko kundoku," in *Kokugogaku ronshū*, ed. Saeki Umetomo Hakase Koki Kien Kangyōkai, p. 67.

221. Nakata Norio, "Nihon no kanji," in *Nihongo no sekai (4)*, ed. Ono Susumu, vol. 4, pp. 94–95 and 141.

222. *TD*, 185, p. 986.

223. Ō no Yasumaro, *Kojiki*, a, p. 49; B. H. Chamberlain, trans., *The Kojiki: Records of Ancient Matters*, vol. 1, p. 5. *Man'yōgana* were Japanese syllables created by employing the sounds and forms but not the meanings of some Chinese characters.

224. Tsuda Sōkichi, "Shoki no kakikata oyobi yomikata," in *Tsuda Sōkichi zenshū*, ed. Tsuda Sōkichi Zenshū Henshūshitsu, vol. 2, pp. 291–292, 305.

225. Satō Kiyoji, *Nihon no kango*, pp. 27–28. Preserved at the Ō Tokyū Kinen Bunko, this document is titled *Kegon kanteiki*. It bears detailed reading marks *(kunten)* that the Japanese used when reading Chinese or Buddhist writings.

226. Kobayashi Yoshinori, "Nihon shoki kokun to kanseki no ko kundoku," p. 65. This edition was compiled in 1004–1012. It contains only volume 22 and volume 24 of the *Nihon shoki*. The old markings *(koten)* and the Japanese syllables *(kana)* are colored red and appear on the right side of the text. In volume 24, the *koten* are in black. They were added to the text in about 1451.

227. Hayashi Tsutomu, "Iwazakihon Nihon shoki kunten no keigo hyōgen," in *Ronshū jōdai bungaku*, ed. Man'yō Shichiyōkai, vol. 7, p. 245. Hayashi points

out that the *kunten* in the 1474 edition of the *Nihon shoki* are very similar to those in the 987 edition, showing a considerable degree of consistency in the pronunciations of certain *kanji* terms during different periods.

228. The Tang monk Xuanzang, for example, used this term in his work *Da Tang Xiyu ji*. Other Tang works whose titles used the term include the *Da Tang kaiyuan zhanjing* and the *Da Tang liudian*. For Tang scholars using "Da Tang" in their works, see Zhang Yue, *Zhang Yuezhi wenji* (*SBCK* edn.), 1, p. 1a; and 12, p. 1a; and Yuan Jie, *Yuan Cishan wenji* (*SBCK* edn.), 6, p. 1b.

229. Toneri Shinnō et al., *Nihon shoki*, 22, p. 157, 614/6/13, p. 161, 623/7; 23, p. 181, 631/8; 25, p. 255, 654/2; 26, p. 262, 655/5/1, p. 264, 656; 29, p. 375, 685/12/6; and 30, p. 401, 689/6/19, p. 421, 694/1/23; *Man'yōshū*, 8, p. 333, no. 1594; and Urabe Kanekata, *Shaku Nihongi*, 19, p. 255.

230. Kishi Toshio, "Kodai Nihonjin no Chūgokukan," in *Kodaigaku sōron*, ed. Heian Hakubutsukan Kenkyūbu, p. 317.

231. Omodaka Hisataka et al., *Jidaibetsu kokugo daijiten (jōdaihen)*, s.v. *morokoshi*. *Morokoshi* can also be rendered in the Chinese characters *zhuyue*. See Keikai, *Nihon ryōiki* (*Nihon koten bungaku taikei* edn.), vol. a, p. 64. Therefore, another argument is that *morokoshi* refers to the area where the various "Yue tribes" in China used to live. This area also extended roughly from modern Zhejiang province down to northern Vietnam.

232. Toneri Shinnō et al., *Nihon shoki*, 22, p. 151, 608/9/11; Urabe Kanekata, *Shaku Nihongi*, 19, p. 255; Matsushita Kenrin, *Ishō Nihonden* (*Shiseki shūran* edn.), a1, p. 28.

233. Urabe Kanekata, *Shaku Nihongi*, 20, p. 264.

234. Toneri Shinnō et al., *Nihon shoki*, 25, p. 256, 654/7/24; and 26, p. 264, 656; Urabe Kanekata, *Shaku Nihongi*, 20, p. 266.

235. Urabe Kanekata, *Shaku Nihongi*, 19, p. 257.

236. *Man'yoshū*, 19, p. 365, no. 4240, p. 377, no. 4262; *Kaifūsō* (*Nihon koten bunka taikei* edn.), pp. 12 and 17. Strictly speaking, Kara refers only to southern Korea. See Toneri Shinnō et al., *Nihon shoki*, 15, p. 306, 493/9/4. Later Karakuni came to refer to China as well.

237. Kōbō Daishi Zenshū Henshū Iinkai, *Kōbō daishi zenshū*, vol. 15, p. 423.

238. Omodaka Hisataka et al., *Jidaibetsu kokugo daijiten*, s.v. "Karakuni."

239. Toneri Shinnō et al., *Nihon shoki*, 22, p. 149, 608/6/15; Urabe Kanekata, *Shaku Nihongi*, 19, p. 255. *Daguo* sometimes appears as *shangguo* (superior country) in Chinese records. See *ZZTJ*, 182, p. 5669. A record in the *JTS*, 196a, p. 5221, further indicates that *daguo* and *shangguo* are interchangeable.

240. *JTS*, 196a, p. 5221; 196b, pp. 5245 and 5250; 198, p. 5296; and 199b, p. 5361. In 821, the Tang court reluctantly called the Tibetan empire Dafan when the two foes made peace with each other. Unwilling to give up China's superiority, the Tang ambassador to Tibet called China Ju Tang. In Chinese, the term *ju* carried a sense of superiority over *da*. See *JTS*, 196b, p. 5265.

241. *JTS*, 196a, p. 5231.

242. Those countries were also known as "peer states" *(diguo)*. Tibet, Koguryŏ, and the Xueyantuo were examples. See *JTS*, 196a, p. 5225; 196b, pp. 5247 and 5267; 197, p. 5274; 198, p. 5295; and 199b, p. 5361; and *CFYG*, 997, p. 12b. For a discussion of the Chinese world order, see Kaneko Shūichi, "Tōdai no kokusai bunsho keishiki ni tsuite," p. 44.

243. Nakamura Jihei studied 118 uses of the term *silin* in the *Quan Tang shi*. The results indicate that the term refers to either neighboring countries, neighbors, or near places. See his "Tōdai no sonraku to rimpo," in *Chūgoku ritsuryōsei no tenkai to sono kokka shakai to no kankei*, ed. Tōshi Kenkyūkai, p. 118.

244. Ichikawa Seinei, *Quan Tang shi yi*, b, p. 1091. In 778 Emperor Taizong dispatched Zhao Baoying to "establish neighborly friendship" with Japan. But the Tang emperor certainly did not regard his Japanese counterpart as a peer. See Sugano no Mamichi et al., *Shoku Nihongi*, 35, p. 445, 778/11/13.

245. Peng Dingqiu, *Quan Tang shi*, 205, p. 2142.

246. Kōbō Daishi Zenshū Henshū Iinkai, *Kōbō daishi zenshū*, vol. 15, pp. 357–358.

247. Wang Wei, *Wang youcheng ji*, 12, p. 3b.

248. Ishimoda Shō, "Tennō to shoban," in his *Nihon kodai kokka ron (1)*, p. 352.

249. Ono no Minemori, *Ryōunshū* (*Nihon koden zenshū* edn.), p. 13.

250. Ennin, *Nittō guhō junrei kōki*, 2, p. 48.

251. Toneri Shinnō et al., *Nihon shoki*, 26, p. 271, 659/7/3.

252. In Japanese sources *i* and *jō* are also geographic terms. For example, the Japanese reading f or both *i* and *jō* is *hina*, meaning "places far away from the capital." See Toneri Shinnō et al., *Nihon shoki*, 14, p. 389, 479/8/1; and 17, p. 25, 527/6/1.

253. Koremune no Naomoto, *Ryō no shūge*, 13, pp. 409 and 410; 31, p. 774; and Ishimoda Shō, "Tennō to shoban," pp. 330–332.

254. Koremune no Naomoto, *Ryō no shūge*, 4, p. 91. By contrast, other foreigners in Japan were regarded as *iteki* (tribesmen), the same as such local tribesmen as the Hayato people. See ibid., 13, p. 403.

255. *Kaifūsō*, pp. 10, 18, and 33; Yoshimine no Yasuyo, Shigeno no Sadanushi, *Keikokushū*, 11, p. 146; Ono no Minemori, *Ryōunshū*, p. 69; Fujiwara no Fuyutsugu et al., comps., *Bunka shūreishū*, a, pp. 82–83.

256. Toneri Shinnō et al., *Nihon shoki*, 9, p. 248, 201/10/3, p. 261, 249/3; 15, p. 406, 485/1/1; 17, p. 18, 512/12, p. 27, 529/3, p. 28, 529/4/7; and 19, p. 51, 540/8, p. 77, 552/10; Urabe Kanekata, *Shaku Nihongi*, 17, p. 239; and 18, p. 247; Hirano Kunio, "Kiki ritsuryō ni okeru 'kika' 'gaiban' no gainen to sono yōrei," p. 125. The Japanese court, for example, called its ambassadors dispatched to Tang, Parhae, and Silla *nyūban shi* and the rulers of these countries *bankyaku*. See Fujiwara no Tokihira, *Engi shiki*, 30, pp. 737–738. See also Omodaka Hisataka et al., *Jidaibetsu kokugo daijiden*, s.v. *tonari*.

257. Borgen, "The Japanese Mission to China," p. 16. But Kojima Noriyuki sug-

gests that the term *ban* should read *ebisu* and that the term *tōban* is a self-degrading expression for Japan, meaning "the eastern tribe." See his *Kokufū ankoku jidai no bungaku*, p. 1734.

258. *Shōtoku Taishi denreki* (*Zoku gunsho ruijū* edn.), b, p. 25; *Man'yōshū*, 5, p. 91, no. 870; *Nihon kiryaku (zenhen)*, 13, pp. 269, 759/7/16, p. 272, 798/6/20; Fujiwara no Fuhito et al., *Ritsu*, 1, p. 5; *Meireiritsu uragaki*, in *Ritsu*, p. 88; Sugano no Mamichi et al., *Shoku Nihongi*, 3, p. 21, 704/7/1; Kōbō Daishi Zenshū Henshū Iinkai, *Kōbō daishi zenshū*, vol. 15, p. 423.

259. Urabe Kanekata, *Shaku Nihongi*, 20, p. 268. Aston translated *shōban* as "various frontier states." See his *Nihongi*, vol. 2, p. 262.

260. Cai Yong, *Du duan*, 2, p. 1b.

261. *THY*, 26, p. 505; *DTKYL*, 3, p. 11a; *TLD*, 4, p. 8a; Cai Yong, *Du duan*, a, p. 1b.

262. Koremune no Naomoto, *Ryō no shūgei*, 28, p. 701.

263. Toneri Shinnō et al., *Nihon shoki*, 17, p. 13, 507/2/4; 18, p. 39, 531/7/1; 25, p. 256, 654/7; and 26, p. 271, 659/7/3, p. 274, 660/7/16; Sugano no Mamichi, *Shoku Nihongi*, 13, p. 156, 739/11/3; 16, p. 188, 746/6/18; 19, p. 219, 754/1/17; 21, p. 254, 758/8/9, pp. 257–258, 758/12/10; 25, p. 302, 764/7/9; 33, p. 416, 774/4/11; and 35, pp. 443–444, 778/10/23. Sometimes the title "Tenshi" was reserved for the Tang emperor and the epithet "Tennō" for the Japanese throne. See Toneri Shinnō, *Nihon shoki*, 23, p. 181, 632/10/4; and 25, p. 256, 654/7; Urabe Kanekata, *Shaku Nihongi*, 20, p. 268; and Matsushita Kenrin, *Ishō Nihonden*, 1a, p. 37.

264. Toneri Shinnō et al., *Nihon shoki*, 22, p. 151, 608/9/11; Matsushita Kenrin, *Ishō Nihonden*, 1a, p. 27; Urabe Kanekata, *Shaku Nihongi*, 19, p. 259.

265. Omodaka Hisataka et al., *Jidaibetsu kokugo daijiten*, s.v. *kimi*.

266. In the Japanese state letter to Sui in 600, the Japanese ruler emerged as *abei jimi*, which is the Chinese transliteration for *ōkimi*. For *ōkimi*, see also Toneri Shinnō et al., *Nihon shoki*, 17, p. 13, 507/2/4. Some records address the Japanese emperor as *kimi*. See ibid., 14, p. 367, 461/2, p. 372, 463; and 22, p. 152, 609/4/4. The common practice, however, was to use the title *ōkimi*. Rulers of Korean countries were not even qualified as *kimi*. The Japanese records address them by their native title *kokishi*. See ibid., 6, p. 176, 28 B.C./10; and 14, p. 377, 465/5, p. 387, 476; and Urabe Kanekata, *Shaku Nihongi*, 18, p. 247.

267. Sugano no Mamichi, *Shoku Nihongi*, 21, p. 258, 758/12/10. In the preface to his two poems, Dōji, a Japanese monk who went to China in 701, also called the Chinese emperor "Tōō." By contrast, he referred to the Japanese throne as *tei* (the emperor). See *Kaifūsō*, p. 164.

268. *Chunqiu Zuoshi zhuan*, 19b, p. 1850; 29, p. 1930; and 30, p. 1938. Another explanation is that the Chinese princes came to pay tribute in spring, hence the term *chao*. See Zheng Xuan et al., *Zhou li zhushu* (*SSJZS* edn.), 18, p. 759. *Chao* should be conducted on a regular basis. The princes of the Chinese

states were supposed to pay a visit in person to the court of the Son of Heaven every three or five years. See *Chunqiu Zuoshi zhuan*, 19b, p. 1855.

269. Kong Yingda, *Li ji zhengyi*, 5, p. 1266; *Chunqiu Zuoshi zhuan*, 18, p. 1837; and 40, p. 2015.

270. *Chunqiu Zuoshi zhuan*, 29, p. 1928; and 18, p. 1837, states: "On the accession of Princes of States, their ministers should go everywhere on such friendly missions, maintaining and cultivating old friendships, and forming external alliances of support." The English translation is from Legge, *The Chinese Classics*, vol. 5, p. 230. This was also the case with Li Yuan, founder of the Tang. When he rebelled against the Sui court, he sent one of his generals to "visit" *(pin)* and to ask for support from the Eastern Turkic leader Shibi Qaghan. See *JTS*, 194a, p. 5153.

271. Koremune no Naomoto, *Ryō no shūge*, 1, pp. 39–40.

272. Toneri Shinnō et al., *Nihon shoki*, 22, p. 151, 608/9/11. The Chinese correlative of *toburafu* is *pin*. For the use of *pin* in Japanese sources, see also ibid., 17, p. 27, 529/3; and Oumi no Mifune, *Tō Daiwajō tosei den*, pp. 24 and 65.

273. Toneri Shinnō et al., *Nihon shoki*, 17, p. 17, 508/12; 19, p. 54, 541/4; and 22, p. 161, 632/7.

274. Ibid., 22, p. 150, 608/8/12. The English translation is from Aston, *Nihongi*, vol. 2, p. 137.

275. *Yoriite* is perhaps a compound word made by the gerund form of *yoru* and *iru*.

276. Urabe Kanekata, *Shaku Nihongi*, 19, p. 255. This quotation is from the *Nihon shoki shiki*, a work containing the notes taken by Japanese courtiers who attended lectures on the *Nihon shoki*.

277. This Japanese verb is *ori*. See Ichiko Teiji, *Shin kogo jiten*, s.v. *mashimasu*.

CHAPTER 8: INFORMATION GATHERING

1.   Toneri Shinnō et al., *Nihon shoki*, 26, pp. 274–275, 660/9/5, 660/10; and 27, p. 286, 663/8/17, 663/8/27. For English translations of these accounts, see Aston, *Nihongi*, vol. 2, pp. 279–280. See also Sugano no Mamichi et al., *Shoku Nihongi*, 27, p. 333, 766/6/28. For studies of this battle, see Suzuki Osamu, *Hakusonkō*. See also Mori Kimiyuki, *Kodai Nihon no taigai ninshiki to tsūkō*, pp. 273–287. The exact location of the battle has been a scholarly issue. Some suggest the mouth of the Hakusonkō River (present-day Kūm River); others, the banks of the Hakusonkō River near the Paekche capital Sabi. See Wang Xiaofu, "Tangchao yu Xinluo guanxi shi lun," p. 168, note no. 24. Based on extensive field trips to southern Korea, documentary and philological studies, Jeon Young-rae arrives at a more convincing conclusion: the battle in question was fought at the present-day Dongjing River. See his *Kudara metsubō to kodai Nihon*, pp. 90–94.

2. This expression first appeared in *NS*, 10, p. 307.

3. Sugano no Mamichi et al., *Shoku Nihongi*, 3, p. 21, 704/7/1.

4. Fujiwara no Fuhito et al., *Ritsu*, 3, pp. 44 and 45. See also Zhangsun Wuji, *Gu Tanglü shuyi*, pp. 208 and 209; Johnson, *T'ang Code*, vol. 2, pp. 93–94.

5. For reports by Japanese and foreign ambassadors that also contained "news on Tang," see Sugano no Mamichi et al., *Shoku Nihongi*, 21, p. 257, 758/12/10; 30, p. 374, 770/3/4; and 35, p. 444, 778/10/23. Dong Zhiqiao, citing Buddhist works, suggests that *Tang xiaoxi* means "the exact news." See his *Ru Tang qiufa xunli xingji cihui yanjiu*, p. 295. His conclusion is questionable, since records in other Japanese works indicate that "news on Tang" was a special feature in an ambassador's report to the Japanese court.

6. Sugano no Mamichi et al., *Shoku Nihongi*, 21, pp. 257–258, 758/12/10. For discussions of Japan's relations with Parhae, see Verschuer, *Relations officielles*, pp. 131–152.

7. Sugano no Mamichi et al., *Shoku Nihongi*, 24, p. 292, 763/1/17.

8. Ibid., 25, p. 302, 764/7/19.

9. Ibid., 30, p. 374, 770/3/4.

10. This is an error for "Chu."

11. Sugano no Mamichi et al., *Shoku Nihongi*, 35, p. 444, 778/10/23.

12. Fujiwara no Otsugu et al., *Nihon kōki*, 12, p. 43, 805/6/8.

13. For an account of this incident, see *JTS*, 124, pp. 3537–3538; and *XTS*, 213, p. 5991.

14. Fujiwara no Otsugu et al., *Nihon kōki*, 12, p. 43, 805/6/8. For Wu Shaocheng, see *JTS*, 145, pp. 3945–3946; and *XTS*, 214, pp. 6002–6004.

15. Fujiwara no Otsugu et al., *Nihon kōki*, 12, p. 43, 805/6/8.

16. Ennin, *Nittō guhō junrei kōki*, 1, p. 8. For a discussion of information on Tang brought back to Japan by Enchin, another Japanese monk, see Zhou Yiliang, "Ru Tang seng Yuanzhen yu Tangchao shi liao," in his *Zhong Ri wenhua guanxi lun*, pp. 96–103.

17. Ibid.

18. Ibid., 2, p. 46.

19. Ibid., 2, p. 46; and 4, p. 97.

20. Ibid., 1, p. 9. For Chinese records on this event, see *JTS*, 17b, p. 575; and *ZZTJ*, 246, p. 7935.

21. Ennin, *Nittō guhō junrei kōki*, 1, p. 29; and 2, pp. 48 and 52.

22. Ibid., 3, p. 88: "The Uighur army has entered China, invading the frontiers, and at present is at Qinfu. The nation has drawn troops from six regional commanderies and is sending them to the Uighur frontier. There are several hundred Uighurs in the capital, and they have all been executed in accordance with an imperial command. The same is also being done in the various prefectures and commanderies." The English translation is from Reischauer, *Ennin's Diary*, p. 314.

23. Ennin, *Nittō guhō junrei kōki*, 1, p. 23; and 2, pp. 29, 30, and 36.

24. Ibid., 1, pp. 8–9.

25. For a study of information gathering by Japanese ambassadors dispatched to Tang China, see Yamaguchi Shinji, *Nara Heian ki no Nippon to Ajia*, pp. 36–66.

26. For a recent work on the cultural exchange between Tang China and Japan, see Ikeda On, *Higashi Ajia no bunka kōryūshi*, pp. 45–321.

27. *JTS*, 199a, p. 5241; *XTS*, 220, p. 6209.

28. Song Minqiu, *Tang dazhaoling ji*, 128, p. 2726.

29. Situo, *Enryaku sōroku*, p. 21; and see Ichikawa Seinei, *Quan Tang shi yi*, a, p. 10173.

30. An accomplished musician, Fujiwara Sadatoshi was attached to the Japanese delegation to China in 835 as an administrative officer. While in Changan, he studied for three months under Mr. Liu, a specialist in *pipa*, a lutelike stringed instrument with a fretted fingerboard. Impressed by the talent of his Japanese disciple, Mr. Liu not only presented him with volumes of music notation, but also gave his daughter in marriage to Sadatoshi. Sadatoshi stayed in China for a year before returning home. He eventually became head of the Bureau of Music and Dancing in 847. See Fujiwara no Yoshifusa et al., *Shoku Nihon kōki*, 4, p. 42, 835/10/19; and 17, p. 196, 843/2/11; and Fujiwara no Tokihira et al., *Nihon Sandai jitsuroku*, 14, pp. 221–222, 867/10/4.

31. For the composition of a Japanese delegation, see Fujiwara no Tokihira, *Engi shiki*, 30, pp. 737–738.

32. Japanese monks who had remained in China for more than nine years to pursue their study needed to re-register themselves with the Office of Daoist Worship (Chongxuan Shu). See *XTS*, 48, p. 1252.

33. Peng Dingqiu, *Quan Tang shi*, 127, pp. 1288–1289; 129, p. 1320; 138, p. 1405; and 205, p. 2142.

34. *JTS*, 199a, p. 5341; Peng Dingqiu, *Quan Tang shi*, 772, p. 8375.

35. *Kokin wakashū mokuroku* (*Gunsho ruijū* edn.), 285, pp. 503–504.

36. Chen Shangjun, ed., *Quan Tang shi bubian*, p. 558.

37. Sugano no Mamichi et al., *Shoku Nihongi*, 35, p. 449.

38. Li Bai, *Li Taibai shi*, 25, pp. 29a–b.

39. *JTS*, 199a, p. 5341; Peng Dingqiu, *Quan Tang shi*, 772, p. 8375; and Lê Tắc, *Annan zhilüe*, p. 216. For a brief account of Nakamaro's tenure at Annan, see Keith W. Taylor, *The Birth of Vietnam*, p. 198.

40. Fujiwara no Yoshifusa et al., *Shoku Nihon kōki*, 5, p. 52.

41. Ibid. For a detailed study of Nakamaro, see Sugimoto Naojirō, *Abe no Nakamaro den kenkyū*. See also Pierre Daudin, "Un Japonais à la Cour des T'ang."

42. The exact time of Kūkai's ordination is uncertain. A record in Fujiwara no Yoshifusa et al., *Shoku Nihon kōki*, 4, p. 38, 835/3/25, reports that he was thirty-one years old when he became a monk.

43. For a discussion of the life of Kūkai, see Yoshito S. Hakeda, *Kūkai: Major Works*, pp. 13–33; Yamasaki Taikō, *Shingon: Japanese Esoteric Buddhism*, pp. 26–33; and Martin Collcutt et al., *Cultural Atlas of Japan*, pp. 87–90. See also Abé Ryūichi, *The Weaving of Mantra*, pp. 71–75, 81, and 83.

44. For problems relating to the historical records on Kūkai, see Hakeda, *Kūkai*, p. 15, note 8; and p. 16, note 12.

45. The birthday of Kūkai is one such example. The commonly used birthday, the fifteenth day of the sixth month of 774, is based on the assumption that Kūkai was the reincarnation of Bukong, the patriarch of Esoteric Buddhism. Since Bukong died on the date in question, that date became Kūkai's birthday. For discussions of this issue and problems related to the primary sources on Kūkai, see Joseph M. Kitagawa, *On Understanding Japanese Religion*, pp. 182–185.

46. Wang Liqi, *Wenjing mifu lun jiaozhu*, p. 15.

47. Shiba Ryōtarō, however, suggests that Kūkai's family were of Ainu origin and had no relation with the Saeki family in the capital. The family could therefore not have been involved in the murder of Tanetsugu. See his *Kūkai no fūkei*, vol. 2, pp. 3–6.

48. Kūkai, *Sangō shiiki*, p. 85; Fujiwara no Yoshifusa et al., *Shoku Nihon kōki*, 4, p. 38, 835/3/25. This sutra is known as *Xukongzang pusa nengman zhuyuan zuishengxin tuoluomi qiuwen chifa*. It was first translated into Chinese in 717 by Shanwuwei, a visiting Indian monk in China, and was brought to Japan in 718 by Dōji (?–744). Japanese scholars hold diverse opinions on who introduced Esoteric Buddhism to Kūkai. Abé regards this issue as one of secondary importance. He also suggests that the person in question did not have to be a distinguished monk. See his *The Weaving of Mantra*, p. 75.

49. Kūkai, *Sangō shiiki*, p. 85. The English translation is by Yoshito S. Hakeda. See his *Kūkai: Major Works*, pp. 19–20.

50. For a discussion of this work, see Keene, *Seeds in the Heart*, pp. 183–185.

51. For discussions of Kūkai's journey to China, see Abé, *The Weaving of Mantra*, pp. 113–127.

52. For a full English translation of this letter, see Appendix 2.

53. Kūkai, *Seireishū*, p. 271.

54. Ibid., pp. 267–271.

55. Ibid., pp. 229 and 279; "Shang xin qinglaijing deng mulubiao," in Wang Liqi, *Wenjing mifu lun jiaozhu*, p. 627.

56. Kūkai, *Seireishū*, pp. 151–152. The two sutras are the *Huayan jing* and the *Dacheng liqu liuboluomi duojing*.

57. Ibid., pp. 233 and 239.

58. Chen Shangjun, *Quan Tang shi bubian*, vol. 22, p. 980.

59. Tachibana had also studied in China and was well versed in Chinese literature and calligraphy. The Chinese called him a "cultivated talent" *(xiucai)*.

Fujiwara no Mototsune et al., *Nihon Montoku tennō jitsu roku*, 1, p. 12, 850/5/15.

60. Fujiwara no Yoshifusa et al., *Shoku Nihon kōki*, 4, p. 38, 835/3/25.

61. *Honchō shinsen den* (*Nihon shisō taikei* edn.), p. 582. *Konjaku monogatari shū* (*Nihon koten bungaku taikei* edn.), p. 76; Terajima Ryōan, *Wa-Kan sansai zue*, pp. 76 and 1067. The term "five brushes" is probably a metaphor for the five major Chinese scripts: the regular script, the official script, the semi-cursive script, the cursive script, and the seal script.

62. Kūkai, *Seireishū*, pp. 231 and 235.

63. The Three Vehicles are considered the means to bring people to salvation. Mahayana and Hinayana Buddhism have different interpretations of this terminology.

64. Chen Shangjun, *Quan Tang shi bubian*, vol. 22, pp. 977–978.

65. For the poem, see Kōbō Daishi Zenshū Henshū Iinkai, *Kōbō daishi Kūkai zenshū*, vol. 7, p. 129.

66. Ichikawa Seinei, *Quan Tang shi yi*, b, p. 10191.

67. Chen Shangjun, *Quan Tang shi bubian*, vol. 22, p. 979. See also the poems presented to Kūkai by Zhu Shaorui, Yunjing, and Hongjian in ibid., pp. 978–979.

68. Kōbō Daishi Zenshū Henshū Iinkai, *Kōbō daishi Kūkai zenshū*, vol. 7, p. 132. The English translation is by Beatrice Lane Suzuki, quoted in Kitagawa, *On Understanding Japanese Religion*, pp. 189–190.

69. Kūkai, *Seireishū*, pp. 273–277.

70. Kōbō Daishi Zenshū Henshū Iinkai, *Kōbō daishi Kūkai zenshū*, vol. 7, p. 132.

71. "Shang xin qinglaijing deng mulubiao," in Wang Liqi, *Wenjing mifu lun jiaozhu*, pp. 628–629. For an English translation of this document, see Hakeda, *Kūkai: Major Works*, pp. 140–150.

72. For a study on this sect, see Minoru Kiyota, *Shingon Buddhism*. See also Taikō Yamasaki, *Shingon*. Abé, however, argues that Kūkai did not establish a new sect in Japan. His aim was "the creation of a new type of religious discourse grounded in his analysis of the ritual language of mantra." For that purpose, Kūkai used an approach of "complementarity of the esoteric and exoteric" which bridged the gap between textual study and ritual practice. To gain acceptance of his teaching, Kūkai worked with the Nara clergy to maintain a cooperative relationship between the Buddhist establishment and the state. See Abé, *The Weaving of Mantra*, pp. 4–11 and 237–259.

73. Kūkai, *Seireishū*, pp. 421–460. The last five subjects are known in Buddhist terminology as the "five studies" (*pañcavidyā*).

74. For a study of this work, see Richard W. Bodman, *Poetics and Prosody in Early Medieval China: A Study and Translation of Kūkai's Bunkyō Hifuron*.

75. For discussions of the invention of *kana*, see Keene, *Seeds in the Heart*, pp. 218–220. See also Komatsu Shigemi, *Kana*, pp. 63–65 and 148. Abé exam-

ines the invention of *kana* in terms of the disintegration of the Japanese legal system based on the Chinese model and of the efforts by Japanese clergy to use a new language that would allow them more power when defining their relations with the state. See Abé, *The Weaving of Mantra,* pp. 3–4 and 388–398.

76. For discussion of handwritten books, see Frederick W. Mote, "Handwritten Books—before and after the Invention of Block Printing"; and Peter F. Kornicki, *The Book in Japan,* pp. 8–111. See also Denis C. Twitchett, *Printing and Publishing in Medieval China,* pp. 13–18.

77. Ō no Yasumaro, *Kojiki,* b, p. 256. See also Basil Hall Chamberlain, trans., *The Kojiki,* p. 313. For discussions of the spread of Chinese books to Japan, see Yan Shaodang, *Hanji zai Riben de liubu yanjiu,* pp. 13–35; Wang Yong, "Hanji dongchuan zhushuo kaobian," in *Zhongguo dianji zai Riben de liuchuan yu yingxiang,* ed. Lu Jian and Wang Yong; and Ōba Osamu, *Kanseki yunyū no bunka shi,* pp. 23–38.

78. Motoori Norinaga (1730–1801) argued that the book in question was a work of philology *(xiao xue),* a subcategory in the traditional Chinese book classification system to which the *Thousand-Character Text* also belongs. Modern scholars such as Ogihara Asao and Kōnosu Hayao agree with this argument. See Ō no Yasumaro, *Kojiki,* p. 257, note 13. Arai Hakuseki (1657–1725), in contrast, suggested that the work in question might have been the *Ji jiu pian (Quick mastery of the characters),* which was compiled by the Western Han Dynasty scholar Shi You. For a discussion, see Seki Akira, *Kikajin,* p. 40.

79. For instance, a sentence in the first article of the constitution reads, "Harmony is to be valued," which is a quotation from the *Confucian Analects.* See Legge, *The Chinese Classics,* vol. 1, p. 143. A sentence in the third article reads, "The lord is Heaven, the vassal is Earth," which is a basic principle of Confucianism. The English quotations from the constitution in this and the following notes are from R. Tsunoda et al., eds., *Sources of Japanese Tradition,* pp. 50–53. Two sentences in the fifth and the eleventh articles, in contrast, show the influence of Legalism. They read, "Deal impartially with the suits which are submitted to you," and "Give clear appreciation to merit and demerit, and deal out to each its sure reward or punishment." For a detailed study of the "Seventeen-Article Constitution," see Umehara Takeshi, *Kempō jūshichi-jō.* See also Asakawa Kanichi, *The Early Institutional Life of Japan: A Study in the Reform of 645 A.D.,* pp. 25–70.

80. Toneri Shinnō et al., *Nihon shoki,* 19, pp. 76–77, 552/10. A Paekche ambassador came "with a present to the [Japanese] emperor of an image of Shaka Butsu (Buddha Sākyamuni) in gold and copper... and a number of volumes of 'sutras.'" The English translation is from Aston, *Nihongi,* vol. 2, p. 65. The *Gangōji engi,* completed in 747, and the *Jōgū shōtoku hōō teisetsu,* written in the middle of the Heian period (794–1185), suggest that Buddhist works

were brought to Japan in 538. See Takeuchi Rizō et al., eds., *Nara ibun*, pp. 383 and 873.

81. Wei Zheng et al., *Sui shu*, 81, p. 1827. The English translation is from Goodrich and Tsunoda, *Japan in the Chinese Dynastic Histories*, p. 40. See also a record of this Japanese mission by the Tang monk Daoshi in his *Fayuan zhulin* (*SBCK* edn.), 51, p. 22a.

82. In the meantime, the Japanese court continued to request that Paekche present books to Japan. A Paekche priest, for example, arrived in Japan in 602 and "presented by way of tribute books on calendar-making, on astronomy, and on geography, and also books on the art of invisibility and on magic." See Toneri Shinnō et al., *Nihon shoki*, 22, p. 140, 602/10. The English translation is from Aston, *Nihongi*, vol. 2, p. 126. During the Tang dynasty, Parhae was also instrumental in Japan's effort to acquire Chinese books. For a discussion, see Kawaguchi Hisao, "Tō Bokkai tono kōtsu to Nihon genzaisho mokuroku," in his *Heian chō Nihon kanbungakushi no kenkyū*, vol. a. The spread of Chinese books to Japan is also discussed in English by Yu-ying Brown in "The Origins and Characteristics of Chinese Collections in Japan."

83. Toneri Shinnō et al., *Nihon shoki*, 22, p. 137, 595/5/10. See also Inoue Mitsusada, *Nihon kodai no kokka to bukkyō*, pp. 15–23; William E. Deal, "Buddhism and the State in Early Japan," in *Buddhism in Practice*, ed. Donald S. Lopez, pp. 216–227.

84. Sugano no Mamichi et al., *Shoku Nihongi*, 16, p. 188, 746/6/18.

85. See Ikeda On, "Gudai Riben shequ Zhongguo dianji wenti," in *Zhongyang yanjiu yuan guoji Hanxue huiyi lunwenji lishi kaogu zu (shangce)*, pp. 350–351, for a chart of the names of the Eight Masters, the catalogs that they created for the Buddhist works they obtained in China, the number of *juan* of these Buddhist works, and other related information. For a discussion of this issue, see also Verschuer, *Relations officielles*, pp. 109–111.

86. Toneri Shinnō et al., *Nihon shoki*, 25, p. 256, 654/7.

87. Tuotuo et al., *Song shi*, 491, p. 14132.

88. *CFYG*, 974, p. 18a.

89. *JTS*, 199a, p. 5341; *XTS*, 220, p. 6209; *THY*, 100, p. 1729.

90. Zhangsun Wuji, *Gu Tanglü shuyi*, 9, p. 196; *TLD*, 10, pp. 65b–66a; Johnson, *T'ang Code*, vol. 2, p. 78. Du Yan, an official of emperor Daizong's time, was reported to the court for having taken the liberty to teach his son astronomy and to possess astronomical instruments. See Tian Tao and Guo Chengwei, *Longjin fengsui pan jiaozhu*, p. 154. For Du Yan, see *JTS*, 66, p. 2470; and *XTS*, 96, p. 3860.

91. *THY*, 36, p. 667. The collectanea, which comprises one thousand volumes, is titled *Wenguan cilin* and was completed in 658. For a brief discussion of the compilation of the work, see Yong Rong, *Siku quanshu zongmu*, appendix, p. 1852.

92. *QTW*, 281, pp. 1277–1278.
93. Kong Yingda, *Mao shi zhengyi*, 10.a, pp. 425–431.
94. For discussions of these activities, see Kong Yingda, *Li ji zhengyi*, pp. 1352–1387.
95. *JTS*, 196a, p. 5232.
96. *THY*, 36, p. 667.
97. Martin Collcutt, "Japan: The Limits of Confucianization" (unpublished paper), pp. 1–8.
98. This catalog is also known as the *Honchō genzaisho mokuroku,* the *Genzaisho mokuroku,* and the *Sukeyo roku.* Japanese scholars have produced a number of detailed studies of this work. See, for example, Yajima Genryō, *Nihonkoku genzaisho mokuroku: shūshō to kenkyū,* and Kohase Keikichi, *Nihonkoku genzai-sho mokuroku kaisetsu kō.* See also Wang Liqi, "Riben guo jianzai shumu tiyao," in his *Wang Liqi lunxue zazhu,* pp. 442–448.
99. A scholar-official, Sukeyo earned the title "Prize-Winning Student in Literature" (Monjō Tokugyōsei) in the civil service examination during the Jōgan reign period (858–876). He then served Emperor Yōzei (r. 877–883) as tutor. In 884, Sukeyo was appointed head of the Great Learning Bureau. Two years later, he was promoted to junior assistant minister, Ministry of Ceremonies. Sukeyo held the position for five years. It was perhaps during this period that he, taking advantage of access to the imperial library, compiled the catalog.
100. The figure is given by Ikeda On. He also suggests that because of mistakes in Sukeyo's listing, the actual number of books should be 16,967. See his "Gudai Riben shechu Zhongguo dianji wenti," p. 362. Sukeyo's work was not the earliest catalog of Chinese books in Japan. The Great Learning Bureau had produced a catalog for its own collection, which Sukeyo consulted. Another was a catalog for the collection housed at the residence of the abdicated emperor in Kyoto (Reizei In).
101. The original catalog is lost. Only a simplified version from sometime during the late twelfth to early thirteenth centuries still exists. The forty subcategories of the catalog are identical to those in the bibliographic section of the *Sui shu,* indicating that Sukeyo referred to the *Sui shu* while compiling his categories. He, however, revised the subcategory of "geography" *(dili)* in the *Sui shu* to "works of geologists" *(tudi jia).* For a study of the scholarly achievement and defects of Sukeyo's catalog, see Wang Zhenping, "Manuscript Copies of Chinese Books in Ancient Japan," pp. 47–49. For discussion of Chinese books in Japan, see Verschuer, *Relations officielles,* pp. 216–223.
102. Ikeda On, "Gudai Riben shequ Zhongguo dianji wenti," p. 363. Based on the records in the bibliographic section of the *Jiu Tang shu,* the imperial collection of the Tang court amounts to 51,852 *juan* of books.
103. Ibid., p. 362. Chikazawa Keiichi gives a slightly different figure for books in

each of the categories. See his "Nihonkoku genzaisho mokuroku ni tsuite," pp. 2–6.

104. *CFYG*, 99, p. 18b.

105. Fujiwara no Fuhito, *Ritsuryō*, pp. 265–266.

106. Sugano no Mamichi et al., *Shoku Nihongi*, 20, p. 243, 757/11/9.

107. Fujiwara no Fujito, *Ritsuryō*, pp. 262–264. For a discussion of the teaching of the *Book of Filial Piety* at the state and provincial universities, see Yaegashi Naohiko, "Nihon kodai no daigaku ni okeru 'Kōkyō.'"

108. For example, doctors in astrology, astronomy, and medicine were usually of senior seventh rank, lower grade, while doctors in Chinese phonetics, mathematical arts, writing, and the calendar were of the junior seventh rank, upper grade.

109. Kiyohara no Natsuno, *Ryō no gige*, 22, p. 645.

110. Sugano no Mamichi et al., *Shoku Nihongi*, 33, p. 423, 775/10/2.

111. The *Thousand-Character Text* was one such work. Phrases from this work appear on wooden strips recently unearthed from the site of the Fujiwara Palace, where the Japanese court remained until 710. These wooden strips were used as paper by low-ranking court officials when practicing calligraphy. The phrases on them indicate that the work in question was available in Japan before the eighth century. See Tōno Haruyuki, "Rongo, Senjibun to Fujiwarakyū mokkan," in his *Shōsōin monjo to mokkan no kenkyū*, pp. 125–148.

112. For a pioneering study of the influence of the Chinese legal system on Japan, see Takigawa Masajirō, "Ryō no shūge ni mietaru Tō no hōritsu shiryō." For the best studies that provide documentary evidence of the spread of Chinese legal works to Japan, see Niida Noboru, *Tōryō shūi*, and Ichijima Kenkichi, ed., *Honchō hōka monjo mokuroku* (*Zokuzoku gunsho ruijū* edn.). For more recent studies, see Rikō Mitsuo, "Wagakuni ni hakusai sareta Tōritsu no chūshakusha to sono itsubun." See also his "'Tōrikuten' no Nihon ni okeru kōyō ni tsuite." Chinese works on rites also spread to Japan. See Tokigawa Masajirō, "Kōto shūrei to Nihon no gishiki," in *Tenseki ronshū*, ed. Iwai Hakase Koki Kinen Jigyōkai, pp. 342–347; and Sakamoto Tarō, "Gishiki to tōrei," in his *Nihon kodaishi no kisoteki kenkyū (2)*, pp. 67–75.

113. Liu Su, *Da Tang xinyu*, pp. 127–129.

114. *JTS*, 149, p. 4023.

115. See the late Tang work by Mo Xiufu *Guilin fengtu ji* (*Congshu jicheng chubian* edn.), pp. 16–17. It has a preface dated 899. See also *JTS*, 149, p. 4024; and Liu Su, *Da Tang xinyu*, p. 129.

116. *JTS*, 149, p. 4024; Liu Su, *Da Tang xinyu*, p. 129.

117. For a general discussion of literary works written in classical Chinese by Japanese writers, see Kawaguchi Hisao, *Heianchō Nihon kanbungakushi no kenkyū*. The Chinese cultural influence on Japanese literature was so persistent that traces of it can be found even in works of later times written in

the Japanese language. See Kojima Noriyuki, *Jōdai Nihon bungaku to Chūgoku bungaku,* vol. a; and *Kokufū ankoku jidai no bungaku.* See also the case study by Masako Nakagawa, *The Yang Kuei-fei Legend in Japanese Literature.*

118. Of the "general collections," the *Wen xuan* was most frequently consulted by the Japanese. Some of the wooden strips unearthed from the Heijō palace bear phrases from this work. See Tōno Haruyuki, "Heijōkyū shutsudo mokkan shoken no Bunsen Ri Zen chū," in his *Shōsōin monjo to mokkan no kenkyū,* pp. 149–153.

CHAPTER 9: ACQUIRING FOREIGN TALENT

1. Toneri Shinnō et al., *Nihon shoki,* 10, pp. 276–277, 284/8/6, 285/2; Aston, *Nihongi,* vol. 1, pp. 261–262. For a discussion of the introduction and use of Chinese characters in Japan, see Ide Itaru, "Reimeiki no kanji shiyō," in *Zemināru Nihon kodaishi (ge),* pp. 426–431.

2. The five classics are *The Classic of Changes, The Book of Historical Documents, The Classic of Poetry, The Book of Rites,* and the *Spring and Autumn Annals.*

3. Tan Yangni (Chinese: Duan Yanger), Kao Anmu (Chinese: Gao Anmao), and Wang Liugui were some of the scholars that Paekche presented to Japan. See Toneri Shinnō et al., *Nihon shoki,* 17, p. 19, 513/6, p. 23, 516/9; 19, p. 79, 553/6, and p. 83, 554/2. See also a record of 758 in Sugano no Mamichi et al., *Shoku Nihongi,* 20, pp. 246–247, 758/4/28, in which eleven medical professionals in Nara traced their origin to Koryŏ. Their ancestors had surrendered themselves to Paekche. They were then presented to Emperor Yūryaku. The most famous of them was Enichi, who was later sent to Tang China to study medicine and came back to Japan in 623. For a discussion of Chinese and Koreans in Japan. See Ueda Masaaki, *Kikajin.* See also Seki Akira, *Kikajin.*

4. Toneri Shinnō et al., *Nihon shoki,* 10, p. 276, 283/2, p. 282, 306/2/1, p. 284, 310/2; and 14, pp. 383–384, 470/1/1.

5. Ibid., 13, p. 339, 414/1/1.

6. Ibid., 15, p. 415, 493/9/1.

7. Ō no Yasumaro, *Kojiki,* c, p. 272 and pp. 282–283; Toneri Shinnō et al., *Nihon shoki,* 10, p. 272, 276/9; and 14, p. 372, 463, p. 380, 467/7, p. 383, 470/1/1, p. 386, 472/12.

8. Toneri Shinnō et al., *Nihon shoki,* 10, p. 276, 283/2, p. 277, 285/8; Aston, *Nihongi,* vol. 1, p. 261. An early-ninth-century work, *Kogo shūi,* suggests that migrants from Paekche and China amounted to several thousand during the reign of Emperor Ōjin (r. 270–309). See Inbe no Hironari, *Kogo shūi,* p. 137.

9. Toneri Shinnō et al., *Nihon shoki,* 9, p. 256, 205/3/1.

10. Kim Pu-sik, *Samguk sagi,* 3, p. 4b.

11. Ibid., 3, p. 9a.

12. Toneri Shinnō et al., *Nihon shoki*, 14, pp. 371–372, 463.

13. Ibid., 26, p. 278, 661/11/7; and 27, p. 285, 663/2.

14. Ibid., 30, p. 401, 689/6/19, p. 411, 691/9/4, p. 417, 692/12/14.

15. Ibid., 19, p. 51, 540/8. The other two major Chinese migrant groups were the Eastern Aya (Dong Han Zhi) and the Western Aya (Xi Han Zhi). Assuming each also had 7,000 households, the number of households of the three Chinese migrant groups alone would reach 20,000.

16. Ibid., 22, p. 158, 618/8/1; and 26, p. 275, 660/10.

17. Sugano no Mamichi et al., *Shoku Nihongi*, 12, p. 137, 735/5/5, p. 141, 736/8/23.

18. Ibid., 9, p. 92, 722/4/21.

19. Ibid., 27, p. 337, 766/10/21. Dongchao came to Japan in 736. He was made auxiliary assistant director of the Bureau of Music and Dancing in 767. In 769, he was promoted to junior fifth rank, upper grade. And in 770, he was appointed assistant governor of Etchū (in present-day Toyama prefecture). See ibid., 12, p. 141, 736/11/3; 28, p. 341, 767/3/20; 30, p. 367, 769/8/9; and 31, p. 387, 770/12/28.

20. Ibid., 18, p. 209, 750/2/16; 23, p. 283, 761/12/16; and 24, p. 291, 763/1/7.

21. See, for example, Zhang Daoguang, Chen Huaiyu, Zhu Zheng, Lu Rujin, Ma Qingchao, Meng Huizhi, Wang Xiyi, Wang Weijing, Wu Shuier, and Yan Ziqin in Sugano no Mamichi et al., *Shoku Nihongi*, 11, p. 134, 734/9/10; 38, p. 500, 784/6/2, 784/6/14; 39, p. 521, 786/8/21, p. 524, 787/4/1, p. 529, 788/5/10; and 40, p. 554, 791/5/16; and Li Fawan in Fujiwara no Otsugu et al., *Nihon kōki*, 8, p. 16, 799/1/29.

22. Feng Zhi, *Yunxian sanlu*, p. 2.

23. *XTS*, 202, p. 5770.

24. Li Fang, *Taiping guangji*, 179, p. 1333. For Vice-Minister Wang Qiu, see *JTS*, 100, p. 3132; *XTS*, 129, pp. 4481–4482; *THY*, 75, p. 1357.

25. *XTS*, 202, p. 5768.

26. See, for example, *Tang zhiyan, Bianyi zhi, Jiyi ji, Yinhua lu, Nanbu xinshu*, and *Qingyi lu*. Records on Xiao Yingshi in these works have been collected in Zhou Xunchu, *Tangren yishi huibian*, pp. 707–710.

27. *JTS*, 190c, pp. 5048–5049; *XTS*, 202, pp. 5767–5768; Ji Yougong, *Tang shi jishi*, 27, p. 16b; *QTW*, 395, p. 1803. Ikeda On, however, suggests that Xiao Yingshi was not invited to Japan but to Silla. See his "Shō Inshi shōhei wa Shiragi ka Nihon ka," in *Enoki hakase shōju kinen Tōyōshi ronshū*, ed. Enoki Hakase Shōju Kinenkai, pp. 1–19. See also Chen Tiemin, "Xiao Yingshi xinian kaozheng."

28. Earlier, in 769, Yuan was made governor of Awa (in present-day Chiba prefecture). See Sugano no Mamichi et al., *Shoku Nihongi*, 27, p. 337, 766/10/21; 30, p. 368, 769/8/19; and 35, pp. 445–446, 778/12/18. See also Han

Sheng, "Konghai yu Yuan Jinqing"; and Mori Kimiyuki, *Kodai Nihon no taigai ninshiki to tsūkō*, pp. 118–138.

29. Ibid., 19, p. 219, 754/1/16. The following description of the life of Jianzhen and his efforts to travel to Japan is based on Oumi no Mifune, *Tō Daiwajō tōsei den*, pp. 34–91 passim. Inoue Yasushi adapted the travels of Jianzhen to Japan into a novel. See *The Roof Tile of Tempyō*, trans. James T. Araki. See also Andō Kōsei, *Ganji Daiwajō den no kenkyū*; and Kuranaka Susumu, *Tō Daiwajō tōseisen no kenkyū*.

30. See the poem in Peng Dingqiu, *Quan Tang shi*, 732, p. 8325.

31. Zhangsun Wuji, *Gu Tanglü shuyi*, 8, pp. 177–178; Johnson, *T'ang Code*, vol. 2, p. 55.

32. Zhangsun Wuji, *Gu Tanglü shuyi*, 5, p. 106; 8, pp. 172 and 177; Johnson, *T'ang Code*, vol. 1, p. 209; and vol. 2, pp. 47 and 55.

33. Huili and Yancong, *Da Ciensi Sanzang fashi zhuan*, pp. 10 and 128. See also Yang Tingfu, *Xuanzang nianpu*, pp. 86 and 213. For a recent study on Xuanzang in English, see Sally H. Wriggins, *Xuanzang: A Buddhist Pilgrim on the Silk Road*.

34. For this pirate attack in 744, see *JTS*, 9, p. 218; and *XTS*, 5, p. 144.

CHAPTER 10: THE MULTIPOLAR NATURE
OF THE INTERNATIONAL SYSTEM IN ASIA

1. Legge, *The Chinese Classics*, vol. 5, p. 360.

2. *Wufu* has also been translated as "five zones." See Yü Ying-shih, "Han Foreign Relations," in *The Ch'in and Han Empires, 221 BC–AD 220*, ed. Denis C. Twitchett and Michael Loewe, vol. 1 of *The Cambridge History of China*, ed. John K. Fairbank and Denis C. Twitchett, pp. 379–381.

3. This constituted the sine qua non for staying in the system. A Chinese lord who failed to send ambassadors regularly to the Zhou court would be deprived of title and fief, and face punitive expeditions from Zhou. See Zhao Qi and Sun Bi, *Mengzi zhushu*, 12, p. 2759; *Chunqiu Zuoshi zhuan*, 6, p. 1748; and 18, pp. 1837–1838; and Guliang Chi, *Chunqiu Guliang zhuan* (*SSJZS* edn.), 6, p. 2388.

4. Major principles of the "tributary system" are outlined in the *Zhou li*. See Zheng Xuan et al., *Zhou li zhushu* (*SSJZS* edn.), 37, p. 892. For discussion of the characteristics and technical details of the tributary system, see Yang Lien-sheng, "Historical Notes on the Chinese World Order," in *The Chinese World Order*, ed. John K. Fairbank, p. 21; and Mark Mancall, "The Persistence of Tradition in Chinese Foreign Policy," p. 14. See also his *China at the Center*, pp. 14–39.

5. *CFYG*, 972, p. 10b.

6. *WYYH*, 508, pp. 2b–3a.

7. Ibid., 551, p. 7a.

8. For major Western works on the tributary relations between China and Japan, see Verschuer, *Relations officielles;* P. A. Herbert, "Japanese Embassies and Students in T'ang China"; and Reischauer, *Ennin's Travels in T'ang China,* pp. 39–47. For Chinese and Western works on Tang China's tributary relations with other countries, see Li Hu, *Han Tang waijiao zhidu shi;* Larry W. Moses, "T'ang Tributary Relations with the Inner Asian Barbarians," in *Essays on T'ang Society,* ed. John C. Perry and Bardwell L. Smith, pp. 61–89; and Hilda Ecsedy, "Trade and War Relations between the Turks and China in the Second Half of the Sixth Century." Western scholars have also studied China's external relations in the widely separated Han and Qing periods. See Yü Ying-shih, "Han Foreign Relations," pp. 381–383. See also his *Trade and Expansion in Han China,* pp. 43 and 59–60; J. K. Fairbank and S. Y. Teng, "On the Chinese Tributary System," and "Ch'ing Administration: Three Studies"; and Warren I. Cohen, *East Asia at the Center: Four Thousand Years of Engagement with the World,* pp. 62–88. These works are characterized by analyses of the economic reasons for contact with China. Such analyses, however, may not apply to relations among East Asian countries, which had agrarian economies and were thus freed from the economic pressure of entering into relations with China.

9. Naitō Konan (1866–1934) was representative of these Japanese scholars. See Miyakawa Hisayuki, "An Outline of the Naitō Hypothesis and Its Effect on Japanese Studies of China."

10. For discussion of studies on China by European scholars and their influence on Japanese scholars, see Joshua A. Fogel, *Politics and Sinology: The Case of Naitō Konan,* pp. 2–8.

11. Nishijima Sadao, "Higashi Ajia sekai no keisei (1): Sōsetsu," in *Iwanami kōza sekai rekishi (kodai 4),* ed. Ienaga Saburō et al., pp. 3–19. See also his *Chūgoku kodai kokka to Higashi Ajia shakai,* pp. 415–512; and *Nihon rekishi no kokusai kankyō,* pp. 4–17.

12. Nishijima Sadao, "Roku-hachi seiki no Higashi Ajia," in *Iwanami kōza Nihon rekishi (kodai 2),* ed. Ienaga Saburō et al., pp. 275–276 and 278. See also his *Nihon rekishi no kokusai kankyō,* pp. 4–5 and 239.

13. Nishijima Sadao, *Nihon rekishi no kokusai kankyō,* pp. 238–239.

14. Kitō Kiyoaki, "Chūgoku kodai kokka to Higashi Ajia shakai" (book review), p. 145.

15. See, for example, Fu Sinian, "Zhi Wu Jingchao shu," in *Fu Sinian quanji,* ed. Chen Pan, vol. 7, pp. 109–135. In his letter dated October 11, 1942, Fu elaborated the structure of a Chinese "empire" in the Qin-Han period. Kurihara Tomonobu further developed Fu's ideas into an elaborate theory. See his "Kan teikoku to shūhen shominzoku," in Ienaga Saburō et al., eds., *Iwanami kōza sekai rekishi (kodai 4),* pp. 445–486; and *Shin Kan shi no kenkyū.*

16. Max Weber, *The Religion of China,* trans. Hans H. Gerth, p. 37; John K. Fair-

bank, "A Preliminary Framework," in *The Chinese World Order*, ed. John K. Fairbank, p. 12.

17. Du Zhengsheng, "Xizhou fengjian de tezhi," in *Zhongguo shixue lunwen xuan-ji*, ed. Wang Shounan et al., vol. 4, pp. 115–117.

18. Kikuchi Hideo, "Sōsetsu," in *Zui Tō teikoku to Higashi Ajia sekai*, ed. Tōdaishi Kenkyūkai, p. 32.

19. Richard L. Walker, *The Multi-State System of Ancient China*, p. 74.

20. Xing Yitian, "Handai de yiyi zhiyi lun," in *Zhongguo shixue lunwen xuanji*, ed. Ruan Zhisheng et al., vol. 2, p. 229.

21. Yü Ying-shih, *Trade and Expansion in Han China*, pp. 10, 42, and 57; Yang Lien-sheng, "Historical Notes on the Chinese World Order," p. 30. Some modern scholars doubt that a mature and consistent tributary system existed during the Han dynasty. See Xing Yitian, "Handai zhongwai jingji jiaotong yishu de shangque," p. 177.

22. Denis Twitchett, "Sui and T'ang China and the Wider World," in *Sui and T'ang China, 589–906*, ed. Denis C. Twitchett, vol. 3, part 1 of *The Cambridge History of China*, ed. John K. Fairbank and Denis C. Twitchett, pp. 157–158.

23. Pugu Huaien rebelled in 764 and lured the Uighurs and the Tibetans to attack Changan. Guo Ziyi, the legendary Tang general, had to travel to the Uighur headquarters in person to persuade them to abandon the campaign and to join the Tang forces to beat the Tibetans. After the victory, China sent a large amount of silk as a reward to the Uighurs. *JTS*, 195, pp. 5205–5206; and 196b, pp. 5243–5267; *XTS*, 217a, pp. 6119–6120. On this incident see Charles A. Peterson "P'u-ku Huai-en and the T'ang court: The Limits of Loyalty."

24. Herrlee G. Creel, *The Origins of Statecraft in China*, vol. 1, p. 213.

25. Wang Gung-wu, "Early Ming Relations with Southeast Asia," in *The Chinese World Order*, ed. John K. Fairbank, pp. 38–44.

26. The tributary system "demonstrated a capacity of adjustment to the power reality." See Yü Ying-shih, *Trade and Expansion in Han China*, p. 58.

27. Kikuchi Hideo, "Sōsetsu," p. 18.

28. Twitchett, "Sui and T'ang China and the Wider World," p. 38.

29. The king of Paekche, for instance, stopped official contact with China when he had successfully expanded his territories. He needed no Chinese help and wanted no Chinese interference with the status quo on the Korean peninsula. See Jonathan W. Best, "Diplomatic and Cultural Contacts between Paekche and China," pp. 485–486.

30. China's war against Koguryŏ in the early Tang, for example, was not a simple result of the military ambitions of Emperor Gaozu and his successor, Emperor Taizong. It was the outcome of a deliberate Paekche policy to involve China in a war with Koguryŏ so as to reduce the military pressure of Koguryŏ on Paekche. See ibid., pp. 476–484.

31. Gari Ledyard, "Yin and Yang in the China-Manchuria-Korea Triangle," in *China among Equals,* ed. Morris Rossabi, pp. 321–322.

32. Criticism of the "investiture theory" has led some Japanese scholars to examine China-Japan relations in terms of Japan's efforts to "gain equal footing" with China. See, for example, Kurihara Tomonobu, "Nihon kara Zui e okutta kokusho," in *Jōdai Nihon taigai kankei no kenkyū,* ed. Kurihara Tomonobu, pp. 175–205; and Masumura Hiroshi, "Jo Sengyō kyōju no 'Sui Wo bangjiao xinkao: Woshi chao Sui bingfei suowei duideng waijiao' oyobi 'Zui-Wa kokkō no taitōsei ni tsuite' o yomu." This theory of equality raises the important question of Japan's motives in contacting China and properly points to self-interest as the answer.

   Unfortunately, the key concept of "equality" in this theory is historically untenable. A fairly modern term that came into use with the rise of the bourgeoisie in Europe in the sixteenth century, equality had never been the aim of Japan's diplomacy toward China. The equality theory becomes particularly vulnerable when it fails to specify the form of diplomatic contacts acceptable to both China and Japan when Japan is said to have gained an equal footing with China. Nor is the theory able to explain how, when dealing with China, a country of tremendous political, cultural, and military power, any Japanese ambassador could act in a manner that would imply that his country enjoyed dignity and privileges equal to those of China. Furthermore, China certainly had never treated Japan as an equal partner. The theory has invited much criticism. See Xu Xianyao, "Sui Wo bangjiao xinkao (5)." See also his "Wakoku kara Zui ni okutta kokusho no mondaiten." The theory in question is an effort to interpret China-Japan relations by an unsuitable modern concept. I therefore consider it irrelevant to the present discussion.

   Another unsuitable interpretation of China-Japan relations during the Sui-Tang period is that Japan "displayed independence" from China. See Verschuer, *Relations officielles,* p. 10. While Japan did quietly disengage itself from the China-centered world order, its ambassadors to China, nevertheless, did not openly display any sense of such independence when visiting China. And despite what Verschuer has suggested, Japan's state letters to the Sui court did not employ the term "Tennō" as a reference for Japanese rulers, and the Japanese court did not unilaterally decide that its ambassadors should not present a state letter when calling on the Tang court.

33. Hirano Kunio, "Nichi-Chō-Chū sangoku kankeiron ni tsuite no oboegaki," p. 61.

34. For a discussion of national interest in diplomacy, see Samuel S. Kim, "The Traditional Chinese Image of World Order," in his *China, the United Nations and World Order* p. 26; and Hirano Kunio, "Nichi-Chō-Chū sangoku kankeiron ni tsuite no oboegaki," p. 58.

35. *HS*, 99a, p. 4051.
36. Yü Ying-shih, *Trade and Expansion in Han China*, pp. 36–43.
37. *JTS*, 63, p. 2406; *ZZTJ*, 180, p. 5627.
38. *JTS*, 194a, p. 5158.
39. Ibid., 199b, p. 5352; *XTS*, 215b, p. 6069.
40. *XTS*, 217b, p. 6151.
41. *ZZTJ*, 209, p. 6626.
42. *XTS*, 222a, p. 6272.
43. Local Han officials reported some thirty visits by Wo representatives. See *HS*, 28b, p. 1658; *HHS*, 85, p. 2820; and *SGZ*, 30, p. 854. The Chinese commandery at Lelang roughly covered northern Korea, including the provinces of South Pyongan, North Hwanghae, South Hwanghae, Kangwon, and South Hamgyong. Its administrative center was located to the south of the modern city of Pyongyang. There were altogether four Chinese commanderies in Korea: Lelang, Zhenfan, Xuantu, and Lintun.
44. *HHS*, 1b, p. 84; and 85, p. 2821. These are the earliest Chinese records that describe official China-Wo relations in detail. Some modern scholars therefore regard 57 as the year in which such relations were formally established. See Reischauer, *Ennin's Travels in T'ang China*, p. 41.
45. *HHS*, 85, p. 2821.
46. *SGZ*, 30, p. 857.
47. The Chinese sources, however, do not specify the exact time of this Wo delegation's visit to the Wei court. See *SGZ*, 30, p. 858.
48. Toneri Shinnō et al., *Nihon shoki*, 10, p. 282, 306/2/1.
49. *JS*, 10, p. 264.
50. *SS*, 97, pp. 2394–2395. Records indicate that Wo ambassadors arrived at the Southern Song court in 421, 425, 430, 438, 443, 451, 460, 462, 477, and 478.
51. *NQS*, 58, p. 1012; *NS*, 79, p. 1975.
52. *LS*, 2, p. 36; and 54, p. 807; *NS*, 6, p. 185; and 78, p. 1975.
53. They arrived in China in 600, 607, 608, 610, and 614. See Wei Zheng et al., *Sui shu*, 81, pp. 1826–1827; and Toneri Shinnō et al., *Nihon shoki*, 22, pp. 148, 151, and 157.
54. They were appointed in 630, 653, 654, 659, 665, 667, 669, 701, 716, 732, 750, 759, 761, 762, 775, 778, 801, 834, and 849. Those appointed in 761, 762, and 894 did not in the end go to China. For a chart with more information about these ambassadors, see Mori Katsumi, *Ken Tō shi*, pp. 25–27. For a discussion of the reasons for the Japanese court to abandon the mission to China in 894, see Robert Borgen, *Sugawara no Michizane and the Early Heian Court*, pp. 240–254. For a summary of the different opinions of Japanese scholars on this issue, see Verschuer, *Relations officielles*, pp, 161–180.
55. Ma Duanlin, *Wenxian tongkao*, 331, p. 2602.

56. Confucius urged statesmen not publicly to make benefit the aim of their activities at home or abroad. He asserted, "The mind of the superior man is conversant with righteousness; the mind of the mean man is conversant with gain." See Xing Bing, *Lun yu zhushu* (*SSJZS* edn.), 4, p. 2471; Legge, *The Chinese Classics*, vol. 1, p. 170. King Hui (r. 369–319 B.C.) of Liang once asked Mencius how his counsels would profit Liang. "Why must Your Majesty use that word profit?" replied Mencius. "What I am provided with are counsels to benevolence and righteousness, and these are my only topics." See Zhao Qi and Sun Bi, *Mengzi zhushu*, 1a, 2665; and Legge, *The Chinese Classics*, vol. 2, pp. 125–126. Early Tang courtiers such as Wei Zheng and Li Yanshou also advocated "governing the universe by virtue [of the Tang emperor]." *ZZTJ*, 197, pp. 6200–6201.

57. As a means for diplomacy, "virtue" was efficacious only when China handled a weaker country. And strength was always the basis of "virtue." Tang proclaimed "virtue" to be its guiding principle of governance after a succession of military victories in the northeast, the north, and the northwest. China had to rely on force, not virtue, when faced with a hostile country. See *JTS*, 198, p. 5371. A comment on the relations between Tang and the Turks in *JTS*, 196b, p. 5266, further explains: "When they [the Turks] are strong, they would assault our borders. However, they would [pretend to] accept our culture when they are weakened." And when China was weak and threatened by a strong enemy, Chinese rulers had to turn to foreign countries for support. "Virtue" would not help much. See *HHS*, 89, p. 2946.

58. Mozi (470–391 B.C.?) made this argument. He also argued for "accomplishment," "benefit," and "utilitarianism" as principles for state conduct. See Fung Yu-lan, *A History of Chinese Philosophy*, vol. 1, pp. 85–86 and 248–249.

59. For a discussion of this issue, see Wang Zhenping, "Act on Appropriateness and Mutual Self-Interest."

60. Fung Yu-lan, *A History of Chinese Philosophy*, vol. 1, p. 179. See also Arthur Waley, *The Analects of Confucius*, p. 33; and Jay Saily, "A. C. Graham's Disputers of the Tao and Some Recent Works in English on Chinese Thought."

61. Liu Xi, *Shi ming*, 4, p. 25a.

62. Kong Yingda, *Shang shu zhengyi* (*SSJZS* edn.), 8, p. 162; Legge, *The Chinese Classics*, vol. 3, p. 182. A righteous ruler, for example, should let people who can resist cold weather live in cold areas and those who can endure hot weather live in tropical areas. See Kong Yingda, *Li ji zhengyi*, 12, p. 1338.

63. Kong Yingda, *Li ji zhengyi*, 48, p. 1598; and 52, p. 1629. See also Liu Xi, *Shi ming*, 4, p. 25a.

64. Ma Qichang, ed., *Han Changli wenji jiaozhu*, vol. 1, p. 13. Appropriateness is a principle applied to both foreign and domestic affairs. If someone's parents, brothers, and elders were humiliated, it was justifiable for him to kill

the perpetrator. This action is referred to as "appropriate killing" (*yisha*). See Zheng Xuan et al., *Zhou li zhushu*, 14, p. 732; and Kong Yingda, *Shang shu zhengyi*, 14, p. 204.

65. *Chunqiu Zuoshi zhuan*, 30, p. 1942; and 51, p. 2107; Legge, *The Chinese Classics*, vol. 5, p. 440. See also Kong Yingda et al., *Zhou yi zhengyi*, 1, p. 15.

66. *Chunqiu Zuoshi zhuan*, 25, p. 1894; Legge, *The Chinese Classics*, vol. 5, p. 334.

67. *Chunqiu Zuoshi zhuan*, 45, p. 2059; Legge, *The Chinese Classics*, vol. 5, p. 629; Kong Yingda, *Li ji zhengyi*, 60, p. 1675.

68. *Chunqiu Zuoshi zhuan*, 28, p. 1917; Legge, *The Chinese Classics*, vol. 5, p. 395.

69. Nishijima Sadao also considered investiture relations reciprocal in nature. This reciprocity, however, was based on China's centrality. See his "Roku-hachi seiki no Higashi Ajia," p. 276. See also his *Nihon rekishi no kokusai kankyō*, pp. 5–6 and 239–240.

70. Mo Di, *Mozi* (*SBCK* edn.), 4, pp. 4a–b and 13b; and 9, p. 3b. Another expression used by Mozi is *xiangli* (mutual benefit). See ibid., 1, p. 8b. For a brief discussion of Mozi, see Wm. Theodore de Bary et al., eds., *Sources of Chinese Tradition*, vol. 1, pp. 34–35.

71. *Chunqiu Zuoshi zhuan*, 29, p. 1933; and 31, p. 1951; Legge, *The Chinese Classics*, vol. 5, pp. 424 and 453. See also Bai Juyi, *Baishi liutie shilei ji*, 14, p. 26b; and 16, p. 65b.

72. *SJ*, 117, p. 3049. For *ji*, see also Shi You, *Ji jiu pian*, p. 48a.

73. *HHS*, 89, p. 2946.

74. *TD*, 185, p. 985; *CFYG*, 997, p. 8a.

75. *JTS*, 199b, p. 5364. If a country did not benefit much from its conquest of another country, this conquest was compared to "acquiring a piece of stony field." See *Chunqiu Zuoshi zhuan*, 58, p. 2167.

76. *TD*, 185, p. 985.

77. Liu Xiang, *Xin xu* (*SBCK* edn.), 10, p. 15b.

78. Ban Gu, *Baihu tongde lun* (*SBCK* edn.), 6, p. 1b.

79. *SS*, 97, pp. 2392 and 2393–2394.

80. Wang Wei, *Wang youcheng ji*, 12, p. 2b. Verschuer, however, asserts that the primary goal of the Japanese missions to China during the Sui-Tang period "was of diplomatic nature" and that cultural exchanges were "of secondary importance" for these missions. See her *Relations officielles*, pp. 252–253 and 255. However, she seems to have revised her opinion on this issue when she writes: "The commercial pragmatism of the Japanese in the various historical periods can be summarized into the following themes. Up to the eighth century: assimilate know-how and foreign techniques; up to the twelfth century: import luxury products." See her *Commerce Extérieur*, pp. 153–154. In fact, there was no real diplomatic issue between the two countries after they clashed militarily in 663 at the Hakusonkō River in Korea. Thereafter, Japan disengaged itself from politics in Korea.

81. Fairbank, "A Preliminary Framework," p. 12.
82. For recent studies of the international system in East Asia, see Warren I. Cohen, *East Asia at the Center,* pp. 1–61; Yongjin Zhang, "System, Empire and State in Chinese International Relations," in *System, Empire and States: Great Transformation in International Politics,* ed. Michael Cox, Tim Dunne, and Ken Booth, pp. 43–63.
83. Denis C. Twitchett, "Sui and T'ang China and the Wider World," p. 37.
84. Each Korean state maneuvered to swing China to its own side in its pursuit of ultimate power in the Korean peninsula. The king of Silla used paying tribute, asking for Chinese official robes, and offering eulogies as means to persuade the Chinese court to dispatch troops against Koguryŏ. In 626, ambassadors from both Silla and Paekche attempted to involve China in Korean politics. They complained that Koguryŏ had blockaded roads to China, making it difficult for them to come to pay tribute. Koguryŏ was also accused of raiding Silla and Paekche borders towns. China sent an official to mediate their disputes. Koguryŏ responded by delivering a state letter to China, apologizing for its action. See *JTS,* 199A, pp. 5321 and 5329; *XTS,* 220, pp. 6187 and 6199; and *ZZTJ,* 192, p. 6030. In 660, Tang eventually decided to recover northwestern Korea by launching a joint expedition with Silla against Koguryŏ. See R. W. L. Guisso, *Wu Tse-t'ien and the Politics of Legitimation in T'ang China,* pp. 114–115; and Pyŏn In-sŏk, "Cong suyu zhidu kan Tangdai Zhongguo yu Xinluo de guanxi," pp. 3–10. See also his "Tang Xuanzong shidai yu dongyi guanxi zhi yipie," pp. 2, 23, and 31.
85. Silla had once had a close alliance with Tang China against Paekche and Koguryŏ. This alliance was broken as soon as the Korean peninsula was unified under the king of Silla, who rejected the Chinese title "Commander of Kyerim," which put him under the authority of a Chinese commissioner.
86. *JTS,* 199a, p. 5340; *XTS,* 220, p. 6208. To the Tang court, however, Japan's action was a humble political gesture. In Tang political thinking, only a "lesser country" would attach its ambassador to the delegation of a "greater country" when conducting diplomacy with China. And only junior administrative officers would entrust their memorials to the courier of prefectural authorities dispatched to Changan when communicating with the court. See Han Yu, *Han Changli quanji,* 21, p. 4a; and Zhangsun Wuji, *Gu Tanglü shuyi,* 10, p. 209. In 659, the Emishi people attached their ambassador to a Japanese delegation, and they paid a visit to the Tang court together. See *THY,* 100, p. 1792; and *CFYG,* 970, p. 15b. Earlier, in 413, when resuming diplomatic ties with the Eastern Jin, the Wo court did the same with a delegation of Koguryŏ. See *JS,* 10, p. 264.
87. *XTS,* 220, p. 6208.
88. These relations originated as early as the Western Han. The Xiongnu, for example, developed both political and economic relations with the settled

and seminomadic communities in the Western Region in order to acquire the agricultural products they needed. See Nicola Di Cosmo, "Ancient Inner Asian Nomads: Their Economic Basis and Its Significance in Chinese History," pp. 1094–1095 and 1116. See also his recent book, *Ancient China and Its Enemies.*

89. From 755 until 842, for example, the Qidan became vassals of their menacing Uighur neighbors but still continued to send regular embassies to the Tang. There were at least forty such embassies. The Tang court received them but no longer granted Chinese titles to the Qidan leaders. See Denis C. Twitchett and Klaus-Peter Tietze, "The Liao," in *Alien Regimes and Border States, 907–1368,* ed. Herbert Franke and Denis C. Twitchett, vol. 6 of *The Cambridge History of China,* ed. John K. Fairbank and Denis C. Twitchett, pp. 49–50.

90. For the names of these Tang merchants and the time of their departure for and return from Japan, see Mori Katsumi, *Nissō bōeki no kenkyū,* p. 71. For a recent archaeological study of this issue, see Chang Lan, *Qi-shisi shiji Zhong Ri wenhua jiaoliu de kaoguxue yanjiu,* pp. 205–223.

APPENDIX 2: THE LETTER TO
THE SURVEILLANCE COMMISSIONER
AT FUZHOU DRAFTED FOR THE AMBASSADOR

1. This letter was drafted by Kūkai for presentation by Kadonomaro, who referred to himself as Kanō (Chinese: Heneng). This is a Chinese-style name.

2. Koremune no Naomoto, *Ryō no shūge* says: "*Qi* could substitute for *zou* [report] when informing [the court] of less important matters" (31, p. 795). In China, from the Eastern Jin dynasty, *qi* was widely used by subjects to communicate with the emperor. It was not until Song that *qi* was employed only in correspondence between subjects. See Gao Cheng, *Shiwu jiyuan,* 2, p. 5a. For records about *qi,* see also *JS,* 43, pp. 1226 and 1230; and *NQS,* 40, p. 699.

3. A term used to refer to people living in modern Qinghai province. For detailed discussions of the Xiqiang, see *HHS,* 87, pp. 2869–2908.

4. An allusion to the *Zhou yi zhengyi:* "Huangdi, Yao and Shun rule the world by establishing the official costume system, [by which they differentiate the noble from the humble]" (Kong Yingda, *Zhou yi zhengyi,* 8, p. 87).

5. A term used to refer to people living to the south of Mt. Wuling and Jiaozhi (modern Vietnam). See Fan Ning, ed., *Bowu zhi jiaozheng,* 1, p. 9.

6. This term applies to an emperor under whose rule people enjoy a peaceful and prosperous life. Since people seldom commit crimes, the emperor has no need to punish criminals. See *HS,* 4, p. 135.

7. Lü Buwei, *Lüshi chunqiu* (*SBCK* edn.), 13, pp. 1a–b. The Chinese divided the sky into nine parts and assigned names to each of them: the central *(juntian),* the east *(cangtian),* the northeast *(biantian),* the north *(xuantian),*

the northwest *(youtian)*, the west *(haotian)*, the southwest *(zhutian)*, the south *(yantian)*, and the southeast *(yangtian)*. They were referred to collectively as *jiuye*. See Wang Liqi, *Lüshi chunqiu zhushu*, pp. 1224–1230.

8. Detailed descriptions of the *bahong* can be found in Liu An, *Huainan zi*, 4, pp. 3b–4a. Both *jiuye* and *bahong* were used in a general sense, referring to the whole world. For the use of *bahong* in other Japanese records, see, for example, Toneri Shinnō, *Nihon shoki*, 3, p. 130, 662 B.C./3/7.

9. A metaphor for ambassadors. For the use of *huanghua*, see Kong Yingda, *Mao shi zhengyi* (*SSJZS* edn.), 9, p. 407: "Brilliant are the flowers; on those level heights and the low grounds. Complete and alert is the messenger [i.e., the ambassador], with his suite; ever anxious lest he should not succeed." Legge, *The Chinese Classics*, vol. 4, p. 249. See also Fujiwara no Fuyutsugu et al., *Bunka shūreishū*, b, p. 315.

10. A mystical island that, according to Chinese legend, was inhabited by immortals. Emperor Qin Shihuang (r. 221–210 B.C.) was said to have sent Xu Fu, a necromancer, and thousands of boys and girls to find this place. See Sima Qian, *Shi ji*, 6, p. 247; and 28, p. 1369; and Guo Pu, *Shan hai jing* (*SBCK* edn.), 12, p. 57b.

11. Mt. Kunlun in modern Xinjiang province. Penglai and Kunyue are used as remote magical sources of treasures at opposite ends of the world.

12. Using the term *guozhu*, rather than *huangdi*, to refer to the emperor of one's own country is a humble, if not self-deprecating, action. Similar records can also be found in Sugano no Mamichi et al., *Shoku Nihongi*, 40, p. 546, 790/7/17; and Ouyang Xiu, *Xin Wudai shi*, 62, pp. 775–776. *Guozhu* is not, as Yuasa Yukihiko has suggested, only a mistake for *guowang*. See his "Ken Tō shi kōben nisoku," pp. 20–21.

13. Modern Fukui in Honshū.

14. Modern Chejudo, which is an island located to the south of the Korean peninsula.

15. *Shusi* sometimes substitutes for *shuchong*. See Peng Dingqiu, *Quan Tang shi*, 59, p. 1259.

16. For the origin of the term *qucheng*, see Kong Yingda, *Zhou yi zhengyi*, 7, p. 77. The annotation to the text reads: "The so-called *qucheng* means to deal with things by varied means without sticking to only one of them so that things can be handled properly." See also Xun Kuang, *Xunzi* (*Nianerzi* edn.), 9, p. 310. Here, this term apparently refers to the special treatments that the Tang court granted to the Japanese envoys.

17. In Chinese classics, *shangke* is used in contrast with *xiake* (ordinary guests). See Kong Yingda, *Li ji zhengyi*, 2, p. 1240; *Zhanguo ce*, 7, p. 288; and Xun Kuang, *Xunzi* (*Nianerzi* edn.), 4, p. 166.

18. An abbreviation for *zhu shifu*, which is a tally made of bamboo. For *zhu shifu*, see also *JTS*, 1, p. 5.

19. A *tongqi* is a bronze tally in the shape of a tiger. Both *zhu shifu* and *tongqi* consist of two pieces. One was kept at the central court; the other was granted to commandery governors. They would obey the order of an imperial envoy only after he showed his tally, and the two pieces matched with each other. See *SJ*, 10, p. 424; *HHS*, 26, p. 3599; and *JS*, 24, p. 739.

20. A bronze tally in the shape of a fish was used in Tang court's relations with countries in the "Western Region." The fish contained two pieces, each bearing a number and the name of a foreign country. Every year, twelve fish were granted to each country for its ambassador to use. An ambassador coming to visit in January should bring the number one fish. He would not be received unless his fish matched with the one kept by the Chinese court. See *THY*, 100, p. 1795. Verschuer mistakes the bronze tally in the shape of a fish for an "emblem" that the Tang court universally issued to tribute-paying countries for their ambassadors to use when calling on China. This misunderstanding leads her to believe that the Japanese court purposely refused to comply with the code of diplomatic conduct by the Tang court. See her *Relations officielles,* p. 7.

21. An allusion to statements in Chinese works such as *Huainan zi.* See Liu An, *Huainan zi,* 4, p. 5a; Wang Liqi, ed., *Fengsu tongyi jiaozhu,* p. 487; and Fan Ning, ed., *Bowu zhi jiaozheng,* p. 21.

22. For the use of *chutu,* see also *Yanshi jiaxun jijie,* ed. Wang Liqi, pp. 287 and 327.

23. Shun is regarded as one of the sage emperors in Chinese history. Here "Shun's sea" refers to the Chinese court.

24. Yao is another sage emperor. Similarly, here "Yao's sun" refers to the Chinese court or the contemporary Chinese emperor.

25. An allusion to Zhuang Zhou, *Zhuangzi,* 8, p. 28a: "Mutton does not adore ants, but ants adore mutton."

26. A letter to officials that takes on the form of *qi* should begin with "[name of the sender] writes" and end with "earnestly write." For a detailed discussion of *qi,* see Patricia Ebrey, "T'ang Guides to Verbal Etiquette," pp. 604–606. For other Japanese records using the term *qi,* see a letter written in 730 by Yoshida no Yoroshi in *Man'yōshū,* 5, p. 86, no. 863. This letter has been translated into English. See Cranston, *A Waka Anthology,* pp. 556–557.

Glossary

abei jimi amei duolisibigu 阿輩雞彌阿
每多利思比古
Abaoji 阿保機
Abe no Nakamaro 阿倍仲麻呂
Abo Qaghan 阿波可汗
Aki 安藝
Amakutararetaokata 天降られた御方
Amami 奄美
Amei 阿每
An Lushan 安祿山
Anaho 穴穂
Andong Jiangjun Wowang Woji 安東
將軍倭王倭濟
Ankō 安康
Annan 安南
Arai Hakuseki 新井白石
Aramikami to Ame no shita shirasu
Hinomoto no subera ga
ohomugotorama 明神と御宇らす
日本の天皇が詔旨らま
Asuka Kiyomihara Ryō 飛鳥淨御原令
Ato no Ōtari 阿刀大足
Awa (in Chiba prefecture) 安房
Awa (in Tokushima prefecture) 阿波
Awada no Ason Mahito 粟田朝臣真人
ba 八
badi 八狄
bafan 八蕃
bahong 八紘
bai 白
Bai Juyi 白居易
Baicun Jiang. *See* Hakusonkō
Baling (prince) 巴陵王
baman 八蠻
ban 蕃
Ban Gu 班固
bangguo 邦國
banjin 蕃人

bankoku 蕃國
bankyaku 蕃客
banrei 蕃禮
banrui sijin 班瑞肆覲
Bao Ji 包佶
Baocheng 襃城
baoshu 報書
Beihai 北海
Beiyan 北燕
benguo biaozhang 本國表章
Benshō 辨正
bi 璧
biantian 變天
Bianyi zhi 辯疑志
biao 表
Biaoxin 驃信
bie shangbiao 別上表
biegong 別貢
bifan 彼蕃
Bilgä 毗伽
biluo 畢羅
bin 賓
bincong 賓從
binfu 賓服
Bingcao Sibing Canjun 兵曹司兵參軍
bingong 賓貢
binke 賓客
binli 賓禮
Bixia 陛下
Bizen 備前
Bo Tiao 波調
Bosi 波斯
boyi 駁議
bubin 不賓
Bukong 不空
buneng zhuandui 不能專對
Bunkyō hifu ron 文鏡秘府論
Byōbugaura 屏風浦

caifu 采服
Caizhou 蔡州
cangtian 蒼天
Cefu yuangui 冊府元龜
ceshu 冊書
Champa 占婆
Changan 長安
changcan guan 常參官
changcao 罻草
Changle 長樂
changshi liao 常食料
Changxi 長溪
Changxing 長興
chao 朝
Chao Heng 晁衡
chaogong 朝貢
Chean Guo 車安國
Chejia 車駕
Chen Huaiyu 陳懷玉
Chengdi 成帝
Chengtian 承天
Chengyu 乘輿
chengzhi jiashou 承制假授
Chenhan 辰韓
Chian 赤岸
chidie 敕牒
chijie 持節
Chika 值嘉
Chiku 竹島
Chin 秦
Chishō 智証
Chitu 赤土
chizhi 敕旨
Chōgen 朝元
Chōkei 朝慶
choku 敕
Chongren 崇仁
Chongxuan Shu 崇玄署
chu (dispatch) 出
chu (grant a Chinese title formally) 除
Chu (name of Emperor Daizong) 俶

Chu Guangxi 儲光羲
Chūai 仲哀
chuang 幢
Chūgoku 中國
chuiyi jun 垂衣君
chūka shisō 中華思想
Chuluo Qaghan 處羅可汗
Chun 純
chūnaiki 中內記
Chunqiu Zuoshi zhuan 春秋左氏傳
Chunyu 淳于
chutu 觸途
Chuzhou 楚州
ci 賜
cifan 次蕃
cishu 賜書
Cixiao 慈孝
Consort Yang 楊貴妃
da 大
Dacheng liqu liuboluomi duojing 大乘理趣六波羅密多經
dafan 大蕃
dafu 大夫
daguo 大國
Dahuo 達貨
Daifang 帶方
Daigaku Ryō 大學寮
daijō daijin 太政大臣
Daijō Tennō. *See* Taishang Tianhuang
Daijōkan 太政官
daikō 大工
dainagon 大納言
dainaiki 大內記
Dairei 大禮
Daizhao Yuan 待詔院
Daizong 代宗
Dajiang 大將
Dali 大理
Dali Si 大理寺
Daming Palace 大明宮
Daming Temple 大明寺
Dangchang Wang 宕昌王

Dangxiang 黨項
Dao de jing 道德經
Daoan 道安
Daohang 道航
Dashi 大食
Dashuai 大率
Da Tang 大唐
Da Tang Kaiyuan zhanjing 大唐開元占經
Da Tang liudian 大唐六典
Da Tang Xiyu ji 大唐西域記
Dawo 大倭
Daxing Cheng 大興城
Dayuezhi 大月氏
Dazai Headquarters 大宰府
de 德
deng 等
Dengzhou (in Henan province) 鄧州
Dengzhou (in Shandong province) 登州
denko 傳戶
Dezong 德宗
Di (error for name of Emperor Daizong) 迪
Di (nomads in northern China) 狄
dianfu 甸服
Dianke Shu 典客署
didie 遞牒
die 牒
diguo 敵國
Dihuang 地皇
dili 地理
Dōji 道慈
dokutei sen 獨底船
Dong Han Zhi 東漢直
Dong Tianhuang 東天皇
Dōshō 道照
Du Yan 杜淹
Duan Yanger 段楊爾
Duanzhou 端州
duice 對策
Duima 對馬
Duke of Xi 鄎公
Duolisibigu 多利斯比古
Duting 都亭
Eastern Han 東漢
Eastern Jin 東晉
ebisu 夷
Echizen 越前
Emishi 蝦夷
enban 遠蕃
Enchin kankei bunsho 圓珍關係文書
Enchin 圓珍
Enichi 惠日
Ennin 圓仁
Enryakuji 延曆寺
er Wang 二王
Er ya 爾雅
eryi 而已
Etchū 越中
fachi 發敕
Fahua jing 法華經
Fahua Temple 法華寺
fan 蕃
Fan Ye 範曄
fanfu 蕃服
fanguo 蕃國
fanjun 蕃君
fanwang 蕃望
Fanyang 范陽
feibai 飛白
Feng Ao 封敖
Feng Changqing 封常清
Fengyi 豐邑
Fengzhong 奉終
Former Yan 前燕
Fucai 阜財
Fuguo jiangjun 輔國將軍
Fujiwara no Ason Kanō 藤原朝臣賀能
Fujiwara no Fuhito 藤原不比等
Fujiwara no Kadonomaro 藤原葛野麻呂

Fujiwara no Kiyokawa 藤原清河 (706–778)

Fujiwara no Kuzunomaro. *See* Fujiwara no Kadonomaro

Fujiwara no Matsukage 藤原松影

Fujiwara no Momokawa 藤原百川

Fujiwara no Sadatoshi 藤原真敏

Fujiwara no Sukeyo 藤原佐世

Fujiwara no Tamaro 藤原田麻呂

Fujiwara no Tanetsugu 藤原種繼

Fujiwara no Tasuke 藤原助

Fujiwara no Teika 藤原定家

Fujiwara no Tsunetsugu 藤原常嗣

Fujiwara no Umakai 藤原宇合

Fukui 福井

Fukuoka 福岡

funadana 船棚

fuquan 符券

Furu 布留

fusang 扶桑

Fuse no Ason Kiyonao 布勢朝臣清直

Fushō 普照

Fuxing 輔興

Fuzhou 福州

gaiban 外蕃

Gangōji engi 元興寺緣起

Ganjin. *See* Jianzhen

gao 告

Gao Anmao 高安茂

Gao Biaoren 高表仁

Gao Helin 高鶴林

Gao You 高誘

Gaochang 高昌

Gaozong (emperor) 高宗

Gaozu (emperor) 高祖

Genbō 玄昉

Genzaisho mokuroku 見在書目錄

Geshu Han 哥舒翰

gong 貢

Gong Zun 弓遵

gongcheng 宮城

Gongsun 公孫

gongxian 貢獻

Gongyue 弓月

Gonzō 勤操

Goon 吳音

Gotō 五島

Gou Jian 勾踐

Goudun shu 鉤盾署

Gounu. *See* Kunu

Great Liang 大梁

Great Yan 大燕

Great Zhou 大周

guan 館

guan fengsu 觀風俗

Guangling 廣陵

Guangling (prince) 廣陵王

Guanglu Si 光祿寺

Guangping (prince) 廣平王

Guangzhou 廣州

Guanjun jiangjun 冠軍將軍

guanyi 館驛

Guanzi 管子

guidao 鬼道

guixian 歸獻

gun 郡

guo 國

Guo Wuzong 郭務悰

Guo Ziyi 郭子儀

Guoqing Temple 國清寺

guosuo 過所

guowang 國王

guoxin 國信

guoxin biegong 國信別貢

guozhu 國主

Guozi Jian 國子監

guxi 姑洗

Hainan 海南

Haizhou 海州

Hakata 博多

Hakuri no Yoshimaro 羽栗吉麻呂

Hakusonkō 白村江

Han Wei Nuguo Wang 漢委奴國王

Han Wudi 漢武帝

Han Zhaodi 漢昭帝
Han Zhixing 韓智興
Hanfei zi 韓非子
Hangzhou 杭州
hanka 反歌
Hanlin daizhao 翰林待詔
Hanlin xueshiyuan jiugui 翰林學士院
    舊規
Hanyuan Hall 含元殿
Hanzei 反正
haotian 顥天
Harima 播磨
Harima Hayatori 播磨速鳥
Hata 秦
Hata no Ōmaro 秦大麻呂
Hayato 隼人
Hebei 河北
Heguri no Ason Hironari 平群朝臣
    廣成
Heiankyō 平安京
Heika. *See* Bixia
Heiyi Dashi 黑衣大食
Henan 河南
Heneng. *See* Kanō
Hengjie 橫街
Hequan 閤勸
Hetian 和田
Hexi Wang 河西王
Hezhi 荷知
Himiko 卑彌呼
hina ヒナ
Hitachi 常陸
Hitachi fudoki 常陸風土記
Hizan 肥前
Hōki 寶龜
Hokkaidō 北海道
Honchō genzaisho mokuroku 本朝見在書
    目錄
Honchō shojaku mokuroku 本朝書籍目錄
Hong Zun 洪遵
Hongjian 鴻漸
Hongjing 弘景

honglu 鴻臚
Honglu Si 鴻臚寺
Honshū 本州
houfu 侯服
Hu Bochong 胡伯崇
huang 皇
huang yu sun ming 皇御孫命
huangcheng 皇城
huangdi 皇帝
huangfu 荒服
Huangfu Dongchao 皇甫東朝
Huangfu Shengnü 皇甫昇女
huanghua 皇花
Huanghui 黃麾
huangzhong 黃鍾
Huayan jing 華嚴經
Hui (King of Liang) 惠
Hui (Korean tribe) 濊
Huiguo 惠果
Huisi 惠思
Hyūga 日向
i 夷
Ichijō 一條
ihō 異邦
Iki 壹岐
Iki no Muraji Hakatoko 伊吉連博德
Illig 頡利
Ingyō 允恭
Inukami no Mitasuki 犬上御田鍬
irō shōsho 慰勞詔書
iru いる
Ise 伊勢
Ishikawa no Ason Michimasu 石川朝
    臣道益
Isonokami no Otomaro 石上乙麻呂
Isonokami no Yakatsugu 石上宅嗣
    (729–781)
Itafuri no Kamatsuka 板振鎌束
iteki 夷狄
Iwabuchi Temple 石淵寺
iwaku 曰
Iwazaki Bunko 岩崎文庫

Iyo 伊予

Izanagi 伊弉諾

Izanami 伊弉冉

Izumo 出雲

ji (abbreviation for Emperor Ingyō's first name) 濟

ji (halter) 羈

Ji jiu pian 急就篇

Ji Qiaorong 紀喬容

jia 假

jia Honglu qing 假鴻臚卿

Jia Wowang 假倭王

Jiabu langzhong yuanwailang 駕部郎中員外郎

jiajue 假爵

jiali (current subofficial functionary) 假吏

jiali (raise the level of reception) 加禮

Jialuo 加羅

Jialuoshe 加羅舍

Jiang Huan 蔣渙

Jiangdong Circuit 江東道

jiangjun 將軍

Jiangzuo Jian 將作監

Jianjiao Taichangqing 檢較太常卿

Jiankang 建康

Jiankun 堅昆

jianmu 監牧

Jiannan 劍南

Jianzhen 鑑真

Jianzhong 建中

jiao xiang li 交相利

jiaoshu 校書

jiaoza 交雜

Jiaozhi 交趾

jiapin 假品

jiashou (acting grand protector) 假守

jiashou (grant temporarily) 假授

jie 節

jie ju 介居

Jiji Temple 既濟寺

jimi 羈縻

jimi zhi yi li wu buda 羈縻之義禮無不答

jin (Chinese unit of weight) 斤

jin (music of northern barbarians) 禁

jin (protocol) 覲

jin (present) 進

Jin (265–420) 晋

Jin (State of) 晋

Jin Heiei 甚兵衛

Jin Lansun 金蘭蓀

Jin Renwen 金仁問

Jincheng 金成

Jindi 金堤

jinduan se 禁斷色

Jingang jie 金剛界

Jingangzhi 金剛智

jingbai 敬白

jingwen 敬問

Jinjikan 神祇官

jinqi 謹啟

Jinsi 金肆

Jinwu Wei 金吾衛

Jisetsu Taishi 持節大使

Jitō 持統

jiu 舅

jiubin li 九賓禮

jiufu 九服

jiuye 九野

Jiyi ji 集異記

jō 戎

Jōgū shōtoku hōō teisetsu 上宮聖德法王帝說

Jōyo. *See* Chengyu

ju (to live) 居

ju (superior) 巨

Ju Tang 巨唐

juan 卷

Juegang 掘港

jueyu 絕域

jun 郡

juntian 鈞天

juru bielu 具如別錄

Juten 儒典
ka 華
kado 華土
Kaifūsō 懷風藻
Kaihuang 開皇
Kaiyuan Temple 開元寺
kaka 華夏
Kammu 桓武
Kamo 賀茂
Kamunabi no Mahito Kiyono 甘南真
　人清野
Kan 韓
kana 假名
Kangguo 康國
kanji 漢字
Kanō 賀能
Kao Anmu. *See* Gao Anmao
Kara 加羅
Karakuni 韓國
karano 枯野
Kasa no Kanamura 笠金村
Kashiwade no Ōoka 膳大丘
Kasuga 春日
Kawabe no Maro 河邊麻呂
Kawabe no Sakamaro 川部酒麻呂
Kawachi no Aya no Ōmaro 西漢
　大麻呂
Kegon kanteiki 華嚴刊定記
Keikō 景行
Keikokushū 經國集
keishi 輕使
ken Tō shissetsushi 遣唐持節使
Ki no Mitsu 紀三津
Kibi no Makibi 吉備真備
kimi 君
Kinai 畿內
Kishi no Nagani 吉士長丹
Kitano 北野
Kiyokawa 清川
Kiyomi 清海
Kiyonao. *See* Xingneng
Kiyono 清野

Kiyowara no Toshikage 清原俊蔭
Kiyowara no Yorinari 清原賴業
Kō Gentaku 高元度
Kōbō Daishi 弘法大師
Kōbō nimo fude no ayamari 弘法にも
　筆の誤り
Koguryŏ 高勾麗
Kōken 孝謙
kokishi 王
Kōko nichiroku 考古日錄
Kong Xuanfu 孔宣父
Kōnosu Hayao 鴻巢隼雄
koshi 越
kōtei. *See* huangdi
koten 古點
kugatachi 盟神探湯
Kujō no Kanezane 九條兼實
Kūkai 空海
Kume no Wakume 久米連若賣
kundoku 訓讀
Kunlun 崑侖
kunten 訓點
Kunu 狗奴
Kunyue 崑越
Kyerim (commander of) 雞林總管
Kyoga. *See* Chejia
Kyūshū 九州
laichao 來朝
Laizhou 萊州
Lantian 藍田
Laozi 老子
Later Tang 後唐
Lelang 樂浪
li 里
Li Bai 李白
Li Fawan 李法琬
Li Gui 李軌
Li Hua 李華
Li ji 禮記
Li Linfu 李林甫
Li Longji 李隆基
Li Shen 李紳

Li Shigu 李師古
Li Shimin 李世民
Li Xiu 李秀
Li Yanshou 李延壽
Li Yong 李邕
Li Yuan 李淵
Li Yuanhuan 李元環
Liang Wendi 梁文帝
Liangyi Hall 兩儀殿
Liangyun Shu 良醖署
Liangzhou 涼州
lianyi yi zhiyi 聯夷以制夷
Libin Yuan 禮賓院
lihe shi 離合詩
lin 鄰
Lingnan 嶺南
lingqu 領取
linguo 鄰國
lingye 領也
Lingyou 靈祐
lingzhi 領之
Lintun 臨屯
linxuan 臨軒
Linyi 林邑
Linzong (李)林宗
lishu youwo 禮數優渥
Liu Mao 劉茂
Liu Renyuan 劉仁願
Liu Xia 劉夏
Liu Xiu 劉秀
Liu Yu 劉裕
Liuqiu 流求
Longmen Grottoes 龍門石窟
Longyou 隴右
lu (official salary) 祿
Lu (state) 魯
Lu Deming 陸德明
Lu Rujin 盧如津
Lu Zhi 陸贄
Lun yu 論語
lunshi chishu 論事敕書
Luo 洛

Luoyang 洛陽
Luzhou 潞州
Ma Duanlin 馬端臨
Ma Qingchao 馬清朝
Ma Zong 馬總
Mahan 馬韓
manfu 蠻服
manyi zhidi 蠻夷之邸
man'yōgana 萬葉假名
Man'yōshū 萬葉集
mashimashite ましまして
mashimasu まします
matsu 待つ
Matsuchi Mountain 真土山
Matsura 松浦
Matsura no miya monogatari 松浦宮
　　物語
mei 䅗
Meng Huizhi 孟惠芝
Menxia Sheng 門下省
Menxia shizhong 門下侍中
mi 縻
Miantu guo 面土國
Miaofa lianhua jing 妙法蓮花經
Michinoku 陸奧
Mikado 御門
Mimana 任那
Mimasaka 美作
Mimune no Imatsugu 三棟今嗣
min 民
Minamoto no Shitagō 源順
Mine no Masato 岑萬里
Ming (emperor) 明帝
mingshen 明神
Mingshen yuyu Riben tianhuang
　　zhaozhi 明神御宇日本天皇詔旨
Mingshen yuyu Riben Zhu ming le
　　mei yu de jingbai Da Tang huangdi
　　明神御宇日本主明樂美御德敬白大
　　唐皇帝
Mingzhou 明州
Mishu Jian 祕書監

Mitsu 三津

Mizuhawake 瑞齒別

Mochuo 默啜

Mohe 靺鞨

Monjō Tokugyōsei 文章得業生

moro 諸

moroki fune 母慮紀舟

Mt. Kunlun 崑崙山

Mt. Long 隴山

Mt. Tairyū 大瀧嶽

Mt. Tiantai 天臺山

Mt. Wuling 五嶺

mouwu 某物

Mozi 墨子

Mozi 墨子

Muhan 慕韓

Muroto Cape 室戶崎

muyi 慕義

Myōgyō Hakase 明經博士

Nagamine no Takana 長岑高名

Nagaoka 長岡

Nagaya (prince) 長屋王

nai youguo zhi buke fei zhe 乃有國之
    不可廢者

naiki 內記

Naitō Konan 內藤湖南 (1866–1934)

Naka no Mahito Ihatomo 仲真人石伴

Nakatomi 中臣

Nakatomi no Ason Nashiro 中臣朝臣
    名代

Nakatomi no Takanushi 中臣鷹主

Nakatsukasashō 中務省

Namba 難波

Nanbu xinshu 南部新書

nanfu 男服

Naniwa. *See* Namba

Nanyi 南裔

Nanyue 南越

Nanzhao 南詔

Nara 奈良

Nashōme 難昇米

neidian 內典

Nihon shoki 日本書紀

Nihonkoku genzaisho mokuroku 日本國
    見在書目錄

Nimmyō 仁明

Ningbo 寧波

Nintoku 仁德

Nishijima Sadao 西島定生

Northern Wei 北魏

nu 怒

Nuguo 奴國

nyūban shi 入蕃使

Ō no Yasumaro 太安萬呂

Ō Tokyū Kinen Bunko 大東急紀念
    文庫

Ōasa Tsumawakuko no Sukune 雄朝
    津間稚子宿彌

Ogihara Asao 荻原淺男

Ōhatsuse no wakatakeru 大泊瀨幼武

Ōjin 應神 (r. 270–309)

Oki 隱岐

ōkimi 大君

Ōkimi Ametarashihiko. *See* abei jimi
    amei duolisibigu

Ōmi 近江

Ono 小野

Ono no Imoko 小野妹子

Ono no Iwane 小野石根

Ono no Takamura 小野篁

Osaka 大阪

Ōsaki 大崎

Ōsazaki 大鷦鷯

Ōtarashihikooshirowake 大足彥忍
    代別

Ōtomo 大伴

Ōtomo no Furumaro 大伴古麻呂

Ōtsu 大津

Ouyang Xun 歐陽詢

Ōyashima no kuni 大八洲國

Paekche 百濟

pan 判

Parhae 渤海

Pei Ju 裴矩

Pei Shiqing 裴世清
Penglai 蓬萊
pin 聘
Pingkang 平康
pipa 琵琶
Pugu Huaien 樸固懷恩
qaghan 可汗
Qapaghan. *See* Mochuo
qi (write) 啓
Qi (479–502) 齊
Qi (a warring state) 齊
qianshu 遣書
Qianzi wen 千字文
Qidan 契丹
Qimin. *See* Yami
Qin 秦
Qin fu 秦府
Qin Shihuang 秦始皇
Qin Wei Wowang 親魏倭王
Qin Yanqi 秦衍期
qing 卿
qingli 請吏
Qinglong Temple 青龍寺
Qingyi lu 清異錄
Qinhan 秦韓
qirong 七戎
Quanzhou 泉州
qucheng 曲成
Rajōmon 羅城門
Reizei In 冷泉院
ren 任
Riben 日本
Riben Zhu ming le mei yu de jingbai
   Da Tang huangdi 日本主明樂美御
   德敬白大唐皇帝
Riben Zhu ming le mei yu de 日本主
   明樂美御德
Ridong 日東
rinkoku 鄰國
Ron 戎
Rouran 柔然
Ruhai 如海

Ryō no gige 令義解
Ryūkyū 流求
Sa Hongke 薩弘恪
Sabi 泗沘
Sado 佐渡
Saeki 佐伯
Saeki no Imaemishi 佐伯今毛人
Saga (prefecture) 佐賀
Saga (r. 809–823) 嵯峨
Sagami 相模
Sakaibe 阪合布
Sakaibe no Ishinuno 阪合布石布
Sakaibe no Iwatsumi 阪合布石積
Sakaibe no Ōkida 阪合布大分
Sakiyama 榮山
sakuhō taisei 冊封體制
Sangō shiiki 三教指歸
sangong 三公
sanguan 散官
sanyue 散樂
sei 西
seido 西土
seikai 西海
Seimu 成務
semmyō 宣命
semu rubie 色目如別
sen 宣
setsu 節
settō 節刀
shakui 借位
Shang shu 尚書
shangguo 上國
Shangjiezan 尚結贊
shangke 上客
Shanwuwei 善無畏
shanyu 單于
Shayuan Directorate 沙苑監
shehui liao 設會料
Shen Weiyue 沈惟岳
Shen Yue 沈約
sheng 甥
shengliao 生料

Shengman jing 勝鬘經

Shengping 昇平

Shengwu 聖武

sheshi liao 設食料

shi (ambassador) 使

shi (missing character from Pei
    Shiqing's name) 世

Shi (name of Prince of Yong) 適

Shi Chaoyi 史朝義

Shi jing 詩經

Shi You 史游

Shibi 始畢

shidie 食牒

shijie 使節

Shikanoshima 志賀島

Shikoku 四國

Shimousa 下總

Shingon 真言

Shishinden 紫宸殿

shoban 諸蕃

Shoku Nihon kōki 續日本後紀

shōnaiki 少內記

Shōtoku (prince) 聖德太子

Shōtoku Taishi denryaku 聖德太子傳曆

shou 授

shouliao 熟料

shu 書

Shuaishan Jiaoyu 率善校尉

Shuaishan Zhonglang Jiang 率善中郎
    將

Shuaizhong Wang 率眾王

shuchō 主帳

shuchong 殊寵

Shugei Shuchi In 綜藝種智院

Shuhan 蜀漢

shuli 殊禮

Shun 舜

Shunzong 順宗

shusi 殊私

shuyi 書儀

Sibin Si 司賓寺

sibing 司兵

sidi guan 私覿官

sidi wu 私覿物

silin 四鄰

Sima Dewen 司馬德文

Sima Qian 司馬遷

Sima Yan 司馬炎

Sinong qing 司農卿

Sinong Si 司農寺

Sishan Si 司膳寺

Sishan Yuanwai Lang 司膳員外郎

Siyi Shu 司儀署

So Inkō 蘇因高

Southern Liang 南梁

Southern Qi 南齊

Southern Song 南宋

Southern Tang 南唐

Sugawara no Kajinari 菅原尾成

Sugawara no Kiyotomo 菅原清公

Sugawara no Michizane 菅原道真

Sugawara no Yoshinushi 菅原善主

Sui 隋

Sui Wendi 隋文帝

Suifu 綏服

Suiko 推古 (r. 593–628)

Suishō 帥升

Sukeyo roku 佐世錄

Sun Xingjin 孫興進

Suō 秦王(國)

Suzhou 蘇州

Suzong 肅宗

Tachibana no Hayanari 橘逸勢

tai banshi shō 對蕃使詔

Taiheira 大平良

Taihuang 泰皇

Taiji Hall 太極殿

Taipu Si 太僕寺

Taishan 泰山

Taishang Tianhuang 太上天皇

taishi 大使

Taizang Jie 胎藏界

Taizhou 臺州

Taizong (emperor) 太宗

Tajihi no Mahito Agatamori 多治比真人縣守

Tajihi no Mahito Hironari 多治比真人廣成

Takada no Nemaro 高田根麻呂

Takamuko no Genri 高向玄理

Tamba 丹波

Tamna 耽羅

Tan Yangni. *See* Duan Yanger

Tane 多褹

Tang 唐

Tang xiaoxi 唐消息

Tang zhiyan 唐摭言

Tara. *See* Tamna

Tarashinakatsuhiko 足仲彦

Tatara 蹈鞴

tei 帝

Tejin 特進

Tenchō 天長

Teng 滕

tenshi. *See* tianzi

Ti Jun 梯儁

tianer 天兒

Tianhou 天后

Tianhuang 天皇

Tianmu 天睦

tianshu 天書

tianzi 天子

Tianzi xinbao 天子信寶

Tianzi xingbao 天子行寶

Tianzi zhibao 天子之寶

tiao 調

Tiaoyin 調音

tōban 遠蕃

toburafu 聘

Tōdaiji 東大寺

Tōji 東寺

Toji Gori 都市牛利

Tokunoshima 德之島

Tong Garrison 潼關

tong qiju 通起居

tongqi 銅契

Tongshang 通商

Tōō 唐王

Tōon 唐音

Tosa 土佐

Tōshōdaiji 唐招提寺

Touma 投馬

Toyo mike kashikiya hime 豐御食炊屋姬

Tsubasa 翼

Tsukushi 筑紫

Tsumori no Kiza 津守吉祥

Tsushima 對馬(都斯麻)

Tudi jia 土地家

Tufan 吐蕃

Tuhuoluo 吐火羅

Tuqishi 突騎施

Tuyuhun 吐谷渾

Ujitada 氏忠

Utsubo monogatari 宇津保物語

Wa. *See* Wo

Wada (port) 輪田

waizhai 外宅

Waka tarashi hiko 稚足彦

wang 王

Wang Changling 王昌齡

Wang Dao 王導

Wang Guofu 王國父

Wang Jun 王駿

Wang Liugui 王柳貴

Wang ming le mei yu de 王明樂美御德

Wang Qiu 王丘

Wang Ren 王仁

Wang Wei 王維

Wang Weijing 王維倩

Wang Xianzhi 王獻之

Wang Xiu 王秀

Wang Xiyi 王希逸

Wang Xizhi 王羲之

Wang Yuanzhong 王元仲

Wangcheng Guo 王城國

wangyan 王言

Wanikishi 和邇吉師

Wannian 萬年

Washū 和臭

Wazui 倭隋
Wei Xu 韋頊
Wei Zheng 魏征
Wei zhi 魏志
wei (prestige) 威
wei (grant a Chinese title formally) 為
Wei (220–265) 魏
weibin 未賓
Weicheng dianxun 維城典訓
weifu 衛服
weiguo 微國
weilao zhishu 慰勞制書
Weimo jing 維摩經
Weiwei Qing 衛尉卿
weiyuan ying 威遠營
wen 問
Wen xuan 文選
Wencheng (princess) 文成公主
Wenguan cilin 文館詞林
Wenlin Lang 文林郎
wenshu 文書
Wenxuan Wang 文宣王
Wenzhou 溫州
Wenzong 文宗
Western Han 西漢
Western Jin 西晉
Western Zhou 西周
Wo 倭
Wo Zan 倭讚
Wonari 乎那利
Wowang 倭王
Wowang Shizi Xing 倭王世子興
Wowang Zhen 倭王珍
Wu (220–280) 吳
Wu (abbreviation for first name of Emperor Yūryaku) 武
Wu (emperor) 武帝
Wu Huaishi 吳懷實
Wu Lingguang 吳令光
Wu Shaocheng 吳少誠
Wu Shuier 吾稅兒
Wu Zetian 武則天

Wudu Wang 武都王
wufu 五服
wuse zhao 五色詔
Wuwei 武威
wuyang 無恙
Xi Han Zhi 西漢直
Xi Huangdi 西皇帝
Xi Tujue 西突厥
xiaguo 下國
Xiajiasi 黠戛斯
xiake 下客
Xian 咸
xiang 餉
xiangli 相利
Xiangyan 祥彥
Xiangyang 襄陽
Xianyang 咸陽
Xiao Bolü 小勃律
Xiao jing 孝經
xiao xue 小學
Xiao Yingshi 蕭穎士
xieben 寫本
Xiematai 邪馬臺
Xieyu Guo 謝颶國
Ximing Temple 西明寺
Xin 新
Xing 興
xing cuo di 刑厝帝
xing wang 行王
Xingneng 興能
Xiongnu 匈奴
Xiqiang 西羌
xishu 璽書
xiucai 秀才
Xu Di 徐逖
Xu Fu 徐福
Xu Gongqing 徐公卿
xu mai liang mei ji zhi 須賣良美己止
xu mai mi ma nai mei ji deng 須賣禰麻乃美己等
xu ming le mei yu de 須明樂美御德
Xu Shouyan 續守言

Xuanhe jigu yinshi 宣和集古印史
Xuanping 宣平
xuantian 玄天
Xuantu 玄菟
Xuanyang 宣陽
Xuanzang 玄奘
Xuanzheng Hall 宣政殿
Xuanzong (r. 712–756) 玄宗
Xuanzong (r. 846–859) 宣宗
Xue 薛
Xue Deng 薛登
Xueyantuo 薛延佗
*Xukongzang pusa nengman zhuyuan
    zuishengxin tuoluoni qiuwen chifa*
    虛空藏菩薩能滿諸願最勝心陀羅尼
    求聞持法
ya 八
Yaku 掖久
Yakushi Enichi 藥師惠日
Yamanoue no Okura 山上憶良
Yamashiro 山城
Yamatai. *See* Xiematai
Yamato 倭
Yamato no Kuni 倭國
Yamato no Nagaoka 大和長岡
Yami 啟民
Yan Jimei 閻濟美
Yan Shigu 顏師古
Yan Zhenqing 顏真卿
Yan Ziqin 晏子欽
Yancheng 鹽城
Yang (emperor) 煬帝
Yang Guifei 楊貴妃
Yan Ju 楊鉅
Yang Yan 楊炎
yangtian 陽天
Yangu 延酷
Yangzhou 揚州
Yanqi 焉耆
Yanshou 延壽
yantian 炎天
Yao 堯
yaofu 要服

yashima 八洲
Yellow Emperor 黃帝
yi (barbarians) 夷
yi (relay service) 驛
yi (righteousness) 義
yi … wei 以…為
yi yidai shui 一衣帶水
Yicao 義操
Yicheng 宜城
Yidu 伊都
yifu 夷服
yiguan 驛官
yima 驛馬
yingke shi 迎客使
Yinhua lu 因話錄
yinshu 印書
Yinyang 陰陽
Yiqi. *See* Iki
yisha 義殺
yishu 遺書
yitian 驛田
Yixing 義興
yizhang 驛長
yizhuan 驛傳
yizi 驛子
Yōei 榮叡
Yong (prince) 雍王
Yongchun 永淳
yoriite 介居
Yōrō Code 養老令
yoru よる
Yoshida no Yoroshi 吉田宜
Yoshinogari 吉野ケ里
yotsu no fune 四舶
youlao 優勞
youli 優禮
youtian 幽天
Youzhou 幽州
Yu Xiulie 于休烈
Yuan (emperor) 元帝
Yuan Jinqing 袁晉卿
Yuan Zhen 元稹
Yuanhe 元和

Yue 越
yueling 月令
Yuelü 樂律
Yuezhi 月氏
Yuezhou 越州
Yuki no Muraji Hakatoko 伊吉連博德
Yumen Guan 玉門關
Yunhui jiangjun 雲麾將軍
Yunjing 曇靖
Yunnan 雲南
Yūryaku 雄略
yuyu 御宇
Zangge 牂牁
zeiiki 絕域
zhang 章
Zhang Chujin 張楚金
Zhang Daoguang 張道光
Zhang Ji 張籍
Zhang Jiuling 張九齡
Zhang rGyal tsan. *See* Shangjiezan
Zhang Shoujie 張守節
Zhang Yue 張說
Zhang Zhi 張芝
Zhang Zhuo 張鷟
Zhanghuai (prince) 章懷太子
zhangke 掌客
Zhangye 張掖
Zhangyun Shu 掌醞署
Zhao Baoying 趙寶英
Zhao Xuanmo 趙玄默
Zhen 珍
Zhenfan 真番
zhenfu 鎮服
Zheng Ren 鄭壬
Zhenglu jiangjun 征虜將軍
zhengzhang 爭長
Zhengzhou 鄭州
Zhenla 真臘
Zhenxiu shu 珍饈署
Zhenzhou 振州
zhi (dictation) 制
zhi (send) 致

Zhifang langzhong 職方郎中
Zhishang 治觴
zhishu (dictation) 制書
zhishu (send a letter) 致書
zhongfan 中蕃
Zhongshu Menxia 中書門下
Zhongshu shilang 中書侍郎
Zhou 周
Zhou Xingsi 周興嗣
Zhoushan 舟山
zhu 柷
Zhu Ci 朱泚
zhu ming le mei yu de 主明樂美御德
Zhu Qiancheng 朱千乘
Zhu Shaorui 朱少瑞
zhu shifu 竹使符
Zhu Zheng 朱政
zhuan 傳
zhuandie 傳牒
zhuandui 專對
zhuanma 傳馬
zhuanzhi guan 專知官
zhufu 竹符
zhufu tongqi ben bei jianzha 竹符銅
    契本備奸詐
zhuli 株離
Zhuque Jie 朱雀街
zhutian 朱天
zhuyue 諸越
Zichen Hall 紫宸殿
zijia 自假
Ziqing 淄青
Zishu 字書
zongji 總集
zongli 總曆
zou 奏
Zuda 頭陀
Zuikei Shūhō 瑞溪周鳳
Zuo Buque 左補缺
Zuo Sanqi Changshi 左散騎常侍
Zuo Shiyi 左拾遺
Zuo zhuan 左傳

Bibliography

PRIMARY SOURCES AND WORKS OF
PRE-TWENTIETH-CENTURY SCHOLARSHIP

Bai Juyi 白居易. *Bai Juyi ji* 白居易集. Beijing: Zhonghua Shuju, 1979.

———. *Bai Kong liutie* 白孔六帖. Song edition. Facsimile rpt. Taibei: Xinxing Shuju, 1969.

———. *Baishi changqing ji* 白氏長慶集. *SBCK* edition.

———. *Baishi liutie shilei ji* 白氏六帖事類集. Southern Song edition. Facsimile rpt. Beijing: Wenwu Chubanshe, 1987.

Bai Xingjian 白行簡. *Li wa zhuan* 李娃傳. *Tangren xiaoshuo* edition. Hong Kong: Zhonghua Shuju, 1985.

Ban Gu 班固. *Baihu tongde lun* 白虎通德論. *SBCK* edition.

———. *Han shu* 漢書. Beijing: Zhonghua Shuju, 1962.

Cai Yong 蔡邕. *Du duan* 獨斷. *SBCK* edition.

Chen Pengnian 陳彭年. *Guang yun* 廣韻. *SBBY* edition.

Chen Shou 陳壽. *San guo zhi* 三國志. Beijing: Zhonghua Shuju, 1959.

Chen Zhensun 陳振孫. *Zhizhai shulu jieti* 直齋書錄解題. Shanghai: Shanghai Guji Chubanshe, 1987.

Cheng Hongzhao 程鴻詔. *Tang liangjing chengfang kao jiaobu ji* 唐兩京城坊考校補記. In *Tang liangjing chengfang kao*. Beijing: Zhonghua Shuju, 1985.

Chunqiu Zuoshi zhuan 春秋左氏傳. Attributed to Zuo Qiuming 左丘明. *SSJZS* edition.

Chūshi shō 柱史抄. Rpt. in vol. 106 of *Gunsho ruijū*. Tokyo: Zoku Gunsho Ruijū Kanseikai, 1939–1943.

Cui Zhiyuan 崔致遠. *Guiyuan bigeng ji* 桂苑筆耕集. *SBCK* edition.

Dairi shiki 大裏式. Ninth century. Rpt. in vol. 33 of *Zōho kojitsu sōsho*. Tokyo: Meiji Tosho Shuppan Kabushiki Kaisha, 1954.

Daoshi 道世. *Fayuan zhulin* 法苑珠林. *SBCK* edition.

Ding Du 丁度. *Ji yun* 集韻. Shanghai: Shanghai Guji Chubanshe, 1985.

Dong Gao 董誥. *Quan Tang wen* 全唐文. Taibei: Dahua Shuju, 1987.

Dou Yi 竇儀 et al. *Song xingtong* 宋刑統. Tianyige edition. Rpt. Beijing: Zhongguo Shudian, 1990.

Du Mu 杜牧. *Fanchuan wenji* 樊川文集. *SBCK* edition.

Du You 杜佑. *Tong dian* 通典. *Shitong* edition. Shanghai: Shangwu Yinshuguan, 1935. Beijing: Zhonghua Shuju, 1984, reprint.

Duan Anjie 段安節. *Yuefu zalu* 樂府雜錄. *Siku quanshu* edition.

Duan Chengshi 段成式. *Youyang zazu* 酉陽雜俎. *SBCK* edition.

Dugu Ji 獨孤及. *Piling ji* 毗陵集. *SBCK* edition.

Ennin 圓仁. *Nittō guhō junrei kōki* 入唐求法巡禮行記. Taibei: Wenhai Chubanshe, 1971.

Er ya 爾雅. Annotated by Guo Pu 郭璞. *SSJZS* edition.

Fan Ye 範曄. *Hou Han shu* 後漢書. Beijing: Zhonghua Shuju, 1973.

Fang Bao 方苞. *Fang Wangxi quanji* 方望溪全集. Taibei: Xinlu Shuju, 1963.

Fang Risheng 方日升. *Gujin yunhui juyao xiaobu* 古今韻會舉要小補. 1606 edition.

Fang Xuanling 房玄齡 et al., comps. *Jin shu* 晉書. Beijing: Zhonghua Shuju, 1974.

Feng Zhi 馮贄. *Yunxian sanlu* 雲仙散錄. Beijing: Zhonghua Shuju, 1998.

Fujiwara no Fuhito 藤原不比等 et al., comps. *Ritsu* 律. Rpt. in vol. 1 of *Shintei zōho kokushi taikei*. Tokyo: Yoshikawa Kōbunkan, 1964.

———. *Ritsuryō* 律令. Rpt. in vol. 3 of *Nihon shisō taikei*. Tokyo: Iwanami Shoten, 1976.

Fujiwara no Fuyutsugu 藤原冬嗣 et al., comps. *Bunka shūreishū* 文華秀麗集. Rpt. in vol. 69 of *Nihon koten bungaku taikei*. Tokyo: Iwanami Shoten, 1964.

Fujiwara no Mototsune 藤原基經 et al., comps. *Nihon Montoku Tennō jitsuroku* 日本文德天皇實錄. Rpt. in vol. 3 of *Shintei zōho kokushi taikei*. Tokyo: Yoshikawa Kōbunkan, 1934.

Fujiwara no Otsugu 藤原緒嗣 et al., comps. *Nihon kōki* 日本後紀. Rpt. in vol. 3 of *Shintei zōho kokushi taikei*. Tokyo: Yoshikawa Kōbunkan, 1934.

Fujiwara no Sanesuke 藤原實資. *Shōyūki* 小右記. Rpt. in vol. 10 of *Dai Nihon kokiroku*. Tokyo: Tokyo Daigaku Shiryō Hensanjo, 1959.

Fujiwara no Takanori 藤原孝範. *Meibūnshō* 明文抄. Rpt. in vol. 886 of *Zoku gunsho ruijū*. Tokyo: Zoku Gunsho Ruijū Kankōkai, 1928.

Fujiwara no Tokihira 藤原時平. *Engi shiki* 延喜式. Rpt. in vol. 26 of *Shintei zōho kokushi taikei*. Tokyo: Yoshikawa Kōbunkan, 1937.

Fujiwara no Tokihira et al., comps. *Nihon Sandai jitsuroku* 日本三代實錄. Rpt. in vol. 4 of *Shintei zōho kokushi taikei*. Tokyo: Yoshikawa Kōbunkan, 1934.

Fujiwara no Yoshifusa 藤原良房 et al., comps. *Shoku Nihon kōki* 續日本後紀. Rpt. in vol. 3 of *Shintei zōho kokushi taikei*. Tokyo: Yoshikawa Kōbunkan, 1934.

Gao Cheng 高承. *Shiwu jiyuan* 事物紀原. Taibei: Shangwu Yinshuguan, 1971.

Gao huangdi yuzhi wenji 高皇帝御制文集. Attributed to Zhu Yuanzhang 朱元璋. Edition of the Jiajing period (1522–1566).

Gongyang Gao 公羊高. *Chunqiu Gongyang zhuan* 春秋公羊傳. *SSJZS* edition.

Gu Yewang 顧野王. *Yu pian* 玉篇. *SBBY* edition.

Guliang Chi 穀梁赤. *Chunqiu Guliang zhuan* 春秋穀梁傳. *SSJZS* edition.

Guo Pu 郭璞. *Shan hai jing* 山海經. *SBCK* edition.

Guo yu 國語. Attributed to Zuo Qiuming 左秋明. *SBCK* edition.

Han Yu 韓愈. *Changli xiansheng ji* 昌黎先生集. *SBCK* edition.

———. *Changli xiansheng ji waiji* 昌黎先生集外集. *SBCK* edition.

———. *Han Changli quanji* 韓昌黎全集. *SBBY* edition.

———. *Shunzong shilu* 順宗實錄. *Haishan xianguan congshu* edition. Rpt. Taibei: Yiwen Yinshuguan, 1967.

Henan zhi 河南志. Yuan dynasty. Rpt. in *Song Yuan fangzhi congkan*. Beijing: Zhonghua Shuju, 1990.

Hitachi no kuni fudoki 常陸國風土記. Eighth century. Rpt. in vol. 2 of *Nihon koten bungaku taikei*, ed. Akimoto Kichirō 秋本吉郎. Tokyo: Iwanami Shoten, 1958.

Honchō monzui 本朝文粹. Attributed to Fujwara no Akihira 藤原明衡. *Nihon bunka taikei* edition. Tokyo: Kokumin Tosho Kabushiki Kaisha, 1925–1928.

Honchō shinsen den 本朝神仙傳. Rpt. in vol. 7 of *Nihon shisō taikei*, ed. Inoue Mitsusada et al. Tokyo: Iwanami Shoten, 1974.

Hong Mai 洪邁. *Rongzhai suibi* 容齋隨筆. *SBCK* edition.

Hong Zun 洪遵. *Hanyuan qunshu* 翰苑群書. *Zhibuzuzhai congshu* edition.

Huang Zunxian 黃遵憲. *Ribenguo zhi* 日本國志. Shanghai: Shanghai Shudian, 1902.

Huangfu Zeng 皇甫曾. *Tang Huangfu Zeng shiji* 唐皇甫曾詩集. *SBCK* edition.

Huili 惠立 and Yancong 彥悰. *Ta Ciensi Sanzang fashi zhuan* 大慈恩寺三藏法師傳. Beijing: Zhonghua Shuju, 1983.

Ichijima Kenkichi 市島謙吉, ed. *Honchō hōka monjo mokuroku* 本朝法家文書目錄. Rpt. in vol. 16 of *Zokuzoku gunsho ruijū*. Tokyo: Kokusho Kankōkai, 1909.

Ichikawa Seinei 市河市寧. *Quan Tang shi i* 全唐詩逸. In *Quan Tang shi*. Beijing: Zhonghua Shuju, 1960.

Il Yŏn 一然. *Samguk yusa* 三國遺事. Tokyo: Gakushuin Daigaku Tōyō Bunka Kenkyūjo, 1984.

Inbe no Hironari 齋部廣成. *Kogo shūi* 古語拾遺. Tokyo: Iwanami Shoten, 1985.

Itō Shō 伊藤松. *Rinkō chōsho* 鄰交征書. Tokyo: Kokusho Kankōkai, 1975.

Ji Yougong 計有功. *Tang shi jishi* 唐詩紀事. Beijing: Zhonghua Shuju, 1965.

Ji Yun 紀昀. *Siku quanshu* 四庫全書. 1781 edition. Facsimile rpt. Taibei: Taiwan Shangwu Yinshuguan, 1983.

Jia Changchao 賈昌朝. *Qunjing yinbian* 群經音辯. *SBCK* edition.

Kaifūsō 懷風藻. Eighth century. *Nihon koten bungaku taikei* edition. Tokyo: Yoshikawa Kōbunkan, 1964.

Keikai 景戒. *Nihon ryōiki* 日本靈異記. Rpt. in vol. 70 of *Nihon koten bungaku taikei*. Tokyo: Yoshikawa Kōbunkan, 1967.

Keiō 敬雄. *Kōbō daishi shō* 弘法大師抄. In *Tendai kahyō*, vol. 41 of *Dai Nihon bukkyō zensho*. Tokyo: Suzuki Gakujutsu Zaidan, 1970–1973.

Ki no Tsurayuki 紀貫之 et al., comps. *Kokin waka shū* 古今和歌集. Rpt. in vol. 8 of *Nihon koden bungaku taikei*. Tokyo: Iwanami Shoten, 1958.

Kim Pu-sik 金富軾. *Samguk sagi* 三國史記. Tokyo: Gakushuin Daigaku Tōyō Bunka Kenkyūjo, 1984.

Kiyohara no Natsuno 清原夏野 et al., comps. *Ryō no gige* 令義解. Rpt. in vol. 2 of *Shintei zōho kokushi taikei*. Tokyo: Yoshikawa Kōbunkan, 1964.

Kōbō Daishi Kūkai Zenshū Henshū Iinkai 弘法大師空海全集編輯委員會. *Kōbō daishi Kūkai zenshū* 弘法大師空海全集. Tokyo: Chikuma Shobō, 1984.

Kōbō Daishi Zenshū Henshū Iinkai 弘法大師全集編輯委員會. *Kōbō daishi zenshū* 弘法大師全集. Wakayama: Mikkyō Bunka Kenkyūjo, 1965–1968.

Kokin wakashū mokuroku 古今和歌集目錄. Attributed to Fujiwara no Nakazane 藤原仲實. Rpt. in vol. 285 of *Gunsho ruijū*, ed. Hanawa Hokiichi. Tokyo: Zoku Gunsho Ruijū Kanseikai, 1939–1943.

Kong Yingda 孔穎達. *Li ji zhengyi* 禮記正義. *SSJZS* edition.

———. *Mao shi zhengyi* 毛詩正義. *SSJZS* edition.

———. *Shang shu zhengyi* 尚書正義. *SSJZS* edition.

Kong Yingda et al. *Zhou yi zhengyi* 周易正義. *SSJZS* edition.

Konjaku monogatari shū 今昔物語集. Rpt. in vol. 24 of *Nihon koten bungaku taikei*, ed. Yamade Yoshio et al. Tokyo: Iwanami Shoten, 1984.

Koremune no Naomoto 惟宗直本. *Ryō no shūge* 令集解. Rpt. in vols. 3–5 of *Shintei zōho kokushi taikei*. Tokyo: Yoshikawa Kōbunkan, 1964.

Kujō no Kanezane 九條兼實. *Gyokuyō* 玉葉. Tokyo: Kokusho Kankōkai, 1906–1907.

Kūkai 空海. *Sangō shiiki* 三教指歸. Rpt. in vol. 71 of *Nihon koten bungaku taikei*. Tokyo: Iwanami Shoten, 1965.

———. *Seireishū* 性靈集. Rpt. in vol. 71 of *Nihon koten bungaku taikei*. Tokyo: Iwanami Shoten, 1965.

———. *Shūi zatsushū* 拾遺雜集. Rpt. in vol. 7 of *Kōbō daishi Kūkai zenshū*. Tokyo: Chikuma Shobō, 1984.

Lê Tắc 黎崱. *Annan zhilüe* 安南志略. Beijing: Zhonghua Shuju, 1995.

Li Bai 李白. *Li Taibai shi* 李太白詩. *SBCK* edition.

Li Deyu 李德裕. *Li Wenrao wenji* 李文饒文集. *SBCK* edition.

Li Fang 李昉. *Taiping guangji* 太平廣記. Beijing: Zhonghua Shuju, 1959.

———. *Taiping yulan* 太平御覽. *SBCK* edition.

———. *Wenyuan yinghua* 文苑英華. Beijing: Zhonghua Shuju, 1966.

Li Jifu 李吉甫. *Yuanhe junxian tuzhi* 元和郡縣圖志. Beijing: Zhonghua Shuju, 1983.

Li Linfu 李林甫. *Tang liudian* 唐六典. *Siku quanshu zhenben* edition. Taibei: Shangwu Yinshuguan, 1976.

Li Qunyu 李群玉. *Li Qunyu shiji* 李群玉詩集. *SBCK* edition.

Li Shangyin 李商隱. *Li Yishan wenji* 李義山文集. *SBCK* edition.

Li Tai 李泰. *Guadi zhi* 括地志. *Chongding Han Tang dili shuchao* edition.

Li Yanshou 李延壽. *Bei shi* 北史. Beijing: Zhonghua Shuju, 1974.

———. *Nan shi* 南史. Beijing: Zhonghua Shuju, 1975.

Li Yong 李邕. *Li Beihai quanshu* 李北海全書. Taibei: Yiwen Yinshuguan, 1968.

Li Zhao 李肇. *Hanlin zhi* 翰林志. *Baichuan xuehai* edition. Rpt. Taibei: Yiwen Yinshuguan, 1983.

———. *Tang guoshi bu* 唐國史補. Shanghai: Shanghai Guji Chubanshe, 1957.

Liang Zhangju 梁章鉅. *Chengwei lu* 稱謂錄. In vol. 2 of *Ming Qing suyu cishu jicheng*, ed. Nagasawa Kikuya. Tokyo: Kyūko Shoin, 1974.

———. *Langji congtan* 浪跡叢談. Beijing: Zhonghua Shuju, 1981.

———. *Langji xutan* 浪跡續談. Beijing: Zhonghua Shuju, 1981.

Lin Bao 林寶. *Yuanhe xingzuan* 元和姓纂. *Siku quanshu zhenben bieji* edition. Taibei: Shangwu Yinshuguan, 1975.

Liu An 劉安. *Huainan zi* 淮南子. *SBCK* edition.

Liu Changqing 劉長卿. *Liu Suizhou shiji* 劉隨州詩集. *SBCK* edition.

Liu Dabin 劉大彬. *Maoshan zhi* 茅山志. 1887 edition. Rpt. Taibei: Wenhai Chubanshe, 1971.

Liu Su 劉餗. *Da Tang xinyu* 大唐新語. Beijing: Zhonghua Shuju, 1984.

———. *Sui Tang jiahua* 隋唐嘉話. *Shuofu sanzhong* edition. Shanghai: Shanghai Guji Chubanshe, 1988.

Liu Xi 劉熙. *Shi ming* 釋名. *SBCK* edition.

Liu Xiang 劉向. *Xin xu* 新序. *SBCK* edition.

Liu Xu 劉煦 et al., comps. *Jiu Tang shu* 舊唐書. Beijing: Zhonghua Shuju, 1975.

Liu Yiqing 劉義慶. *Shishuo xinyu* 世說新語. *SBCK* edition.

Liu Yuxi 劉禹錫. *Liu Mengde wenji* 劉夢得文集. *SBCK* edition.

Liu Zongyuan 柳宗元. *Liu Hedong ji* 柳河東集. *SBCK* edition.

Lu Xinyuan 陸心源. *Tang wen shiyi* 唐文拾遺. Taibei: Dahua Shuju, 1987.

Lu Zhi 陸贄. *Tang Lu Xuangong hanyuan ji* 唐陸宣公翰苑集. *SBCK* edition.

Lü Buwei 呂不韋. *Lüshi chunqiu* 呂氏春秋. *SBCK* edition.

Lü Wen 呂溫. *Lü Heshu wenji* 呂和叔文集. *SBCK* edition.

Luo Jun 羅濬. *Baoqing siming zhi* 寶慶四明志. *Song Yuan fangzhi congkan* edition. Beijing: Zhonghua Shuju, 1990.

Ma Duanlin 馬端臨. *Wenxian tongkao* 文獻通考. *Shitong* edition. Rpt. Shanghai: Shangwu Yinshuguan, 1935; rpt. Beijing: Zhonghua Shuju, 1986.

Man'yōshū 萬葉集. Eighth century. Rpt. in vols. 4–7 of *Nihon koten bungaku taikei*. Tokyo: Iwanami Shoten, 1957–1962.

Matsushita Kenrin 松下見林. *Ishō Nihonden* 異稱日本傳. Rpt. in vol. 20 of *Shiseki shūran*. Tokyo: Kondō Shuppanbu, 1924–1938.

Meireiritsu uragaki 名例律裏書. In *Ritsu*, vol. 1 of *Shintei zōho kokushi taikei*. Tokyo: Yoshikawa Kōbunkan, 1964.

Minamoto no Tsunenori 源經範. *Daishi go gyōjō shūki* 大師御行狀集記. Rpt. in vol. 206 of *Zoku gunsho ruijū*. Tokyo: Zoku Gunsho Ruijū Kanseikai, 1904.

Miyoshi no Tameyasu 三善為康. *Chōya gunsai* 朝野群載. Rpt. in vol. 29 of *Shintei zōho kokushi taikei*. Tokyo: Yoshikawa Kōbunkan, 1964.

Mo Di 墨翟. *Mozi* 墨子. *SBCK* edition.

Mo Xiufu 莫休符. *Guilin fengtu ji* 桂林風土記. *Congshu jiecheng chubian* edition. Shanghai: Shangwu Yinshuguan, 1935.

Motoori Norinaga 本居宣長. *Gyojū gaigen* 馭戎慨言. Rpt. in vol. 8 of *Motoori Norinaga zenshū*. Tokyo: Chikuma Shobō, 1972.

Nara ibun 寧樂遺文. Ed. Takeuchi Rizō 竹內理三. Tokyo: Tokyodō, 1962.

Nihon kiryaku 日本紀略. Eleventh century. Rpt. in vols. 10–11 of *Shintei zōho kokushi taikei*. Tokyo: Yoshikawa Kōbunkan, 1929.

Ō no Yasumaro 太安萬侶. *Kojiki* 古事記. Rpt. in vol. 1 of *Nihon koten bungaku zenshū*, ed. Ogihara Asao and Kōnosu Hayao. Tokyo: Shogakkan, 1973.

Ono no Minemori 小野岑守 et al., comps. *Ryōunshū* 凌雲集. Rpt. in vol. 13 of *Nihon koten zenshū*. Tokyo: Nihon Koten Zenshū Kankōkai, 1925–1929.

Oumi no Mifune 淡海三船. *Tō Daiwajō tōsei den* 唐大和上東征傳. Beijing: Zhonghua Shuju, 1979.

Ouyang Xiu 歐陽修. *Xin Wudai shi* 新五代史. Beijing: Zhonghua Shuju, 1974.

Ouyang Xiu 歐陽修 and Song Qi 宋祁. *Xin Tang shu* 新唐書. Beijing: Zhonghua Shuju, 1975.

Peng Dingqiu 彭定求. *Quan Tang shi* 全唐詩. Beijing: Zhonghua Shuju, 1960.

Qian Qi 錢起. *Qian Kaogong ji* 錢考功集. *SBCK* edition.

Quan Deyu 權德輿. *Quan Zaizhi wenji* 權載之文集. *SBCK* edition.

Ren Fan 任昉. *Shuyi ji* 述異記. *Siku quanshu* edition.

Ruan Yuan 阮元. *Shisanjing zhushu* 十三經注疏. Taibei: Dahua Shuju, 1982.

Ruijū sandai kyaku 類聚三代格. Eleventh century. Rpt. in vol. 25 of *Shintei zōho kokushi taikei*. Tokyo: Yoshikawa Kōbunkan, 1965.

Ryōshō 令抄. Rpt. in vol. 78 of *Gunsho ruijū*, ed. Hanawa Hokiichi 塙保己一. Tokyo: Zoku Gunsho Ruijū Kanseikai, 1939–1943.

Saichō 最澄. *Kenkairon engi* 顯戒論緣起. In Itō Shō, *Rinkō chōsho*. Tokyo: Kokusho Kankōkai, 1975.

Sanfu huangtu 三輔黃圖. Han dynasty. *SBCK* edition.

Shamen Guanding 沙門灌頂. *Guoqing bailu* 國清百錄. Rpt. in vol. 46 of *Taishō Tripitaka*. Tokyo: Taishō Shinshu Daizokyō Kankōkai, 1924.

Shen Jiji 沈既濟. *Renshi zhuan* 任氏傳. *Tangren xiaoshuo* edition. Hong Kong: Zhonghua Shuju, 1985.

Shen Yue 沈約. *Song shu* 宋書. Beijing: Zhonghua Shuju, 1974.

Shi You 史游. *Ji jiu pian* 急就篇. *SBCK* edition.

Shiban 師蠻. *Honchō kōsō den* 本朝高僧傳. Rpt. in vol. 63 of *Dai Nihon bukkyō zensho*. Tokyo: Suzuki Gakujutsu Zaidan, 1970–1973.

Shin gishiki 新儀式. Rpt. in vol. 80 of *Gunsho ruijū*. Tokyo: Zoku Gunsho Ruijū Kanseikai, 1932.

Shōtoku Taishi denreki 聖德太子傳曆. Rpt. in vol. 189 of *Zoku gunsho ruijū*. Tokyo: Zoku Gunsho Ruijū Kanseikai, 1897.

Sima Guang 司馬光. *Zizhi tongjian* 資治通鑒. Beijing: Zhonghua Shuju, 1956.

Sima Qian 司馬遷. *Shi ji* 史記. Beijing: Zhonghua Shuju, 1959.

Sima Zhen 司馬貞. *Bu shi ji* 補史記. In *Shi ji*. Shanghai: Wuzhou Tongwen Ju, 1903.

Situo 思託. *Enryaku sōroku* 延曆僧錄. Preserved in vol. 1 of *Tōdaiji yōroku*, ed. Tsutsui Eishun. Osaka: Zenkoku Shobō, 1934.

Song Minqiu 宋敏求. *Changan zhi* 長安志. *Song Yuan fangzhi congkan* edition. Beijing: Zhonghua Shuju, 1990.

———. *Tang dazhaoling ji* 唐大詔令集. Shanghai: Shangwu Yinshuguan, 1959.

Sugano no Mamichi 菅野真道 et al., comps. *Shoku Nihongi* 續日本紀. Rpt. in vol. 2 of *Shintei zōho kokushi taikei*. Tokyo: Yoshikawa Kōbunkan, 1935.

——— et al., comps. *Shoku Nihongi*. Ed. Aoki Kazuo 青木和夫 et al. *Shin Nihon koten bungaku taikei* edition. Tokyo: Iwanami Shoten, 1989–1998.

Sugawara no Michizane 菅原道真. *Ruijū kokushi* 類聚國史. Rpt. in vols. 2–3 of *Shintei zōho kokushi taikei*. Tokyo: Yoshikawa Kōbunkan, 1933–1934.

Sun Qi 孫棨. *Beili zhi* 北里志. *Shuo fu sanzhong* edition. Shanghai: Shanghai Guji Chubanshe, 1988.

Sun Qiao 孫樵. *Sun Qiao ji* 孫樵集. *SBCK* edition.

Takakusu Junjirō 高楠順次郎, ed. *Dai Nihon bukkyō zensho* 大日本佛教全書. Tokyo: Bukkyō Zensho Kankōkai, 1912. Rpt., Tokyo: Suzuki Gakujutsu Zaidan, 1970–1973.

Takamura monogatari 篁物語. Late Heian period. Rpt. in vol. 77 of *Nihon koten bungaku taikei*. Tokyo: Iwanami Shoten, 1964.

Terajima Ryōan 寺島良安. *Wa-Kan sansai zue* 和漢三才圖繪. 1715 ed. Rpt. Tokyo: Wa-Kan Sansai Zue Kankō Iinkai, 1970; facsimile rpt. Tokyo: Wa-Kan Sansai Zue Kanko Iinkai, 1979.

Toneri Shinnō 舍人親王. *Nihon shoki* 日本書紀. Rpt. in vols. 67–68 of *Nihon koten bungaku taikei*, ed. Sakamoto Tarō et al. Tokyo: Iwanami Shoten, 1976.

——— et al., comps. *Nihon shoki* 日本書紀. Rpt. in vols. 1–2 of *Shintei zōho kokushi taikei*. Tokyo: Yoshikawa Kōbunkan, 1964–1966.

Tuotuo 脫脫 et al., comps. *Liao shi* 遼史. Beijing: Zhonghua Shuju, 1974.

———. *Song shi* 宋史. Beijing: Zhonghua Shuju, 1977.

Urabe Kanekata 卜部兼方. *Shaku Nihongi* 釋日本紀. Rpt. in vol. 8 of *Shintei zōho kokushi taikei*. Tokyo: Yoshikawa Kōbunkan, 1932.

Utsubo monogatari 宇津保物語. Late tenth century. Rpt. in vols. 10–12 of *Nihon koten bungaku taikei*. Tokyo: Iwanami Shoten, 1959–1962.

Wang Chang 王昶. *Jinshi cuibian* 金石萃編. *Shike shiliao congshu* edition, series 1, no. 6. Taibei: Yiwen Yinshuguan, 1966.

Wang Chong 王充. *Lun heng* 論衡. *SBCK* edition.

Wang Dang 王讜. *Tang yulin* 唐語林. Shanghai: Shanghai Guji Chubanshe, 1978.

Wang Jia 王嘉. *Shiyi ji* 拾遺記. *Siku quanshu* edition.

Wang Pijiang 汪辟疆. *Tangren xiaoshuo* 唐人小說. Xianggang: Zhonghua Shuju Xianggang Fenju, 1985.

Wang Pu 王溥. *Tang huiyao* 唐會要. *Congshu jicheng chubian* edition. Shanghai: Shangwu Yinshuguan, 1936.

———. *Wudai huiyao* 五代會要. Shanghai: Shangwu Yinshuguan, 1938.

Wang Qi 王圻 and Wang Siyi 王思義. *Sancai tuhui* 三才圖會. 1609 edition. Facsimile rpt. Shanghai: Shanghai Guji Chubanshe, 1988.

Wang Qinruo 王欽若. *Cefu yuangui* 冊府元龜. Beijing: Zhonghua Shuju, 1960.

Wang Renyu 王仁裕. *Kaiyuan Tianbao yishi* 開元天寶遺事. In *Kaiyuan Tianbao yishi shizhong*. Shanghai: Shanghai Guji Chubanshe, 1985.

Wang Wei 王維. *Wang youcheng ji* 王右丞集. *SBCK* edition.

Wang Yinglin 王應麟. *Yu hai* 玉海. 1226 edition. Facsimile rpt. Taibei: Huawen Shuju, 1967.

Wang Yucheng 王禹偁. *Xiao chu ji* 小畜集. *SBCK* edition.

Wei Shou 魏收. *Wei shu* 魏書. Beijing: Zhonghua Shuju, 1974.

Wei Zheng 魏徵 et al., comps. *Sui shu* 隋書. Beijing: Zhonghua Shuju, 1973.

Xiao Song 蕭嵩 et al., comps. *Da Tang kaiyuanli* 大唐開元禮. *Siku quanshu zhenben* edition. Taibei: Shangwu Yinshuguan, 1978.

Xiao Tong 蕭統. *Wen xuan* 文選. *SBCK* edition.

Xiao Yi 蕭繹. *Jin louzi* 金樓子. *Zhibuzu zhai congshu* edition.

Xiao Zixian 蕭子顯. *Nan Qi shu* 南齊書. Beijing: Zhonghua Shuju, 1972.

Xie Zhaozhi 謝肇制. *Wu za zu* 五雜俎. 1618 edition.

Xing Bing 邢昺. *Lun yu zhushu* 論語注疏. *SSJZS* edition.

Xu Jian 徐堅. *Chuxue ji* 初學記. Beijing: Zhonghua Shuju, 1962.

Xu Jingzong 許敬宗. *Wenguan cilin* 文館詞林. Kōnin period (810–824) edition. Facsimile rpt. Tokyo: Koten Kenkyūkai, 1969.

Xu Ling 徐陵. *Xu Xiaomu ji* 徐孝穆集. *SBCK* edition.

Xu Shen 許慎. *Shuowen jiezi* 說文解字. Beijing: Zhonghua Shuju, 1963.

Xu Shizeng 徐師曾. *Wenti mingbian xushuo* 文體明辨序說. Beijing: Renmin Wenxue Chubanshe, 1962.

Xu Song 徐松. *Tang liangjing chengfang kao* 唐兩京城坊考. Beijing: Zhonghua Shuju, 1985.

Xu Yin 徐寅. *Xu gong Diaoji wenji* 徐公釣磯文集. *SBCK* edition.

Xun Kuang 荀況. *Xunzi* 荀子. *Nianerzi* edition. Rpt. Taibei: Xianzhi Chubanshe, 1976.

Yan Kejun 嚴可鈞. *Quan Jin wen* 全晉文. In *Quan Shanggu Sandai Qin Han Sanguo Liuchao wen*. Beijing: Zhonghua Shuju, 1958.

Yang Ju 楊鉅. *Hanlin xueshiyuan jiugui* 翰林學士院舊規. In *Hanyuan qunshu*. *Zhibuzuzhai congshu* edition.

Yang Xuanzhi 楊衒之. *Luoyang qielan ji* 洛陽伽藍記. *SBCK* edition.

Yao Runeng 姚汝能. *An Lushan shiji* 安祿山事跡. 1857 edition.

Yao Silian 姚思廉. *Liang shu* 梁書. Beijing: Zhonghua Shuju, 1973.

Yao Xuan 姚鉉. *Tang wencui* 唐文粹. 1890 edition. Rpt. Hangzhou: Zhejiang Renmin Chubanshe, 1986.

Yong Rong 永瑢. *Siku quanshu zongmu* 四庫全書總目. Beijing: Zhonghua Shuju, 1965.

Yoshimine no Yasuyo 良岑安世 and Shigeno no Sadanushi 滋野貞主. *Keikokushū* 經國集. Rpt. in vol. 125 of *Gunsho ruijū*. Tokyo: Zoku Gunsho Ruijū Kanseikai, 1939–1943.

Yu Shinan 虞世南. *Beitang shuchao* 北堂書抄. Song edition. Facsimile rpt. Tokyo: Chūbun Shuppansha, 1979.

Yuan Jie 元結. *Yuan Cishan wenji* 元次山文集. *SBCK* edition.

Yuan Kang 袁康. *Yue jue shu* 越絕書. *SBCK* edition.

Yuan Zhen 元稹. *Yuan Zhen ji* 元稹集. Beijing: Zhonghua Shuju, 1982.

———. *Yuanshi changqing ji* 元氏長慶集. *SBCK* edition.

Yue Ke 岳珂. *Kui tan lu* 愧郯錄. *SBCK* edition.

Yue Shi 樂史. *Yang Taizhen waizhuan* 楊太真外傳. In *Kaiyuan Tianbao yishi shizhong*. Shanghai: Shanghai Guji Chubanshe, 1985.

Zhang Chujin 張楚金. *Hanyuan* 翰苑. *Liaohai congshu* edition. Rpt. Taibei: Yiwen Yinshuguan, 1971.

Zhang Ji 張籍. *Zhang Siye shiji* 張司業詩集. *SBCK* edition.

Zhang Jiuling 張九齡. *Tang chengxiang Qujiang Zhang xiansheng wenji* 唐丞相曲江張先生文集. *SBCK* edition.

Zhang Junfang 張君房. *Yunji qiqian* 雲笈七籤. *SBCK* edition.

Zhang Yi 張揖. *Guangya shuzheng* 廣雅疏証. Taibei: Zhonghua Shuju, 1982.

Zhang Yuanji 張元濟. *Sibu congkan* 四部叢刊. Shanghai: Shangwu Yinshuguan, 1919.

Zhang Yue 張說. *Zhang Yuezhi wenji* 張說之文集. *SBCK* edition.

Zhang Zhuo 張鷟. *Chaoye qianzai* 朝野僉載. *Tang Wudai biji xiaoshuo daguan* edition. Shanghai: Shanghai Guji Chubanshe, 2000.

Zhangsun Wuji 長孫無忌. *Gu Tanglü shuyi* 故唐律疏議. Beijing: Zhonghua Shuju, 1983.

Zhanguo ce 戰國策. Warring States period. Rpt., ed. Liu Xiang 劉向. Shanghai: Shanghai Guji Chubanshe, 1978.

Zhao Qi 趙岐 and Sun Bi 孫奭, eds. *Mengzi zhushu* 孟子注疏. *SSJZS* edition.

Zhao Yi 趙翼. *Gaiyu congkao* 陔余叢考. 1852 edition.

Zheng Chuhui 鄭處誨. *Minghuang zalu* 明皇雜錄. Beijing: Zhonghua Shuju, 1994.

Zheng Xuan 鄭玄 et al. *Zhou li zhushu* 周禮注疏. *SSJZS* edition.

Zheng Yuan 鄭元 and Jia Gongyan 賈公彥, eds. *Yi li zhushu* 儀禮注疏. *SSJZS* edition.

Zhonghua Shuju 中華書局, comps. *Sibu beiyao* 四部備要. Shanghai: Zhonghua Shuju, 1931.

Zhu Junsheng 朱駿聲. *Shuowen tongxun dingsheng* 說文通訓定聲. 1833 edition. Rpt. Wuhan: Wuhan shi Guji Shudian, 1983.

Zhu Qingyu 朱慶餘. *Zhu Qingyu shiji* 朱慶餘詩集. *SBCK* edition.

Zhuang Zhou 莊周. *Zhuangzi* 莊子. Rpt. and annotated by Guo Xiang in *Nianerzi*. Taibei: Xianzhi Chubanshe, 1976.

Zuda shinnō nittō ryakki 頭陀親王入唐略記. Rpt. in vol. 68 of *Dai Nihon bukkyō zensho*. Tokyo: Suzuki Gakujutsu Zaidan, 1970–1973.

Zuikei Shūhō 瑞溪周鳳. *Zenrin kokuhōki* 善鄰國寶記. Rpt. in vol. 21 of *Shiseki shūran*. Tokyo: Kondō Shuppanbu, 1924–1938.

WORKS OF MODERN SCHOLARSHIP

Abé Ryūichi. *The Weaving of Mantra: Kūkai and the Construction of Esoteric Buddhist Discourse.* New York: Columbia University Press, 1999.

Adachi Kiroku 足立喜六 and Shioiri Ryōdō 鹽入良道, eds. *Nittō guhō junrei kōki* 入唐求法巡禮行記. Tokyo: Heibonsha, 1970–1985.

Aikens, C. Melvin, and Akazawa, Takeru. "Fishing and Farming in Early Japan: Jomon Littoral Tradition Carried into Yayoi Times at the Miura Caves on Tokyo Bay." In *Pacific Northeast Asia in Prehistory: Hunter-Fisher-Gatherers, Farmers, and Sociopolitical Elites*, ed. C. Melvin Aikens and Song Nai Rhee, pp. 75–82. Pullman, Wash.: WSU Press, 1992.

Akazawa, Takeru. "Maritime Adaptation of Prehistoric Hunter-Gatherers and Their Transition to Agriculture in Japan." *Senri Ethnological Studies*, 9 (1981), pp. 213–258.

Anazawa Wakou and Manome Jun'ichi. "Two Inscribed Swords from Japanese Tumuli." In *Windows on the Japanese Past: Studies in Archaeology*, ed. R. Pearson, G. L. Barnes, and K. Hutterer, pp. 375–395. Ann Arbor: Center for Japanese Studies, University of Michigan, 1986.

Anderson, E. N. *The Food of China.* New Haven: Yale University Press, 1988.

Andō Kōsei 安藤更生. *Ganjin Daiwajō den no kenkyū* 鑒真大和上傳の研究. Tokyo: Heibonsha, 1960.

Aoki, Michiko Y. *Records of Wind and Earth: A Translation of Fudoki with Introduction and Commentaries.* Ann Arbor: Association for Asian Studies, 1997.

Aoyama Sadao 青山定雄. *Tō Sō jidai no kōtsū to chishi chizu no kenkyū* 唐宋時代の交通と地誌地圖の研究. Tokyo: Yoshikawa Kōbunkan, 1963.

Asakawa Kanichi. *The Early Institutional Life of Japan: A Study in the Reform of 645 A.D.* New York: Paragon Book Reprint Corp., 1963.

Aston, W. G., trans. *Nihongi: Chronicles of Japan from the Earliest Time to A.D. 697.* Tokyo: Charles E. Tuttle, 1972.

Barat, Kahar. *The Uygur-Turkic Biography of the Seventh-Century Buddhist Pilgrim Xuanzang: Ninth and Tenth Chapters.* Bloomington: Research Institute for Inner Asian Studies, Indiana University, 2001.

Barnes, Gina L. *China, Korea, and Japan: The Rise of Civilization in East Asia.* New York: Thames and Hudson, 1993.

———. *Protohistoric Yamato: Archaeology of the First Japanese State.* Ann Arbor: Museum of Anthropology and Center for Japanese Studies, University of Michigan, 1988.

Best, Jonathan W. "Diplomatic and Cultural Contacts between Paekche and China." *HJAS*, 42, no. 2 (1982), pp. 443–501.

Birrell, Anne. *The Classic of Mountains and Seas.* New York: Penguin, 2000.

Bischoff, F. A. *La forêt des princeaux: Étude sur l'Académie du Han-lin sous la dynastie des T'ang, et traduction du Han-lin tche*. Paris: Presses Universitaires de France, Bibliothèque de l'Institut des Hautes Études Chinoises, 1963, vol. 18.

Bodman, Richard W. *Poetics and Prosody in Early Medieval China: A Study and Translation of Kūkai's Bunkyō Hifuron*. Ann Arbor: University Microfilms, 1978.

Borgen, Robert. "The Japanese Mission to China (801–806)." *Monumenta Nipponica*, 37, no. 1 (1982), pp. 1–28.

———. *Sugawara no Michizane and the Early Heian Court*. Cambridge, Mass.: Harvard University Press, 1986. Paperback edition, Honolulu: University of Hawai'i Press, 1994.

Brown, Yu-ying. "The Origins and Characteristics of Chinese Collections in Japan." *Journal of Oriental Studies*, 21, no. 1 (1983), pp. 19–31.

Campany, Robert Ford. *Strange Writing: Anomaly Accounts in Early Medieval China*. Albany: State University of New York Press, 1996.

Cao Xun 曹汛. "Tangren shiti zhong de 'Ridong' houshi you ewei 'Riben' zhe" 唐人詩題中的'日東'後世有訛為'日本'者. *Zhonghua wenshi luncong*, 3 (1983), p. 198.

Carter, Steven D. *Traditional Japanese Poetry: An Anthology*. Stanford: Stanford University Press, 1991.

Cen Zhongmian 岑仲勉. *Langguan shizhu timing xin kaoding* 郎官石柱題名新考訂. Shanghai: Shanghai Guji Chubanshe, 1984.

Chamberlain, Basil Hall, trans. *The Kojiki: Records of Ancient Matters*. Tokyo: Charles E. Tuttle, 1982.

Chang, K. C., ed. *Food in Chinese Culture: Anthropological and Historical Perspectives*. New Haven: Yale University Press, 1977.

Chang Lan 萇嵐. *Qi-shisi shiji Zhong Ri wenhua jiaoliu de kaoguxue yanjiu* 7–14 世紀中日文化交流的考古學研究. Beijing: Zhongguo Shehui Kexue Chubanshe, 2001.

Chen Jianxian 陳建憲. "Jing Chu wufeng yu Riben gusu" 荊楚巫風與日本古俗. In *Zhong Ri minsu de yitong he jiaoliu*, ed. Jia Huixuan and Shen Renan. Beijing: Beijing Daxue Chubanshe, 1993.

Chen Shangjun 陳尚君, ed. *Quan Tang shi bubian* 全唐詩補編. Beijing: Zhonghua Shuju, 1992.

Chen Shangsheng 陳尚勝. "Tangdai de Xinluo qiaomin qu" 唐代的新羅僑民區. *Lishi yanjiu*, 1996, no. 1, pp. 161–166.

Chen Tiemin 陳鐵民. "Xiao Yingshi xinian kaozheng" 蕭穎士繫年考證. *Wen shi*, no. 37 (1993), pp. 187–212.

Chen Wenjing 陳文經. "Tangdai Xinluo qiaomin de huodong" 唐代新羅僑民的活動. In *Gudai Zhong Han Ri guanxi yanjiu*, ed. Lin Tianwei and Huang Yuese, pp. 27–38. Xianggang: Xianggan, Daxue Yazhou Yanjiu Zhongxin, 1987.

Cheng Xilin 程喜霖. *Tangdai guosuo yanjiu* 唐代過所研究. Beijing: Zhonghua Shuju, 2000.

Chikazawa Keiichi 近澤敬一. "Nihonkoku genzaisho mokuroku ni tsuite" 日本國見在書目錄について. *Fukuoka daigaku jimbun ronsō*, 14, no. 1 (1982), pp. 2–6.

Cohen, Warren I. *East Asia at the Center: Four Thousand Years of Engagement with the World*. New York: Columbia University Press, 2001.

Collcutt, Martin. "Japan: The Limits of Confucianization." Unpublished paper.

Collcutt, Martin, Marius Jansen, and Isao Kumakura. *Cultural Atlas of Japan*. New York: Facts on File, 1988.

Cranston, Edwin A. "Atemiya: A Translation from the Utsubo Monogatari." *Monumenta Nipponica*, 24, no. 3 (1969), pp. 289–313.

―――. *A Waka Anthology*, volume 1: *The Gem-Glistening Cup*. Stanford: Stanford University Press, 1993.

Creel, Herrlee G. *The Origins of Statecraft in China*. Chicago: The University of Chicago Press, 1970.

Daudin, Pierre. "Un Japonais à la cour des T'ang: Gouverneur du Protectorat d'Annam Abe-no Nakamaro alias Tch'ao Heng." *Bulletin de la Société des Études Indochinoises*, 40 (1965), pp. 215–280.

de Bary, Wm. Theodore, et al., eds. *Sources of Chinese Tradition*. New York: Columbia University Press, 1960.

Deal, William E. "Buddhism and the State in Early Japan." In *Buddhism in Practice*, ed. Donald S. Lopez. Princeton: Princeton University Press, 1995.

Di Cosmo, Nicola. *Ancient China and Its Enemies*. Cambridge: Cambridge University Press, 2001.

―――. "Ancient Inner Asian Nomads: Their Economic Basis and Its Significance in Chinese History." *JAS*, 53, no. 4 (1994), pp. 1092–1126.

Ding Ruming 丁汝明. *Tang Wudai biji xiaoshuo daguan* 唐五代筆記小說大觀. Shanghai: Shanghai Guji Chubanshe, 2000.

Dong Zhiqiao 董志翹. *Ru Tang qiufa xunli xingji cihui yanjiu* 入唐求法巡禮行記詞彙研究. Beijing: Zhongguo Shehui Kexue Chubanshe, 2000.

Du Zhengsheng 杜正勝. "Xizhou fengjian de tezhi" 西周封建的特質. In *Zhongguo shixue lunwen xuanji*, ed. Wang Shounan et al., vol. 4, pp. 83–127. Taibei: Youshi Wenhua Shiye Gongsi, 1981.

Ebersole, Gary L. *Ritual Poetry and the Politics of Death in Early Japan*. Princeton: Princeton University Press, 1989.

Ebrey, Patricia. "T'ang Guides to Verbal Etiquette." *HJAS*, 45, no. 2 (1985), pp. 581–613.

Ecsedy, Hilda. "Trade and War Relations between the Turks and China in the Second Half of the Sixth Century." *Acta Orientalia Hungaricae*, 21 (1968), pp. 131–180.

Fairbank, John K., ed. *The Chinese World Order.* Cambridge, Mass.: Harvard University Press, 1968.

————. "A Preliminary Framework." In *The Chinese World Order*, ed. John K. Fairbank, pp. 1–19. Cambridge, Mass.: Harvard University Press, 1968.

Fairbank, John K., and S. Y. Teng. "Ch'ing Administration: Three Studies." *Harvard-Yenching Institute Studies*, 19 (1960), pp. 107–246.

————. "On the Chinese Tributary System." *HJAS*, 6, no. 2 (1941), pp. 135–246.

Fan Bangjin 范邦瑾. "Tangdai fanfang kaolüe" 唐代蕃坊考略. *Lishi yanjiu*, 1990, no. 4, pp. 149–154.

Fan Ning 範寧, ed. *Bowu zhi jiaozheng* 博物志校正. Beijing: Zhonghua Shuju, 1980.

Farris, William W. *Population, Disease and Land in Early Japan, 645–900.* Cambridge, Mass.: Harvard University Press, 1985.

Fogel, Joshua A. *Politics and Sinology: The Case of Naitō Konan.* Cambridge, Mass.: Harvard University Press, 1984.

Friday, Karl. "Pushing beyond the Pale: The Yamato Conquest of the Emishi and Northern Japan." *Journal of Japanese Studies*, 23, no. 1 (1997), pp. 1–24.

Fu Sinian 傅斯年. "Zhi Wu Jingchao shu" 致吳景超書. In *Fu Sinian quanji*, ed. Chen Pan, pp. 109–135. Taibei: Lianjing Chuban Shiye Gongsi, 1980.

Fu Xinian 傅熹年. "Tang Changan Daminggong Hanyuandian yuanzhuang de tantao" 唐長安大明宮含元殿原狀的探討. *Wen wu*, 1973, no. 7, pp. 30–48.

Fukunaga Mitsuji 福永光司. "Kōten Jōtei to Tennō Taitei to Genshi Tenson" 昊天上帝と天皇大帝と元始天尊. *Chūtetsubun gakkaihō*, 1976, no. 2, pp. 1–34.

Fung Yu-lan. *A History of Chinese Philosophy.* Trans. Derk Bodde. Princeton: Princeton University Press, 1983.

Furuse Natsuko 古瀬奈津子. *Ken Tō shi no mita Chūgoku* 遣唐使の見た中國. Tokyo: Yoshikawa Kōbunkan, 2003.

Gardiner, K. H. J. "The Kung-sun Warriors of Liaodong (189–238)." *Papers on Far Eastern History*, no. 5 (1972), pp. 59–107.

Geddes, Ward. "Takamura Monogatari." *Monumenta Nipponica*, 46, no. 3 (1991), pp. 275–291.

Goodrich, L. C., and R. Tsunoda, *Japan in the Chinese Dynastic Histories.* South Pasadena, 1951; rpt., Kyoto: Perkings Oriental Books, 1968.

Guisso, R. W. L. *Wu Tse-t'ian and Politics of Legitimation in T'ang China.* Occasional Papers. Bellingham: Washington University, 1978.

Gulik, Robert van. *Irezumi: The Pattern of Dematography in Japan.* Leiden: E. J. Brill, 1982.

Hakeda, Yoshito S. *Kūkai: Major Works.* New York: Columbia University Press, 1972.

Hamada Kōsaku 濱田耕策. "Tōchō ni okeru Bokkai to Shiragi no sōchō jiken ni tsuite" 唐朝における渤海と新羅の爭長事件について. In *Kodai Higashi Ajiashi ronshū (2)*, ed. Suematsu Yasukazu Hakase Koki Kinenkai, pp. 339–360. Tokyo: Suematsu Yasukazu Hakase Koki Kinenkai, 1978.

Han Sheng 韓昇. "Konghai yu Yuan Jinqing" 空海與袁晋卿. *Wenxian*, 1997, no. 2, pp. 214–227.

Hashikawa Tokio 橋川時雄. "Wajin ga chōsō o mitsuida koto" 倭人が㟢草を貢いだこと. In *Ishihama sensei koki kinen Tōyōgaku ronsō*, ed. Ishihama Sensei Koki Kinenkai, pp. 449–458. Osaka: Ishihama Sensei Koki Kinenkai, 1958.

Hayashi Tsutomu 林勉. "Iwazakihon Nihon shoki kunten no keigo hyōgen" 岩崎本日本書紀訓點の敬語表現. In *Ronshū jōdai bungaku*, ed. Man'yō Shichiyōkai, vol. 7, pp. 171–248. Tokyo: Kasama Shoin, 1972.

Heng, Chye Kiang. *Cities of Aristocrats and Bureaucrats: The Development of Medieval Chinese Cityscapes*. Honolulu: University of Hawai'i Press, 1999.

Herbert, P. A. "Japanese Embassies and Students in T'ang China." In *Occasional Papers*, 4, pp. 1–20. Perth: University of Western Australia, Center for East Asian Studies, 1970.

———. *Under the Brilliant Emperor*. Canberra: Australian National University Press, 1978.

Higuchi Kiyoyuki 樋口清之. "Yon-roku seiki no i shoku jū" 四－六世紀の衣食住. In *Zemināru Nihon kodaishi (ge)*, ed. Ueda Masaaki et al., pp. 553–562. Tokyo: Kōbunsha, 1980.

Hirano Kunio 平野邦雄. "Kiki ritsuryō ni okeru 'kika' 'gaiban' no gainen to sono yōrei" 記紀律令における"歸化" "外蕃"の概念とその用例. *Tōyō bunka*, 60 (1980), pp. 101–130.

———. "Nichi-Chō-Chū sangoku kankei ron ni tsuite no oboegaki" 日、朝、中三國關係論についての覺書. *Tōkyō Joshi Daigaku Fuzoku Hikaku Bunka Kenkyūjo kiyō*, 41 (1980), pp. 54–69.

———. "The Yamato State and Korea in the Fourth and the Fifth Centuries." *Acta Asiatica*, 31 (1977), pp. 51–82.

Hirano Takuji 平野卓治. "Ritsuryō ikaisei to shoban" 律令位階制と「諸蕃」. In *Nihon kodai no seidi to seido*, ed. Hayashi Rokurō Sensei Kanreki Kinenkai, pp. 95–136. Tokyo: Zoku Gunsho Ruijū Kanseikai, 1985.

Honda, Heihachirō. *The Manyoshu: A New and Complete Translation*. Tokyo: Hokuseido Press, 1967.

Honiden Kikushi 本位田菊士. "Kodai Nihon no kunshugō to Chūgoku no kunshugō" 古代日本の君主號と中國の君主號. *Shigaku zasshi*, 90, no. 12 (1981), pp. 1747–1784.

———. "Zui Tō kōshō to Nihon kokugō no seiritsu" 隋唐交渉と日本國號の成立. *Shikan*, no. 120 (1989), pp. 26–44.

Hori Toshikazu 堀敏一. "Nihon to Zui, Tō ryōkoku tono aida ni kawasareta kokusho" 日本と隋，唐両国との間に交わされた国書. In his *Ritsuryō sei to Higashi Ajia sedai: Wadashi no Chūgoku shigaku (2)*, pp. 175–201. Tokyo: Kyūko Shoin, 1994.

Hucker, Charles O. *A Dictionary of Official Titles in Imperial China.* Stanford: Stanford University Press, 1985.

Hudson, Mark. "Ethnicity in East Asia: Approaches to the Wa." *Archaeological Review from Cambridge,* 8, no. 1 (1989), pp. 51–63.

―――. "From Toro to Yoshinogari: Changing Perspectives on Yayoi Period Archaeology." In *Bibliographic Reviews of Far Eastern Archaeology: Hoabinhinan, Jōmon, Yayoi, Early Korean States,* ed. Gina L. Barnes, pp. 63–112. Oxford: Oxbow Books, 1990.

―――. *Ruins of Identity: Ethnogenesis in the Japanese Islands.* Honolulu: University of Hawai'i Press, 1999.

Hudson, Mark, and Gina L. Barnes. "Yoshinogari: A Yayoi Settlement in Northern Kyūshū." *Monumenta Nipponica,* 46, no. 2 (1991), pp. 211–235.

Ichiko Teiji 市古貞次. *Shin kogo jiten* 新古語辭典. Tokyo: Gakushū Kenkyūsha, 1986.

Ide Itaru 井手至. "Reimei ki no kanji shiyō" 黎明期の漢字使用. In *Zemināru Nihon kodaishi (ge),* ed. Ueda Masaaki et al., pp. 422–431. Tokyo: Kōbunsha, 1980.

Ikeda On 池田溫. "Giki kyūnen Wakoku kenhōbutsu o megutte" 義熙九年倭國獻方物をめぐって. In *Egami Namio kyōju koki kinen ronshū,* ed. Egami Namio Kyōju Koki Kinen Jigyōkai, pp. 27–47. Tokyo: Yamakawa Shuppansha, 1977.

―――. "Gudai Riben shequ Zhongguo dianji wenti" 古代日本攝取中國典籍問題. In *Zhongyang yanjiuyuan guoji Hanxue lunwenji lishi kaogu zu (shangce),* ed. Zhongyang Yanjiuyuan Guoji Hanxue Lunwenji Bianji Weiyuanhui, pp. 345–367. Taibei: Zhongyang Yanjiuyuan, 1981.

―――. "Hai Seisei to Kō Byōjin" 裴世清と高表仁. *Nihon rekishi,* 280 (1971), pp. 8–12.

―――. *Higashi Ajia no bunka kōryū shi* 東アジアの文化交流史. Tokyo: Yoshikawa Kōbunkan, 2002.

―――. "Shō Inshi shōhei wa Shiragi ka Nihon ka" 蕭穎士招聘は新羅か日本か. In *Enoki hakase shōju kinen Tōyōshi ronshū,* ed. Enoki Hakase Shōju Kinenkai, pp. 1–19. Tokyo: Kyūko Shoin, 1988.

―――. "Tenhō kōki no Tō, Ragi, Nichi kankei o megutte" 天寶後期の唐、羅、日關係をめぐって. In *Shunshi Ben Rinseki kyōju kanreki kinen Tōshi ronso,* ed. Ben Rinseki Kyōju Kanreki Kinenkai, pp. 208–251. Tokyo: Taishūkan Shoten, 1995.

Ikeuchi Hiroshi 池内宏. "Kōsonshi no Taihōgun setchi to Sō Gi no Rakurō Taihō nigun" 公孫氏の帶方郡設置と曹魏の樂浪帶方二郡. *Man-Senshi kenkyū (jōsei),* vol. 1, pp. 237–250. Kyoto: Sokokusha, 1951.

Imamura Keiji. *Prehistoric Japan: New Perspective on Insular East Asia.* London: UCL Press, 1996.

Inaoka Kōji 稲岡耕二. "Shoku Nihongi ni okeru semmyō" 續日本紀における宣命. In Sugano no Mamichi et al., *Shoku Nihongi* (*Shin Nihon koten bungaku taikei* edn.), ed. Aoki Kazuo et al., vol. 2, pp. 663–703. Tokyo: Iwanami Shoten, 1990.

Inoue Hideo 井上秀雄. "Go Kanjo no Tōikan"《後漢書》の東夷觀. In *Ono Katsutoshi hakase shōjū kinen tōhōgaku ronshū*, ed. Ono Katsutoshi Hakase Shōju Kinenkai, pp. 33–56. Kyoto: Ryūkoku Daigaku Tōyō Shigaku Kenkyūkai, 1982.

———. "Sangokushi no Tōi ōshakan"《三國志》の東夷王者觀. *Tōhoku Daigaku Bungakubu kenkyū nempō*, 31 (1981), pp. 191–248.

Inoue Mitsusada 井上光貞. "Kani jūnikai to sono shiteki igi" 冠位十二階とその史的意義. In his *Nihon kodai kokka no kenkyū*, pp. 283–306. Tokyo: Iwanami Shoten, 1965.

———. *Nihon kodai no kokka to bukkyō* 日本古代の國家と佛教. Tokyo: Iwanami Shoten, 1971.

Inoue Yasushi. *The Roof Tile of Tempyō*. Trans. James T. Araki. Tokyo: University of Tokyo Press, 1991.

Ise Sentarō 伊瀬仙太郎. *Chūgoku seiiki keieishi no kenkyū* 中國西域經營史の研究. Tokyo: Gannandō Shoten, 1969.

Ishii Masatoshi 石井正敏. *Higashi Ajia sekai to kodai no Nihon* 東アジア世界と古代の日本. Tokyo: Yamakawa Shuppansha, 2003.

———. "Ōtomo no Furumaro sōgen ni tsuite" 大伴古麻呂奏言について. *Hōsei shigaku*, 35 (1983), pp. 27–40.

———. "Tō no shōgun Go Kaijitsu ni tsuite" 唐の將軍吳懷實について. *Nihon rekishi*, 402 (1981), pp. 23–37.

Ishimoda Shō 石母田正. "Tennō to shoban" 天皇と「諸蕃」. In his *Nihon kodai kokka ron (1)*, pp. 329–359. Tokyo: Iwanami Shoten, 1973.

Itazawa Takeo 板澤武雄. "Nittō tsūkō ni okeru kokusho mondai ni tsuite" 日唐通交に於ける國書問題について. *Shirin*, 24, no. 1 (1939), pp. 1–23.

Iwami Kiyohiro 石見清裕. *Tō no hoppō mondai to kokusai chitsujo* 唐の北方問題と國際秩序. Tokyto: Kyūko Shoin, 1998.

———. "Tō no kokusho juyo reigi ni tsuite" 唐の國書授予礼儀について. *Tōyōshi kenkyū*, 57, no. 2 (1998), pp. 37–69.

Jeon Young-rae 全榮來. *Kudara metsubō to kodai Nihon* 百濟滅亡と古代日本. Tokyo: Yūzan Kaku, 2004.

Johnson, Wallace. *The T'ang Code*. Princeton: Princeton University Press, 1979–1997.

Kaneko Shūichi 金子修一. "T'ang International Relations and Diplomatic Correspondence." *Acta Asiatica*, 55 (1988), pp. 75–101.

———. "Tōdai kokusai kankei ni okeru Nihon no ichi ni kansuru ichi shiron" 唐代國際關係における日本の位置に関する一試論. *Kodai bunka*, 50, no. 9 (1998), pp. 14–24.

———. "Tōdai no kokusai bunsho keishiki ni tsuite" 唐代の國際文書形式について. *Shigaku zasshi*, 83, no. 10 (1974), pp. 29–51.

———. "Tōdai sakuhōsei ippan" 唐代冊封制一斑. In *Higashi Ajia shi ni okeru kokka to nōmin*, ed. Nishijima Sadaō Hakase Kanreki Kinenkai, pp. 297–326. Tokyo: Yamakawa Shuppansha, 1984.

Kawaguchi Hisao 川口久雄. *Heianchō Nihon kanbungakushi no kenkyū* 平安朝日本漢文學史の研究. Tokyo: Meiji Shoin, 1953.

———. "Tō, Bokkai tono kōtsū to Nihon genzaisho mokuroku" 唐、渤海との交通と日本見在書目録. In his *Heian chō Nihon kanbungakushi no kenkyū*, vol. a, pp. 135–155. Tokyo: Meiji Shoin, 1953. Rpt., 1982.

Keene, Donald. *Seeds in the Heart: Japanese Literature from Earliest Times to the Late Sixteenth Century.* New York: Henry Holt and Company, 1993.

Kidder, Jonathan Edward Jr. "The Earliest Societies in Japan." In *Ancient Japan*, ed. Delmer M. Brown, vol. 1 of *The Cambridge History of Japan*, ed. John W. Hall et al., pp. 48–107. New York: Cambridge University Press, 1993.

———. "Yoshinogari and the Yamatai Problem." *Transactions of the Asiatic Society of Japan*, 4th series, no. 6 (1991), pp. 115–140.

Kikuchi Hideo 菊池英男. "Sōsetsu" 總說. In *Zui Tō teikoku to Higashi Ajia sekai*, ed. Tōdaishi Kenkyūkai, pp. 1–84. Tokyo: Kyūko Shoin, 1979.

Kiley, Cornelius J. "State and Dynasty in Archaic Yamato." *JAS*, 33, no. 1 (1973), pp. 25–50.

Kim, Samuel S. "The Traditional Chinese Image of World Order." In his *China, the United Nations and World Order*, pp. 19–48. Princeton: Princeton University Press, 1979.

Kimiya Yasuhiko 木宮泰彦. *Nisshi kōtsūshi* 日支交通史. Tokyo: Kanasashi Hōryūdō, 1927.

Kin Bunkyo 金文京. "Kanji bunkaken no kundoku genshō" 漢字文化圏の訓讀現象. In *Wa Kan hikaku bungaku kenkyū no sho mondai*, ed. Wa Kan Hikaku Bungaku Kai, pp. 175–204. Tokyo: Kyūko Shoin, 1988.

Kishi Toshio 岸俊男. "Kodai Nihonjin no Chūgokukan" 古代日本人の中國觀. In *Kodaigaku sōron*, ed. Heian Hakubutsukan Kenkyūbu, pp. 313–326. Kyoto: Tsunoda Bunei Hakase Koki Kinenkai, 1983.

Kitagawa, Joseph M. *On Understanding Japanese Religion.* Princeton: Princeton University Press, 1987.

Kitō Kiyoaki 鬼頭清明. "Chūgoku kodai kokka to Higashi Ajia shakai" 中國古代國家と東アジア社會 (book review). *Tōyōshi kenkyū*, 43, no. 2 (1984), pp. 143–149.

———. *Hakusonkō* 白村江. Tokyo: Kyōikusha, 1981.

Kiyokoba Azuma 清木場東. "Tō ritsuryōsei jidai no jōshokuryōsei ni tsuite" 唐律令制時代の常食料制について. In *Ritsuryōsei*, ed. Tōshi Kenkyūkai, pp. 305–331. Tokyo: Kyūko Shoin, 1986.

Kiyota, Minoru. *Shingon Buddhism*. Tokyo and Los Angeles: Buddhist Books International, 1978.

Kobayashi Yoshinori 小林芳規. "Nihon shoki kokun to kanseki no ko kundoku" 日本書紀古訓と漢籍の古訓讀. In *Kokugogaku ronshū*, ed. Saeki Umetomo Hakase Koki Kien Kokugogaku Ronshū Kankōkai, pp. 37–68. Tokyo: Hyōgensha, 1969.

Kohase Keikichi 小長谷惠吉. *Nihonkoku genzaisho mokuroku kaisetsu kō* 日本國見在書目錄解說稿. Tokyo: Komiya Shoten, 1956.

Kojima Noriyuki 小島憲之. *Jōdai Nihon bungaku to Chūgoku bungaku (jō)* 上代日本文學と中國文學(上). Tokyo: Hanawa Shobō, 1962.

———. *Kokufū ankoku jidai no bungaku* 國風暗黑時代の文學. Tokyo: Hanawa Shobō, 1979.

Komatsu Shigemi 小松茂美. *Kana* カな. Tokyo: Iwanami Shoten, 1968.

Konishi, Jin'ichi. *A History of Japanese Literature*. Vol. 1. Trans. Aileen Gatten and Nicholas Teele; ed. Earl Miner. Princeton: Princeton University Press, 1984.

Kornichi, Peter F. *The Book in Japan: A Cultural History from the Beginnings to the Nineteenth Century*. Leiden: E. J. Brill, 1998.

Kuranaka Susumu 藏中進. *Tō Daiwajō tōseiden no kenkyū* 唐大和上東征傳の研究. Tokyo: Ofusha, 1976.

Kurihara Tomonobu 栗原朋信. "Gishi Wajinden ni mieru Yamataikoku o meguru kokusai kankei no ichimen" 魏志倭人傳にみえる邪馬臺國をめぐる國際關係の一面. *Shigaku zasshi*, 73, no. 12 (1964), pp. 1–38.

———. *Jōdai Nihon taigai kankei no kenkyū* 上代日本對外關係の研究. Tokyo: Yoshikawa Kōbunkan, 1978.

———. "Jōdai no Nihon e taisuru Sankan no gaikō keishiki" 上代の日本へ對する三韓の外交形式. In his *Jōdai Nihon taigai kankei no kenkyū*, pp. 237–259. Tokyo: Yoshikawa Kōbunkan, 1978.

———. "Kan teikoku to shūhen shominzoku" 漢帝國と周邊諸民族. In *Iwanami kōza sekai rekishi (kodai 4)*, ed. Ienaga Saburō et al., pp. 445–486. Tokyo: Iwanami Shoten, 1970.

———. "Nichi Zui kōshō no ichisokumen" 日、隋交涉の一側面. In his *Jōdai Nihon taigai kankei no kenkyū*, pp. 206–236. Tokyo: Yoshikawa Kōbunkan, 1978.

———. "Nihon kara Zui e okutta kokusho" 日本から隋へ贈った國書. In *Jōdai Nihon taigai kankei no kenkyū*, ed. Kurihara Tomonobu, pp. 175–205. Tokyo: Yoshikawa Kōbunkan, 1978.

———. "Shichishitō no meimon yori mita Nihon to Kudara Tōshin no kankei" 「七支刀」の銘文よりみた日本と百濟、東晉の關係. *Rekishi kyōiku*, 18, no. 4 (1970), pp. 13–18.

———. *Shin Kan shi no kenkyū* 秦漢史の研究. Tokyo: Yoshikawa Kōbunkan, 1969.

Lammers, Wayne P. *The Tale of Matsura: Fujiwara Teika's Experiment in Fiction.* Ann Arbor: Center for Japanese Studies, University of Michigan, 1992.

Ledyard, Gari. "Yin and Yang in the China-Manchuria-Korea Triangle." In *China among Equals*, ed. Morris Rossabi, pp. 313–350. Berkeley: University of California Press, 1983.

Lee, Sherman E. *A History of Far Eastern Art.* 5th edn. New York: Harry N. Abrams, 1994.

Legge, James. *The Chinese Classics.* Rpt. Hong Kong: Hong Kong University Press, 1960.

Levenson, Joseph R. "T'ien-hsia and Kuo and the Transvaluation of Values." *Far Eastern Quarterly*, 11, no. 4 (1952), pp. 447–451.

Levy, Ian H. *The Ten Thousand Leaves.* Princeton: Princeton University Press, 1981.

Li Bincheng et al. 李斌城. *Sui Tang Wudai shehui shenghuo shi* 隋唐五代社會生活史. Beijing: Zhongguo Shehui Kexue Chubanshe, 1998.

Li Hu 黎虎. *Han Tang waijiao zhidu shi* 漢唐外交制度史. Lanzhou: Lanzhou Daxue Chubanshe, 1988.

Li Jinxiu 李錦秀. *Tangdai caizheng shi gao (shang)* 唐代財政史稿(上). Beijing: Beijing Daxue Chubanshe, 1995.

———. *Tangdai caizheng shi gao (xia)* 唐代財政史稿(下). Beijing: Beijing Daxue Chubanshe, 2001.

———. *Tangdai zhidu shi lüelun gao* 唐代制度史略論稿. Beijing: Zhongguo Zhengfa Daxue Chubanshe, 1998.

Li Tingxian 李廷先. *Tangdai Yangzhou shi kao* 唐代揚州史考. Yangzhou: Jiangsu Guji Chubanshe, 1992.

Liu Dunzhen 劉敦楨. *Zhongguo gudai jianzhu shi* 中國古代建築史. Beijing: Zhongguo Jianzhu Gongye Chubanshe, 1984.

Liu Jianming 劉健明. *Suidai zhengzhi yu duiwai zhengce* 隋代政治與對外政策. Taibei: Wenjin Chubanshe, 1999.

Lü Yifei 呂一飛. *Huzu xisu yu Sui Tang fengyun* 胡族習俗與隋唐風韻. Beijing: Shumu Wenxian Chubanshe, 1944.

Luo Fuyi 羅福頤. *Qin Han Nanbei chao guanyin zhengcun* 秦漢南北朝官印徵存. Beijing: Wenwu Chubanshe, 1987.

Ma Junmin 馬俊民 and Wang Shiping 王世平. *Tangdai mazheng* 唐代馬政. Xian: Xibei Daxue Chubanshe, 1995.

Ma Qichang 馬其昶. *Han Changli wenji jiaozhu* 韓昌黎文集校注. Shanghai: Shanghai Guji Chubanshe, 1986.

Mancall, Mark. *China at the Center.* New York: Free Press, 1984.

———. "The Persistence of Tradition in Chinese Foreign Policy." *Annals of the American Academy of Political and Social Science*, 349 (1963), pp. 14–26.

Masumura Hiroshi 増村宏. "Nisshutsu tokoro tenshi to nichibotsu tokoro tenshi" 日出處天子と日沒處天子. *Shirin*, 51, no. 3 (1968), pp. 30–50.

———. "Jo Sengyō kyōju no 'Sui Wo bangjiao xinkao: Woshi chao Sui bingfei suowei duideng waijiao' oyobi 'Zui-Wa kokkō no taitōsei ni tsuite' o yomu" 徐先堯教授の「隋倭邦交新考－倭使朝隋并非所謂對等外交」及び「隋倭國交の對等性」についてを讀む. *Kadai shigaku*, 16 (1969), pp. 19–28.

———. *Ken Tō shi no kenkyū* 遣唐使の研究. Kyoto: Dōhōsha, 1988.

———. "Kyūshin ryō Tōsho Nihonden no kentō" 舊新兩唐書日本傳の檢討. In *Tōyōshi ronshū*, ed. Uchida Ginpū Hakase Shōju Kinenkai, pp. 471–498. Kyoto: Dōhōsha, 1978.

McCullough, William H., and Helen Craig McCullough. *A Tale of Flowering Fortunes*. Stanford: Stanford University Press, 1980.

Miki Tarō 三木太郎. *Wajinden no yōgo no kenkyū* 倭人傳の用語の研究. Tokyo: Taga Shuppan Kabushiki Kaisha, 1984.

Minagawa, Masao, and Takeru Akazawa. "Dietary Patterns of Japanese Jomon Hunter-Gatherers: Stable Nitrogen and Carbon Isotope Analysis of Human Bones." In *Pacific Northeast Asia in Prehistory*, ed. C. Melvin Aikens and Song Nai Rhee, pp. 59–68. Pullman, Wash.: WSU Press, 1992.

Miyakawa Hisayuki. "An Outline of the Naitō Hypothesis and Its Effects on Japanese Studies on China." *Far Eastern Quarterly*, 14, no. 4 (1955), pp. 533–552.

Miyazaki Ichisada 宮崎市定. *Nazo no shichishitō* 迷の七支刀. Tokyo: Iwanami Shoten, 1983.

———. "Shichishitō meimon shishaku" 七支刀銘文試釋. *Tōhōgaku*, 64 (1982), pp. 1–14.

———. "Tennō naru shōgō no yurai ni tsuite" 天皇なる稱號の由來について. *Shisō*, 646 (1978), pp. 1–24.

Mori Katsumi 森克己. *Ken Tō shi* 遣唐使. Tokyo: Shibundō, 1966.

———. *Nissō bōeki no kenkyū* 日宋貿易の研究. Tokyo: Kokuritsu Shoin, 1948.

Mori Kimiyuki 森公章. *Kodai Nihon no taigai ninshiki to tsūkō* 古代日本の對外認識と通交. Tokyo: Yoshikawa Kōbunkan, 1998.

———. "Tennō gō no seiritsu o megutte" 天皇號の成立をめぐて. *Nihon rekishi*, 418 (1983), pp. 12–29.

Mori Kōichi 森浩一. *Kōkogaku to kodai Nihon* 考古學と古代日本. Tokyo: Chūō Kōronsha, 1994.

Morohashi Tetsuji 諸橋轍次. *Dai Kan Wa jiten* 大漢和辭典. Rev. edn. Tokyo: Taishūkan Shoten, 1986.

Moses, Larry W. "T'ang Tributary Relations with the Inner Asian Barbarians." In *Essays on T'ang Society*, ed. John C. Perry and Bardwell L. Smith, pp. 61–89. Leiden: E. J. Brill, 1976.

Mote, Frederick W. "Handwritten Books—before and after the Invention of Block Printing." *Gest Library Journal*, 2, no. 2 (1988), pp. 49–96.

Mozai Torao 茂在寅男. "Ken Tō shi gaikan" 遣唐使概觀. In *Ken Tō shi kenkyū to shiryō*, ed. Mozai Torao et al., pp. 1–43. Tokyo: Tōkai Daigaku Shuppan Kai, 1987.

———. *Kodai Nihon no kōkaijutsu* 古代日本の航海術. Tokyo: Shōgakkan, 1979.

Murayama Shichiro and Roy A. Miller. "The Inariyama Tumulus Sword Inscription." *Journal of Japanese Studies*, 5, no. 2 (1979), pp. 405–438.

Murry, James A. H., et al. *The Oxford English Dictionary*. Oxford: Clarendon Press, 1978.

Nabeta Hajime 鍋田一. "Roku shichi seiki no hinrei ni kansuru oboegaki" 六－七世紀の賓禮に關する覺書. In *Ritsuryōsei no shomondai*, ed. Takigawa Masajirō Hakase Beiju Kinenkai, pp. 399–426. Tokyo: Kyūko Shoin, 1984.

Nagahiro Toshio 長廣敏雄 and Mizuno Seiichi 水野清一. *Kanan Rakuyō Ryūmon sekkutsu no kenkyū* 河南洛陽龍門石窟の研究. Tokyo: Zauhō Kankōkai, 1941.

Naitō Konan 內藤湖南. *Nihon bunkashi kenkyū* 日本文化史研究. Tokyo: Kōdansha, 1924.

Nakagawa, Masako. "The *Shan-hai ching* and *Wo*: A Japanese Connection." *Sino-Japanese Studies*, vol. 15 (2003), pp. 45–55.

———. *The Yang Kuei-fei Legend in Japanese Literature*. Lewiston, N.Y.: Edwin Mellen Press, 1998.

Nakamura Hidetaka 中村榮孝. *Nihon to Chōsen* 日本と朝鮮. Tokyo: Shibundō, 1966.

Nakamura Hiroichi 中村裕一. "Tōdai no choku ni tsuite" 唐代の敕について. *Mukōgawa Joshi Daigaku kiyō (kyōiku gakkahen)*, 31 (1984), pp. 1–34.

———. "Tōdai no irō seisho ni tsuite" 唐代の慰勞制書に就いて. In *Ritsuryōsei*, ed. Tōshi Kenkyūkai, pp. 333–358. Tokyo: Kyūko Shoin, 1986.

———. "Tōdai no jisho ni tsuite" 唐代の璽書について. *Mukōgawa Joshi Daigaku kiyō (kyōiku gakkahen)*, 28 (1980), pp. 25–40; 29 (1981), pp. 29–56.

———. "Tōdai no seishoshiki ni tsuite" 唐代の制書式に就いて. *Shigaku zasshi*, 91, no. 9 (1982), pp. 39–62.

Nakamura Jihei 中村治兵衛. "Tōdai no sonraku to rimpo" 唐代の村落と鄰保. In *Chūgoku ritsuryōsei no tenkai to sono kokka shakai to no kankei*, ed. Tōshi Kenkyūkai, pp. 116–122. Tokyo: Tōsui Shobō, 1984.

Nakamura Taichi 中村太一. "Kodai suijō kōtsū ni kansuru kisoteki kōsa" 古代水上交通に關する基礎的考察. In *Nihon kodai no kokka to saigi*, ed. Hayashi Rokurō and Suzuki Yasutami, pp. 629–641. Tokyo: Yūzankaku Shuppan Kabushiki Kaisha, 1996.

Nakano Takayuki 中野高行. "Irō shōsho ni kansuru kisoteki kōsa" 慰勞詔書に關する基礎的考察. *Komonjo kenkyū*, 23 (1984), pp. 60–67.

———. "Irō shōsho no ketsugo no hensen ni tsuite" 慰勞詔書の「結語」變遷について. *Shigaku*, 55, no. 1 (1985), pp. 95–102.

———. "Irō shōsho to tai banshi shō no kankei ni tsuite" 慰勞詔書と「對蕃使詔」の關係について. *Komonjo kenkyū*, 27 (1987), pp. 73–77.

Nakata Norio 中田祝夫. "Nihon no kanji" 日本の漢字. In *Nihongo no sekai (4)*, ed. Ono Susumu, pp. 271–296. Tokyo: Chūō Kōronsha, 1983.

Nakata Yūjirō 中田勇次郎. *Ō Gishi o chūshin to suru hōjō no kenkyū* 王羲之を中心とする法帖の研究. Tokyo: Nigensha, 1960.

Naoki Kōjiro 直木孝次郎. *Nihon no rekishi* 日本の歴史. Vol. 1. Tokyo: Shōgakkan, 1973.

Niida Noboru 仁井田陞. *Chūgoku hōseishi kenkyū (4)* 中國法制史研究(四). Tokyo: Tokyo Daigaku Shuppankai, 1964.

———, ed. *Tōryō shūi* 唐令拾遺. Tokyo: Tokyo Daigaku Shuppankai, 1933.

Nishijima Sadao 西島定生. *Chūgoku kodai kokka to Higashi Ajia shakai* 中國古代國家と東アジア社會. Tokyo: Tokyo Daigaku Shuppankai, 1983.

———. *Chūgoku kodai teikoku no keisei to kōzō* 中國古代帝國の形成と構造. Tokyo: Tokyo Daigaku Shuppankai, 1961.

———. "Higashi Ajia sekai no keisei (1): Sōsetsu" 東アジア世界の形成(一): 總説. In *Iwanami kōza sekai rekishi (kodai 4)*, ed. Ienaga Saburō et al., pp. 3–19. Tokyo: Iwanami Shoten, 1970.

———. "Ken Tō shi to kokusho" 遣唐使と國書. In *Ken Tō shi kenkyū to shiryō*, ed. Nishijima Sadao et al., pp. 46–86. Tokyo: Tōkai Daigaku Shuppankai, 1987.

———. "Ken Zui shi to kokusho mondai" 遣隋使と國書問題. *Gakushikai kaihō*, 776 (1987), pp. 39–44.

———. *Nihon rekishi no kokusai kankyō* 日本歴史の國際環境. Tokyo: Tokyo Daigaku Shuppankai, 1985.

———. "Roku-hachi seiki no Higashi Ajia" 六 - 八世紀の東アジア. In *Iwanami kōza Nihon rekishi (kodai 2)*, ed. Ienaga Saburō et al., pp. 229–278. Tokyo: Iwanami Shoten, 1962.

———. "Shin Gi Waō sakuhō ni itaru Higashi Ajia no jōsei" 親魏倭王冊封に至る東アジアの情勢. In *Kodaishi ronsō*, ed. Inoue Mitsusada Hakase Kanreki Kinenkai, pp. 1–48. Tokyo: Yoshikawa Kōbunkan, 1978.

———. "Tōōchō to ken Tō shi" 唐王朝と遣唐使. In *Ken Tō shi jidai no Nihon to Chūgoku*, ed. Egami Namio, pp. 41–62. Tokyo: Shogakkan, 1982.

———. "Yon–roku seiki no Higashi Ajia to Nihon" 四 - 六世紀の東アジアと日本. In *Zemināru Nihon kodaishi (ge)*, ed. Ueda Masaaki et al., pp. 593–614. Tokyo: Kōbunsha, 1980.

Nunome Chōfu 布目潮渢 and Ōno Hitoshi 大野仁. "Haku Kyoi hyakudōhan shakugi" 白居易百道判釋義. *Osaka Daigaku Kyōyōbu kenkyū shūroku (jinbun shakai kagaku)*, 28 (1980), pp. 21–35; 29 (1981), pp. 1–22; 30 (1982), pp. 37–61.

Nunome Junrō 布目順郎. "Dōtakumen no kōjikei kigu o motta jimbutsu gazō ni tsuite" 銅鐸面の工字形器具を持った人物畫像について. *Kōkogaku zasshi*, 36, no. 2 (1950), pp. 25–31.

Ōba Osamu 大庭修. "'Himiko o Shin Gi Waō to suru seisho' o meguru mondai" 「卑彌呼を親魏倭王とする制書」をめぐる問題. In *Suenaga sensei koki kinen kodaigaku ronsō*, ed. Suenaga Sensei Koki Kinenkai, pp. 177–203. Osaka: Suenaga Sensei Koki Kinenkai, 1967.

————. "Kan no chūrōshō kōi to Gi no sozzen chūrōshō sozzen kōi" 漢の中郎將、校尉と魏の率善中郎將、率善校尉. *Shisen*, 42 (1971), pp. 5–31.

————. *Kanseki yunyū no bunkashi* 漢籍輸入の文化史. Tokyo: Kenbun Shuppan, 1997.

————. "Qian Tang shi chuan de xingtai" 遣唐使船的形態. In *Gudai Zhong Han Ri guanxi yanjiu*, ed. Lin Tianwei and Huang Yuese, pp. 47–31. Xianggang: Xianggang Daxue Yazhou Yanjiu Zhongxin, 1987.

————. *Shin Kan hōseishi no kenkyū* 秦漢法制史の研究. Tokyo: Sōbunsha, 1982.

————. "Tō kokushin no kobungakuteki kenkyū" 唐告身の古文學的研究. In *Seiiki bunka kenkyū*, ed. Seiiki Bunka Kenkyūkai, vol. 3, pp. 281–368. Kyoto: Hōzōkan, 1960.

————. "Zen Kan no shōgun" 前漢の將軍. In his *Shin Kan hōseishi no kenkyū*, pp. 357–409. Tokyo: Sōbunsha, 1982.

Ogino Minahiko 荻野三七彦. "Inshō shijō no Nihon to Chūgoku" 印章史上の日本と中國. In *Taigai kankei to shakai keizai*, ed. Mori Katsumi Hakase Kanreki Kinenkai, pp. 69–84. Tokyo: Hanawa Shobō, 1978.

Okazaki, Takashi. "Japan and the Continent." In *Ancient Japan*, ed. Delmer M. Brown, vol. 1 of *The Cambridge History of Japan*, ed. John W. Hall et al., pp. 268–316. Cambridge: Cambridge University Press, 1993.

Okikawa, A., and S. Koyama. "A Jomon Shellmound Database." *Senri Ethnological Studies*, 9 (1981), pp. 187–200.

Omodaka Hisataka et al. 澤瀉久孝. *Jidaibetsu kokugo daijiten (jōdaihen)* 時代別國語大辭典（上代編）. Tokyo: Sanseidō, 1968.

Ono Katsutoshi 小野勝年. *Nittō guhō junrei kōki no kenkyū* 入唐求法巡禮行記の研究. Tokyo: Suzuki Gakujutsu Zaidan, 1964–1969.

Paku Sekisen 朴昔順. "Nihon kodai kokka no tai ban ninshiki" 日本古代國家の對「蕃」認識. *Nihon rekishi*, no. 637 (2001), pp. 1–15.

Pan Lü Qichang 潘呂棋昌. *Xiao Yingshi yanjiu* 蕭穎士研究. Taibei: Wenshizhe Chubanshe, 1983.

Pan Yihong. "Marriage Alliances and Chinese Princesses in International Politics from Han through T'ang." *Asia Major*, 3rd series, 10, nos. 1–2 (1997), pp. 111–131.

————. *Son of Heaven and Heavenly Qaghan*. Bellingham: Center for Asian Studies, Western Washington University, 1997.

Pearson, Richard J. "Ancient Japan." In *Yoshinogari: The World of the Wei Dynasty Annals*, ed. Sahara Makoto, pp. 154–157. New York: George Braziller, 1992.

————. "The Contribution of Archaeology to Japanese Studies." *Journal of Japanese Studies*, 2, no. 2 (1979), pp. 305–334.

Pearson, Richard J., Gina L. Barnes, and K. Hutterer, eds. *Windows on the Japanese Past: Studies on Archaeology.* Ann Arbor: Center for Japanese Studies, University of Michigan, 1986.

Peterson, Charles A. "P'u-ku Huai-en and the T'ang Court: The Limits of Loyalty." *Monumenta Serica,* 29 (1970–1971), pp. 423–455.

Philippi, Donald L. *Norito, a Translation of the Ancient Japanese Ritual Prayers.* Princeton: Princeton University Press, 1990.

Price, Barbara J. "Secodary State Formation: An Explanatory Note." In *Origins of the State,* ed. Ronald Cohen and Elman R. Service, pp. 161–184. Philadelphia: Institute for the Study of Human Issues, 1978.

Pulleyblank, Edwin. *The Background of the Rebellion of An Lu-shan.* London: Oxford University Press, 1951.

Pyŏn In-sŏk 卞麟錫. "Cong suyu zhidu kan Tangdai Zhongguo yu Xinluo de guanxi" 從宿衛制度看唐代中國與新羅的關係. Master's thesis, National University of Taiwan, 1966.

———. "A Study of Disputes among Foreign Envoys over Seating Order at the Court of the T'ang Dynasty." *The Journal of Asiatic Studies,* 10, no. 4 (Seoul, 1967), pp. 129–148.

———. "Tang Xuanzong shidai yu dongyi guanxi zhi yipie" 唐玄宗時代與東夷關係之一瞥. *Dalu zazhi,* 30, no. 12 (1965), pp. 2, 23, 31.

———. "Zhongguo Tangdai yu Xinluo de guanxi" 中國唐代與新羅的關係. *Dalu zazhi,* 32, no. 9 (1966), pp. 273–277.

Quan Hansheng 全漢昇. "Tang Song diguo yu yunhe" 唐宋帝國與運河. In his *Zhongguo jingji shi yanjiu (shang),* pp. 265–395. Xianggang: Xinya Yanjiusuo, 1967.

Reischauer, Edwin O. *Ennin's Dairy.* New York: Ronald Press, 1955.

———. *Ennin's Travels in T'ang China.* New York: Ronald Press, 1955.

———. "Notes on T'ang Dynasty Sea Routes." *HJAS,* 5, no. 2 (1940), pp. 142–164.

Rikō Mitsuo 利光三津夫. "'Tōrikuten' no Nihon ni okeru kōyō ni tsuite" 「唐六典」の日本における行用について. *Hōgaku kenkyū,* 63, no. 5 (1990), pp. 1–28.

———. "Wagakuni ni hakusai sareta Tōritsu no chūshakusha to sono itsubun" 我國に舶載された唐律の注釋者とその逸文. *Shigaku zasshi,* 67, no. 11 (1958), pp. 63–83.

Robinson, G. W. "Early Japanese Chronicles: The Six National Histories." In *Historians of China and Japan,* ed. W. G. Beasley and E. G. Pulleyblank, pp. 213–228. London: Oxford University Press, 1961.

Rodd, Laurel Rasplica, and Mary Catherine Henkenius. *Kokinshū: A Collection of Poems Ancient and Modern.* Princeton: Princeton University Press, 1984.

Rotours, Robert des. "Les Insignes en deux parties (fou) sous la dynastie des T'ang." *T'oung Pao,* 41 (1952), pp. 1–148.

Sabban, Françoise. "The History and Culture of Food and Drink in Asia: China." Trans. Elborg Forsters. In *The Cambridge World History of Food*, ed. Kenneth F. Kiple and Kriemhild C. Ornelas, vol. 2, pp. 1171–1172. Cambridge: Cambridge University Press, 2000.

Sahara, Makoto. "Once There Was a War: Changes in Stone Projectile Points." *Kodaigaku kenkyū*, 78 (1975), pp. 26–28.

———. "Rice Cultivation and the Japanese." *Acta Asiatica*, no. 63 (1992), pp. 40–63.

———. "Yoshinogari, the World of the Wei Dynasty Annals." In *Ancient Japan*, ed. Richard J. Pearson, pp. 154–157. New York: George Braziller, 1992.

Saily, Jay. "A. C. Graham's Disputers of the Tao and Some Recent Works in English on Chinese Thought." *JAOS*, 112, no. 1 (1992), pp. 36–41.

Sakamoto Tarō 阪本太郎. "Gishiki to tōrei" 儀式と唐禮. In his *Nihon kodaishi no kisoteki kenkyū (2)*, pp. 67–75. Tokyo: Tokyo Daigaku Shuppankai, 1964.

———. *Nihon no shūshi to shigaku* 日本の修史と史學. Tokyo: Shibundō, 1969.

———. *Shōtoku Taishi* 聖德太子. Tokyo: Yoshikawa Kōbunkan, 1979.

Sakamoto Yoshitane 阪元義種. *Kodai Higashi Ajia no Nihon to Chōsen* 古代東アジアの日本と朝鮮. Tokyo: Yoshikawa Kōbunkan, 1978.

———. *Wa no goō* 倭の五王. Tokyo: Kyōikusha, 1981.

———. "Wa no goō no shakugō mondai" 倭の五王の爵號問題. In *Zemināru Nihon kodaishi (2)*, ed. Ueda Masaaki et al., pp. 381–392. Tokyo: Kōbunsha, 1980.

Sakayori Masashi 酒寄雅志. "Shichi hachi seiki no Dazaifu" 七、八世紀の大宰府. *Kokugakuin zasshi*, 80, no. 11 (1979), pp. 34–45.

Sansom, G. B. "The Imperial Edicts in the Shoku Nihongi (700–790)." *The Transactions of the Asiatic Society of Japan*, 2nd series, 1 (1924), pp. 5–39.

Sasaki Kōmei. "The Wa People and Their Culture in Ancient Japan: The Cultures of Swidden Cultivation and Padi-Rice Cultivation." *Acta Asiatica*, no. 61 (1991), pp. 24–46.

Satō Kiyoji 佐藤喜代治. *Nihon no kango* 日本の漢語. Tokyo: Kadokawa Shoten, 1979.

Satō Makoto 佐藤信. *Nihon to Bokkai no kodai shi* 日本と渤海の古代史. Tokyo: Yamakawa Shuppansha, 2003.

Schafer, Edward H. "Fusang and Beyond." *JAOS*, 109, no. 3 (1989), pp. 379–400.

———. *The Golden Peaches of Samarkand*. Berkeley: University of California Press, 1963.

———. "Ritual Exposure in Ancient China." *HJAS*, 14 (1951), pp. 130–174.

Seki Akira 關晃. *Kikajin* 歸化人. Tokyo: Shibundō, 1966.

Shaanxisheng Bowuguan Fupingxian Wenhuaguan 陝西省博物館富平縣文化館. "Tang Li Feng mu fajue jianbao" 唐李鳳墓發掘簡報. *Kaogu*, 5 (1977), pp. 313–326.

Shiba Ryōtarō 司馬遼太郎. *Kūkai no fūkei* 空海の風景. Tokyo: Chūō Kōronsha, 1975.

Shimizu, Yoshiaki. *Japan, the Shaping of Daimyo Culture, 1185–1868*. Washington, D.C.: National Gallery of Art, 1988.

Snellen, J. B., trans. "Shoku Nihongi." *The Transactions of the Asiatic Society of Japan*, 2nd series, pt. 1, vol. 11 (1934), pp. 151–239; pt. 2, vol. 14 (1937), pp. 11–278.

Song Nai Rhee. "Secondary State Formation: The Case of Koguryŏ." In *Pacific Northeast Asia in Prehistory*, ed. C. Melvin Aikens and Song Nai Rhee, pp. 191–196. Pullman, Wash.: WSU Press, 1992.

Steinhardt, Nancy S. *Chinese Imperial City Planning*. Honolulu: University of Hawai'i Press, 1990.

Sugimoto Naojirō 杉本直治郎. *Abe no Nakamaro den kenkyū* 阿倍仲麻呂傳研究. Tokyo: Ikuhōsha, 1940.

Sun Guangqi 孫光圻. "Xu Fu dongdu hanglu yanjiu" 徐福東渡航路研究. In *Quanguo shoujie Xu Fu xueshu taolunhui lunwenji*, ed. Zhongguo Hanghai Xuehui et al., pp. 171–193. Beijing: Zhongguo Kuangye Daxue Chubanshe, 1988.

———. "Zhong Ri shuidao zhilu de hanghai xue bianxi" 中日水稻之路的航海學辯析. In *Zhong Ri guangxishi guoji xueshu taolunhui lunwen*, ed. Zhongguo Zhong Ri Guanxishi Yanjiuhui, pp. 79–84. Beijing: n.p., 1988.

Suzuki Osamu 鈴木治. *Hakusonkō* 白村江. Tokyo: Gakusei Sha, 1972.

Tajima Isao 田島公. "Nihon no ritsuryō kokka no 'hinrei'" 日本の律令國家の賓禮. *Shirin*, 68, no. 3 (1985), pp. 35–86.

Takeda Sachiko 武田知子. *Kodai kokka no keisei to ifukusei* 古代國家の形成と衣服制. Tokyo: Yoshikawa Kōbunkan, 1984.

Takeda Yukio 武田幸男. "Heisei shōgun Wazui no kaishaku" 平西將軍倭隋の解釋. *Chōsen gakuhō*, 77 (1975), pp. 1–38.

Takemoto Toru. "The Kyūshū Dynasty: Furuta's Theory on Ancient Japan." *Japan Quarterly*, 30, no. 4 (1983), pp. 383–387.

Takigawa Masajirō 瀧川政次郎. "Kōto shūrei to Nihon no gishiki" 江都集禮と日本の儀式. In *Tenseki ronshū*, ed. Iwai Hakase Koki Kinen Jigyōkai, pp. 342–347. Tokyo: Iwai Hakase Koki Kinen Jigyōkai, 1963.

———. "Ryō no shūge ni mietaru Tō no hōritsu shiryō" 令集解に見えたる唐の法律史料. *Toyō gakuhō*, 18, no. 1 (1929), pp. 25–57.

———. "Shichi seiki no Tōa henkyoku to Nihon shoki" 七世紀の東亞變局と日本書紀. In *Nihon shoki kenkyū*, ed. Yokoda Kenichi, vol. 6, pp. 175–240. Tokyo: Hanawa Shobō, 1972.

Taylor, Keith W. *The Birth of Vietnam*. Berkeley: University of California Press, 1983.

Tezuka Takayoshi 手塚隆義. "Shin Gi Waō kō" 親魏倭王考. *Shien*, 23, no. 2 (1963), pp. 24–37.

Tian Tao 田濤 and Guo Chengwei 郭成偉, eds. *Longjin fengsui pan jiaozhu* 龍筋鳳髓判校注. Beijing: Zhongguo Zhengfa Daxue Chubanshe, 1996.

Tokoro Isao 所功. "Chōga gishikibun no seiritsu" 朝賀儀式文の成立. In *Nihon kodaishi ron'en*, ed. Endō Motoo Sensei Shōju Kinenkai, pp. 571–610. Tokyo: Kokusho Kankōkai, 1983.

Tonami Mamoru 礪波護. *Tōdai seiji shakaishi kenkyū* 唐代政治社會史研究. Kyoto: Dōhōsha, 1986.

Tōno Haruyuki 東野治之. "Heijōkyū shutsudo mokkan shoken no Bunsen Ri Zen chū" 平城宮出土木簡所見の文選李善注. In his *Shōsōin monjo to mokkan no kenkyū*, pp. 149–153. Tokyo: Hanawa Shobō, 1977.

———. *Ken Tō shi to shōsōin* 遣唐使と正倉院. Tokyo: Iwanami Shoten, 1992.

———. "Rongo, Senjibun to Fujiwarakyū mokkan" 論語、千字文と藤原宮木簡. In his *Shōsōin monjo to mokkan no kenkyū*, pp. 125–148. Tokyo: Hanawa Shobō, 1977.

———. "Tennōgō no seiritsu nendai ni tsuite" 天皇號の成立年代について. In his *Shōsōin monjo to mokkan no kenkyū*, pp. 397–402. Tokyo: Hanawa Shobō, 1977.

Tsuboi, Kiyotari. "Issues in Japanese Archaeology." *Acta Asiatica*, no. 63 (1992), pp. 1–20.

Tsuda Sōkichi 津田左右吉. "Shoki no kakikata oyobi yomikata" 書紀の書きかたおよび訓みかた. In *Tsuda Sōkichi zenshū*, ed. Tsuda Sōkichi Zenshū Henshūshitsu, vol. 2, pp. 291–396. Tokyo: Iwanami Shoten, 1963.

Tsukishima Hiroshi 築島裕. *Heian jidaigo shinron* 平安時代語新論. Tokyo: Tokyo Daigaku Shuppankai, 1969.

Tsunoda, Ryusaku, et al., eds. *Sources of Japanese Tradition*. New York: Columbia University Press, 1958.

Twitchett, Denis C. *Printing and Publishing in Medieval China*. New York: Frederic C. Beil Publishers, 1983.

———. "The Problem of Sources." In *Sui and T'ang China, 589–906*, ed. Denis C. Twitchett, vol. 3, part 1 of *The Cambridge History of China*, ed. John K. Fairbank and Denis C. Twitchett, pp. 38–47. Cambridge: Cambridge University Press, 1979.

———. "Sui and T'ang China and the Wider World." In *Sui and T'ang China, 589–906*, ed. Denis C. Twitchett, vol. 3, part 1 of *The Cambridge History of China*, ed. John K. Fairbank and Denis C. Twitchett, pp. 32–38. Cambridge: Cambridge University Press, 1979.

———. "The T'ang Market System." *Asia Major*, n.s., 12, no. 2 (1966), pp. 202–248.

———. *The Writing of Official History under the T'ang*. Cambridge: Cambridge University Press, 1992.

Twitchett, Denis C., and Klaus-Peter Tietze. "The Liao." In *Alien Regimes and Border States, 907–1368*, ed. Herbert Franke and Denis C. Twitchett, vol. 6 of

The Cambridge History of China, ed. John K. Fairbank and Denis C. Twitchett, pp. 43–153. Cambridge: Cambridge University Press, 1994.

Uchida Ginpū 內田吟風. "Gishi Wajinden naka no nettaiteki shokiji ni tsuite" 魏志倭人傳中の熱帶的諸記事について. In *Tōhōgaku ronshū,* ed. Ono Katsutoshi Hakase Shōju Kinenkai, pp. 51–57. Kyoto: Ryūkoku Daigaku Tōyō Shigaku Kenkyūkai, 1982.

Ueda Masaaki 上田正昭. *Kikajin* 歸化人. Tokyo: Chūō Kōronsha, 1965.

———. *Wakoku no sekai* 倭國の世界. Tokyo: Kōdansha, 1976.

Umehara Takeshi 梅原猛. *Kempō jūshichijō* 憲法十七條. Tokyo: Shōgakkan, 1981.

Verschuer, Charlotte von. *Le Commerce Extérieur du Japon des Origines au XVIe Siècle.* Paris: Éditions Maisonneuve & Larose, 1988.

———. *Les relations officielles du Japon avec la Chine aux VIIIe et IXe Siècles.* Geneva: Librairie Droz, S.A., 1985.

Waley, Arthur. *The Analects of Confucius.* London: George Allen and Unwin, 1938.

Walker, Richard L. *The Multi-State System of Ancient China.* Hamden: Shoe String Press, 1953.

Wang Gung-wu. "Early Ming Relations with Southeast Asia." In *The Chinese World Order,* ed. John K. Fairbank, pp. 34–62. Cambridge, Mass.: Harvard University Press, 1968.

———. "The Rhetoric of a Lesser Empire." In *China among Equals,* ed. Morris Rossabi, pp. 47–65. Berkeley: University of California Press, 1983.

Wang Jinlin 王金林. *Han Tang wenhua yu gudai Riben wenhua* 漢唐文化與古代日本文化. Tianjin: Tianjin Renmin Chubanshe, 1996.

Wang Liqi 王利器. *Fengsu tongyi jiaozhu* 風俗通義校注. Taibei: Mingwen Shuju, 1983.

———. *Lüshi chunqiu zhushu* 呂氏春秋注疏. Chengdu: Bashu Shushe, 2002.

———. "Riben guo jianzai shumu tiyao" 日本國見在書目提要. In his *Wang Liqi lunxue zazhu,* pp. 442–448. Beijing: Beijing Shifan Xueyuan Chubanshe, 1990.

———. *Wenjing mifu lun jiaozhu* 文鏡祕府論校注. Beijing: Zhongguo Shehui Kexue Chubanshe, 1983.

———. *Wenxin diaolong jiaozheng* 文心雕龍校証. Shanghai: Shanghai Guji Chubanshe, 1980.

———. *Yanshi jiaxun jijie* 顏氏家訓集解. Shanghai: Shanghai Guji Chubanshe, 1986.

Wang Tao. "A City with Many Faces: Urban Development in Pre-Modern China." In *Exploring China's Past,* trans. and ed. Roderick Whitfield and Wang Tao, pp. 111–121. London: Saffron, 1999.

Wang Weikun 王維坤. "Tang Zhanghuai taizi mu bihua keshi tu bianxi" 唐章懷太子墓壁畫客使圖辨析. *Kaogu,* 1 (1966), pp. 65–74.

Wang Xiaofu 王小甫. "Tangchao yu Xinluo guanxi shi lun" 唐朝與新羅關係史論. *Tang yanjiu*, 6 (2000), pp. 155–177.

Wang Yi-t'ung. *A Record of Buddhist Monasteries in Lo-yang.* Princeton: Princeton University Press, 1984.

Wang Yong 王勇. "Hanji dongchuan zhushuo kaobian" 漢籍東傳諸說考辨. In *Zhongguo dianji zai Riben de liuchuan yu yingxiang*, ed. Lu Jian and Wang Yong, pp. 49–65. Hangzhou: Hangzhou Daxue Chubanshe, 1990.

Wang Zhenping. "Act on Appropriateness and Mutual Self-Interest: Early T'ang Diplomatic Thinking, A.D. 618–649." *Medieval History Journal*, 1, no. 2 (1998), pp. 165–194.

———. "Manuscript Copies of Chinese Books in Ancient Japan." *Gest Library Journal*, 4, no. 2 (1991), pp. 35–67.

———. "Speaking with a Forked Tongue: Diplomatic Correspondence between China and Japan 238–608." *JAOS*, 114, no. 1 (1994), pp. 23–32.

Wang Zhongmin 王重民, Sun Wang 孫望, and Tong Yangnian 童養年, eds. *Quan Tang shi waibian* 全唐詩外編. Beijing: Zhonghua Shuju, 1982.

Weber, Max. *The Religion of China.* Trans. Hans H. Gerth. New York: Free Press, 1951.

Wechsler, Howard J. "T'ai-tsung (reign 626–649) the Consolidator." In *Sui and T'ang China, 589–906*, ed. Denis C. Twitchett, vol. 3, part 1 of *The Cambridge History of China*, ed. John K. Fairbank and Denis C. Twitchett, pp. 188–241. Cambridge: Cambridge University Press, 1979.

Wong Siu-kit, Lo, Allan Chung-hang, and Kwong-tai Lam. *The Book of Literary Design.* Hong Kong: Hong Kong University Press, 1999.

Wriggins, Sally H. *Xuanzang: A Buddhist Pilgrim on the Silk Road.* Boulder: Westview Press, 1996.

Wright, Arthur F. "The Sui Dynasty (581–617)." In *Sui and T'ang China, 589–906*, ed. Denis C. Twitchett, vol. 3, part 1 of *The Cambridge History of China*, ed. John K. Fairbank and Denis C. Twitchett, pp. 48–149. Cambridge: Cambridge University Press, 1979.

———. "Sui Yang-ti: Personality and Stereotype." In *The Confucian Persuasion*, ed. Arthur Wright, pp. 47–76. Stanford: Stanford University Press, 1960.

Wu Yugui 吳玉貴. *Tujue hanguo yu Sui Tang guanxi shi yanjiu* 突厥汗國與隋唐關係史研究. Beijing: Zhongguo Shehui Kexue Chubanshe, 1998.

Xiang Da 向達. *Tangdai Changan yu Xiyu wenming* 唐代長安與西域文明. Taibei: Mingwen Shuju, 1981.

Xiang Zonglu 向宗魯, ed. *Shuoyuan jiaozheng* 說苑校證. Beijing: Zhonghua Shuju, 1987.

Xin Deyong 辛德勇. "Tang Changan Duting yi kaobian" 唐長安都亭驛考辨. In his *Gudai jiaotong yu dili wenxian yanjiu*, pp. 113–116. Beijing: Zhonghua Shuju, 1996.

———. "Tang Changan cheng jianzhi congkao" 唐長安城建置叢考. *Wenshi*, 37 (1993), pp. 93–112.

Xing Yitian 邢義田. "Handai de yiyi zhiyi lun" 漢代的以夷制夷論. In *Zhongguo shixue lunwen xuanji*, ed. Ruan Zhisheng et al., vol. 2, pp. 227–276. Taibei: Youshi Wenhua Shiye Gongsi, 1976.

———. "Handai zhongwai jingji jiaotong yishu de shangque"《漢代中外經濟交通》一書的商榷. *Shi yuan*, 3 (1972), pp. 175–178.

Xu Chen 徐琛. "Ennin no nittō guhō keiro kō—Chūgoku Kōsoshō Nantsu, Jūkō ni okeru jōrikuchi to keiro" 丹仁の入唐求法經路考—中國江蘇省南通、 如皋における上陸地と經路. Trans. Suzuki Yasutami. In *Nihon kodai kokka to saigi*, ed. Hayashi Rokurō et al., pp. 661–682. Tokyo: Yūzankaku Shuppan, 1996.

Xu Tongxin 許同莘. *Gongduxue shi* 公牘學史. Shanghai: Shangwu Yinshuguan, 1947.

Xu Xianyao 徐先堯. *Er Wang chidu yu Riben shuji suozai guoshu zhi yanjiu* 二王尺牘與日本書紀所載國書之研究. Taibei: Huashi Chubanshe, 1979.

———. "Sui Wo bangjiao xinkao (wu)" 隋倭邦交新考(五). *Zhongguo yu Riben*, 61 (1964), pp. 28–31.

———. "Wakoku kara Zui ni okutta kokusho no mondaiten" 倭國から隋に贈った國書の問題點. *Kokusai tōhō gakusha kaigi kiyō*, 17 (1972), pp. 99–101.

Yaegashi Naohiko 八重樫直比古. "Nihon kodai no daigaku ni okeru 'Kōkyō' (jo)" 日本古代の大學における「孝經」(上). *Nōtorudamu Seishin joshi daigaku kiyō*, 5, no. 1 (1981), pp. 17–30.

Yajima Genryō 矢島玄亮. *Nihonkoku genzaisho mokuroku: shūshō to kenkyū* 日本國見在書目錄：集証と研究. Tokyo: Kyūko Shoin, 1984.

Yamada Hideo 山田英雄. "Nichi, Tō, Ragi, Bōtsu aida no kokusho ni tsuite" 日、唐、羅、渤間いだの國書について. In *Nihon kōkogaku kodaishi ronshū*, ed. Itō Nobuo Kyōju Kanreki Kinenkai, pp. 343–366. Tokyo: Yoshikawa Kōbunkan, 1974.

———. "Shogi ni tsuite" 書儀について. In *Taigai kankei to shakai keizai*, ed. Mori Katsumi Hakase Kanreki Kinenkai, pp. 29–44. Tokyo: Hanawa Shobō, 1968.

Yamao Yukihisa 山尾幸久. *Gishi Wajinden* 魏志倭人傳. Tokyo: Kōdansha, 1986.

———. "Kudara sansho to Nihon shoki" 百濟三書と日本書紀. In *Chōsenshi Kenkyūkai rombunshū*, ed. Chōsenshi Kenkyūkai, vol. 15, pp. 5–40. Tokyo: Ryūkei Shosha, 1978.

Yamasaki Taikō. *Shingon: Japanese Esoteric Buddhism*. Trans. Richard and Tynthis Peterson. Boston: Shambhala Publications, 1988.

Yamaguchi Shinji 山内晋次. *Nara Heian ki no Nippon to Ajia* 奈良平安期の日本とアジア. Tokyo: Yoshikawa Kōbunkan, 2003.

Yan Gengwang 嚴耕望. "Tang liangjing chengfang kao" 唐兩京城坊考. In his *Tangshi yanjiu conggao*, pp. 258–303. Xianggang: Xinya Yanjiusuo, 1969.

———. "Tang liangjing guanyi kao" 唐兩京館驛考. In his *Tangshi yanjiu conggao*, pp. 258–303. Xianggang: Xinya Yanjiusuo, 1969.

Yan Shaodang 嚴紹璗. *Hanji zai Riben de liubu yanjiu* 漢籍在日本的流布研究. Nanjing: Jiangsu Guji Chubanshe, 1992.

Yan Wenru 閻文儒 and Yan Wanjun 閻萬鈞. *Liangjing chengfang kao bu* 兩京城坊考補. Zhengzhou: Henan Renmin Chubanshe, 1992.

Yang Kuan 楊寬. *Zhongguo gudai ducheng zhidushi yanjiu* 中國古代都城制度史研究. Shanghai: Shanghai Guji Chubanshe, 1993.

Yang Lien-sheng. "Historical Notes on the Chinese World Order." In *The Chinese World Order*, ed. John K. Fairbank, pp. 20–33. Cambridge, Mass.: Harvard University Press, 1968.

Yang Tingfu 楊廷福. *Xuanzang nianpu* 玄奘年譜. Beijing: Zhonghua Shuju, 1988.

Yang Xianyi and Gladys Yang. *Tang Dynasty Stories*. Beijing: Chinese Literature Press, 1986.

Yokota Ken'ichi 橫田健一. "'Nihon shoki' to 'Jingiryō,' 'Kōshikiryō'"「日本書紀」と「神祇令」、「公式令」. In *Ritsuryōsei no shomondai*, ed. Takigawa Masajirō Hakase Beiju Kinenkai, pp. 577–587. Tokyo: Kyūko Shoin, 1984.

Yokoyama Sadahirō 橫山貞裕. "Waō Bu no jōhyōbun ni tsuite" 倭王武の上表文について. *Nihon rekishi*, 389 (1980), pp. 92–96.

Yoshikawa Shinji 吉川真司. "Nara jidai no sen" 奈良時代の宣. *Shirin*, 71, no. 4 (1988), pp. 1–38.

Yu Xianhao 郁賢皓. *Tang cishi kao quanbian* 唐刺史考全編. Hefei: Anhui Daxue Chubanshe, 2000.

Yü Ying-shih. "Han Foreign Relations." In *The Ch'in and Han Empires, 221 BC–AD 220*, ed. Denis C. Twitchett and Michael Loewe, vol. 1 of *The Cambridge History of China*, ed. John K. Fairbank and Denis C. Twitchett, pp. 377–462. Cambridge: Cambridge University Press, 1986.

———. *Trade and Expansion in Han China*. Berkeley: University of California Press, 1967.

Yuan Ke 袁珂. *Shanhai jing jiaozhu* 山海經校注. Shanghai: Shanghai Guji Chubanshe, 1980.

Yuasa Yukihiko 湯淺幸孫. "Ken Tō shi kōben nisoku" 遣唐使考弁二則. *Nihon rekishi*, 464 (1987), pp. 16–27.

Zhang Zexian 張澤咸. "Tangdai de jieri" 唐代的節日. *Wen shi*, no. 37 (1993), pp. 65–92.

Zhang, Yongjin. "System, Empire and State in Chinese International Relations." In *System, Empire and States: Great Transformation in International Politics*, ed. Michael Cox, Tim Dunne, and Ken Booth, pp. 43–63. Cambridge: Cambridge University Press, 2001.

Zhou Shaoliang 周紹良. *Tangdai muzhiming huibian* 唐代墓誌銘彙編. Shanghai: Shanghai Guji Chubanshe, 1992.

Zhou Xunchu 周勛初, ed. *Tang yulin jiaozheng* 唐語林校證. Beijing: Zhonghua Shuju, 1987.

―――. *Tangren yishi huibian* 唐人軼事彙編. Shanghai: Shanghai Guji Chubanshe, 1995.

Zhou Yiliang 周一良. "Ru Tang seng Yuanzhen yu Tangchao shiliao" 入唐僧圓珍與唐朝史料. In his *Zhong Ri wenhua guanxishi lun*, pp. 96–103. Nanchang: Jiangxi Renmin Chubanshe, 1990.

Zhou Yiliang and Zhao Heping 趙和平. *Tang Wudai shuyi yanjiu* 唐五代書儀研究. Beijing: Shehui Kexue Chubanshe, 1995.

Zhou Zumo 周祖謨. *Luoyang qielan ji jiaoshi* 洛陽伽藍記校釋. Beijing: Zhonghua Shuju, 1963.

Zhu Yafei 朱亞非. "Cong 'Ru Tang qiufa xunli xingji' kan Tangdai Shandong de duiwai jiaowang" 從《入唐求法巡禮行記》看唐代山東的對外交往. *Wenxian*, 1996, no. 4, pp. 123–139.

Index

About the Author

Wang Zhenping, who received his doctorate from Princeton University, is currently associate professor of history at the National Institute of Education, Nanyang Technological University, Singapore. He is the author of *China-Japan Relations during the Han-Tang Period* (in Chinese).